Shakespeare:
Text and Theater

Jay L. Halio

Shakespeare: Text and Theater

Essays in Honor of Jay L. Halio

Edited by
Lois Potter and Arthur F. Kinney

Newark: University of Delaware Press
London: Associated University Presses

© 1999 by Associated University Presses, Inc.

All rights reserved. Authorization to photocopy items for internal or personal use, or the internal or personal use of specific clients, is granted by the copyright owner, provided that a base fee of $10.00, plus eight cents per page, per copy is paid directly to the Copyright Clearance Center, 222 Rosewood Drive, Danvers, Massachusetts 01923. [0-87413-699-7/99 $10.00+8¢ pp, pc.]
Other than as indicated in the foregoing, this book may not be reproduced, in whole or in part, in any form (except as permitted by Sections 107 and 108 of the U.S. Copyright Law, and except for brief quotes appearing in reviews in the public press).

Associated University Presses
440 Forsgate Drive
Cranbury, NJ 08512

Associated University Presses
16 Barter Street
London WC1A 2AH, England

Associated University Presses
P.O. Box 338, Port Credit
Mississauga, Ontario
Canada L5G 4L8

The paper used in this publication meets the requirements
of the American National Standard for Permanence of Paper
for Printed Library Materials Z39.48-1984.

Library of Congress Cataloging-in-Publication Data

Shakespeare, text and theater : essays in honor of Jay L. Halio / edited by Lois Potter and Arthur F. Kinney.
    p.   cm.
Includes bibliographical references and index.
ISBN 0-87413-699-7 (alk. paper)
  1. Shakespeare, William, 1564–1616—Criticism, Textual.
2. Shakespeare, William, 1564–1616—State history.   3. Shakespeare, William, 1564–1616—Adaptations.   I. Halio, Jay L.   II. Potter, Lois.   III. Kinney, Arthur F., 1933–   .
PR3071.S47   1999
822.3'3—dc21   98-49751
                                                                                                         CIP

PRINTED IN THE UNITED STATES OF AMERICA

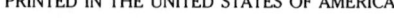

Contents

List of Illustrations	7
Preface and Acknowledgments	9

Part One: Texts

The First Folio: Where Should We Be Without It? STANLEY WELLS	17
"All we like sheep . . ." SUSAN SNYDER	33
Still Babbling of Green Fields: Mr. Greenfields and the Twenty-third Psalm GEORGE WALTON WILLIAMS	45
"So quick bright things come to confusion": or, What Else Was *A Midsummer Night's Dream* About? TOM CLAYTON	62
"The gift is small, / The will is all": Musings for Jay Halio DONALD W. FOSTER	92

Part Two: Performances

A Polish Gentleman's Visit to London Theaters in 1820–1821 JERZY LIMON	109
How Revolutionary *is* Cross-cast Shakespeare? A Look at Five Contemporary Productions GRACE TIFFANY	120
Strands Too Far Remote: A Note on Translating the Political and the Politics of Translation AVRAHAM OZ	136
Beginning with Branagh: *Romeo and Juliet,* Hammersmith, 1986 RUSSELL JACKSON	146
To Know a Shakespeare Character MARVIN ROSENBERG	163

The Readiness Was All: Ian Charleson and Richard Eyre's
   Hamlet   170
   RICHARD ALLAN DAVISON
Stoppard's *Rosencrantz and Guildenstern Are Dead:* The
   Film   183
   H. R. COURSEN
Cori-Ollie-anus: Shakespeare's Last Tragedy and American
   Politics in 1988   195
   R. B. PARKER
Staging *The Tempest* as an Alchemical Experiment in the
   Theater   209
   PEGGY MUÑOZ SIMONDS

Part Three: Text and Performance

Stage Directions as Evidence: The Question of Provenance
   ALAN C. DESSEN   229
Show Business: The Editor in the Theater   248
   JILL L. LEVENSON
"Oh be some other name": Translating *Romeo and Juliet*   266
   LAURIE E. MAGUIRE
Humor Out of Breath: Francis Gentleman and the *Henry IV*
   Plays   285
   LOIS POTTER
Editing Informed by Performance History: The Double
   Ending of *Troilus and Cressida*   298
   DAVID BEVINGTON
Two Lears: Notes for an Actor   310
   ALEXANDER LEGGATT
Staging *The Comedy of Errors*   320
   ARTHUR F. KINNEY

A Checklist: Jay L. Halio   332
   Compiled by BARBARA SILVERSTEIN

Contributors   334
Index to Works by, or Attributed to William Shakespeare   338
General Index   340

Illustrations

Frontispiece: Jay L. Halio 2

Production photograph of *Coriolanus* directed by John Hirsch at San Diego's Old Globe Theatre 194

Tetragram from Isidore of Seville's *De natura rerum* (Augsburg, 1472) 213

The art of making charcoal (from Conrad Gesner's *The Jewell of Health: The Practice of the New and Old Physicke*) 217

The alchemist-magician in his laboratory manipulating the element of fire 218

Alchymia with her laboratory utensils 219

Feeding charcoal into an alchemical furnace 221

The *cauda pavonis* from Salomon Trismosin's *Splendor Solis* 222

A woodcut of an alchemical distillation 223

Preface and Acknowledgments

JAY L. HALIO, AS IS WELL KNOWN, HAS HAD AN EXEMPLARY CAREER AS SCHOLAR and editor. But this is only one of the motives for this collection. From the start of his career, he has shown special talents for discovering and encouraging others: as teachers, as writers, and as colleagues. His collegiality and support for junior members of the university are stressed both by his colleagues and by members of the secretarial and administrative staff. "I am in the English department because of Jay Halio," one declares emphatically. "One thing I will always be grateful to Jay Halio for," writes a colleague, "is his kindness to me as a young assistant professor. [He] helped me to make my academic life one in which teaching remains central." Another confirms his kindness to junior colleagues: "I vividly recall the lively interest he took in my research, my plans, and, most particularly, my ideas about teaching."

A graduate summa cum laude from Syracuse University, with master's and doctor's degrees from Yale and advanced study at the Centro di Cultura per Stranieri at the University of Florence, Jay began his career at the University of California at Davis and then, declining promotion there to professor, came to the University of Delaware in 1973 as the H. Rodney Sharp Professor of Liberal Studies. At Delaware, he soon became known for his formidable combination of high principles and a passion for argument. From 1975 to 1981 he was the Associate Provost for Instruction, where (a current colleague notes) he "really made the needs of the humanities felt." He founded two new university programs, still thriving: the Center for Teaching Effectiveness and the Center for Advanced Study. The former encourages teachers across the campus to share pedagogic techniques; the latter enables them to set aside teaching and administrative duties while they finish major projects of their own. While still performing regular duties in the English Department, Jay acted as Director of the Humanities Semester from 1978 until 1990, coordinated the Comparative Literature Program from 1982 to 1987, directed the Center for Teaching Effectiveness briefly in 1986–87, and in 1994 was Acting Director of the Jewish Studies Program.

Jay's interest in teaching has always been closely involved with his interest in Shakespeare. A Danforth Associate in Teaching himself from 1981 to 1986, between 1985 and 1993 he directed a summer seminar for high school teachers under the auspices of the National Endowment for the Humanities, called "Shakespeare: Enacting the Text." For half of each course the classes were given at Stratford-upon-Avon, where he coordinated lessons with productions of the Royal Shakespeare Company. Since 1975, too, he has been a founding member of the Central Executive Committee of the Folger Shakespeare Library Institute of Renaissance and Eighteenth-Century Studies. He is at present a member of the Academic Council of the Globe Theatre Centre and, through 1998, under still another National Endowment for the Humanities grant, he is completing the New Shakespeare Variorum edition of *All's Well That Ends Well,* a project that will enable teachers and scholars alike. Indeed, anyone who has had the good fortune to use his edition of *The Merchant of Venice* in the New Oxford Shakespeare, or the First Quarto of *King Lear* for the New Cambridge Shakespeare, or his book on *A Midsummer Night's Dream* in the Shakespeare in Performance Series published by the Manchester University Press, will know that for Jay learning and teaching are inseparable—and inseparably bound to the availability of good texts. A contributor to this volume has praised his flair for sensing just how much annotation the reader will need to open rather than close off possibilities of interpretation. His admirable Cambridge edition of *King Lear* is a model in this respect; it is also thoroughly responsive to the theatrical possibilities of the play, including those which are open to the choice of individual players. His love of the theater is passionate and extends even to the practical, as can be seen in *Understanding Shakespeare's Plays in Performance,* where he writes of "the excitement of anticipation" that forms part of theatergoing and then connects it with specific tasks: "Finding what's on, checking the cast and direction, buying the tickets, all contribute to the anticipation of pleasure" (83).

The decade in which he served as chairman of the Delaware Press Board of Editors (1985–95) was crucial in making the Press a central force in publications on Shakespeare's work, his theater, and his plays in performance. He published both established scholars and junior faculty, bringing into print some of the finest dissertations produced in the United States and abroad. A colleague has praised the "truly democratic vision" which allowed new authors to share "recognition and equal billing with many of the profession's most widely published and distinguished members." His limitless interest in the work of others, sometimes at the expense of his own, was from the start matched by his efficiency. A colleague recalls "his dawn-to-late-night round of appointments" at Shakespeare conventions and the energy with which he kept up such enterprises even during the year he spent as Visiting Professor at the University of Malaya: "Long before the age of e-mail and fax machines, Jay was coordinating publishers, contributors, and copyright holders for a collection to be produced almost half a world away from Kuala Lumpur. . . . It is no mystery, but it is nonetheless a marvel to see how he does it." Even more visionary, perhaps, was Jay's editorship and publication of the proceedings of several World Shakespeare Congresses, bringing more closely together the world community of Shakespeareans. Before he left the Press he instituted a second collateral series: English translations of some of the best, largely unavailable, Renaissance essays from other nations and languages.

Another feature of Jay's work for the University Press was his willingness to carry on, when others would not, festschriften paying tribute to those important to Shakespeare studies: to C. L. Barber, O. B. Hardison, Jr., and Sam Schoenbaum. In keeping with Jay's own practice, this volume makes no attempt to disguise its nature. While it is easy to understand the widespread distrust of the old-style festschrift, united only by the contributors' acquaintance with its honoree, we feel that there is still a place for the newer, thematically-organized one. Its celebratory nature provides welcome relief from the notorious competitiveness of the profession, bringing together many distinguished authors who might not otherwise be found within the same covers. Invited to write for a scholar who gave so many others their own start in the scholarly world, our contributors responded warmly. This book could well have been much longer if we had taken account of all the areas on which Jay has published: twentieth-century literature and drama, Jewish literature, and the art and science of teaching. Instead, we have confined it to Shakespeare's text and performance, and the relation between them. We were not otherwise prescriptive: though our "default" edition is the Riverside Shakespeare, we did not insist that all contributors use it, because, as will be apparent, different essays required different editorial policies. We have even allowed differences in both format and length where there seemed a good case for them; and some of the essays are much less formal than others.

Nevertheless, certain patterns have emerged. Plays on which Jay himself has worked or is still working—particularly *Romeo and Juliet* and *King Lear*—get attention from more than one contributor; some are in dialogue with each other and with ongoing scholarly debate. Subjects that he found particularly interesting—the problems of editing and cross-cultural Shakespeare—are well represented here. We hope that the collection will be fun to read, and an appropriate tribute to a scholar who likes a good argument at least as much as he likes reconciling disputes. His has been a lifelong commitment to the humanities and to those who teach and research them. It seems only natural to invite some of those who have benefited from his legendary nurturing to honor him in turn.

* * *

We are grateful to those who have supplied us with the reminiscences of Jay that appear above, and to Graham Clarke, who kindly allowed us to use as our cover illustration his delightful etching, "Full House," from "Mr. William Shakespeare, The Life and Times of," ©copyright reserved Graham Clarke 1995. The folio was originally displayed at the 1996 joint meeting of the International Shakespeare Association and the Shakespeare Association of America, held in Los Angeles, California. The University of Delaware Press, its outside reader, and Associated University Presses (especially Chris Retz) have worked with great care to make this book worthy of its honoree. Rebecca Jaroff gave her help in the early, organizational stages of this project and Paige Harrison helped with the proof-reading and prepared the index. Above all, we should like to thank Barbara Silverstein for her admirably conscientious and thorough copy-editing, a much bigger job than that word suggests, and for compiling the checklist of Jay L. Halio's works.

Shakespeare:
Text and Theater

Part One
Texts

The First Folio: Where Should We Be Without It?

STANLEY WELLS

SHAKESPEARE'S DEATH IN APRIL 1616 WAS MARKED, SO FAR AS WE CAN TELL, BY no published tributes. This may seem odd. When Sir Philip Sidney died in 1586 he was given a state funeral extraordinary in its pomp and circumstance followed by the publication of numerous tributes both in England and on the Continent.[1] Edmund Spenser died in poverty in 1599, but the Earl of Essex paid his funeral expenses and he was buried in Westminster Abbey where, says William Camden, his hearse "was attended by poets, and mournful elegies and poems, with the pens that wrote them, were thrown into his tomb."[2] Memorial verses by a number of poets, some published soon after he died, survive both in print and in manuscript. Ben Jonson too died poor, in 1637, but he too was buried in the Abbey; a volume of memorial verses, *Jonsonus Virbius,* appeared soon after his death, and a subscription started to raise money for a memorial was thwarted only by the Civil War. Even poor Robert Greene's corpse is said to have been honored with a crown of bays, and his death in 1592 was marked by, admittedly, vituperative comments from enemies, as well as by the publication of a eulogy, *Greene's Funerals,* by one R. B. So it is natural to ask why the death of the man now regarded as the greatest artist of them all was not similarly marked.

Various answers are possible. One is that Sidney was an aristocrat with many claims to fame other than his literary achievement—which indeed was relatively little known when he died; that Spenser was a courtier and public servant as well as a poet; and that Jonson had worked extensively for the court and had achieved recognition from the royal family. It is only fair to note too that many other writers of the period now greatly admired, such as John Lyly, Thomas Dekker, Thomas Middleton, John Webster, and John Ford, have no memorial—we don't even know in what year Webster or Ford died. But Shakespeare, as principal dramatist and shareholder of the King's Men, and consequently a member of the royal household, must also have been known at court and had already in his lifetime been the subject of a number of printed and other tributes. If his death itself was not marked in the way of some of his great contemporaries', this is partly, I suggest, because he was the first great literary commuter. Playwrights naturally based themselves in London. But Shakespeare died in Stratford, not London; he could have been buried in the Abbey only with difficulty. Of course his work was necessarily based on the capital, and he certainly had lodgings there, although he seems to have changed them often enough to have been regarded as having no fixed address—certainly the tax inspectors had difficulty in keeping track of him. But I suspect that he had done a good deal more of his writing in Stratford than is generally supposed: he had bought a fine, large house there early in his career, and I should be surprised if, in spite of the difficulties of travel, he did not contrive to spend long periods of creative time in the peace and quiet of a study in New Place.

But in fact Shakespeare was commemorated; only a time lag creates a mistaken impression of indifference. He has two main memorials. One is the bust in Holy Trinity Church with its laudatory inscriptions in both Latin and English. This was in place by 1623, seven years after he died; inevitably it took time to commission, execute, and set in place in Stratford a sculpture made in a London workshop. The other, far greater memorial is the Folio volume *M[aste]r William Shakespeare's Comedies, Histories and Tragedies* published in the same year. This too could not have appeared rapidly after Shakespeare died. We do not know when plans to publish it were inaugurated. It is surely significant that the only theater people mentioned in Shakespeare's will are John Heminges and Henry Condell, who signed the Epistle Dedicatory to the Folio, along with Richard Burbage, who had died before the book went to press. All three were colleagues of long standing who had worked with Shakespeare through most of his career. Shakespeare himself may have discussed with them the possibility of a collection of his plays, and the bequests to them of money to buy mourning rings may mark some kind of bond that they would memorialize as well as mourn him. It would not be at all surprising if the project took seven years to come to fruition; as anyone who has edited the *Complete Works* has reason to know, big books take a long time to prepare. The Folio is a very big book, and a lot of work had to go into its preparation even before a start could be made on its printing, which itself lasted for nearly two years.

It is also worth remarking that although the Folio is the first printed tribute to Shakespeare, this was an age in which poems circulated extensively in manuscript as well as in print. There is, for instance, a memorial poem to Shakespeare by William Basse which, although not printed until 1633, when it was attributed to John Donne in his *Poems,* survives in a large number of manuscripts—twenty-seven are recorded in the Oxford *Textual Companion,* with the statement that "No doubt a further search would uncover further copies."[3] This poem makes the suggestion that Shakespeare, like some of his illustrious forebears, might have been buried in the Abbey beside them:

> Renownèd Spenser, lie a thought more nigh
> To learnèd Chaucer; and rare Beaumont, lie
> A little nearer Spenser, to make room
> For Shakespeare in your threefold, fourfold tomb.

The lines go on to suggest that, if room cannot be found for Shakespeare in the Abbey, they may themselves appear upon "this carvèd marble of thine own," which seems to indicate that their author was submitting his verses for possible publication by the monument makers. Although they had not appeared in print when the Folio was published, Ben Jonson had clearly read them since in his poem in praise of Shakespeare he writes:

> My Shakespeare, rise; I will not lodge thee by
> Chaucer, or Spenser, or bid Beaumont lie
> A little further to make thee a room.

Perhaps, then, there is no real reason to suggest that Shakespeare's death was less adequately commemorated than his later admirers might have hoped. And the great Folio is a monument whose importance cannot be exaggerated but is in danger of being underestimated. In this essay I should like to say something about the way that its compilers worked and the effect that this has had upon later ages' perception of Shakespeare.

II

We must consider first the situation at the time of his death. All his poems had appeared in print except for a few disputed lyrics, including "Shall I die?" He had clearly authorized the publication of the narrative poems and "The Phoenix and Turtle"; the *Sonnets* had appeared in 1609 under less certain auspices, and in *The Passionate Pilgrim* of 1599 William Jaggard had caused offense by ascribing to Shakespeare poems that he certainly did not write.

With the plays, the situation is different. None of his plays had appeared with the kind of authorizing documents represented by the dedications to the narrative poems; indeed it is generally supposed that Shakespeare had had nothing to do with the publication by printing of any of his plays. For him, it would seem, publication was performance. Nevertheless, quarto editions of reasonably high textual authority had appeared of thirteen plays now generally ascribed to him: they are *Titus Andronicus* (1594), *Love's Labor's Lost* (1598), *Richard III* (1597), *A Midsummer Night's Dream* (1600), *Romeo and Juliet* (1597), *Richard II* (1597), *The Merchant of Venice* (1600), *Henry IV, Part One* (1598), *Henry IV, Part Two* (1600), *Much Ado About Nothing* (1600), *Hamlet* (1604), *Troilus and Cressida* (1609), and *King Lear* (1608). *Othello* was to follow, in 1622. Another four plays—those now known as *Henry VI, Parts Two and Three* (1594, 1595), *The Merry Wives of Windsor* (1602), and *Henry V* (1600)—had appeared in texts that differ seriously enough from those later published in the Folio for them to have been regarded as unauthorized, "bad" quartos. To these eighteen texts we may add *The Troublesome Reign of King John* (1594), which a few scholars have believed to be derived from Shakespeare's *King John*, although it is more generally regarded as a source play, and *The Taming of a Shrew* (1594), of which the reverse is true. Neither bears a close relationship to the texts printed in the Folio. Many of these texts had been reprinted by 1616, some several times, and *Richard II* had been reissued with the addition in 1608 of the episode of Richard's abdication that had been absent from the three editions printed while Queen Elizabeth was alive.

In addition to these texts, at the time of Shakespeare's death certain others had been printed with an ascription to him. These are *The London Prodigal,* a citizen comedy published in 1605, in which posterity has taken little interest; the short but powerful domestic tragedy known as *A Yorkshire Tragedy,* entered as Shakespeare's in the Stationers' Register in 1608 and published as by him in the same year, but now ascribed to Thomas Middleton and occasionally performed; and *Pericles,* published in 1609.

As time passed, other publishing projects materialized. The most important is Thomas Pavier's aborted attempt, along with the printer William Jaggard, to publish an incomplete collection of Shakespeare's plays in 1619. It was a shady venture, as is witnessed by the fact that some of the volumes were falsely dated, apparently in an attempt to evade copyright restrictions. Ten volumes had appeared before the Lord Chamberlain intervened, obtaining an injunction from the Stationers' company that "no plays that His Majesty's players do play shall be printed without consent of some of them."[4] All the volumes were reprints of existing quartos, and they included *A Yorkshire Tragedy* and *The First Part of Sir John Oldcastle,* a history play exploiting the popularity of Shakespeare's Falstaff plays, which had been published anonymously in 1600 but was now, in a falsely dated reprint of the 1600 quarto, declared to have been "Written by William Shakespeare."

The Lord Chamberlain's intervention was almost certainly prompted by the King's Men. This may, as Gary Taylor suggests, have been "because Pavier's attempt persuaded them that they should oversee the publication of Shakespeare's work personally," but even more suggestive is his alternative hypothesis, that "their plans for the Folio were already under way."[5] There is no objective evidence for this, but my suspicion is based upon my hunch that Shakespeare's colleagues had long intended to memorialize him with a volume that would rival, if not surpass, the great Folio of Ben Jonson's *Works*— not, be it noted, simply plays—which had appeared in the year Shakespeare died. The Pavier project may have hastened their rate of progress, and it may be significant that the printer, Jaggard, was the same for both. To some extent the Folio must have been a labor of love, a pious act of memorialization; but it was also a commercial venture that could bring financial profit to the King's Men as well as to the publishers and printers.[6] We are accustomed to think of Heminges and Condell as the editors of the volume, and in the dedication they accept responsibility for its "faults . . . if any be committed," describing themselves as "a pair . . . careful to show their gratitude both to the living [i.e., the dedicatees] and the dead," but editing was only a sideline for them. Heminges was a founder-member of the Lord Chamberlain's company in 1594, and, like Shakespeare, stayed with it throughout his career; like Shakespeare, he made a good deal of money out of it. An actor, he seems also to have been one of the company's main businessmen. He is caricatured in verses on the burning of the Globe in 1613 as "old stuttering Heminges" and three years later is described as "old Master Heminges" in a masque by Ben Jonson. The last reference to him as an actor is in 1611, which may mean that he gave himself up to business after that; but literary editing can at best have been only a part-time activity. Condell too was not a young man, and appears to have gone on acting until around 1619, at least. It is not surprising that some people have suspected that a share of the editorial duties may have been undertaken by Ben Jonson, who contributed lines on the portrait and his famous, if qualified, eulogy on Shakespeare, and possibly even by Ralph Crane, who has been identified as the scribe responsible for making transcripts of some of the plays especially executed for the volume (and whom one sometimes suspects of being several different men masquerading as one).[7] In speaking of Heminges and Condell, and even of Ben Jonson, as editors of the Folio, we must be using the term to mean those who took the more important decisions rather than those who performed the more mundane but demanding tasks of, for example, transcription, copyediting, and proofreading, some of which were no less laborious and demanding of scholarly ability than those undertaken by the editors of scholarly editions at the present time. But it is not always easy to distinguish between decisions which might have been made by, as it were, overseers of the project and others which might have been the responsibility of the publishers and printers.

What exactly were the more important decisions? The first was to publish the book at all. It was a bold thing to do, a declaration of faith in Shakespeare's selling power as a dramatist for reading as well as performing. No Folio edition made up entirely of plays by an English dramatist had previously appeared. The closest precedent was the Folio of Ben Jonson's works of 1616. Jonson was mocked for this in an epigram entitled "To Mr Ben Jonson demanding the reason why he called his plays 'works'":

> Pray tell me, Ben, where doth the mystery lurk:
> What others call a play you call a work.[8]

But this is rather unfair, since the volume included non-dramatic writings as well as plays. The publishers' faith in Shakespeare was justified by the success of the volume, in spite of its high selling price of around £1 (depending on, for example, whether it was bought bound or unbound): a reprint was called for after nine years, in 1632, whereas the Jonson Folio was not reprinted until twenty-four years after first publication, in 1640.

Another important task was to decide on the preliminaries to the book, including the engraving of Shakespeare by Martin Droeshout which, along with the bust in Holy Trinity Church, Stratford-upon-Avon, provides us with our principal evidence of Shakespeare's physical appearance. Even Ben Jonson's volume had not been adorned with a portrait of the author. Probably Shakespeare's was specially commissioned; it may have been made from a pre-existent drawing that has not survived. Other tasks were the composition of the dedication, to the Earls of Pembroke and Montgomery, and the epistle "To the great variety of readers," both signed by Heminges and Condell, as well as the assembling of the commendatory verses by Jonson, Hugh Holland, Leonard Digges, and James Mabbe. It would be interesting to know whether these, too, were commissioned; Digges, at least, had a personal association with Shakespeare and so may well have written mainly out of personal affection: his stepfather, Thomas Russell, lived at Alderminster, near Stratford, and was the executor of Shakespeare's will.

The preliminaries to the Folio are of genuine interest, but of far greater consequence were the editors' decisions about what to include and to exclude. This has had a paramount influence upon our perception of the canon of Shakespeare's work. The decision to exclude poems seems particularly perverse, in that these were the only works that Shakespeare clearly intended to be read. There may well have been problems about copyright. The *Sonnets,* published in 1609, had not been much of a success, judging by the absence of reprints, so Thorpe probably still had unsold copies; *Venus and Adonis* and *The Rape of Lucrece,* on the other hand, had been reprinted regularly since they first appeared in 1593 and 1594 respectively, so their publishers too would not wish to part with the rights. So the title chosen for the volume, *M[aste]r William Shakespeare's Comedies, Histories and Tragedies,* may reflect a desire not so much, as has been suspected, to avoid Jonson's term "works" as to emphasize the range of Shakespeare's achievement. But, paradoxically, the decision not to include the poems in a volume that otherwise aimed at completeness had the effect for centuries of reducing the impression of Shakespeare's range by drawing attention away from his achievement as a nondramatic poet. The poems were excluded from reprints of the Folio throughout the seventeenth century, and the content of eighteenth-century editions continued to reflect that of the Folio, with the poems issued at best in supplementary volumes, until Malone's edition of 1780. Partly, no doubt, for this reason, the sonnets were relatively little known until the Romantic period, and there is no serious critical discussion of the narrative poems before Coleridge's, in the *Biographia Literaria* of 1817.

The choice of plays for inclusion and exclusion must have reflected Heminges and Condell's familiarity with Shakespeare's production during the greater part of his career. Their omission of certain plays that had already been ascribed to Shakespeare has been taken ever since as evidence that he did not write them: it would be difficult to deny that he wrote both *A Yorkshire Tragedy* and *The London Prodigal* if they had been printed in the Folio. But Heminges and Condell's implicit testimony has not always been believed. They also omitted *Pericles* and *The Two Noble Kinsmen,* both now ascribed in whole or in part to Shakespeare. The omission of

Pericles cannot be attributed simply to the fact that the edition printed in 1608 is corrupt; the play remained in the repertory during the 1620s, so the company should have been able to supply a good text. Perhaps Heminges and Condell omitted both plays because they knew that in them Shakespeare had a collaborator. Their decision had a damaging effect on the reputation of *The Two Noble Kinsmen*, which until recently has been treated as part of the Beaumont and Fletcher canon instead of being included in editions of Shakespeare. Shakespeare and Fletcher's joint authorship of this play is attested to in the 1634 quarto; no such testimony survives to the now largely accepted joint authorship of a play that was included in the Folio, *All is True*, or *Henry VIII*; if we believe in this (as I, for one, do), we must suppose that the anomaly is accounted for by the editors' desire to complete the cycle of plays about English history. Unfortunately, they also omitted the other play on which we have good reason to believe that Shakespeare collaborated with Fletcher, *Cardenio*, and so may well be held responsible for its failure to survive. Might they also have included a play called *Love's Labor's Won?* Probably we shall never know.

Heminges and Condell included in the Folio eighteen plays that had not previously appeared in print (if we regard *The Troublesome Reign of King John* and *The Taming of a Shrew* as independent plays). This is their single most important influence on our perception of Shakespeare. It is not possible to say with absolute certainty that if some of the most highly regarded of Shakespeare's plays, including *Julius Caesar, As You Like It, Twelfth Night, Macbeth, Coriolanus,* and *Antony and Cleopatra,* had not been printed in the Folio, they would not have survived: after all, one of Shakespeare's plays, *Othello*, appeared for the first time in print in 1622, after he died and before the Folio was published, and there is no absolute reason that other unpublished plays might not have reached the bookstalls, with or without the King's Men's permission, if the Folio had not appeared. On the other hand, there is no guarantee that they would, and it may be worth contemplating what would have been the nature of our loss if they had not.

Without the plays first printed in the Folio, Shakespeare's comedies would have been greatly depleted. We should have lacked three of the earliest: *The Two Gentlemen of Verona, The Taming of the Shrew,* and *The Comedy of Errors;* two of the greatest: *As You Like It* and *Twelfth Night;* the two that have been designated "problem comedies": *Measure for Measure* and *All's Well that Ends Well;* and all the "last plays", or romances, except *Pericles*. In addition, *The Merry Wives of Windsor* would have been represented only by the grossly inferior short quarto of 1602. The English history plays would have lacked their beginning—*1 Henry VI*—and their end— *All is True* (as we should certainly have called the lost play, though we should have had no external evidence that Shakespeare had anything to do with it); we should have lacked *King John*; Parts Two and Three of *Henry VI* would have been represented only by their anonymously printed early texts and again would have been known by the titles restored by the Oxford editors, *The First Part of the Contention* and *The True Tragedy of Richard, Duke of York;* and *Henry V* would have been known only in the truncated, garbled and anonymously printed text of 1600, lacking, for example, all the speeches of the Chorus. Without the Folio, Shakespeare's only play about Roman history would have been *Titus Andronicus*—no *Julius Caesar, Coriolanus,* or *Antony and Cleopatra;* in the absence of *Macbeth* there would have been only three "great tragedies," not four; *Timon of Athens* would have been unknown, *King Lear* would have been represented only by the badly printed quarto, and *Othello* would have lacked the willow song and other passages unique to the Folio text.

Perhaps the most impressive witness to the Folio editors' declared ambition to "keep the memory of so worthy a friend and fellow alive as was our Shakespeare" is the care which they bestowed on the texts they printed. It is not easy to estimate how much they did to the texts unique to the Folio. They must have received manuscripts of these texts, presumably from the players (unless any of them had come directly from Shakespeare or his executors); it is clear that some, such as *The Comedy of Errors* and *All's Well that Ends Well*, were set up from the author's pre-performance manuscripts, which the company may have held. Others, such as *The Tempest* and *The Winter's Tale,* came from transcripts, usually supposed to have been undertaken by Ralph Crane, possibly at the instigation of the editors, who were perhaps unable to obtain a prompt book for those plays still in the repertoire. The two Folio-only plays that seem closest to theatrical copy are *Julius Caesar* and *Macbeth,* but a transcript may have been used. (It is worth bearing in mind that the process of preparing a manuscript for printing, along with its treatment in the printing house, may have rendered it worthless for any purpose other than the lining of pie dishes or other such base uses. For this reason, as Peter Blayney writes, "the manuscript supplied would not usually have been 'the allowed book' then being used for performance."[9] In other words, the theory that any play was printed directly from a promptbook implies belief that it had been discarded by the players.)

For the plays that had previously appeared in print, on the other hand, we have points of comparison. It would presumably have been possible for the editors simply to hand over to the printers a copy of a printed text of each of these plays and tell them to get on with it. Rarely, if ever, did they do this, even though to have done so would have saved both the editors and their printers a great deal of trouble. Their normal practice seems to have been to select a printed copy (not necessarily of the first edition, which of course may not have been easily available) and to have this annotated with changes derived from a theatrical copy (probably a manuscript, but conceivably a printed text used as a prompt copy). The selection was itself an important matter. For no play did the editors choose one of those versions which twentieth-century scholars have designated "bad" quartos. These texts are currently a matter of controversy, but the fact that Heminges and Condell avoided, for example, the 1600 quarto of *Henry V* and the 1603 *Hamlet* is enough to cast suspicion on the authenticity of these editions, though not to deny their intrinsic interest.

The task of comparison and annotation seems not always to have been executed with exemplary thoroughness. For some plays, such as *Love's Labor's Lost* and *Much Ado about Nothing*, the changes are slight and fail to make corrections or provide information about staging, which must be presumed to have existed in any manuscript from which a performance could adequately have been regulated. For others, changes are more substantial, though not pervasive. *Titus Andronicus*, for example, was printed from a copy of the third quarto of 1611, but with the addition of a scene that had not appeared in any of the quartos, (the "fly" scene), and with other changes, some of which reflect theatrical practice after the introduction of act intervals, around 1608. And for a few plays the process of annotation was remarkably thorough, resulting in copy that the printers must have found difficult to read. For *Troilus and Cressida*, for example, a copy of the 1609 quarto appears to have been marked up with some 500 variants, an average of between seventeen and eighteen changes on each page—or one every two to three lines—made after comparison with a scribal promptbook on which revisions for production at the Globe had been marked. Most pains were taken over *King Lear*, for which, if we have writ our annals true (a phrase that I should not have been able to use had it not been for the Folio), a copy of the second quarto was marked up with the addition from a promptbook of around 100 full lines that are not in the quarto. The copy was also marked for omission of close to 300 lines, including an entire scene, that *are* in the quarto, and contains over 850 verbal variants, including changes and additions to stage directions and reassignment of several speeches to different speakers. The result, with deletions, additions, interlineations, and interleaved sheets, must have been a compositor's nightmare.

It is hard to believe that the editors would have gone to all this trouble, and have caused so much trouble to their printers, had they not believed that they would have failed to do justice to the man they wished to commemorate if they had printed his plays from the quartos—even from the "good" quartos—which many subsequent editors have preferred over the Folio texts. They must also have believed that the promptbooks that they used as a basis for what they regarded as necessary correction more closely represented the form in which their author would have wished to see them in print. The result of all their work is that for a number of Shakespeare's plays we have far better evidence of the form and manner in which these plays were actually performed than if only the quartos had survived, or if Heminges and Condell had taken the easier way out and simply reprinted quartos. The Folio is a tribute to Shakespeare the dramatist, an affirmation of the belief that his plays reached full fruition only in the theater.

There is a corollary of this to which I should like to draw attention. Some of Shakespeare's plays are much longer than others, and than most of the other plays written around the same time. This has given rise to a belief on the part of some scholars that the longest plays could never have been acted in their entirety. Richard Dutton writes, "There is substantial evidence of a Shakespeare who regularly wrote, with some facility, plays too long and complex to be staged in the theater of his day, plays for which the only plausible audience was one of readers."[10] This idea seems to me to be decisively disproved by the Folio. It is true that the Folio versions of certain plays, including *Hamlet* and *King Lear*, are shorter by two or three hundred lines than their quarto counterparts, but they are still long plays, much longer than, for instance, *A Midsummer Night's Dream* or *The Tempest*; and *Troilus and Cressida*, which was also revised by comparing it with a theater manuscript, was not shortened in the process and is the third longest of the plays, shorter only than *Richard III* and *Hamlet*. Yet if, as bibliographical scholarship has amply demonstrated, the Folio texts of these plays were prepared from theater manuscripts, there are no grounds for arguing that Shakespeare was writing in the knowledge that any of his plays, even the longest, would necessarily be shortened before they reached the stage. We must accept the idea not merely that Shakespeare wrote long plays but that his company performed them and his audiences accepted them, even if they did last longer than the "two hours" that the Prologue to *Romeo and Juliet* optimistically set forth as the length of the performance.[11]

Another corollary of the Folio editors' desire to bring the texts into line with theatrical practice is, of course, that the evidence most readily available to them, at least for plays still in the repertory of the King's Men, related to the manner in which the plays were presented in their time, rather than that at which the plays were first performed. It is for this reason that they print, for example, what is pretty certainly an adapted text of *Macbeth*, rather than the play as first acted.

An important effect of changes in theater practice is the presence, in the Folio, of act and scene divisions in a number of plays. None of the plays printed during Shakespeare's lifetime is divided into either acts or scenes (though it is clear that in some plays he had the classically derived five-act structure in mind as he wrote); there is every reason to believe that until about 1608, plays in the public theaters, even the longest, were acted without interruption.[12] The editors of the Folio, however, clearly set out with the intention of dividing all the plays into acts, although they abandoned this practice in the later part of the volume. Some of the subdivisions indicated in Folio texts undoubtedly reflect theatrical practice, but others are no less clearly editorial, and some are grotesquely inappropriate, as readers will testify who have had the experience of coming, possibly with relief, to what is marked as the end of Act IV of *Love's Labor's Lost* only to find that they are only half way through the play. Although the Folio editors' intention to divide all the plays was not carried through—some plays, such as *Romeo and Juliet* and *Antony and Cleopatra*, were printed with no divisions, others, such as *Hamlet*, were only partially divided—what they did encouraged later editors to complete the process. Thus, the presentation of the plays was brought closer to that of classical drama, resulting in printed texts that misrepresent the manner in which most of the plays were originally given, breaking the flow of the action. Recognizing this, modern editors during the past thirty or forty years have done what they can to minimize act and scene breaks; had it not been for the Folio, they would very likely be printing the plays continuously, as in the quartos, a policy that might well have had far-reaching effects on theatrical practice—and, indeed, on theater economics as affected by bar receipts during intervals.

The other single most important decision facing the editors of the Folio was how to arrange the volume's contents. They might have arranged the plays according to order of composition. They might even have told their readers when the plays were written, thus saving scholars of later generations an enormous amount of trouble. Regrettably, they decided instead to group the plays according to the categories named in the title of their volume: comedies, histories, and tragedies. This was not a straightforward task, and the manner in which they approached it has had far-reaching effects. On quarto publication, only six of the plays had been assigned more or less precisely to the categories in which they were to be placed in the Folio: *Titus Andronicus* was "A Roman tragedy," *Romeo and Juliet* an "excellent conceited tragedy" in 1597 and a "most lamentable tragedy" in 1599, *Love's Labor's Lost* a "pleasant conceited comedy," *The Merry Wives of Windsor* a comedy, *Hamlet* a tragical history on the title pages of the first and second quartos, and a straightforward tragedy on the headtitle of the second quarto, and *Othello* a tragedy. You may note that this list includes none of the histories. Another five plays were assigned to no category—these are the first printed version of Part Two of *Henry VI*, the second part of *Henry IV*, and three comedies: *A Midsummer Night's Dream, Much Ado About Nothing,* and *The Two Noble Kinsmen.* One play, *Pericles,* was described simply as a "play." Two of the plays were classed as histories in both the Folio and the quarto: Part One of *Henry IV* and *Henry V* (a Chronicle History), but three of the Folio histories were called tragedies on first publication: the first printed version of *3 Henry VI, Richard II,* and *Richard III.* One of the Folio comedies, *The Merchant of Venice,* was a history on its title page and a comical history according to its headtitle, and two of the Folio tragedies started off as histories: *King Lear* was a chronicle history on its title page and a history on its headtitle, and *Troilus and Cressida* was a "famous history."

The most conspicuous anomalies in the Folio's classification relate to the plays there classified as histories. The word "history" had a broad signification; it could be used of any narrative, not just an historical one. The Folio editors chose to use it only in the historical sense, and they also restricted it to plays based on medieval and Tudor English history. In doing so, they obscured the tragical nature of Shakespeare's treatment of the final part of the reign of Henry VI and the reigns of Richard II and Richard III, and ignored the historical aspects of the reign of King Lear as well as those of the plays based on Roman history that had not appeared in quarto. They were clearly intent on emphasizing the biographical aspects of the history plays— only one, *Richard III,* is described as a tragedy, and even that is "The Life and Death of Richard III" in the running titles. To this extent, their procedure takes the plays away from the theater in the direction of narrative history. To this end, they pretty certainly altered the titles under which some of the plays had been performed: the second and third parts of *Henry VI* seem to have been known in the theaters of the 1590s as the First and Second Parts of *The Contention betwixt the two Famous Houses of York and Lancaster* (or some equally unwieldy variant of this), and the play printed as *Henry VIII* in the Folio is three times alluded to as *All is True,* never unequivocally as *Henry VIII,* in accounts of the burning of the Globe: indeed the ballad commemorating that occasion has as the last words of its refrain the words "and yet all this is true."

Editorial decisions about genre affect other plays than those that had already appeared in print: the Roman tragedies and *Macbeth* are no less historical narratives than the plays centered on the lives of English kings, and *Cymbeline* is an historical as well as a comical play. Shakespeare's work is essentially eclectic, often drawing on a wide variety of literary and dramatic traditions and conventions within a single play. In attempting to confine it within the straitjacket of three categories, Heminges and Condell were less true to his memory than they might have wished.

There are, then, two principal ways in which the First Folio has affected our image of Shakespeare. One derives from its editorial procedures: its selection of editions and manuscripts to reprint, its employment of Ralph Crane as a transcriber, its imposition of act and scene divisions on many of the plays, its groupings of the plays according to generic divisions, and its varying of their original titles to fit this grouping. For good and for ill, these and related matters have shaped the way in which succeeding generations have thought and written about their author, and in which the plays have been presented, both in print and on the stage.

But most important of all is the inclusion in the Folio of all those plays that had not previously reached print, and that might never have done so had it not been for the efforts of Heminges, Condell, and their colleagues. Without them, it is not too much to say, the history of the world would have been different. Shakespeare, shorn of eighteen of his plays, would not have been the pre-eminent dramatist that he now is. The English language would be far less rich. Countless works of art in many kinds that have been inspired by the plays could not have come into existence: Verdi, for instance, could not have composed *Macbeth,* or Schubert, "Who is Sylvia?" and "Hark, hark the lark." W. H. Auden could not have written "The Sea and the Mirror," or Marina Warner *Indigo;* for better or for worse, we should be without *The Forbidden Planet* and *Return to the Forbidden Planet.* Thomas Hardy's *Under the Greenwood Tree,* Julian Slade's musical comedy *Salad Days,* and Noël Coward's *Present Laughter* would have had different titles; so would Dorothy Sayers' *Gaudy*

Night, Aldous Huxley's *Brave New World,* and R. C. Sherriff's *Journeys End.* The careers of most of our greatest actors and directors would have been different. How many young actresses could have made their mark without being able to play Perdita or Miranda, Rosalind or Viola, Isabella or Helen? Where would the reputations of David Garrick, Sarah Siddons, and W. C. Macready be without *Macbeth*, or John Philip Kemble without *Coriolanus,* Helena Faucit without *The Winter's Tale*, Laurence Olivier and Kenneth Branagh without *Henry V,* or John Gielgud without *The Winter's Tale* and *The Tempest?* Should we have had the Shakespeare Institute or the Shakespeare Birthplace Trust or the Royal Shakespeare Company if Shakespeare were known as the author of only fourteen or so plays? Would all the thousands of books on Shakespeare have been merely a lot shorter, or would they never have come into being? If not, would the University of Delaware Press have existed? Would Sam Wanamaker have wanted to reconstruct the Globe? Would Jay Halio have devoted his life to the works of Shackerley Marmion? It doesn't bear thinking about.

Notes

1. Elegies in English, Latin and Greek are reproduced in facsimile in *Elegies for Sir Philip Sidney (1587),* with an introduction by A. J. Colaianne and W. L. Godshalk (Delmar, NY: Scholar's Facsimiles and Reprints, 1980).
2. Quoted in the entry for Spenser in the *Dictionary of National Biography,* ed. Sir Sidney Lee, 63 vols. (London: Oxford University Press, 1895–1900), 53: 396.
3. Stanley Wells and Gary Taylor, with John Jowett and William Montgomery, *William Shakespeare: A Textual Companion* (Oxford: Oxford University Press, 1987), 163.
4. Ibid., 34–6; quotation modernized from p. 36.
5. Ibid., 36.
6. Peter W. M. Blayney, *The First Folio of Shakespeare* (Washington, D. C.: Folger Shakespeare Library Publications, 1991), 2.
7. " . . . we should recognize that his involvement with the First Folio was so extensive and of such a kind that it is Ralph Crane rather than the playwright Nicholas Rowe whom we should acknowledge as the first person to confront the problems of translating Shakespeare's plays from the stage to the study: Shakespeare's earliest editor." T. Howard-Hill, "Shakespeare's Earliest Editor: Ralph Crane," *Shakespeare Survey* 44 (1992): 129.
8. Cited in *Ben Jonson,* ed. C. H. Herford, Percy and Evelyn Simpson, 11 vols. (Oxford: Oxford University Press, 1925–52), 9: 13.
9. Peter Blayney, "The Publication of Playbooks," in *A New History of Early English Drama,* ed. John D. Cox and David Scott Kastan (New York: Columbia University Press, 1997), 392.

10. Richard Dutton, "The Birth of the Author," in *Elizabethan Theater: Essays in Honor of S. Schoenbaum*, ed. R. B. Parker and S. P. Zitner (Newark: University of Delaware Press, 1996), 87.

11. We have evidence, of course, that plays were sometimes shortened in performance, and that omitted passages were sometimes restored in printing; Humphrey Moseley, for instance, states in the Beaumont and Fletcher Folio of 1647 that the texts there published include "both all that was acted and all that was not"; what persuades me that the editors of the Folio brought their texts into line with the plays as acted is the very fact that in a number of instances they omit passages present in alternative versions.

12. The 1597 quarto of *Romeo and Juliet* marks the end of a number of scenes in the later part of the play with a type ornament; *Pericles* prints a rule after the ends of Acts One and Two, which of course immediately precede Choruses. In the 1622 *Othello*, the beginnings of Acts Two, Four, and Five are marked, and the 1634 edition of *The Two Noble Kinsmen* is fully marked into Acts and Scenes.

"All we like sheep . . ."

Susan Snyder

THINGS SHOULD BE NAMED CORRECTLY, SAID CONFUCIUS, "SO THAT THE HUMAN spirit is not beset by misunderstanding." For the correct names of Shakespeare's characters, the early printed texts are the chief authority. But sometimes Quarto and Folio show Shakespeare to have been a lax godfather, inattentive or indecisive in his naming. On occasion he offered more than one designation for the same figure; often he failed to provide any. Once in a while he gave us a name without a functioning body to go with it (Violenta in *All's Well*, for example, or Leonato's wife Innogen in *Much Ado*): as if the godparent performed his naming duty at the christening but forgot to bring the baby. In the afterlife of Shakespeare's plays, generations of editors have had to step in as auxiliary godparents, trying to make sense of what he did and didn't do in the way of christening characters, following their own interpretations and notions of correctness—and bowed down, as time went on, by an ever-more-weighty tradition of what earlier editors had done. Through such time-honored character designations in the Dramatis Personae, and especially in the stage directions and speech headings that by constant repetition fix any label in the reader's consciousness, users of these editions may be "beset by misunderstanding" without even knowing it.

As Barbara Mowat has shown, it is editorial tradition that has kept the label of *Puck* rather than *Robin Goodfellow* so tenaciously fastened to Oberon's right-hand sprite in *A Midsummer Night's Dream*. At the very beginning of the editing tradition, Nicholas Rowe settled on *Puck,* and generations of editors have followed, apparently without question.[1] There is certainly room for question, since *Robin* appears more often than *Puck* in both Q and F stage directions and speech headings. Indeed, Richard Kennedy has argued that Shakespeare's copy for Q1 used *Robin* throughout and that the compositor changed some to *Puck* because of type shortages.[2] *Puck* in Shakespeare's usage functions as a generic designation for a mischievous and at times malicious spirit, *Robin Goodfellow* as an individual name. When Oberon addresses him with the first, he accompanies it with an adjective: "my gentle puck," analogous to "my gentle lord." The second needs no qualifier: "Hie therefore, Robin," "Robin, take off this head." Speaking to the audience at the end of the play, he refers to himself first as "an honest puck," i.e., not like the more devilish pucks, and then simply as "Robin."[3]

Neither the greater textual claim of *Robin* over *Puck* nor the precedence that should be given it if proper names are preferred over generic titles is news. Some nineteenth-century editors record the fluctuations in Q and F speech headings and stage directions between *Robin* and *Puck,* and a few more recent ones even incorporate these fluctuations (see Variorum, Kittredge, Penguin). On the question of category label and individual name, Rowe's choice to regularize with *Puck* is perhaps easier to understand when we know that the clearest textual indication of the word's generic status was not available to him: the telltale "an" in "as I am an honest puck" does not appear in the edition he worked from. It was omitted in F3, by accident or design, and therefore does not appear in F4. Capell some decades later restored the missing "an," but by then the designation *Puck* was well established, and Capell did not change it in his own text. Nor did anyone else through generations of editing, though some included a note pointing out the generic nature of the designation.[4] Not until 1906 did an editor reject the Rowe tradition: William Alan Neilson regularized speech headings and stage directions to *Robin* and listed in the Dramatis Personae "Robin Goodfellow, a puck." That should have made some kind of impact, especially since Neilson's edition, and those derived from it,[5] were widely used in American schools and universities. But subsequent editions, in this country as elsewhere, still march obedient to Rowe's command.[6] Only very recently, in the Oxford *Complete Works* and single-play editions for the New Folger and Oxford series, has *Robin* begun displacing *Puck*. Even before Kennedy made his case based on type shortage, *Robin Goodfellow* was a marginally better choice than *Puck*. Not decisively, perhaps, since the early texts seem to support both, and generic character designations are common in Q and F stage directions. The point is that one alternative of the two nearly equal ones, arguably the preferable one, was effectively wiped out for two hundred years, really almost three hundred years, by a choice made in 1709 by one editor.

Most generic labels, unlike *Puck,* are easily distinguished from personal names. Generics abound in F stage directions, especially at the top and the bottom of the social ladder, designating rulers—*King, Duke*—and menials—*Servant, Messenger, Clown*. Especially Clown. Of the twenty-five comedies and tragedies in the First Folio, twelve have at least one part headed this way. Why so many? Mainly because "clown" in Elizabethan usage can mean not only a kind of comic role, the ignorant bumpkin, but also the principal comedian of the acting company. The designation thus extends beyond the bumpkin to other kinds of roles the comedian would play: Bottom in *A Midsummer Night's Dream* and Pompey in *Measure for Measure* are labeled *Clown*, but so is Touchstone in *As You Like It*.[7] For some in this group, Shakespeare never offers a personal name; in *Othello* and *Antony and Cleopatra* we have no choice but to designate them "Clown." Others are named in the dialogue, sometimes with considerable underlining. To these, editors have eventually awarded speech headings in their own names. It is surprising, though, how long they took about it in some cases. The Folio text of *Measure for Measure* repeats Pompey's name twenty-six times, but he remains *Clown* in editions for more than two hundred years. The Schlegel-Tieck translation does label him *Pompeius,* probably because there is no German equivalent for the "clown" of Elizabethan English. But in the English speaking world Pompey had to wait until the Dyce edition of 1857 to appear in the Dramatis Personae and textual paraphernalia in his own name.

What should we make of the fact that editors of *Measure for Measure* were so slow to register a tapster's name, however stressed in the text, while their Dramatis Personae lists never failed to name the Duke in the same play as *Vincentio?* The name "Vincentio" derives neither from the dialogue, where it never appears, nor from the Folio stage directions and speech headings, which employ only *Duke.* It comes from one of those "names of the actors" lists that are appended to seven of the Folio plays, especially—as in this case— plays thought to be printed from Ralph Crane's transcripts. We don't know who compiled these lists, or with what authority; they are not very accurate, omitting several minor but significant characters (see Appendix). But the name "Vincentio," for all its doubtful provenance, clings burr-like to the Duke in every Dramatis Personae list through the centuries. The same is true for the name "Claudius" in the more or less parallel case of *Hamlet.* This ruler, too, is never named in the dialogue of his play, although Q2 and F have a first entrance for "*Claudius, King of Denmarke.*" Editors unanimously take up the suggestion for their Dramatis Personae lists, perhaps relieved to be able to assign the King a personal name in a play that also contains a former king and a masquerade king.[8] When we consider how influential is the bare whisper of a name for a ruling monarch and what trouble editors have in taking seriously the name of a commoner even when it's repeatedly shouted, it is hard to escape the class implication: if you're a king or a duke, your personal name is important, but if you belong to the lower classes, it doesn't matter. Common nouns for common people.

I may seem to be reversing the position I took a few years ago when I was editing *All's Well that Ends Well*.[9] I argued then for retaining generic speech headings for the clown in that play. But I still favor using generics instead of what I call nonce-names, appellations that are given late and casually when the dramatic situation requires some kind of name to be used, but not dwelt on or repeated. (On the class question, my argument was neutral, including the two French lords as well as the steward and the clown.) Among clowns, I distinguish between the repeated and significant names *Bottom* and *Pompey* on the one hand, and on the other *Lavatch* and *Feste*, each specified once, for an immediate practical purpose, and never mentioned again. For these, it seems better for editors to stay with a generic label rather than create a spurious significance for the nonce-name by repeating it over and over in speech headings and stage directions, a practice that renders the reader's experience of the play needlessly different from the playgoer's.

Twelfth Night presents an additional problem, however. The Folio designation *Clown* endures through almost the whole editorial history, though in recent times often with the name *Feste* added, at least in the Dramatis Personae. *Clown* here clearly points to a kind of actor rather than to a traditional role. This character is not a bumpkin but a professional wit, a household retainer who makes his living by amusing people. When the Duke needs to have him identified (this is the one occasion when he's named), Curio answers "Feste the jester, my lord, a fool that the Lady Olivia's father took much delight in" (2.4.11–12). The name "Feste," suggesting holiday humor, seems almost an extension of the occupational labels "jester" and "fool." The generic title *Fool* makes more sense for this character than any pseudo-individual one, since we see him only at his professional activities: performing stand-up comedy routines, singing songs, wittily angling for tips, doing impersonations. We know nothing of his private desires and needs. Even his wish to be revenged on Malvolio is motivated by Malvolio's slur on his abilities *as a fool*. In the dialogue, people address him and refer to him, never as "Clown," or "Feste," but as "Fool," the same way he refers to himself. In a typical Folio sequence, the stage direction "*Enter* Clowne" is followed immediately by Sir Andrew's line "Here comes the Fool" (2.3.15). He is in fact at the center of a web of fool-allusions in this play, which counts 87 instances of *fool, folly* and derivatives, and gathers in all the major characters. Recent editors have gone from

Clown to *Feste.* Since they have already ventured away from the Folio designation, why not attend to the shout of the text, that insistently repeated *fool,* rather than the single murmur of *Feste?* That is, follow the lead of the New Folger editors, and adopt *Fool* in the speech headings and stage directions.

Feste and Lavatch, along with Claudius and Vincentio, focus a question for us: should editors use every scrap of evidence the early texts provide to identify characters for the reader? Surely such minimally supported designations should not be given great prominence by repetition in stage directions and speech headings. Non-dialogue names like "Claudius" and "Vincentio" perhaps have a place in the initial Dramatis Personae lists; at least nothing in the text contradicts them. But what about another label, not a name this time but a title: Montano as "*Gouernour of Cyprus*"? This description comes from the "Names of the Actors" compilation at the end of the Folio text of *Othello* (see Appendix), which in this case may derive in turn from a single stage direction in Q1, at the beginning of Act 2: "*Enter* Montanio, *Gouernor of* Cypres." E. A. J. Honigmann thinks Shakespeare first conceived of Montano as having this position but then changed his mind in the course of composition.[10] Certainly no one in the play as we have it treats Montano like a governor, even a governor who is giving up his post. He appears with other local gentry in the first Cyprus scene, included in the general greetings and not singled out in any way. In the drinking scene he seems very much one of the boys, not a senior statesman. And when he is then wounded by Cassio, wouldn't we expect some comment if he were really the former governor? Steevens questioned the description in 1793, pointing to the unclear provenance of the Folio character lists as well as counterindications in the text (Steevens-Reed, 376). An additional note by Steevens on the drinking scene adds tartly, "If Montano was Othello's predecessor in the government of Cyprus, (as we are told in the Personae Dramatis,) he is not very characteristically employed in the present scene, where he is tippling with people already *fluster'd,* and encouraging a subaltern officer who commands a midnight guard, to drink to excess" (482). The "governor" label is actively misleading, and Steevens clearly knows he should delete it. But tradition is too strong: the 1793 edition, like all its predecessors, lists in the Dramatis Personae "Montano, Governor of Cyprus." So do all nineteenth-century and almost all twentieth-century editions, though some also reprint Steevens's doubting notes.[11] Walker and Wilson observe that the identification of Montano as governor is based only on the Q stage direction "and may have no authority" (139); but, although they think Q1 an untrustworthy text, they leave

Montano's title intact in the Dramatis Personae. Even Sanders cannot quite get rid of it, although he puts it in skeptical quotation marks. The New Folger editors are the first I know to demote Montano from deputy head of state to simply an official. Why did it take so long? Editors who feel free to remove "ghost characters" like Innogen from their texts, adding a note of explanation, could do the same with "ghost titles." But it is hard to throw off the weight of precedent.

While tradition encourages consistency with our predecessors, it can also perpetuate strange *in*consistencies. Why do editors of *Macbeth* regularly standardize the Folio designation *Seyward* to *Siward,* but leave the parallel *Seyton* in its unmodernized form? Here the trendsetter was Theobald, who changed the *Seyward* references to *Siward* and added a genealogical note explaining Malcolm's relation to that family.[12] He also changed *Seyton* to *Siton*—but only in the Dramatis Personae, not in the text. The first effort prevailed; the second, somewhat feeble stab at consistency did not. Generations of editors have reproduced *Siward* (modernized spelling) and *Seyton* (original spelling), and by doing so have foreclosed on the possibilities of symbolic opposition that are opened by the Folio's parallel-but-different spellings. Shakespeare likes to put radically opposed moral values in focus by pairing such characters by their names, having them share a common first syllable and diverge in the second. Think of Macbeth and Macduff in the same play, or Edgar and Edmund in *King Lear.* Seyward and Seyton are minor figures, to be sure, but their very lack of personal dimension makes them useful in a symbolic register. Both are introduced in the last phase of the action, Seyton by the side of an increasingly isolated Macbeth while Seyward helps to lead the forces massed against him. In the dialogue Seyward is associated verbally with Christendom, goodness, grace, and "the powers above," while the sound of Seyton's name unavoidably links this final sole companion of Macbeth with "the common enemy of man" to whom he has given up his eternal jewel.[13] A note by G. R. French, cited in the Variorum (271) and several later editions, points out the aptness of having this character arm Macbeth, since "the Setons of Touch were (and are still) hereditary armour-bearers to the kings of Scotland." But although the note uses the name in its modern form, no one transfers that form to the text until Wilson in 1947. And we have had to wait even longer for the alternative model of consistency, to me the preferable one in allowing for more richness of meaning: Hunter in 1967 leaves both Seyward and Seyton in their original form, as does Nicholas Brooke in 1990.

My title for this essay comes from the Book of Isaiah, though many of us know it better from Handel's *Messiah.* "All we like sheep have gone astray" (Isa. 53:6, RSV). The verse continues, "we have turned every one to his own way." I am arguing, however, that maybe we *should* turn more to our own ways, not rejecting tradition for the sake of novelty but also resisting the temptation to follow tradition for its own sake, trying not to go astray in a herd. Trying, in short, to think every detail afresh, which is so easy to say and so very hard to do.

Appendix: Dramatis Personae lists in the First Folio

Character lists are appended to seven plays (*The Tempest, Two Gentlemen of Verona, Measure for Measure, The Winter's Tale, 2 Henry IV, Othello, Timon of Athens*), the first four of which came through the hands of the scrivener Ralph Crane.[14] If the copy for *The Merry Wives of Windsor,* the only Crane-transcript play that lacks such a list, contained a character list like the others, it may have been omitted in printing for lack of space; the text of the play ends close to the end of the page. In any case, similar lists in a Crane transcript of Middleton's *The Witch* and in the 1623 quarto of *The Duchess of Malfi,* also based on a Crane manuscript, suggest to T. H. Howard-Hill that "it was his practice to supply his transcripts with lists of characters, though whether he compiled them himself or copied them cannot be determined."[15] The provision of such lists may be seen as part of Crane's general tendency to render the texts he transcribed in more "literary" form, perhaps specifically influenced by the example of Jonson. Noting that the earliest Crane transcript known is a Jonson one (1618), Howard-Hill speculates that "Jonson's Folio of 1616, in which the plays were preceded by 'Names of the Actors' and locality indications and regularly divided into acts and scenes, must have supplied useful example to a scribe who sought a model for his literary transcripts."[16] W. W. Greg ascribed the Folio lists to an editor who was perhaps the bookkeeper or Isaac Jaggard himself.[17] In those pre-Hinman days he could hold the somewhat contradictory opinions that lists "were specially drawn up by the editor when preparing the copy for the collection" and that some of them "were obviously supplied as padding when it was found that the plays would not fill the space allotted to them" (355). Greg thought only the *Tempest* list was certainly in the copy and not specially supplied to fill up space (418). J. H. P. Pafford speculates that the *Winter's Tale* list, like those for *Two Gentlemen, Measure,* and *Othello,* "was probably drawn up and put in at the printing house to fill a page which would otherwise be largely blank."[18] But Howard-Hill counters that

> it is hardly conceivable that a compositor would have held up work on the Folio to allow space-filling lists to be compiled if they were not already part of the copy, and the order of printing gives no support for the view that this happened. Whatever the reason they were printed, they were already available in the compositors' copy: when they were not, the compositors did not hesitate to leave a blank page if the sequence of printing made it necessary. The character of the lists and the provision of the name of the duke in *Measure for Measure* makes it highly improbable that the compositors compiled them themselves as necessary.[19]

If they were space-fillers to meet an immediate need, these lists could only have been made up in the printing house, and since such compiling—even when done carelessly—takes time, it is more likely that they were already part of the copy received from the players.

But what purpose could the lists have served in the playhouse? Most of them have significant omissions. Nine characters are missing from the *Winter's Tale* compilation, including Mopsa, Dorcas, and Time. All the other lists, except those for *Tempest* and *Two Gentlemen*, are incomplete. The characters omitted are minor (except Flavius in *Timon of Athens,* possibly confused by the compiler with Flaminius), and appear in one scene only. Such characters might conceivably have been omitted from a playhouse list as easy to double, not requiring extra actors. But some of those included in the lists are also one-scene characters easy to double: in *2 Henry IV,* for example, Beadle, Fang and Snare, Lady Northumberland, Lady Percy, Mouldy, Wart, and Bullcalf; in *Measure,* Francisca, Barnardine, and Froth; in *Two Gentlemen,* Eglamour and Antonio. Some of the absentees are important to the plots, like Barnardine, though many are not. It is unlikely, in any case, that such faulty lists could have had a practical function in production.

Honigmann pushes provenance for the lists further back beyond the playhouse, to Shakespeare himself. He argues that such lists would have been useful for keeping track of characters in the process of composition.[20] But Honigmann does not here address two problems with his theory: the lists' inaccuracies, which would presumably diminish their value to the working playwright as well as to the stage presenters, and the occurrence of four out of seven of them in texts based on Crane's transcripts, a preponderance too great for coincidence. In his later *Texts of "Othello",* he does take account of the Crane link, and indeed uses it to support his contention that F *Othello* is based on a Crane MS.[21]

The best guess is that someone in an editorial capacity with only a superficial acquaintance with the plays compiled the lists, overlooking some single-appearance characters. If such lists were drawn up for all the Folio plays, it is hard to see why more of them were not used, since only a few plays lack space at the end that might be filled with character names. It seems they were done for only a few, in four cases probably by the scrivener Crane; in others, perhaps, in imitation of Crane. As to what their purpose was, and why they were added to these plays, we as yet have no answers.

Notes

This paper was originally presented at a panel chaired by Jay Halio at the World Shakespeare Congress, Los Angeles, 1996: "Editing Shakespeare: Then and Now."

1. Barbara A. Mowat, "Nicholas Rowe and the Twentieth-Century Shakespeare Text." In *Shakespeare and Cultural Traditions: The Selected Proceedings of the International Shakespeare Association World Congress, Tokyo, 1991*, ed. Tetsuo Kishi, Roger Pringle, and Stanley Wells (Newark: University of Delaware Press, 1994), 317.

2. Richard Kennedy, "Speech Prefixes in Some Shakespeare Quartos," paper presented at the "Editing Shakespeare" seminar of the World Shakespeare Congress, Los Angeles, 1996, 3–5. Kennedy contends that personal names are the norm for speech headings in Q1 *MND*, and that all variations into the generic are alternatives resorted to by compositors because of type shortages.

3. 2.1.148; 3.2.355; 4.1.79; 5.1.426, 433. Quotations here and elsewhere are from the Bevington edition. Bevington, like most editors, gives a capital letter to *puck* in the first and fourth of these citations.

4. See Steevens, 1773, Grant White, Cambridge; also, later, Wilson, Wells, Foakes.

5. The Tudor Shakespeare and the Neilson and Hill versions.

6. In his Dramatis Personae Wilson also lists "Robin Goodfellow, the Puck." The commentary likewise insists that "Robin Goodfellow is a name; Puck is strictly speaking a title for a class of mischievous or malicious sprites, and it is noticeable that Robin is never addressed simply as 'puck' in the text" (103). Nevertheless, he follows tradition in regularizing to "Puck," making use of the QF fluctuations between *Robin* and *Puck* instead to construct one of his elaborate revision hypotheses. Arden editor Brooks's explanation that the shifts between these two in the speech headings point to a distinction between Robin, the prankster of folklore, and Puck, Oberon's lieutenant, is no more convincing.

7. David Wiles, *Shakespeare's Clown: Actor and Text in the Elizabethan Playhouse* (Cambridge: Cambridge University Press, 1987), 12. Wiles goes on to observe that bumpkin and wit could merge in theatrical practice: "In *Cambises* the functions of rustic and Vice were distinct: Hob and Lob, the 'country patches', are given a risible Mummerset accent, and are the objects of the Vice's mockery. In Tarlton, the Vice and the rustic are fused."

8. Early texts of *Hamlet* have speech headings in the Mousetrap scene for the fictive Gonzago and Baptista that do not differ from those of the actual King and Queen of Denmark: *King* and *Queen* (Q2), *King* and *Bap* (F1), *King* and *Queen* (F2),

etc. Theobald distinguishes the fictional pair by using "Duke" and "Dutchess" for their stage directions and speech headings, and is followed by Warburton, Capell, Johnson, and Steevens 1773. Steevens 1778, however, inaugurates the now standard "P. King" and "P. Queen."

9. Susan Snyder, "Naming Names in *All's Well that Ends Well*," *Shakespeare Quarterly* 43 (1992): 265–79.

10. E. A. J. Honigmann, *The Stability of Shakespeare's Text* (London: Edward Arnold, 1965), 37–39. Honigmann adduces as traces of the early plan an allusion (1.3.41–44) to Montano's seeking to be relieved, the Q1 entrance direction, and Montano's gladness (2.1.32) at Othello's appointment as governor. But his first indication of Montano's "original" status depends on accepting Capell's suggestion that "Signor Montano . . . prays you to believe him" should read "relieve him," an emendation that has not been widely accepted by modern editors. And the last instance, a possible contrast to Iago's resentment at being passed over for the lieutenancy in Montano's gracious assent to his loss of office, is hardly independent evidence. The more general point (45), that Shakespeare frequently individualizes characters on first entrance with a name of which he makes no further use (Solinus in *Comedy of Errors*, Prince Escalus in *Romeo and Juliet*, Ferdinand in *Love's Labour's Lost*, etc.), may have more valid application in regard to Montano's anomalous Q1 entrance designation, though the individualization is by title rather than by name.

11. The "governor" designation caused production problems as well. Furness in the Variorum edition reports that Edwin Booth delayed Montano's entrance in the drinking scene until just before Cassio's drunken exit, presumably finding Montano's earlier carousing unseemly (129).

12. Theobald 1733 reads *Siward* in each case except the first (3.6.31), which was changed to match the others in the 1740 edition. Capell changes the name back to *Seyward*. Steevens in 1773 has *Siward* in the Dramatis Personae and 3.6 but *Seyward* in four later scenes; but by 1778 he has regularized to *Siward*. The tradition is fairly well set by this time, with the partial exception of Rann, who has *Siward* in the text but confusingly refers to *Seyward* in a note on 3.6.31.

13. 4.3.190–93, 240–41; 3.1.69–70.

14. The number should posssibly be five or even six: some have suspected a Crane transcript behind F *2 Henry IV,* and Honigmann has recently argued convincingly for Crane's hand in F *Othello* (*Texts of "Othello,"* especially ch. 5).

15. T. H. Howard-Hill, *Ralph Crane and Some Shakespeare First Folio Comedies* (Charlottesville, Va.: University Press of Virginia, 1972), 78.

16. Ibid., 10.

17. W. W. Greg, *The Shakespeare First Folio: Its Bibliographical and Textual History* (Oxford: Clarendon Press, 1955), 77–79.

18. J. H. P. Pafford, ed. *The Winter's Tale*, 2.

19. Howard-Hill, *Ralph Crane*, 77–78.

20. Honigmann, *Stability*, 45–46.

21. Honigmann, *The Texts of "Othello" and Shakespearean Revision* (London and New York: Routledge, 1996), 70–72.

Abbreviated references to Shakespeare plays indicate the following:

Q: Quarto editions of *A Midsummer Night's Dream, Hamlet,* and *Othello,* cited from Kenneth Muir and Michael J. B. Allen, eds., *Shakespeare's Plays in Quarto* Berkeley and Los Angeles: University of California Press, 1981.

F: *Comedies, Histories, & Tragedies.* London: Isaac Jaggard and Edward Blount, 1623.

Rowe: Nicholas Rowe, ed. *Works.* 7 vols. London: J. Tonson, 1709.

Theobald 1733: Lewis Theobald, ed. *Works.* 7 vols. London: A Bettesworth etc., 1733.

Theobald 1740: 2nd ed. 8 vols. London: H. Lintott, 1740.

Warburton: William Warburton, ed. *Works.* 8 vols. London: J. & P. Knapton etc., 1747.

Johnson: Samuel Johnson, ed. *Plays.* 8 vols. London: J. & R. Tonson etc., 1765.

Capell: Edward Capell, ed. *Comedies, Histories, and Tragedies.* 10 vols. London: Dryden Leach etc., 1768.

Steevens 1773: George Steevens, ed. *Plays.* 10 vols. London: C. Bathurst etc., 1773.

Steevens 1778: 2nd ed. 10 vols. London: C. Bathurst, 1778.

Rann: Joseph Rann, ed. *Dramatic Works.* 6 vols. Oxford: Rivington etc., 1786.

Steevens-Reed: George Steevens and Isaac Reed, eds. *Plays.* 4th ed. 15 vols. London: T. Longman, 1793.

Schlegel-Tieck: A. W. von Schlegel and Ludwig Tieck, trans. and ed. *Dramatische Werke.* 9 vols. Berlin: G. Reimer, 1825–33.

Grant White: Richard Grant White, ed. *Works.* 12 vols. Boston: Little, Brown, 1857–66.

Cambridge: W. G. Clark and W. A. Wright, eds. *Works.* 9 vols. Cambridge: Cambridge University Press, 1863–66.

Neilson: W. A. Neilson, ed. *Complete Dramatic and Poetic Works.* Boston and New York: Houghton, Mifflin, 1906.

Neilson and Hill: W. A. Neilson and C. J. Hill, eds. *Complete Plays and Poems.* Boston and New York: Houghton, Mifflin, 1942.

Oxford: Stanley Wells and Gary Taylor, eds. *Complete Works.* Oxford: Clarendon Press, 1986.

Bevington: David M. Bevington, ed. *Complete Works.* 4th ed. New York: HarperCollins, 1992.

A Midsummer Night's Dream

Variorum: H. H. Furness, ed. *A Midsommer Nights Dreame.* New Variorum ed. Philadelphia: Lippincott, 1895.

Tudor: W. A. Neilson and A. H. Thorndyke, eds. *A Midsummer Night's Dream.* Tudor Shakespeare. New York: Macmillan, 1921.

Wilson: John Dover Wilson and Sir Arthur Quiller-Couch, eds. *A Midsummer-Night's Dream.* New Shakespeare. Cambridge: Cambridge University Press, 1924.

Kittredge: G. L. Kittredge, ed. *A Midsummer Night's Dream.* Boston: Ginn, 1939.

Penguin: G. B. Harrison, ed. *A Midsummer Night's Dream.* Penguin Shakespeare. London: Penguin, 1953.

Wells: Stanley Wells, ed. *A Midsummer Night's Dream.* New Penguin Shakespeare. Harmondsworth, Middlesex: Penguin, 1967.

Brooks: Harold F. Brooks, ed. *A Midsummer Night's Dream.* Arden Shakespeare. London: Methuen, 1979.

Foakes: R. A. Foakes, ed. *A Midsummer Night's Dream.* New Cambridge Shakespeare. Cambridge: Cambridge University Press, 1984.

New Folger: Barbara A. Mowat and Paul Werstine, eds. *A Midsummer Night's Dream.* New Folger Library Shakespeare. New York: Washington Square Press, 1993.

Holland: Peter Holland, ed. *A Midsummer Night's Dream.* Oxford Shakespeare. Oxford: Clarendon, 1994.

Macbeth

Wilson: John Dover Wilson, ed. *Macbeth.* New Shakespeare. Cambridge: Cambridge University Press, 1947.

Hunter: G. K. Hunter, ed. *Macbeth.* New Penguin Shakespeare. Harmondsworth, Middlesex: Penguin, 1967.

Brooke: Nicholas Brooke, ed. *The Tragedy of Macbeth.* Oxford Shakespeare. Oxford: Clarendon, 1990.

Othello

Variorum: H. H. Furness, ed. *Othello.* New Variorum ed. Philadelphia: Lippincott, 1886.

Walker and Wilson: Alice Walker and John Dover Wilson, eds. *Othello.* New Shakespeare. Cambridge: Cambridge University Press, 1957.

Sanders: Norman Sanders, ed. *Othello.* New Cambridge Shakespeare. Cambridge: Cambridge University Press, 1984.

New Folger: Barbara A. Mowat and Paul Werstine, eds. *Othello.* New Folger Library Shakespeare. New York: Washington Square Press, 1993.

The Winter's Tale

Pafford: J. H. P. Pafford, ed. *The Winter's Tale.* Arden Shakespeare. London: Methuen, 1963.

Still Babbling of Green Fields:
Mr. Greenfields and the Twenty-third Psalm

GEORGE WALTON WILLIAMS

THIS ESSAY DISCUSSES THE HISTORY AND THE RAMIFICATIONS OF THE MOST CELE-brated textual crux in Shakespeare's plays. The Folio text of *Henry V,* thought by many critics to have been set from Shakespeare's holograph, gives Mrs. Quickly's account of Falstaff's death in this prose passage:

> a parted eu'n iust betweene Twelue and One, eu'n at the turning o'th'Tyde: for after I saw him fumble with the Sheets, and play with Flowers, and smile vpon his fingers end, I knew there was but one way: for his Nose was as sharpe as a Pen, and a Table of greene fields.
> (2.3.12–16; TLN 835–39)

The Quarto edition of 1600, a version briefer and of doubtful provenance and authority, gives the account in verse:

> He went away as if it were a crysombd childe,
> Betweene twelue and one,
> Iust at turning of the tide:
> His nose was as sharpe as a pen:
> For when I saw him fumble with the sheetes,
> And talk of floures, and smile vpon his fingers ends
> I knew there was no way but one.
> (B4v)

The Folio phrase, "and a Table of greene fields" (TLN 839), lacking in the Quarto, has given much trouble to critics for nearly three hundred years. It is arguable that it was difficult for some of Shakespeare's contemporaries also.

The full account of the death of Falstaff from "Nay sure, hee's not in Hell" to "as cold as any stone" (832–847) consists of a series of twenty-six separate and separable phrases and clauses, the cumulative effect of which is very powerful. The Quarto account lacks five of these items, repeats one, and transposes one.

Lacking in Q:	832	Nay sure, hee's not in Hell:
	833–4	a made a finer end,
	839	a Table of greene fields.
	840	be a good cheare:
	845	put my hand into the Bed,
Repeated in Q:	[846]	and they were as cold as any stone.
Transposed in Q:	838–9	for his Nose was as sharpe as a Pen,

Of these seven variants, it is evident that three of the Quarto's lackings (833–34, 840, 845) comprise concepts fully realized in the Folio passages and that the repeated phrase ([846]) simply repeats again what has already been said twice. The first variant (832) is an accommodation to the change in the cue given by the preceding speaker. Nothing in these variants seems particularly remarkable or abnormal in a comparison of the two texts.

On the other hand, the transposition of the phrase "for his Nose was as sharpe as a Pen" from 838–39 to follow line 836 is remarkable; it is the only transposition in the entire series. That is an achievement of some ninety-five percent identity in the Quarto rendition of the sequence of phrases, which represents the sixty lines of Folio prose in the entire scene by forty-eight lines of verse, a notable difference. Furthermore, that accuracy has occurred in a sequence many of the units of which could be transposed without significant damage to the integrity of the passage and with no loss to the overall effect. Still more remarkable is the fact that the phrase "for his Nose was as sharpe as a Pen" transposed in the Quarto and the phrase "and a Table of greene fields" absent in the Quarto are contiguous in the Folio.

It is not easy to accept the premise that the conjunction of these two extraordinary variants is no more than coincidental; nor is it easy to imagine how the dislocations arose. It would almost seem necessary to postulate a difficulty in Shakespeare's original holograph that caused one or another of the agents responsible for the Quarto, rendering holograph prose as verse, to omit the phrase that the Folio compositor was later to print as "a Table of greene fields"—as presenting some difficulty in comprehension or not intelligible in the manuscript or written out of sequence in the margin later—and hence also to transpose out of its normal order the immediately preceding phrase.

As it is unlikely that speculation in the cloudy origins of the Quarto will be very illuminating, it might be of interest to examine what critics and editors have made of the phrase through the centuries. The Folio phrase remained unchanged in the received text in the seventeenth-century folios and in the editions of Nicholas Rowe in 1709 and 1714. Alexander Pope's edition of 1723 (1725) and 1728 simply deleted it, and ever since Pope's slashing hook so violently emended the text, critics and editors have been engaged in spirited controversy. They have divided into two camps: critics have been adventurous, suggesting many different emendations; editors have in the main been conservative, retaining the emendation "babbled" for "Table" advanced by Lewis Theobald in 1726 and recording but not adopting the suggestions of the critics. Between them, they have over the years reached three solutions.

The first solution to the problem has been to reform it altogether by simply removing the phrase from the text, considering it an intrusive stage direction. This was Pope's way. In his edition of 1723 and in later editions he deleted the words from the text, placing them "in the Margin" (at the foot of the page). He did so, having satisfied himself that they were a stage direction: "A Table was here directed to be brought in, . . . and this direction crept into the text from the margin. *Greenfield* was the name of the Property-man . . . who furnish'd implements &c. for the actors." Warburton followed suit in his edition (1747), vigorously supporting his predecessor for giving "So reasonable an account of this blunder." No other editors have deleted the phrase completely from the dialogue as if it were a stage direction, but some have proposed other interpretations of the "direction." Theobald in his *Shakespeare Restored* (1726) offered an alternate: "*Chairs,* and a Table off. Green Fields"; he continued: "I therefore believe This was intended as a Direction . . . to remove the *Chairs* and *Table* . . . and to shift the Scene, from the *Tavern* to a Prospect of *green Fields* representing Part of [*France*]" (138). Roberts, in his *Answer* of 1729, supported Theobald's suggestion, but refined it by supposing that Green and Field were the names of actors (25); Fitzgerald, in *Notes and Queries* (1888), understands "Table" to mean "a paper of some sort" and conceives the direction as a warning for Mr. Greenfields, the actor who was to play Exeter, to have ready for the next scene the document of the royal descent that he would need to show the French King (84).

It is doubtful that Theobald would have found Roberts' "support" helpful, for he was probably advancing this "stage direction" theory disingenuously, merely as a preamble to his own emendation to the text; to which Pope alludes in the appendix to his edition of 1728: "The Restorer Theobald . . . would have a meer Conjecture admitted" (Vol. 8, sig. Aa3). Although Johnson read this as Pope's seeming "to admit Theobald's emendation" (ed. 1765), Pope did not, in fact, change his text in the editions of 1728 or of 1735. Later editors Singer (1853) and Collier (ed. 1876) misunderstood Johnson, and without examining Pope's later editions thought that Pope had accepted Theobald's emendation. He never did, of course; and for his pains in denouncing Pope, "pidling Tibald," as is well known, was duncified. Knight (ed.1839) proposed that Pope's conjecture "can only have been meant as a hoax upon the general reader"; this charitable interpretation is indeed a possibility, but Pope's response to Theobald's emendation in his comment in the edition of 1728 and, indeed, to Theobald generally in *The Dunciad* does not to this reader seem to have the tone of the continuation of a joke.

The second solution to the problem has been to do nothing about it: to follow the First Folio and its successors through Rowe (ed. 1714) without question. Of all the early editors, only Delius (in his second [1857] and subsequent editions, including the "Leopold" Shakespeare), has retained the reading of the Folio. Glossing "Table" as a piece of furniture, Delius has attempted to explain the difficult reading thus: "The comic . . . may consist then in this, . . . that the Hostess compares the nose simultaneously with a pointed quill and with a flat table"; he has set off as parenthetical "as sharp as a pen and" in his explanatory note (48). Among subsequent editors, Charlotte Porter and Helen Clarke (1903–1912) and recently John F. Andrews in his Guild Shakespeare Edition (1989) have followed that example. Andrews explains the Folio reading thus:

> The Hostess could be referring to a pen on a decorated writing tablet . . . ; or . . . to a pen (enclosure) on a picture (tabula) . . . [; or to] a writing pen on a table covered with green baize. . . . If so, both objects could be equally distinct to her, the pen with its fine point, the table with its keen edges and sharp corners. (348)

Jenkins (1996) argues that "the supreme objection to *Table* . . . is that it fails to fit the sense. . . . It adds nothing significant to the image to have the pen on a table, still less a green table. Shakespeare would never be so feeble," and he adds (1997b): the fact that the quarto omits "and a Table . . ." "is clear evidence against [having] . . . the pen on a table[;] . . . the reporter had no image of a pen on a table."

In spite of the reluctance of the great variety of editors to retain the Folio text in their editions, critics have been vigorous and imaginative in arguing for its retention, offering many explanations for that text. The earliest explanation for the word "table"—other than that it is a piece of furniture—is that it signifies a tablet or table-book. William Smith (1754) suggested that "On table-books, silver... pens were formerly... fixed either to the backs or covers. Mother Quickly compares Falstaff's nose... to one of those pens... and she meant probably to have said, on a table-book, with a shagreen-cover... but ... she calls it a table of green fells, or turn'd into green fields" (381).

Other explanations have been offered: Tuckey (1956) suggests that "pen" and "table" are nouns of topographical reference, signifying "mountain peak" and "tableland"; Falstaff's nose "juts above his other features as sharply as a mountain peak juts above a flat countryside" (486–91). Bateson replies (1957): "It is a good story, but it doesn't wash" (225). Nathan (1959) offers two ideas: "The sharp nose that signified imminent death also brought to the Hostess' mind a picture of a burial ground... a cemetery" for which "green fields" might be regarded as a euphemism. "There is some slight possibility of an intentional ambiguity. *Table* could also refer to a tombstone. Falstaff's nose... a miniature tombstone on the face of a dying man" (92–94). Hulme (1956b) suggests that the context is prominently sexual, *pen* and *table* being slang or popular terms for the sexual organs, male and female (284). Or, to consider more curiously, Hall (1889): "The word might symbolize a vegetarian repast of... salads, &c, while the 'sharpness' may stand for the pickles *ad lib.*" (163).

The interpretation most frequently found in the criticism, however, defines "table" as a picture. Malone (ed. 1790, App., 643) was the first to suggest this possibility: "I once had a conjecture that... the word *table* is right and that the corrupted word is *and,* which may have been misprinted for in.... A *pen* may have been used for a pinfold [formed of pointed stakes], and a *table* for a picture." To which, Ritson replied in *Cursory Criticisms* (1792): "Such miserable nonsense" (103). Ritson was objecting primarily to the pinfold; he did not inhibit the idea of a picture, which continues in the minds of critics to the present day. Rann (ed. 1791), reading "babbled," provides a gloss "as green as grass" to explain "table." Caldecott proposes as "*possible,* that amongst the household furniture of the day... coarsely painted... pictures of green fields with green trees shooting up in a spiral and pointed form were in use: and it is enough for us that *some such thing* is not impossible" to encourage the editor to see the Folio text as the correct reading, although he recognizes that no course can be taken for performance other than to adopt Theobald's emendation. Critics of this interpretation have relied on the authority of art historians such as Waterhouse who points out that pictures of fields, that is, landscapes, were very rare in England in Shakespeare's day, and if known, would not have been known to someone of Mrs. Quickly's understanding. Landscape as a recognized genre derived from Dutch painting, not yet common in England (1978, 48, 154–61). However, although the word is not in Shakespeare's dramatic vocabulary, the *OED* dates it from 1598: (1.) "a table . . . [of] painted Landskips" (R. Haydocke).

A more sensitive, complete, and very learned explanation of the interpretation of "table" as picture or image is that of Ephim C. Fogel (1958). He recalls the traditional signs of approaching death as described by Hippocrates—first noticed by Creighton (1889)—and repeated constantly thereafter: "a sharp nose . . . the colour of the whole face being green" (489). "Falstaff's symptoms," he writes, "are hyperbolic in a Quicklian manner. Falstaff's nose is not merely sharp, but as sharp as a pen; . . . and his color is not merely green, but the very picture of greenness, a 'Table of greene fields'" (490). Eagle (1957, 240) also cited that source, specifying the translation of Galen as the closest origin of Shakespeare's series of the signs of death. Fogel's assiduous supporter, R. F. Fleissner, has confirmed the Galenic source (1983, 58–60) and maintained the validity of Fogel's interpretation in many articles. He has noted particularly the emphasis on greenness which admits a mock parody of Falstaff and the Green Knight (1986, 1992), and on greenness (*chlorosis*) in "male green-sickness," marked in Falstaff's love for the Prince (1961); on the frequency of greenness in ballads, especially in association with death (1976), the greenness of fields and vegetation as emblems of human transience (1985) and as used in depicting human faces by Arcimboldo (1992); on green fields as the background of hunting scenes such as might appear in painted cloths or tapestries (1983); on a "table" as anticipating *Hamlet* (1976) and as an item in discussions of painting (1996).

Hulme (*N&Q*, 1956) (supported by Eagle [1957] and by Fleissner [1991]) suggests that "Table" is another kind of image, a coat of arms: Mrs. Quickly "sees the nose tapering, like a pen against a green background . . . a device on a coat of arms, the field vert translated into green fields," and she remembers that Falstaff promised to marry her and make her a Lady. Bateson objects (1957): "Miss Hulme's coat of arms is an intolerably abrupt interruption—in its context an almost unintelligible one."

The most specific explanation and the one to have produced the most heat is that of Leslie Hotson, interpreting "Table" as portrait (*TLS*, 6 April 1956, 212, with letters supporting and objecting in 1956 and 1958). Hotson proposes: "The Hostess, then, is telling Falstaff's stricken crew that his sharpened nose as he lay a-dying was a 'picture', or as it might be, the 'spitten image' of 'greene fields'" i.e., of

Sir Richard Grenville's, dying at Flores in 1591. Hotson supported this interpretation with the observations that "play with Flowers" (in Q—"talk of floures") suggests talking of Flores and "his fingers end" suggests the famous One against Fifty-three, the odds confronting Grenville at Flores, a parallel picked up in *1 Henry IV* (2.4.179–80), Falstaff's description of the robbery at Gadshill (first noted by Stewart [1935]). The correspondence on this theory was vigorous, Hotson's position being supported by Coulson and Gittings (two letters), and being rejected by Barker, Young, Walker, and Williamson. The historian A. L. Rowse observed near the end of the controversy (1958) that there is "no evidence that Grenville was pronounced Greenfield at all" (313).

Bateson (1972) rejects all such interpretations because "*they ruin the Hostess's part* . . . with such laboured and quite uncharacteristic witticisms. . . . In three plays the Hostess [uses only] eight similes . . . , and they are all short, simple, familiar" (131–32; cf. 1962, 57–58). (Fleissner counters, observing that two of these compare the human body to plant life [1992, 326]). Jenkins (1997a) argues that "since four centuries of ingenuity have failed to find a satisfactory meaning for 'a Table of' . . . the case [for emending it] is very strong."

The third solution to the problem has been to emend, and critics have been inventive, suggesting many options to their colleagues engaged practically in editing the text. Five only—to "Table" and to "fields"—have been printed in editions. Since it was adopted in his edition in 1733, Theobald's emendation to "babbled" has been the received text. The Bowdlers' edition (1807) adopted "he fabled." G. B. Harrison's English Penguin edition (1931, 1951) adopted "'a talk" which is thus justified: "the passage in the Quarto reads—' . . . talk of floures . . . '. In my own proofs I have thrice met the misprint '*table*' for '*talk*' (or vice-versa)"; this justification does not, however, explain the grammar of the resulting clause. Mowat and Werstine printed "talked" (ed. 1995). J. P. Collier's fanciful emendations in the Perkins Folio of 1632, adopted in his editions of 1853 and 1856, include the notation that the line should be "on a table of green frieze": "Mrs Quickly likens the nose of the dying wit . . . to the sharpness of a pen, as seen in strong relief on a [writing] table [covered with green cloth]" (1853, 258). Delius adopted the reading in his first edition (only; 1854), and Keightley in correspondence with Halliwell (1853), and Moberly (ed. 1880), Barker (1956), and Creighton (1889) supported this explanation, but Davenport Adams (ed. 1876) thought "frieze" a "lection worthy of a railway director."

Other suggestions of the critics have been less well received by editors. These have seen Folio *Pen* as "pin"; *and* as "in" or "on" or "one" or "like"; *a* as the article, as the unstressed indeterminate vowel [a] (= of, have), or as the pronoun (= he); *Table* as "carold," "stable," "talked," "tatle," "tattled"; *fields* as "feald," "fell(s)," or "field." Wylie (1889, 163) suggested "pin" as an item "more likely to occur to Mrs. Quickly [than a pen], and because it would certainly stand out in stronger relief on the green table." For *Table* Heyworth proposed "carold": Falstaff is "singing snatches of . . . the Bellman's Song," with the line "The fields were green as green could be" (1972, 129, supported by McFarland [1972]). Delius (ed. 1857), attempting to support Malone further with the idea of a pen as a pin as a pinfold as a sheepfold, thought that Mrs. Quickly might have wished to extend "this parallel . . . with a *stable* of green fields (48)."

For *fields* Bradley (1894) proposed "feald," meaning "cloth." Steevens suggested (ed. 1778): "Green fells and green fields might anciently have had the same meaning." The proposed emendation to the singular "field" takes us back to the idea of table as a piece of furniture, particularly a counting house table (Bradley, 1894, and Hulme, *N&Q,* 1956b).

More imaginative constructions quoted in the Cambridge edition (1864) give us: "a table of greasy fell" (Bailey), "stubble on shorn fields" (*Fraser's Magazine*), and "and the bill of a green finch" (Spence, 1889, 302). Other efforts are perhaps jokes—"as green as the fields of the Thebaid" (Nicholson, 1889, 163) and "his noise was as sharp as a wren in a treble of Green Sleeves" (Bulloch, 1878, 159).

The first of all emendations to *Table* is that of "a Gentleman sometime deceas'd," Theobald tells us (1726, 138), who annotated his copy of this play with the marginalium "to Correct this Passage thus; ' . . . a' talked of . . . .'" As no such copy has as yet come to light, it is not impossible that Theobald was cautiously inventing a situation to protect himself against a captious critic, although he may, of course, have seen such a note. Styan Thirlby had indeed written some annotations in his copies of the editions of Rowe (now lost) and Pope which Theobald might have seen, but Thirlby was still alive when Theobald offered this attribution; Thirlby went on to jot down in his copies of Theobald (ed. 1733) and again in that of Warburton (ed. 1747) his own suggestions "talk'd" and "fabled."

"Talked" appears in the Folio some 18 times as "talk'd," eight times as "talkt." (In this passage, just twenty lines below, it has the form "talk'd" [TLN 859]). (And such a "repetition" might seem to argue against the use of the word here; if it appears at 859, it could be argued, as Fleissner too has argued [1994], that it should not appear also at 839.) Spedding (quoted in the Cambridge ed. 1864) suggested that "talk'd" received some support from the fact that the phrase "talk of floures" appears in the Q, but Greg (1928, 46) disallowed this link, pointing out that the two uses are "not directly parallel at all, for ["talk of floures"] is a perversion of the words 'and play with Flowers' in F" at line 837. (In fact, the erroneous appearance of the concept of "talk" in conjunction with flowers at line [837] in Q may have assisted in the omission of the concept in conjunction with green fields. "Babled"—or some word of speaking—was so strong a term that it displaced "play" and thus occasioned its own omission from its proper place. See also Jackson, 251, and Nicholson, 163). Johnson (1959), supporting "talked," found, as he thought, the same error in Ford's *Love's Sacrifice* (1633), but that error is in the reverse, and the argument for "talked" is thus not strong. Bateson (1972) has presented the most extended and persuasive argument for "talked"; he noticed that in Shakespeare's hand medial *k* could easily be misread as *b* (329; Kellner, sec. 59. Stone lists five *b* [Q] / *k* [F] variants in *King Lear* [p. 177]). Keightley (1867), on second thought, approved of "talk'd" for "it also better suits the metre" (247). (As the passage is in prose, it is not clear what Keightley meant; perhaps he was thinking of rhythm?—as Fleissner has noted [1992].) In fact, the reverse is true: a monosyllable in this location destroys the meter which requires a dissyllable to render one of Shakespeare's most extraordinary and powerful verse lines embedded in prose—

| For his nose | was as sharp | as a pen | and a' - | - of green | fields |

—a line of anapestic pentameter followed by a single stressed syllable.

Taylor (ed. 1982, 295), rejecting "table," sees the choice of emending as reduced to a "purely aesthetic decision" between "talked" and "babbled." In fact, editorial history has already made the decision. Although Mowat and Werstine have adopted "talked" (ed. 1995), other editors have found it, presumably, "all too prosaic" and aesthetically distracting (Fleissner, 1976, 146); and no critic has brought forward either an explanation for "table" or an emendation to it, that has been accepted by editors, superior to the emendation of Theobald. All editors, excepting those few cited, from the mid-eighteenth century to our own time, have adopted this emendation.

Theobald (*Shakespeare Restored*, 137–38) extended the suggestion of the "Gentleman sometime deceas'd" by supposing that "we may [come still] nearer to the Traces of the Letters [than by reading "talk'd"], by restoring it thus; ' . . . a' *babled* of. . . . ' To *bable*, or *babble*, is to mutter, or speak indiscriminately, like . . . dying Persons . . . [or like] those in a Calenture, when they are losing the Use of Speech. . . . It is certainly observable . . . of People near Death, when they are delirious by a Fever, that they . . . have their heads run on green Fields." And in his edition (1733), he adopted his "meer Conjecture," with some trepidation, we may suppose. Fleissner (1976) has suggested that Theobald "read in" his emendation unconsciously, as the second syllable of the emendation is the same as the second syllable of his own name (144); but, indeed, "Tibald" is as close to "table" as to "babbled." Bateson (1955) finds that the weakness in the emendation is "the suggestion of mental deficiency (second childhood) that it injects into the Hostess's account" (93), for, by his analysis, in Shakespeare's plays "babbling" always signifies talking like a baby (1972, 129). Others dispute that analysis, agreeing with Schanzer (1956) who considers that a term describing "any aimless or inconsequential chatter . . . becomes depreciatory only when applied to an adult in full possession of his mental powers" (120). Jenkins (1996) praises the "suggestion of dimly conscious undisciplined chatter which *babbled* gives." Fleissner (1992) regards "babbled" as a verb that deprives Falstaff of "the right to death with dignity" (326).

In spite of objections, some deeply felt, and of contrary arguments, the tributes to Theobald's "babbled" have been legion. The series begins with Roberts in 1729 and continues through the editions of Capell (1783), Malone (1790), Caldecott, Singer (1826), the Clarkes (1866), Gollancz (1895), Herford (1896), and so on without impediment up to and including modern critics Barker (1956), Jackson (1987, 251) and three of the most recent editors of our time: Taylor (1982), Gurr (1992), Craik (1995). Knight (ed. 1839) terms it "one of the most beautiful examples of the conjunction of poetry and truth"; and R. G. White, the editor of the first "Riverside Shakespeare" and the first American Shakespearean of international renown, writes (1865) of it as "the most felicitous conjectural emendation ever made of Shakespeare's text." In more than a century, no one has disagreed; even those who hesitate, admire.

Nevertheless, paleographical arguments have continued. Theobald supposed that in reading "babled" instead of "talk'd" he was coming "nearer to the Traces of the Letters," and as an attorney his training in reading legal documents would have qualified him (Seary, 1990, 214) to read the Elizabethan secretary hand in which Shakespeare presumably wrote this passage. The problems are two: "Ta" misprinted for "ba/Ba"; "ble" misprinted for "bld/bled/bl'd/beld."

Early critics assigned significance to the presence of a capital letter in the Folio (e.g., Malone, Caldecott), but modern critics accept the premise that, as the compositor of this page of the Folio (Comp. A) is in the habit of setting important nouns with capitals, nothing specific may be derived from the presence of one here, beyond the obvious fact that the compositor thought that the difficult word was a noun: "a Table" (e.g., Dawson, 1989, 123). Greg is confident that "in the hands of the time 'b' and 't' . . . are often difficult to distinguish" (1928, 4); but Sisson (1956) argues that "in fact Shakespeare, if we accept Hand D in *Sir Thomas More* . . ., does not post-link *b*, and does not write a *t* that is to be confused with a *b*" (2: 59–60). That is—again—to see the difficulty in reverse. Dawson has similarly erred (124). This particular misreading is not automatically reversible. What is needed to support this theory is examples of readings in which a manuscript *b* has been read and printed as a *t* (Kellner, 1925, 42). Such examples do not exist. But Taylor argues to the contrary that in Hand D "sometimes the crowding of letters obscures the distinction [of the post-linked *b*,] . . . [and] the downstroke on the *t* is often looped—particularly with initial *t*—while the *b* downstroke is itself sometimes rather faint . . . , these traits producing the possibility of *t* [printed for] /*b* misreadings, particularly at the beginning of a word, and when followed by a crowded vowel" (ed. 1982, 294–95) (see also Dawson). Nevertheless, although the secretary *b* may *in theory* be misread as a *t*, Shakespeare has not written a *b* that has *in fact* been misread as a *t* (Kellner, 1926, 42, 105). Nowhere in the canon is there an emendation, generally accepted by editors, of a printed initial *t* for a presumed MS *b*, and none of the modern editors of *Sir Thomas More* has been guilty of misreading Hand D's initial *b* as *t* (Williams, 1978, 196). There remains, of course, the possibility that *b* is not at all the correct reading of the initial manuscript letter. Heyworth argues that capital "*B* would be impossible [in MS] to misread as *T* and, despite Greg's authority, I do not see *t* for small *b* as an easy misreading. [Contrariwise, secretary] initial *c* [is] a letter which is often indistinguishable from [and often misread as] the equivalent *t* graph." He is correct, but no one has accepted his "carold" (*TLS*, 1972).

Similarly the second half of the word presents problems, although not in the final letter; scholars have accepted as regular and easy the confusion between terminal *e* and *d*. (Modern editors emend original "talke" to "talk'd" in at least two instances: *Richard III*, 3.2.91, and *Romeo and Juliet*, 4.1.7.) Theobald adopted the spelling "babled," as nearer to the traces of the letters (modernizing editors usually print "babbled"; Oxford Old-Spelling "babeld" [attributed to

Theobald (!)]); but "babld," the preterite form nearest of all to the traces of the letters, is a form that nowhere appears in Shakespeare. Of some thirty examples of preterites in print of verbs ending in "ble"—e.g., cobble, dabble, double, scribble, table, tremble, trouble—no instance in quarto or folio printing of authorial or compositorial orthography uses the collocation "bld," a preterite marked without an *e* or an apostrophe (Williams, 1978, 196; *pace* Dawson, Taylor). The word "babbled" appears in Shakespeare only in this emendation, although in the Folio "babling" occurs six times, always spelled with one medial "b"; "babble" occurs twice, with two medial "b's", and "bibble babble" occurs twice, once in *Twelfth Night* (TLN 2081–82, so spelled) and once in this play (TLN 1919–20; Fluellen refers to "pibble ba-| ble" in the camp [an example neutralized by the line break and by the conceivable association with "Babel"]). Thus, although no paleographical evidence can be brought to contribute positively to the validity of Theobald's emendation of *b* for *T*, or to the substitution of *bb* for *b*, none can be brought forward in refutation. Regardless of the precise spelling in the manuscript, then, as Jenkins (1996) has suggested, the compositor, "forming an impression by seizing on some [letters] and half-guessing the rest, . . . could have leapt to *table*, especially as the preceding *a*, taken as the indefinite article, would lead to the expectation of a noun" (so also Dawson, 127) and Taylor has observed that "pen" would suggest to the Hostess the idea of a table (ed. 1982). The emendation is a unique phenomenon.

Support for "babbled" has, however, been found in unlikely places. Bateson thought "babbling" had been suggested by the notion of brooks babbling in green fields (1955, 94). Cutts (1968) proposes that there is an association between "babbling" and the whore of Babylon. Porter (1986), citing links between this English/ French play and John Eliot's *Ortho-epia Gallica* (1593), a handbook for English/ French speakers, notes that in one of the English/ French dialogues of a language lesson, two speakers called in the English "prattlers," chatting "among greene fields," are called in the French "Babillards" (488). Gurr (ed. 1992) terms this association "likely."

Babbling of green fields suggested to Theobald the desire of feverous people in their final moments for green fields, but Warburton ridiculed that notion: Falstaff was "far from wanting cooling in green fields, [for] his feet were cold." R. G. White (1854) envisions the green fields in another way: "Falstaff had been a boy . . . a merry boy surely, and an innocent one perhaps; and now as the end of his ill-spent life rapidly approaches, amid his confused ravings about the dreadful future and the ill-spent past, come up visions of the green and sunlit meadows over which he chased his childhood's happy hours. There is not in so few words a passage of such tearful pathos in the language, as this" (329). The sentiment of this interpretation is echoed a century later by Schanzer (1954): "Falstaff, in his delirium, has returned to his prelapsarian days and sees himself again as a child, playing with flowers in a green meadow.... This picture ... seems to me a stroke of genius" (120). Ure (1957), rejecting such a notion, launches out to see the green fields as a sick man's delusion for the sea. Other critics, returning to land, see these green fields as a recollection specifically of the "green pasture" of the Twenty-third Psalm (Coverdale, BCP, Geneva; "pastures faire" Sternhold and Hopkins [1562]; "pastures full" Bishops'). Although some modern critics object to the "sentimentality" of this interpretation (see Fleissner, 1976, 145), others do not; recent editors include in their notes the possibility of this interpretation (Walter 1954, Wilson 1955, Bevington 1992, Craik 1995). In spite of the paleographical difficulties in accepting the validity of this allusion, the psalmodic association has commanded the support of generations of critics and readers. A "stroke of genius"—to borrow a phrase—which adds a dimension of the pathetic, the mysterious, and the eternal to the solution of a crux that, as it stands, is merely confusing.

The argument that the reference in Falstaff's hesitant and uncertain babbling is to the Psalm was first given to criticism by two critics in the same issue of *Notes and Queries* (1853, 314): J. B. argues that "Shakespeare, as the only means of gaining our forgiveness, makes [Falstaff] die in repentance for his sins, and seems to have had the Twenty-third Psalm in mind." But an even earlier critic records in that issue that "as a school boy [i.e., about 1823] ... he jotted down [as a gloss] in the margin of his Shakespeare *'i.e.,* singing snatches of the twenty-third Psalm.'" This youthful prodigy deserves our thanks: but we shall never be able to acknowledge him: he signed his name as "Nemo."

Strangely enough, the reference to the Psalm gives comfort to all, both to those who hold with "babbled" and to those who hold with "Table"—Thou shalt prepare a table before me in the presence of them that trouble me" (verse 5; Coverdale, BCP). Richmond (1956): "'No way but one' [Quarto text], the walk through the valley of the shadow of death; thereabouts ... were the green pastures in which he was to lie and pluck flowers, thereabouts a table was prepared." Hulme (*N&Q,* July 1956): "*table* in conjunction with *green fields* and 'I knew there was but one way' [Folio text] cannot but evoke in English hearers of Christian upbringing the comfort of the twenty-third Psalm." It is well known that Falstaff quotes the Scriptures more than does any other character in the canon (Poole, 65). That he misquotes or quotes flippantly cannot obscure the fact that he is familiar with many Biblical passages, and it is not improbable that the pattern of quotation carefully presented in the two *Henry IV* plays should be continued here in *Henry V.* Had he been a Lollard, or a weaver, there would have been an easy explanation for this knowledge; as he was, presumably, neither, we must look elsewhere for its source. Falstaff claims to have lost his voice in singing of anthems (*2 Henry IV,* 1.2.180). If we choose to believe him, and if we wish to imagine that this character would have been singing anthems in the manner of Shakespeare's Anglican contemporaries, his statement must indicate that in his youth, when he had been "page to Thomas Mowbray, Duke of Norfolk" (*ibid.*, 3.2.23–24), he had been a choirboy, the only activity that would have included the singing of anthems; it would have included also listening to readings of the Scriptures and would have necessitated the singing of psalms (in English—the "recollection" is in English) as a part of the daily office. The Twenty-third Psalm would have been sung in normal rotation once a month.

Falstaff has rejected Doll Tearsheet's suggestion that he remember his end (*2 Henry IV,* 2.4.218), and Mrs. Quickly has rejected any need now for Falstaff to call on God; but in his last speech to Falstaff, the newly crowned King Henry V had said: "Fall to thy prayers." Perhaps that royal command has at last been obeyed.

Works Cited

The various editions are indicated in the text by the name of the editor and the date of the edition; where the page reference is to the crux *in loco,* no page numbers are given. Critical works are listed here; multiple entries by a single author are listed in chronological order.

Anon. in *Fraser's Magazine,* cited in Samuel Neil, ed. 1878.
B., J. *Notes and Queries* vol. 8 (1853), 314.
Bailey, Samuel. Quoted in Cambridge edn. 1864.
Barker, Ernest. "The Death of Falstaff." *Times Literary Supplement,* 13 April 1956, 221.
Bateson, F.W. "Editorial Commentary." *Essays in Criticism* 5 (1955): 92-95; "A Table of Green Fields," *ibid.* 7 (1957): 225–26.
———. "Shakespeare's Laundry Bills: The Rationale of External Evidence." *Shakespeare Jahrbuch* (Heidelberg) 98 (1962): 51–63.
———. *The Scholar-Critic.* London: Routledge, 1972.
Bradley, Herbert. "Table of Green Fields." *Academy,* 21 April 1894, 331.
Bulloch, John. *Studies on the Text of Shakespeare.* London, 1878.

Caldecott, Thomas. Manuscript Notations in a copy of the Variorum edition of 1813; latest datable entry about 1821. (British Library, 11762.dd.)

Collier, J. P. *Notes and Emendations*. London, 1853.

Coulson, E. G. "Falstaff and Sir Richard Grenville." *Times Literary Supplement*, 20 June 1958, 345.

Creighton, C. "Falstaff's Deathbed." *Blackwood's Edinburgh Magazine* 145 (1889): 325–36.

Cutts, John P. *American Notes and Queries* 6 (1968): 133–35.

Davidson, Chalmers H. *Times Literary Supplement*, 30 May 1958, 297.

Dawson, Giles E. *Times Literary Supplement*, 22 April 1977, 484.

———. "Shakespeare's Handwriting." *Shakespeare Survey* 42 (1989): 119–28, esp. 123–25.

Eagle, Roderick. "The Death of Falstaff." *Notes and Queries* 202 (1957): 240.

Fitzgerald, Percy. *Notes and Queries* 7th Ser., vol. 6 (1888): 84.

Fleissner, R. F. "Falstaff's Green Sickness Unto Death." *Shakespeare Quarterly* 12 (1961): 47–55.

———."'A Table of Greene Fields': Grasse–Greene/Table and Balladry." *Shakespeare Jahrbuch* (Weimar) 112 (1976): 146.

———. "Putting Falstaff to Rest: 'Tabulating' the Facts." *Shakespeare Studies* 16 (1983): 57–74

———. "Sir John's Flesh was Grass: A Necrological Note on Falstaff and the Book of Isaiah." *American Notes and Queries* 23 (1985): 97–98.

———. "Sir John Falstaff Atilt with Sir Gawain." *Arthurian Interpretations* 1 (1986): 35–38.

———. *Shakespeare and the Matter of the Crux*. Lewiston, Maine: Edwin Mellen Press, 1991.

———. "Theobald Tabled: More on the Picture of Falstaff's Death." *Notes and Queries* 237 (1992): 326–28.

———. "The Round Knight of the Table: Sir John Falstaff's Final Moments." A paper presented to the Textual Seminar, International Shakespeare Conference, Stratford, 1994.

Fogel, Ephim C. "'A Table of Green Fields' A Defence of the Folio Reading." *Shakespeare Quarterly* 9 (1958): 481–92.

Gittings, Robert. "Falstaff and Sir Richard Grenville." *Times Literary Supplement*, 9 May 1958, 255; 6 June 1958, 313.

Greg, W. W. *Principles of Emendation in Shakespeare* (Annual Shakespeare Lecture of the British Academy). London: British Academy, 1928.

Grey, Zachary. *Critical, Historical, and Explanatory Notes on Shakespeare*. London, 1754.

Hall, A. *Notes and Queries*, 7th Ser., vol. 8 (1889), 163.

Heyworth, P. L. "Falstaff's Green Fields." *Times Literary Supplement*, 4 February 1972, 29.

Hotson, Leslie. "Falstaff's Death and Greenfields'." *Times Literary Supplement*, 6 April 1956, 212; "Falstaff and Sir Richard Grenville." 16 May 1958, 269.

Hulme, Hilda M. "The Table of Green Fields." In "The Critical Forum." *Essays in Criticism* 6 (1956): 117–19; *ibid.* 7 (1957), 222–23.

———. "Falstaff's Death: Shakespeare or Theobald?" *Notes and Queries* 201 (1956): 283–87.

———. *Explorations in Shakespeare's Language.* London: Longmans, 1962. (This study incorporates the comments of the preceding items.)

Jackson, MacDonald P. "The Year's Contributions . . . Textual Studies." *Shakespeare Survey* 39 (1986): 236–52.

Jenkins, Harold. Correspondence, 29 August 1996; 1 January 1997, 15 March 1997.

Johnson, S. F. "A Table of Green Fields Once More." *Shakespeare Quarterly* 10 (1959): 450–51.

Keightley, Thomas. Correspondence with J. O. Halliwell in Marvin Spevack, ed. "James Orchard Halliwell and Friends. . . ." *The Library* 18 (1996): 230–45.

———. *The Shakespeare–Expositor.* London, 1867.

Kellner, Leon. *Restoring Shakespeare.* New York: Knopf, 1925.

McFarland, Thomas. *Shakespeare's Pastoral Comedy.* Chapel Hill: University of North Carolina Press, 1972.

Nathan, Norman. "'A Table of Green Fields.'" *Notes and Queries* 204 (1959): 92–94.

Nemo. *Notes and Queries*, 6th Ser., vol. 8 (1853): 314.

Nicholson, Brantley. *Notes and Queries*, 7th Ser., vol. 8 (1889): 163.

Poole, Kristen. "Saints Alive! Falstaff, Martin Marprelate, and the Staging of Puritanism." *Shakespeare Quarterly* 46 (1995): 47–75.

Porter, Joseph A. "More Echoes from Eliot's *Ortho-epia Gallica.*" *Shakespeare Quarterly* 37 (1986): 486–88.

Richmond, Oliffe. "The Death of Falstaff." *Times Literary Supplement*, 27 April 1956, 253.

Ritson, Joseph. *Cursory Criticisms.* London, 1792.

Roberts, John. *An Answer to Mr. Pope's Preface to Shakespeare.* London, 1729.

Rowse, A. L. *Times Literary Supplement*, 6 June 1958, 313.

Schanzer, Ernest. "The Table of Green Fields." In "The Critical Forum." *Essays in Criticism* 6 (1956): 119–21.

Seary, Peter. *Lewis Theobald and the Editing of Shakespeare.* Oxford: Clarendon Press, 1990.

Singer, S. W. *The Text of Shakespeare Vindicated.* London, 1853.

Sisson, C. J. *New Readings in Shakespeare.* 2 vols. Cambridge: University Press, 1956.

Smith, William. Quoted in Grey 1754.

Spedding, James. Correspondence quoted in the Cambridge edn. 1864.

Spence, R. M. *Notes and Queries*, 7th Ser., vol. 7 (1889): 302.

Stewart, G. R. "Three and Fifty upon Poor Old Jack." *Philological Quarterly* 14 (1935): 274–75.

Stone, P. W. K. *The Textual History of 'King Lear'.* London: Scolar Press, 1980.

Taylor, Gary. "Appendix B 2," in *Henry V* (The Oxford Shakespeare). Oxford: Oxford University Press, 1982.

Theobald, Lewis. *Shakespeare Restored.* London, 1726.

Thirlby, Styan K. Manuscript notations in editions of Theobald (1733) and Warburton (1747) (Folger Shakespeare Library).

Thistleton, A. E. *Notulae Criticae* No. 12 (1904), 14.

Tuckey, John S. "'Table of Green Fields' Explained." In "The Critical Forum." *Essays in Criticism* 6 (1956): 486–91.

Ure, Peter. "A Table of Green Fields." In "The Critical Forum." *Essays in Criticism* 7 (1957): 223–24.

Walker, Roy. *Times Literary Supplement,* 23 May 1958, 283.

Waterhouse, Ellis. *Painting in Britain 1530–1790* (Pelican History of Art). Harmondsworth: Penguin Books, 1978.

White, Richard G. *Shakespeare's Scholar.* New York, 1854.

Williams, G. W. "The Year's Contributions . . . Textual Studies." *Shakespeare Survey* 31 (1978): 191–98.

Williamson, Hugh Ross. *Times Literary Supplement,* 6, 27 June 1958, 313, 361.

Wylie, Charles. *Notes and Queries,* 7th Ser., vol. 8 (1889): 163.

Young, N. "The Death of Falstaff." *Times Literary Supplement,* 20 April 1956, 237; "Falstaff and Richard Grenville." 23 May 1958, 283.

"So quick bright things come to confusion": or, What Else Was *A Midsummer Night's Dream* About?[1]

Tom Clayton

IN THE NOW ANCIENT HISTORY OF SHAKESPEARE'S BIRTH-QUATERCENTENARY YEAR of 1964, it would not have been easy to find in the year's publications a pair of perspectives less alike than those of R. W. Dent,

> Rather than being a foe to good living, poetic imagination can be its comfort and its guide, far "more yielding" than most dreams. Whether *A Midsummer Night's Dream* has an unplumbed "bottom" as well as its inescapable Bottom, I hesitate to say. But it provides us "a most rare vision," one that offers us a disarmingly unpretentious defense of poetry by the greatest of England's poets;

and Jan Kott: "The *Dream* is the most erotic of Shakespeare's plays. In no other tragedy or comedy of his, except *Troilus and Cressida*, is the eroticism expressed so brutally."[2]

Each essay was original in its own way. Dent's is historical in emphasis, modest in assertion, and consistently illuminating, a classic. Kott's was groundbreaking, rough—"brutal"?—and provocative, and has been widely influential, especially as partial source of what is probably the most famous production of the century, Peter Brook's, in 1970 (see Halio 48–69). Brook's preface to Kott's book suggests why: it "is Poland that in our time has come closest to the tumult, the danger, the intensity, the imaginativeness and the daily involvement with the social process that made life so horrible, subtle and ecstatic to an Elizabethan" (x–xi).[3] True or not, the perception had its sway. Kott revealed and dwelt on the darker side of Shakespeare— or he projected it, or both. In any case, it was a side especially congenial to the time and has become durably postmodern. Accordingly, something of the character of Shakespeare's *Dream* has been thrust into the shade in succeeding decades, and critical editions as well as productions have undergone their own notable, not always unquestionable, alterations in the past decade or so.[4] My aim here is to try to restore light and a measure of balance of perspective in a few of *Dream*'s quarters that have suffered neglect or occasionally worse.

Theatrical production cannot stand still, of course, and by no means every *Dream* should ring changes on moonlight, roses, and transcendental imagination. But some recent professional productions have seemed to perform everything but the script, often adhering to the letter but relentlessly violating the spirit, something few living playwrights would readily permit. "Adaptation . . . of one sort or another seems to be the rule, . . . but how far can one carry this process and still call it Shakespeare?" (Halio 7). A view current among post-literary academics at present is that nothing has perennial value because all is culturally determined, including "Shakespeare" and his (currency) value. But this view is routinely falsified by individual and collective experience in the reading and often in the theater.

Performance and understanding begin with the script and text. For plays with more than one substantive text, the ultimate witness is the one inferred to be closer to holograph, usually but not always the longer—with *Hamlet* the longest—version.[5] "Holograph" may be foul papers (most often), fair copy, or revised manuscript; with inferred scribal transcript (Shakespeare's, anonymous, or by Ralph Crane) intervening between print and holograph (of whatever kind). Revisionists argue that "revised" versions showing signs of "promptbook" influence and accordingly closer to theatrical practice are more authoritative, at least as far as their additions, cuts, and other alterations are concerned. But the assumption that the "more theatrical" text is the "better" is circular and rests on a somewhat limited view of genre, intention, and effect.

The modern textual situation of *Dream* was "stable" until 1986, when the *Oxford Shakespeare* innovated in incorporating F's—the Folio's—assignment to Egeus and Lysander of speeches in 5.1 that are Philostrate's and Theseus', respectively, in Q1 (1600), the sole wholly substantive text and the most authoritative as the source of Q2, in turn the source of most of F. The received explanation is that Q1 came from autograph foul papers, and F from Q2 altered here and there from a playhouse promptbook. It is easy enough to see expediency as a hypothetical reason for such changes in performance, but not as a good reason to adopt them, much less as revisions supposed to be by Shakespeare. In fact, they serve well enough to open up anew the question of *extent* in so-called Shakespearean revision.

"'Tis Strange, My Theseus" (5.1.1)

The critical and performing fate of these dramatic and mythical lovers has been mixed, especially in the past quarter century: not infrequently, Hippolyta has been aggrandized, Theseus demonized.[6] The script seems to give them about equal measure, a suggestion Shakespeare didn't need but Plutarch supplied in explaining the end of the war brought to Athens "within the precinct of the very cittie it selfe" by the Amazons:

> at the ende of foure moneths, peace was taken betwene them by meanes of one of the women called Hyppolita. . . . Nevertheles, some saye that she was slayne (fighting on Theseus side). . . . In memorie whereof, the piller which is joyning to the temple of the Olympian ground, was set up in her honour. *We are not to marvell, if the historie of things so auncient, be founde so diversely written.* (Bullough 386, 387)

Amen. So much context explains the mythic site and character of Theseus' recently most infamous lines, the first two of

> Hippolyta, I woo'd thee with my sword,
> And won thy love doing thee injuries;
> But I will wed thee in another key,
> With pomp, with triumph, and with revelling.
> (1.1.16–19)

His subject is the familiar progress of wooing, winning, wedding, with the paradox that the wars of myth were paradoxically the scene of contest turned to courtship; but the wedding will be triumphant "in another" and its own traditional "key."

The plotline of the impending nuptials of Theseus and Hippolyta constitutes *Dream*'s opening; it is joined in 2.1 by the alienation-reconciliation and amatory-management plotline of Oberon, Titania, and Puck/Robin that constitutes the closing. The parallels are obvious enough, and significant; and much has been written that is sensitive and wise about the propriety of doubling Theseus/Oberon and Hippolyta/Titania, which was certainly done as early as 1661 (Holland 96–97). But two points need making about doubling. First, doubling (to economize, for example) does not entail special affinities between the characters doubled. Second, and just as important, affinities between two characters may be seen without their doubling.

Theseus was clearly intended to be overshadowed at the end by Oberon and company, the inescapable effect of the order of events, with the diurnal world of waking reason giving way to the nocturnal world of dreamtime and imagination. But Theseus is no less important for that: if the day needs the night for rest and dreaming, night needs the day for enlightenment and exercise; and Theseus' reason transcends its own limitations, through his imagination (sic) and sentiment, which it is partly the business of his two act-5 set-pieces—"More strange than true" and "The kinder we"—to demonstrate. One might say that if there were not a Theseus to deliver these speeches, a speaker might have had to be created from scratch. Not, of course, that the speeches came first, but they have a primacy and significance that *Dream* would be different and the worse for being without.

Theseus and Hippolyta are never separated, appearing together in 1.1, 4.1, and 5.1; and their dialogue is very much reciprocal from the opening exchange to their last banter on "Pyramus and Thisbe" (5.1.300–05).[7] Her mere four-and-a-half lines in the opening sub-scene have served every interpretative purpose, but they are sufficient in content and context to convey mutuality more readily than they can, without strain, express discontent and aloofness:

> Four days will quickly steep themselves in night;
> Four nights will quickly dream away the time;
> And then the moon, like to a silver bow
> [New] bent in heaven, shall behold the night
> Of our solemnities.
>
> (1.1.7–11)

In *Dream*, Theseus has a good deal of the country squire about him, and Hippolyta herself is on the horsy side, the two of them dog-fanciers together in their telling exchange in 4.1, just before they come upon the sleeping lovers. The pair's mutuality, similarity of expression, and shared "lifestyle"—as Anglo-Athenian-mythical country gentry—are far more in evidence than is a raw or even cooked competitiveness here, where their speeches even run to nearly equal length: Theseus has three lines opening (4.1.109–11), then she seven (112–18) and he eight-and-a-half, his last line completed by the transitional "But soft, what nymphs are these?" (119–27). This pattern of easy reciprocity obtains throughout, even when they disagree. Theirs is, on the showing, a civil(ized) relationship of "mutual love and good liking";[8] and *that* is expressed most succinctly by *"my* Theseus" (5.1.1): one doesn't address a stranger to one's affections thus, and this is the opening note of act 5.

The social motion of their duologue here is marked by the echoing of Hippolyta's "'Tis *strange*" in (1) Theseus' extended reply beginning "More *strange* than true," and (2) Hippolyta's closing, "But howsoever, *strange* and *admirable*"—'to be wondered at,' with a trace of 'deserving admiration' (l. 27). The speeches of both express the complementarity of the speakers, as well as their differences, which are also complementary. Theseus' skeptical voice of reason confidently pronouncing in error transcends the limitations of what he "may believe" when it comes to the poet, whose flights of imagination are exquisitely and accurately described; in spite of himself, he speaks for the play and of the play, and of himself at one remove, if not for Shakespeare. But how not?

Some now hastily if not facilely dismiss Theseus and this setpiece by inflating the truisms that (1) his view should not be taken for Shakespeare's; (2) he is wrong about the imagination and much else, and Hippolyta is right; and (3) Theseus himself is an "antique" figment of imagination and therefore a butt of his own joke. But "*antic* fables"—bizarre narratives—is almost certainly correct, despite the fact that most current editions have "*antique* fables," as in Q1.[9] This is a problem of appropriate modern spelling, but it is not clear why editors who often follow F prefer Q1 here. Since "antique" makes inferior sense otherwise, one supposes the preference due to its ready association with Theseus, who is routinely faulted, accordingly, for disbelieving in his own mythical identity. No one can resist this joke who hasn't been pressed to explain how the "fables" *just told* are "antique" meaning ancient.

Theseus is not wrong about the value of "cool reason," even if it has limitations as applied here. But if he is "wrong" about the imagination, he nevertheless brings his own powerful imagination into play to deprecate the poet, who could scarcely be better appreciated by downright eulogy. Did Shakespeare give Theseus these splendid lines to make him risibly pompous and transcendently wrong? The former not really, the latter most certainly, in a special way.

There is general acceptance of Dover Wilson's argument that Shakespeare added the poet to a shorter speech on the imagination of the lover and the madman, which affords a ready explanation for mislining and overcrowded lines in Q1 at that point.[10] Whether the poet arrived at once or on second thought, he dominates the speech as we have it:

> The poet's eye, in a fine frenzy rolling,
> Doth glance from heaven to earth, from earth to heaven;
> And as imagination bodies forth
> The forms of things unknown, the poet's pen
> Turns them to shapes, and gives to aery nothing
> A local habitation and a name.
>
> (12–17)

Even delivered with skepticism and irony, this is breathtaking, a towering tribute to the poet as vates *and* as maker. It is a masterstroke to make Theseus its author, the rational skeptic pronouncing judgment on the irrationality of the imagination by using its highest resources to do so, condemning and commending simultaneously— to its and the poet's credit. Theseus may be talking through his philosopher's hat, but he has been given the poet's own eloquence to do it with. Transported by imagination unawares, he returns to practicalities with his last four lines—*and* those of the original version of the speech (if the poet *was* added). Hippolyta's rejoinder, sound, sympathetic, reasonable, and appreciative, complements Theseus' sweeping survey by bringing "something of great constancy" into the space of the poet's shapes and airy nothing. She is made utterly gracious in joining him at an esthetic distance from the object of their contemplation: "howsoever, strange and admirable." One of the most notable things about the exchange is that Theseus' imagination exceeds his reason here, and Hippolyta's reason her imagination—ultimately to the harmony and credit of them both.

In both exchanges of genial one-upmanship or simple disagreement Hippolyta fares as well as Theseus or better. It is (as always already) easy to read the gender wars into them. But the two characters read and perform most cohesively and intelligibly, and with least strain, as social and personal—and military—equals of partly shared background: mythic nobility from different countries of the classical and post-classical mind joined in late-Renaissance (or Early Modern) English-poetical matrimony.

The only non-fairy in the play who mentions fairies at all—twice— is Theseus. The lovers nowhere show the slightest awareness of their existence, even though Theseus' "fairy toys" implies that fairies figured in the lovers' accounts. For us to supply fairies to their hypothetical account would be to forget about the "discrepant awareness" of dramatic characters and ourselves, who know so much more than they.[11] Bottom alone has "reason" to swear there are fairies, but he does no such thing. The only bare *hint* of fairies by others is Demetrius' "I wot not by what power / (But by some power it is)" (4.1.164–

65): fairy power, but *he* knows not that. Whatever the lovers' fables, as Hippolyta logically infers—she does not intuit—their experience was real and shared, and the fairies are no less real to us or, invisible, to them.

Theseus has *two* setpieces, or "arias,"[12] in act 5, so it might seem curious that the first gets far more attention than the second, "the kinder we" (89–105), which has often been ignored and is now read by some as hypocritical. But the speech seems in earnest for both Shakespeare and Theseus, and there are no textual grounds, as opposed to categorical aprioristic judgments, for taking it otherwise. It is in earnest for good reason, its theme *noblesse oblige,* which might not be necessary in a genuinely classless society of the sort the world has yet to see. Where there are inequalities, their effects are substantially ameliorated when the more fortunate—or powerful— show care for the less. And where there is personal contact between power and vulnerability, kindness finds a way to level differences in some degree. "The kinder we" episode speaks well for Theseus, and it appears to speak also for the play, not pompously preaching but eloquently pleading, with metaphor, anecdote, and subsequent example, advocating compassion of attitude and *noblesse oblige* in behavior, a socioethical message of some importance in Shakespeare's day and once again— rather urgently—in our own. The affluent and socially sophisticated find this banal and bourgeois. Directors who find it so, who wish to concentrate on other matters, or who do not like Theseus, either make the delivery effete and ineffectual or cut the speech.[13]

Both Theseus' speech itself and the dialogue that precedes it make a case for obligatory as well as obliging kindness that is in no way offset by the comic mockery of the courtiers during the performance of "Pyramus and Thisbe," although there is obvious *theoretical* inconsistency. But this entire part of the play is a rich amalgam of the serious and the comic that in a sympathetic production has no trouble with either the serious or the—superficially—inconsistent comedy. Told colorfully and wittily by Philostrate how bad the homespuns' play is (61–70), Theseus asks, "What are they that do play it?" "Hard-handed men that work in Athens here, / Which never labor'd in their minds till now," etc. His response is, "And we will hear it." This is ad hominem with benevolence. Warned a second time by Philostrate that "it is nothing, nothing in the world; / Unless you can find *sport in their intents*" (78–79), Theseus insists that "I will hear that play; / For never any thing can be amiss / When simpleness and duty tender it" (80–82). "Find sport" prepares for the courtiers' comments, and "their intents" stresses the primacy of intentions and the applicability of the golden rule in such cases. The homespuns are honored in having their play preferred, and audiences diverted by shortcomings of which the players are unaware and that they have no need to know.[14]

Hippolyta's "He says they can do nothing in this *kind*" elicits Theseus' cheerful asteism, "The *kind*er we" (85–89), the beginning of Shakespeare's setpiece and Theseus' poetic and substantial reflections on sympathetic imagination illuminated with the colors of rhetoric everywhere present in Shakespeare's earlier plays. "What *poor duty* cannot do, noble respect / Takes it in might, not merit" (91–92) at once defines noblesse oblige ("magnanimous or generous consideration," Foakes 120); gives an allegorical instance with personification; and concludes with an elliptical and emphatic short line strikingly expressive in its use of "might," a signal instance of pointed antanaclasis. "Might" is used to mean both "power" ("might" is more powerful than "merit") and potentiality (what they "might" do).[15] An exemplum follows as a general anecdote based on Theseus' past experience:

> Where I have come, great clerks have purposed
> To greet me with premeditated welcomes;
> Where I have seen them shiver and look pale,
> Make periods in the midst of sentences,
> Throttle their practic'd accent in their fears,
> And in conclusion dumbly have broke off,
> Not paying me a welcome.

Their failure became success, however, because,

> Trust me, sweet,
> Out of this silence yet I pick'd a welcome;
> And in the modesty of *fearful* duty,

complementing the earlier "*poor* duty"

> I read as much as from the rattling tongue
> Of saucy and audacious eloquence.
> Love, therefore, and tongue-tied simplicity
> In least speak most, to my capacity.
>   (5.1.93–105)

Hippolyta's "It must be your imagination then, and not theirs" (5.1.214), though ironic, spells out what is implied throughout this speech, in which Theseus advocates and exercises the very faculty of imagination he decried in theory at the beginning of the scene, a benign inconsistency to his moral credit.

The Amazonian Hippolyta, entirely at home in the Athenian court, joins the men in commenting wittily (and in prose) on the play and performance: "Indeed he [Quince] hath played on this prologue like a child on a recorder—a sound, but not in government" (122–23). When Wall walks off, her "This is the silliest stuff that ever I heard" (210) elicits Theseus'—thematic and didactic—reply, "The best in this kind are but shadows; and the worst are no worse, if imagination amend them. . . . If we imagine no worse of them than they of themselves, they may pass for excellent men" (211–18). Her next comment, "I am a-weary of this moon. Would he would change!" (251), together with Theseus' response, epitomizes the complex of dramatic effects centering on "Pyramus and Thisbe," a theatrical and literary three-ring circus of burlesque (meta)drama, witty commentary, and extemporaneous and illicit dialogue by the players with their immediate audience—with the seriously humane undercurrent rising to the surface here, again, with Theseus' answer concerning Moon: "It appears by his small light of discretion that he is in the wane; but *yet in courtesy, in all reason,* we must stay the time" (254–55). For *this* function of reason Theseus deserves credit that he is now seldom accorded by critics.

The last of Theseus and the courtiers is Theseus' speech concluding,

> This palpable-gross play hath well beguil'd
> The heavy gait of night. Sweet friends, to bed.
> A fortnight hold we this solemnity,
> In nightly revels and new jollity. [*Exeunt.*]
>
> (367–70)

The jokes made by the courtiers about the palpable-gross play can be played as callous and as overheard and taken so by the players, in which case the audience will be disconcerted accordingly; it is just as obvious in the dialogue and often in performance that they are neither.[16] In fact, the entire social event centering on "Pyramus and Thisbe" is at once hugely comic and tacitly serious in its performing and the reasons for its being preferred. The punctuation of the drama by courtiers' comments is made more bond than brake, and this is still more so with the interaction between courtiers and players, notably Pyramus (184–87), Moon (257–59), and Pyramus again, rising from the dead to reassure Demetrius about Wall and offer the options of a terminal epilogue or a Bergomask (351–54).

The latter is shortly forthcoming, bringing to an end "Pyramus and Thisbe" and, soon after, the play of the courtiers of Athens. Then with the fairies the *Dream* resumes.

"Do you amend it then; it lies in you" (2.1.118)

Oberon and Titania are not Theseus and Hippolyta. They are a married king and queen different from their mythical, aristocratic human counterparts in being folkloric supernaturals. Their behavior is that of (im)mortals with higher powers, like Greek-mythical gods except that the fairies are better behaved and motivated. Their estrangement and reconciliation is the central plot-line, even the main plot determining the progress of all other plots; at the center of it, in turn, is the fairy-queen-and-commoner romance of Titania and Bottom, its catalyst the refusal of Titania to give Oberon the changeling boy. Notwithstanding that he is the subject of a custody fight (as well as one with dire meteorological consequences, Titania claims), it is not very common for critics to discuss the *boy*'s interests; and he does not routinely appear, since he is not among the dramatis personae. According to the social norms implicit in the relations between the principals, it must be about the time that the boy would be fairy bar-mitzvahed and join the men—or elder fairies—if he is ready to be a "henchman." So, in the patriarchal fairy culture, *his* interests are best served by his joining Oberon. Moreover, while Oberon "beg"s Titania to give him the boy, she withholds him, not for *his* sake but for the sake of his deceased mother, her late votary. The loyalty part of the sentiment is creditable but the rest and the effects are not: withholding the boy is made a willful refusal to yield responsibly and sympathetically to Oberon's begging: it has no evident benefits for the boy, the boy's deceased mother, herself, or Oberon, now or hereafter.

It is easy and now common to take the situation out of the play or away from the dialogue, anachronize it, and paraphrase it into male bullying and female righteous resistance; but the particular wording of the dialogue stresses the play's principled view of the relative right and wrong of the case, with Oberon given the dialogue to have the better of it, despite Titania's speaking at much greater length and with considerable rhetorical force—and extraordinary poetical eloquence.[17] One could scarcely claim that all of Oberon's responses should be mild in delivery, as most are in phrasing, because some are clearly meant not to be (e.g., 2.1.63);[18] but they are mostly laconic (excepting 74–80) and matter-of-fact; it is Titania's speeches that are lengthy and heated. Oberon is hardly guiltless in his mischievous reaction, but his pitying her and regretting his harshness show him twice "human." To her famous setpiece on the disordered state of the land (2.1.81–117), he replies mildly,

> Do you amend it then; it lies in you.
> Why should Titania cross her Oberon?
> I do but *beg* a little changeling boy,
> To be my henchman.
>
> (2.1.118–21)

He repeats his appeal plaintively and companionably: "Give me that boy, and I will go with thee" (143). He is refused, Titania leaves, and the plot thickens and in degree darkens—more in some productions than in others: "Well, go thy way. Thou shalt not from this grove / Till I torment thee for this injury" (2.1.146–47). If it is his "torment," it is Titania's "injury"; or vice versa.

It is apparently Titania's jealousy that prompts her to accuse him of infidelity in courting the pastoral figment "Phillida" and of coming here from India because

> ... the bouncing Amazon,
> Your buskin'd mistress, and your warrior love,[19]
> To Theseus must be wedded, and you come
> To give their bed joy and prosperity.
>
> (70–73)

A supernatural kindness, *and* they come to share in conferring it. The reciprocal *"forgeries* of jealousy" are important not because they seem true but because they evaporate as soon as the quarrel ceases—with Oberon having the boy as henchman and Titania being released from the effects of love-in-idlness.[20]

Oberon's "I wonder if Titania be awak'd; / Then what it was that next came in her eye, / Which she must dote on in extremity" (3.2.1–3) can be taken to express some solicitude as well as eagerness to hear the worst, but the comic worst is what it heralds: it is an audience incitement with characterological detail. The denouement is 4.1.46–103, in the middle of which is an imperative that cries out for a youth musical, "rock the ground whereon these sleepers be" (86); and I am familiar with at least one rock-musical version, *The Dream*, directed by Chris Bond at the Half Moon Theatre in Mile End Road, London, in the spring of 1984.[21] The reunited couple indeed "will to-morrow midnight solemnly / Dance in Duke Theseus' house triumphantly, / And bless it to all fair prosperity" (4.1.88–90)—and so they do and so ends the play. The reconciliation of Oberon and Titania thus completes the harmonizing of the play's lovers eight and expresses it in the way and spirit of the time of Sir John Davies's nearly contemporary *Orchestra* (1594) in a dance.[22]

Flower Power: The Doting and the Anti-Dote

Three are anointed into redirected affections: Titania and Lysander in 2.2 (27–34, 78–82), and Demetrius in 3.2 (102–09). Oberon initiates the dotings—and later supplies the antidote—with the best intentions, except for his practical joke played on Titania by means of flower power such that "The juice of it on sleeping eyelids laid / Will make or man or woman madly dote / Upon the next live *creature* that it sees" (2.1.170–72). Invisible, he sympathetically apostrophizes Helena, just departed in pursuit of Demetrius: "Fare thee well, nymph. Ere he do leave this grove, / Thou shalt fly him, and he shall seek thy love" (2.1.245–46). And he directs Puck, in disastrously general terms but according to his best lights (he hasn't seen Hermia and Lysander), to anoint the eyes of the "disdainful youth" in "Athenian garments" (2.2.260–66). So much for Hermia's Lysander, for the nonce.

Much concern is expressed by Demetriologists: is he restored to his original love, or is he *compelled* by Oberon's psychopharmacology to love Helena for evermore? He *is* anointed with the doting flower: "Flower of this purple dye, / Hit with Cupid's archery, / Sink in apple of his eye" (3.2.102–4). Both the "flower" and Demetrius' Lysander-like infatuated exclamations of adoration upon awakening and seeing Helena seem to say so. So also says the fact that Lysander is cured of doting by a different, antidotal herb that Puck is supposed to "crush . . . into Lysander's eye," which with its "liquor hath this virtuous property, / To take from thence all error with his might, / And make his eyeballs roll with wonted sight" (3.2.366–69). But though Demetrius is anointed with the flower that makes Titania and Lysander dote, his seems a case of homeopathic medicine, in effect a cure of the infection of doting upon Hermia's eyes (1.1.230) that, unlike the others, he had contracted without floral influence.

And the incantation over Demetrius is different from that over the others. Shakespeare attuned the heptasyllabic incantations accompanying each of the anointings to the individual case and left little room for doubt about any.[23] Sympathetic as before with the young lovers' plight, Oberon sends Puck to fetch Helena, saying he "will charm" Demetrius' "eyes against she do appear" (3.2.99). His incantation is carefully distinctive:

> When *his love* he doth espy,
> Let her shine as gloriously
> As the Venus of the sky.
> When thou wak'st, if she be by,
> Beg of her for remedy.
>
> (3.2.102–09)

"His love" is unequivocally specific, by contrast with the incantation over Lysander, meant for Demetrius but made general in expression by Puck as in Oberon's instructions: "When thou wak'st, let love forbid / Sleep his seat on thy eyelid" (2.2.79–80). "His love" contrasts all the more with the horridly specific incantation over Titania—"What thou seest when thou dost wake, / Do it for thy true-love take; . . . / Wake when *some vile thing* is near" (2.2.27–28, 34). The "apple of his eye" (pupil, but object, too) is equally specific, and "Beg of her for remedy" says that Demetrius needs no other *and* no antidote, which he has had already.

Finally, Demetrius is made to be at pains to explain his case to Theseus (and to us) thus:

> . . . my good lord, I wot not by what power
> (But by some power it is), my love to Hermia
> (Melted as the snow) seems to me now
> As the remembrance of an idle gaud,
> Which in my childhood *I did dote upon;*
> And all the faith, the virtue of my heart,
> The object and the pleasure of mine eye,
> Is only Helena. To her, my lord,
> Was I betrothed ere I [saw] Hermia;
> But like a sickness did I loathe this food;
> *But, as in health, come to my natural taste,*
> Now I do wish it, love it, long for it,
> And will for evermore be true to it.
>
> (4.1.164–76)[24]

These measured but enthusiastic lines have the ring of sincerity and truth, and are some distance from the sheer infatuation and excess of the lovers in a trance.

The others' "doting" is cured by applying the "anti[-]dote"—with an implicit etymological joke; Shakespeare uses "antidote" once only, without jest, in *Macbeth,* who yearns for "some sweet oblivious antidote" to "Cleanse the stuff'd bosom" (5.3.43–44). The spells of curative reanointing are equally differentiated: wittily ironical and generic in Lysander's case (3.2.448–63), personal and affectionate in Titania's.

> Be as thou wast wont to be;
> See as thou wast wont to see.
> Dian's bud [o'er] Cupid's flower
> Hath such force and blessed power.
> Now, my Titania, wake you, my sweet queen.
>
> (4.1.71–75)

But suppose Demetrius *were* in a permanent trance. True love is partly that, and for lasting and reciprocated love it is a small—and unconscious—price to pay. Oberon prophesies (or proclaims), "back to Athens shall the lovers wend / With league whose date till death shall never end" (3.2.372–73).

Bottom's deliverance is Puck's removing of the ass-head with a single line of unceremonious blank verse: "Now, when thou wak'st, with thine own fool's eyes peep" (4.1.84).

Bottom, Bestiality, and Noblesse Oblige

The rise of the phallus in *Dream* production probably dates from Peter Brook's priapic scenario for his post-1960s *Dream* (1970). What still had some shock value then—even after *Hair* (1968) and *Oh, Calcutta!* (1969), but this was Shakespeare—has come to be *de rigueur* in many quarters of the book trade as well as on stage, as witness the covers or dust jackets of (1) Selbourne's *Making of "A Midsummer Night's Dream"* (1982), with its photograph of Bottom borne sitting on the backs of his fellows, one of whom has a fisted, upraised forearm thrust up between Bottom's legs; (2) the Oxford/World's Classics edition (1994), with 1628 woodcut of Robin Goodfellow with notable erection (1628); and (3) *Shakespeare in Performance: "A Midsummer Night's Dream"* (1994), without phallics but with Titania topless (for all practical purposes, near-transparent body stocking notwithstanding). Few major productions since Brook's have failed to show the pressure of Kott and Brook.

But Bottom's conduct as Titania's pampered and enthralling gentle-mortal guest is unexceptionably punctilious and as courtly as it can be, which in its way is very: Titania's "ear is much enamour'd" of "his note" (3.1.138), and he is "a very paramour for a sweet voice," as Quince malapropises later (4.2.11–12). I doubt whether the conceit of Bottom's copulating with Titania much precedes Brook's 1970 production, but it has certainly been rampant since. I agree entirely with part of Holland's comment, "What is so remarkable about Titania's night with Bottom is not a subdued, suppressed sexual bestiality that has only been properly uncovered in the twentieth century but rather the innocence which transforms something that might so easily have been full of animal sexuality into something touchingly naïve" (73); but the "sexual bestiality" seems to me not so much "properly uncovered" as untimely ripped. Such explicit eroticism is distinct from bawdy, a wholly different and typically comic and Shakespearean way of mediating sexuality in art. Titania says presumably with reference to the dewfall that "The moon, methinks, looks with a watery eye, / And when she weeps, weeps every little flower, / Lamenting some enforced chastity" (3.1.198–200). This is not a proclamation of celibacy but neither is it of sex at any price: it explicitly deplores sex by force. In a recent RSC production at the Royal Shakespeare Theatre, by something of a compromise Bottom and Titania, in decorous, half-dressed semi-private, copulated modestly and traditionally in the "missionary position," in a huge, inverted umbrella.[25]

It seems worth noting a quite different form of conceit in a glancing sally of ecclesiastical satire, or witticism without the satire, in Quince's exclamation, "Bless thee, Bottom, bless thee! Thou art translated" (3.1.118–19), from one sort of ass to another, as it were. This must have been accompanied by Quince's making the sign of the cross, and it quite possibly carried an allusion to a bishop's mitre and episcopal "translation" from see to shining see. Robin also uses the word in "I ... left sweet Pyramus translated there" (3.2.31–32).

Bottom rises to the requirements of his courtly translation and himself practices noblesse oblige, the particular form of socially benevolent behavior that Helena speaks for more generally as "manners," a value well above the "honor" of the infatuated young men and their brash devotion to their mistress Helena, and correspondingly harsh rejection of their sometime favorite, Hermia. Perhaps partly because the idea of "manners" has contracted from a stronger moral purport to something close to mere etiquette, it tends to be not much noticed in *Dream*, but, as already noted in connection with Theseus, it is certainly there and important, to Shakespeare as to his characters and some of his contemporaries. Bottom is at his gracious best as an ideal courtier translated favorite of the fairy queen (3.1, 4.1), and she is not wholly fool to find him "as wise as thou art beautiful" (3.1.148)—in manners, if not to the unbiased eye.[26] Titania tells her fairy courtiers to "Be kind and courteous to this gentleman" and "do him courtesies" (164, 174), and Bottom responds in kind with genial humor as he learns the fairies' names (179–96). And so he continues in 4.1 until he has "an exposition of sleep come upon me" (39), when the court fairies leave and Titania ends their dialogue with "Sleep thou, and I will wind thee in my arms. / . . . O how I love thee! How I dote on thee!" (40–45). The lack of stage directions at this point might be taken as performance latitude if not license for licentiousness. But both Q1 and F have Oberon present "behind" (i.e., "unseen," eds.) for the entire action, which could hardly pass uninterrupted if it were played as in some recent productions and Oberon were truly "jealous Oberon." After Titania's last line, both she and Bottom inferentially now sleeping, Oberon bids "Welcome, good Robin. Seest thou this sweet sight? / Her dotage now I do begin to pity" (46–47).

Dream as More than Dream

The manifold ramifications of literary and figurative dream in *Dream* have understandably occupied the attention and sometimes obsessed the imagination of theatrical and academic exponents alike, often with a regrettable suppressing of the play's socioethical implications. That these were important to Shakespeare is evident in the emphasis they receive in *Dream,* comic at one end of the aesthetic scale in Bottom's delightful attempt, like Christopher Sly's, to rise to the greatness thrust upon him; serious at the other end to the point of—near—deadly earnest in the discord between the lovers. Helena as sentient victim is one of Shakespeare's most persuasive spokespersons for the theme:

> *Helena. If you were civil and knew courtesy,*
> You would not do me thus much injury. . . .
> If you were men, as men you are in show,
> You would not use a gentle lady so.
> (3.2.147–48, 151–52)

The sentiment is significant enough—as well as dramatically pertinent and compelling—to be repeated, still more plaintively and with a keen sense of the modes of mockery, when Helena includes her dearest, oldest friend Hermia:

> *If you have any pity, grace, or manners,*
> You would not make me such an argument.
> (3.2.241–42)

What is said here is—again—socially important, unequivocal, and psychologically and philosophically true, not less now than in Shakespeare's day. To bury such humane and ethical sentiments in stage business, gender psychology, and mesmerism is to maim the play and abuse the audience and its civil culture simultaneously.

Demetrius remarks that "It seems to me / That yet we sleep, we dream" (4.1.193–94); and the lovers' experience, including Titania's and Bottom's, is very dreamlike, whereas much of the play's internal experience is less so, even as it centers *on* the fairies. And yet. Bottom's dream "hath no bottom" because he hath it, for good and always.

Bless Thee, *Aegeus,* Bless Thee, *Thou* Art Translated; or Whence and Whither a Paternal *Senex Iratus* and a Pantaloon?

Disappearing without a trace in act 4, Egeus by his incorrigible irritability and intolerance would seem to have written himself out of the script before the matrimonial action of act 5 (in Q1), pronouncing his own epitaph, in effect, with his terminal Shylock-like, epizeuxis-laden lines calling for "the law, the law upon his [Lysander's] head," etc. (4.1.154–59). Among important recent editions, only the Oxford and Norton *Complete Works,* and the Oxford/World's Classics single-play text, replace Q1's act-5 Philostrate with F's Egeus and give some of Theseus' Q1 lines to Lysander (F).[27] The reasons were critical judgment and a belief that Folio changes represent Shakespearean revision, especially if they seem to have a theatrical orientation.[28] The scholarly consensus (both Oxfords included) is that Q1 (1600) derives from autograph foul papers, whereas F derives from Q2 (the 1619 reprint disguised as "1600") to some extent collated with and reflecting the promptbook, "the source for many of F's substantive variants from Q" (279). William B. Long, Randall McLeod, and others have argued that the playbook of Shakespeare's day was nothing like so orderly and consistent as Greg's and textual posterity's theoretical "prompt-book," an entity of importance in modern theatrical practice (see, e.g., Maguire 23 f. and Long 125–43). "If a rule is needed for judging what happened to a playwright's manuscript in the theater, it should be, 'as little as possible'" (Long 127); and only as much as was essential to clarify performance.

There is no very specific evidence for dating act 5 changes involving Egeus and Lysander. F's act divisions postdate 1609;[29] the F stage direction, "'Tawyer with a Trumpet before them'" (5.1.125.1/TLN 1924), probably "originated in a relatively late revival," since there is no known record of Tawyer "(presumably William)" before 1624.³⁰ Yet Taylor argues for other Folio variants:

> Some of these clearly originate in the prompt-book; others are clearly necessary; others involve the alteration of Q readings which seem acceptable to a casual or even an alert reader, and which therefore can hardly have originated in the whims of an unassisted printing-house 'editor'. Without strong evidence to the contrary, one must therefore assume that the prompt-book is the authority for all added or substantially altered Folio directions and speech-prefixes. Some of these variants might derive from late revivals, over which Shakespeare had no control; but none certainly do, and only the act divisions and Tawyer's name can be confidently associated with performances later than those in the mid 1590s. Although each direction has been considered on its merits, we have found no reason to doubt that the bulk of the Folio directions represent the play as originally and authoritatively staged. Those directions which clearly envisage a different staging from that implied by Q seem to us to be dramatic improvements for which Shakespeare was probably responsible. (279–80)

This is a good example of what appears to be the Folio bias in action and effect. If there were no such bias, one might expect the practice described above to be reversed, thus: "Although each [F variant] has been considered on its merits, we have found no reason to doubt that the bulk of the [Q1] directions represent the play as originally and authoritatively staged"—or at least authoritatively conceived and composed, since authority qualifies conception and composition better than it can qualify staging as such. Such quartos as Q1 are (and historically were) certainly—as well as by definition—closer to their authorial origins than was "the prompt-book," a playbook of usually mixed authority lying somewhere between holograph and F. From his study of manuscript playbooks of the period, in this case especially *John a Kent and John a Cumber*, William B. Long concludes,

> On the basis of this earliest surviving example, the difference between the literary document—the fair copy of the play manuscript sold to the company by a fledgling playwright nevertheless aware of an ongoing theatrical tradition—and the theatrical document—the play as adapted to playing needs by the company—was merely seven short annotations indicating how few markings a given company felt it necessary to employ in its playbook. (139–40)

Critical judgment of variants is not easily separated from assumptions or inferences about their origin, and these work in a circle—

hermeneutic, not necessarily vicious: if the F variants are thought superior, they must have come from an authoritative source. Since it has been demonstrated that F was set from Q2 (1619), the ultimate source of "Shakespearean" alterations had to be "the prompt-book," from which details were copied into the copy of Q2. It seems likely that such details were copied from the promptbook, but it seems quite as likely—even more likely, to my way of thinking—that some changes made in Q2 between 1619 and 1623 reflected evolving theatrical practice unconnected with Shakespeare. If so, which changes were Shakespeare's?

Since there is no apparent theatrical reason for Egeus to replace Philostrate—the same actor could have played both parts without altering the script[31]—the purpose must have been to bring back and reconcile Egeus, who otherwise disappears in act 4, very like Shylock in *The Merchant of Venice*—dismissed to unhappiness, as it were. Holland notes that "audiences are unlikely to object if Egeus proves to be the person at court who fulfills that role [of Master of Revels], as in Bill Alexander's 1986 production" (267–68). Alexander went only half way, however; he rejected F's Lysander and "retained the quarto's assignment to Theseus of V.i.44–60" (Halio 82). And "audiences are unlikely to object" is not compelling: is it a reason for making a change? Of course, Egeus' newly and miraculously congenial and solicitous presence can be defended thematically, socially, structurally, symbolically, and otherwise as necessary and transcendently fulfilling, supremely imaginative, and therefore profoundly Shakespearean: nothing comes easier than symmetry, sentiment, and sophistry. Less grandly, it ties up loose ends and satisfies supposed audience expectations or desires—good enough theatrical and commercial reasons for making changes, but slight and arbitrary in this instance.

In F these perfunctory changes of speech assignment could have been made by virtually anyone—especially incompletely (one of the six speeches is still Philostrate's in F at 5.1.76). Shakespeare's complicity cannot in reason be forced much further than Brooks's description of a "change Shakespeare cannot have wished for, though he might acquiesce in it as an expedient" (xxxii). Even if Shakespeare made the change—how shall we know?—he must have done so mechanically and in haste, altering nothing for sense or consonance, merely reassigning speeches. This is hardly what one would expect of the author of the inferred addition of the poet to the company of the lover and madman in Theseus' great setpiece, or of any other addition or revision with content enough to evaluate. In short, there seems no reason to dignify such "revision" by finding Shakespeare guilty of it. It should be axiomatic that a "revision" anyone could execute—above all a cut but any purely mechanical change as well—not only need not but should not be assigned to Shakespeare—or to any other playwright—without strong positive reasons.

The respective stage directions are
> Enter Theseus, Hyppolita, and Philostrate. Q1, TLN 1736
> Enter Theseus, Hippolita, Egeus and his Lords. F, TLN 1792

The sole business assuredly Shakespeare's is Q1's, which opens with a subscene's intimate conversation between Theseus and Hippolyta that Philostrate need not overhear even if "present" for 1–27.

Replying to Theseus' enquiry, Philostrate (or Egeus) says, "There is a brief how many sports are ripe. / Make choice of which your Highness will see first" (42–43). This has no stage direction in Q1 and needs none; it has none in F, which could well use something to explain how not Theseus, to whom the brief is offered (Q1), but Lysander (*Lis.* F), comes to read the titles of the entertainments, with Theseus responding only with a comment on each. In Q1 Theseus both reads the title and makes the comment, which has obvious stageworthiness and makes sense of Philostrate's presentation lines. Theseus is the ruler, after all. Here Brooks follows Q1 but the Oxford et al. follow F. Holland explains,

> While some commentators have worried why Lysander should be given the task, whether Philostrate has had his place usurped or has turned away in a huff, and whether the hierarchies and niceties of court behaviour have been disrupted, the dialogue certainly works more effectively when split between Lysander and Theseus, involving one more character in the action. (265)

Whether F's version works more effectively depends very much upon what confidence and ingenuity are invested in performance, but it seems quite as gratuitous as the reassignment of Philostrate's lines to Egeus. There is no cogent explanation available for either and not much to be said for them in effect, whatever may be said of them in theory, so there is little reason to think they are Shakespeare's. Instances of virtually certain Shakespearean revision there are, Theseus' setpiece poet probably prominent among them.[32] But it requires no strain to conclude that there was less Shakespearean revision than has recently been asserted.

The Epilogue of Puck and Robin

These are one and the same fairy with the significant but long-neglected difference that "Puck" is *a* Puck, a species of fairy.[33] In

Dream he is identified for us first by a nameless fairy as "that shrewd and knavish sprite / Call'd Robin Goodfellow" (2.2.33–34), very likely a propitiatory name.[34] The fairy adds, "Those that Hobgoblin call you, and sweet Puck, / You do their work, and they shall have good luck. / Are not you he?" General awareness of the distinction considerably postdated Katharine Briggs's *Anatomy of Puck* (1959). Both "Puck" and "Robin" occur together as speech headings (with and without abbreviation) in the earliest editions (Qq, F), but "Puck" has been the received normalization. Only recently has "Robin" become the normalized—unambiguous—speech heading, in the Oxford (and Norton) editions. "Puck" may well survive, however, since it is traditional and everyone knows who is intended: though there are many fairies in *Dream*, there is only one Puck.[35]

Shakespeare sometimes seems to mark by name the changing faces and functions of this character obedient to the letter of command but mischief-loving most of the time, who is thoroughly benign in the terminal couplet of the Epilogue, but with darker edges and affinities manifested here and there before. In 3.2, for example, Oberon bids "Robin, overcast the night," and "The starry welkin cover thou anon / With drooping fog as black as Acheron" (355–57). "Puck" (his speech heading in Qq, F) replies,

> My fairy lord, this must be done with haste,
> For Night's swift dragons cut the clouds full fast,
> And yonder shines Aurora's harbinger,
> At whose approach, ghosts, wand'ring here and there,
> Troop home to churchyards. Damned spirits all,
> That in crossways and floods have burial,
> Already to their wormy beds are gone.
> For fear lest day should look their shames upon,
> They willfully themselves exile from light,
> And must for aye consort with black-brow'd Night.
>
> (3.2.378–87)

From this poetical digression into the world of *Hamlet* or *Macbeth* he is quickly recalled by Oberon's reminder that "we are spirits of another sort." "Puck" assumes the darker character again and flirts with a pre-Gothic genre when he enters, alone, after the lovers have gone to bed, beginning, "Now the hungry lion roars," and going on to other gloomy and chilling "Now" events in

> Now it is the time of night
> That the graves, all gaping wide,

> Every one lets forth his sprite,
> In the church-way paths to glide,

a deliberate, spine-tingling, ghost-story warmup (371–82) before he modulates to "we fairies . . . / Now are frolic" and his present office: "I am sent with broom before / To sweep the dust behind the door" (390).

Is anything to be made of the separate names and designations? Is the Puck a sinister species given to recalcitrance at best, and Robin an exceptional member with a better nature made evident as such by the use of his name? Or to put that differently, is anything to be made of the uses of "his" multiple names in the play—in the text, the stage directions, and the speech headings? Brooks notes that the "most striking variations [in speech-prefixes] are between 'Puck' and some version of 'Robin Goodfellow'. These can readily be understood as corresponding each to the aspect of the character then uppermost in Shakespeare's mind" (xxiv). This plausible and intelligent interpretation may well be right. His detailed "explanation of how they came to alternate in the Q1 text" (xxiv–v) distinguishes between "Puck" as Oberon's messenger and "Robin" as the mischief-maker "acting on his own initiative."

I am inclined to see (the) "Puck" as having the darker nature, "Robin" as the more sociable. But the distribution of names in *Dream* does not seem to support the distinction (or Brooks's). The names occur in dialogue only nine times. In stage directions and speech headings they distribute pretty much—not by formes but—by the printer's sheet in Q1, with "Robin" in sheets B, D, and F; and "Puck" in C and E.[36] Uses in the dialogue are not much more evidently deliberate *except* in the Epilogue.

There has been no grave harm done in normalizing to "Puck" (or "Robin") throughout, but doing so—like normalizing to the personal name "Othello" or "Shylock"—obscures a distinction and a conjunction that the inconsistent speech-headings of the early editions emphasize, presumably inadvertently: the identity of the individual and the anomaly of the group ("Moor," "Jew," "Puck"). Shakespeare himself seems to use both in close proximity and interchangeably but for the meter: "Welcome, good Robin. Seest thou this sweet sight?" (4.1.45/TLN 1513), where "Puck" would be unmetrical; "And, gentle Puck, take this transformed scalp" (63/1531), where either name could be used, depending upon "transforme/'d."[37] In that context both names have a positive valence, even if "good" is mainly phatic and "gentle" reflects status more than behavior (oxymoronically), itself as much phatic as flattering.

In any case, editorial normalizing and a sense of the interchangeability of names seem to have prevented readers from noting the Epilogue's—differential—use of both names. The stage direction says "Enter Pucke," and "Pucke"—5.1.370.1–71/TLN 2080–81, H3v—speaks the "prologue" to the fairies' song and dance; but "Robin"—l. 423/2133, H4—speaks the Epilogue.[38] Whether these differential speech headings represent deliberate division of character is doubtful, but in the Epilogue the use of both names appears to make a significant distinction between a threatening generic Puck and the obliging individual Robin. As "an honest Puck"—the Real Thing—the first appeals for "unearned luck / Now to scape the serpent's tongue" (432–33), promising "amends ere long" (434) if favored (cf. 2.1.32–43); but at the same time slyly threatens with "Else *the Puck* a liar call" (435), a very imprudent thing to do. After the Puck-in-effect concludes *his* part with "So, goodnight unto you all," by contrast, Robin-in-effect adds a genial terminal couplet, "Give me your hands, if we be friends, / And *Robin* shall restore amends" (437–38)—a clear advance from "amends ere long" (434).

It is no accident that the Epilogue, characteristically (for fairies) in heptasyllabics, opens with a falling rhythm in a trochaic-tetrameter couplet, and closes with a rising rhythm in an iambic-tetrameter couplet. The only other variation is an iambic-tetrameter line (431) beginning what is in effect the second octave. The first octave is impersonal and collective (beginning "we shadows"), and asks the "Gentles" to "think but this," that they have been asleep and dreaming; and "not [to] reprehend" a "theme / . . . yielding but a dream" (427–28).[39] It concludes equally generally, "If you pardon, we will mend" (430). Then the second octave turns personal with "I . . . an honest Puck" and "me" (Puck and/or Robin), and the semi-formal "Gentles" gives way to "if we be friends" (437), audience and Robin together. One takes "me" to be "Robin" exclusively, because he is named in the next, last line; but the point seems to be that the audience's giving their hands brings out the reciprocating Robin in the Puck. Anyhow, all are one in this conclusion.

Perhaps a pause cueing applause was intended or practiced between "So goodnight unto you all"—which has a terminal ring—and the closing couplet, "Give me your hands," which is affably forthcoming—and does mean "applaud," of course, the practical purport of all epilogues. But here the phrase must surely have been intended also to initiate hand-shaking. It is used in that way by Shakespeare many times with "hand" and four to six other times with "hands." Nearest in sense is *Julius Caesar* with Brutus' "Give me your hands all over, one by one" (2.1.112); and *The Tempest*, where

Alonso says to Ferdinand and Miranda, "Give me your hands. / Let grief and sorrow still embrace his heart / That doth not wish you joy!" (5.1.213–15).[40] The gesture of taking hands is exactly right for Robin here, and it must have been the business of public performance in Shakespeare's day, when "the crowd of 'understanders'" would be "jostling alongside the amphitheatre platforms" (Gurr 179). With an elevated platform like the new Bankside Globe's, the natural action accompanying the lines would be the speaker's bending or kneeling to take the hands of spectators closest to the platform, whether right to right hand or, more likely, one by each hand, two by two.

"At the end" of Brook's *Dream*, "Puck and all his colleagues deliberately broke the magic—the magic created by theatre—by advancing into the audience on his final lines . . . and shaking hands with everyone they could reach. But of course such a tactic subtly continues the magic as well, making it linger in a way analogous to Puck's last speech, which both breaks and extends the illusion" (Dawson 24–25). The notion that *all* Puck does is invite applause is so deeply ingrained that no one seems to have remarked that Brook in effect rediscovered and elaborated on what must have been the original design, though Trewin comes close: "Puck, in his last two lines, . . . is inviting applause. Peter Brook interpreted the first words literally: his Puck (John Kane) jumped from the stage and came through the house, shaking hands left and right, the rest of the company at his heels. That was, and is, a fitting end to *A Midsummer Night's Dream:* all, on stage or off, must be at peace beneath the visiting moon" (105).

Such an "interactive" gesture, rather Michelangelic, makes an energetic kindred connection between the persons in and of the theater, and symbolically between the dramatic "shadows" brought together by the play for communal performance: of roles on the stage by players, and understanding and appreciation—their roles—off the stage by audience and spectators—for we too are shadows as such stuff as dreams—including this one—are made on, whose own little lives are rounded with a sleep. The script itself, itself shared, is the shadow of dialogue passing from actor to auditor and spectator, and through author, scribe, and printer (and editor) to reader: withal from poet-playwright to admirers of his making.

Notes

1. Or perhaps "Like." G. K. Hunter: "The question that is central to my discussion is . . . less 'what is this play about?' than 'what is this play like?'" (5). Unless other-

wise specified, quotations are taken from the *Riverside Shakespeare,* 2nd ed.; and italics used for emphasis within quotations are mine unless otherwise specified. For familiarity's sake, I refer to Robin Goodfellow as "Puck" throughout.

2. Dent, "Imagination in *A Midsummer Night's Dream,*" 129; Kott, "Titania and the Ass's Head," in *Shakespeare Our Contemporary,* published in Poland in 1961 as *Szkice o Szekspirze,* in the U.S. in English in 1964, 175.

3. The two influenced each other, Brook through his 1955 production of *Titus Andronicus,* Kott by his book and through personal association. See Brook's Preface.

4. This is not meant to imply that there were not many—sometimes egregious—departures in preceding centuries, especially in production, on which see Halio, chs. 1–2.

5. The most substantial survey of contemporary thinking is to be found in Wells and Taylor's indispensable *Textual Companion;* see the condensed "Summary of Control-Texts," 145–47; and cf. the introduction to "Shakespeare's Text" in *Riverside* 55–69.

6. Belittling Theseus goes some way back; cf. even Young 138, 139; he quotes Hippolyta's 5.1.23–27 all or in part 4 times: [vii] epigraph with only 5 lines of Theseus' speech immediately preceding, 8, 140, and 180 as the last 2 lines of his book; since the title is *Something of Great Constancy,* this is not surprising.

7. Hippolyta has only 1.56% of *Dream*'s words by comparison with Theseus' 10%. Bottom has the highest percentage of all at 12.6 (10.3 as himself and 2.3 as Pyramus); Helena has 11.3 and Oberon 10. These figures should in general surprise no one, since the speakers variously speak best as well as most, except for Hippolyta, whose paucity of dialogue is quite sufficient in quality and content to articulate the queen she is. The use of *word* counts eliminates the arbitrary disparity between verse and prose arising from "line counts" in editions of different size and design (e.g., quarto vs. folio). Spevack's *Concordance* provides the data for word counts based on *Riverside* (1st ed.).

8. See the section of this title and the whole of Cressy's chap. 10 on "Courtship and the Making of Marriage" (233–66).

9. For example, the New Arden and the Oxfords + Norton read *antique.* Pelican (1959, rev. 1971) and *Riverside* (1974, 1997) read *"antic* fables" (anticke *F*). As *OED2* notes, the spelling "antique" was used sometimes (as presumably in Q1) for the different word, "antic" (see both *antic* and *antique*).

10. "Wilson showed that if the irregular lines were removed, the text would still make excellent sense. . . . As W. W. Greg has said, 'There is no escaping the conclusion that in this we have the original writing, which was supplemented by fresh lines crowded into the margin so that their metrical structure was obscured.' . . . The obvious way of accounting for confusions in lineation in the quarto is to suppose that they result from alterations and reworkings made by the author in the course of composition" (Foakes 137).

11. The useful term is Bertrand Evans's.

12. "Several major speeches in this play are important not because they further the action or elaborate a character, but because they represent an explicit verbal development of ideas hinted at in other parts of the play. They are as it were arias in which snatches of melody heard elsewhere are fully developed" (Wells, ed. *Dream* 24).

13. In two post-1970s productions about a decade apart at the Tyrone Guthrie Theater, Minneapolis, director Liviu Ciulei did the former (1985) and Joe Dowling the latter (1997).

14. "Rude mechanicals" rather than "hempen homespuns" (both borrowed from Puck) is the form of reference preferred by most contemporary commentators.

15. *Might* as the third-person subjunctive of *may* (*OED2* v1). The New Variorum *Dream* records the difficulties of earlier editors with this passage; e.g., Johnson's note begins, "The sense of this passage as it now stands, if it has any sense, is this." Steevens alone seems to have recognized the wordplay, which has persistently gone unnoticed: "'In *might*' is, perhaps, an elliptical expression for *what might have been*" (210). It is apt and usual to gloss by the proverb, "To take the will for the deed" and "Everything is as it is taken" (Tilley, Dent, W393).

16. Demetrius' "No wonder, my lord; one lion may [speak], when many asses do" (153–54) *works* as a joke fitting the ineptitude rather than as a snide judgment on the men playing their parts. It has been suggested that Moon is distraught by the courtiers' comments (232–45) and shows it when to Lysander's "Proceed, Moon" he replies, obligingly, "All that I have to say is to tell you that the lanthorn is the moon, I the man i' th' moon, this thorn-bush my thorn-bush, and this dog my dog" (257–59). He certainly could be played distraught, but at the expense of the manifest comic design, where the jokes and sociability, not the personal feelings of the player, are consistently foregrounded.

17. Notable exchanges and speeches by or about Oberon in this connection are 2.1.18–80, 118–47, 175–85; 3.2.374–77; 4.1.45–63, 70–82, 84–90 (87: "Now thou and I are new in amity").

18. In slanted productions Oberon tends to wax stentorian at every opportunity given or taken, partly on the hint, no doubt, of Puck's telling a fairy that "The King doth keep his revels here to-night; / Take heed the Queen come not within his sight; / For Oberon is passing fell and wrath," etc. (2.1.18–31). Puck's hyperbolical description expresses his swaggering for effect.

19. Neither "mistress" nor "love" implies coition; the case on this evidence is one of courtly courtship.

20. Greenblatt's reading differs: "Oberon and Titania have, we learn, long histories of amorous adventures; they are aware of each other's wayward passions; and, endowed with an extraordinary eroticizing rhetoric, they move endlessly through the spiced, moonlit night" (Norton 810–11). The character with a long history of amorous adventures is Theseus, four of whose liaisons are mentioned by Oberon (Perigenia, Aegles, Ariadne, and Antiopa; 2.1.77–80) in reproaching Hippolyta for her love of Theseus. Hippolyta and Antiopa are plainly differentiated here, but they were alternative names of the same Amazon, Antiopa/e the more common.

21. I saw it on 22 May. As an exuberant adaptation, it was arguably closer to the spirit—and therefore to the original letter—of *Dream* than many a recent "production." Bottom also played electric bass in the rock group providing the music, the "Hempen Homespuns."

22. The *orchestra* in ancient Greek and Greece was a dancing place. Shakespeare's *Rape of Lucrece*, in rhyme royal like *Orchestra*, also was printed in 1594.

23. Heptasyllabics are a distinctive verse-form of the fairies in *Dream* (though Puck usually speaks in pentameters) and of the Shakespearean Weïrd Sisters (but not Hecate) in *Macbeth*, among other uses. It has been written that "the brief waves of verse in other meters" than blank verse "serve mainly to change the rhythm or to provide a verse mode more appropriate for certain kinds of characters. The fairies . . . signal their peculiar status (at least part of the time) through tetrameter couplets" (Wright 114). But (acatalectic, octosyllabic) tetrameters are the exceptions to heptasyllabic lines rather than the rule; and trochaics are still less frequent than occasional iambic tetrameters—e.g., the first two and last two lines of the Epilogue.

Heptasyllabics have a unique and variously exploitable lilt, and they are perhaps the most sense-enforcing kind of verse: the lines are almost invariably regular and the stresses especially serviceable in forcing the sense(s) and emphases intended. But most of Shakespeare's verse, including his blank verse, expresses its intended sense partly through meter, so it is a mistake to decide upon the sense and rhetoric of the words before entertaining the meter's dictates. This is one reason why it is useful for actors to understand versification—not technically, but functionally and semantically.

24. Demetrius' waking declaration of love for Helena (3.2.137–44) is similar to Lysander's (2.2.102–05, 111–22) and is taken so by Helena, but this is part of the (not uneasy) comedy of mistaken identity at midplay: "There's no art / to find the mind's construction in the face" (*Macbeth* 1.4.11–12)—or in the amatory utterance.

25. Dir. Adrian Noble, 1994–95; I saw it at the RST on 25 August 1994. In the 1970s *a tergo* became fashionable in productions of Jacobean tragedy, especially *The Changeling*.

26. Greenblatt finds him "the most flatulently absurd of the mechanicals" (Norton 807).

27. The F-based New Variorum *Dream* reads likewise.

28. So far as I know, no one has made a strong case for the changes. Oxford cites Barbara Hodgdon's "Gaining a Father" as making a critical case for following F with Egeus, but her case is mainly rhetorical. She dismisses Brooks's thoughtful argument in favor of Q1's Philostrate as "mask[ing] only slightly the subjectivity of equating Shakespeare's wishes with his own; I would counter his argument by noting that rejections of the Folio variants as theatrical expediency are themselves speculative" (535). She handles the awkwardness of Egeus as "our usual manager of mirth" by saying that, "since Theseus asks four questions in rapid succession, all of which have to do with the evening's entertainment, *it is most unlikely that an audience will pick up on* only one and thus question Philostrate's absence. Even if they do, the inconsistency is of a kind Shakespeare is all too famous for elsewhere" (538).

29. "The King's men appear not to have made use of such intervals before about 1609 (see Taylor, 'The Structure of Performance')" (*Textual Companion* 279b).

30. *Textual Companion* 279b; if "Tawyer" came so late, why not Egeus and Lysander? "William Tawyer, as we know from the record of his burial ['June 1625, at St. Saviour's, Southwark'], was 'Mr. Heminges man'" (Brooks xxx). Extrapolating backward by way of Heminges, who was associated with Shakespeare's company from 1594 on, Berger infers that "Tawyer and his trumpet . . . could have been added at any time after the composition of the foul papers in the mid-1590s" (xi), whenever he was old enough, but we do not know when he was born.

31. And "Assertions that" the change "was made for reasons of doubling are unfounded and implausible" (*Textual Companion* 285a, 5.1.0.1/1700.1n).

32. Recent writings on revision are by now legion, among the seminal works being those by Warren (1978), Urkowitz (1980), the collection edited by Taylor and Warren (1983), and Ioppolo (1991).

33. In "All we like sheep . . ." elsewhere in this collection Susan Snyder includes consideration of Puck/Robin as an editorial problem in deciding how to designate characters in speech headings and stage directions.

34. Used in full otherwise only—and curiously, given its unnecessary length, which seems not likely to be authorial—in Q1 SDs (2.1.0.1/TLN 367, 3.2.0.1/988, and 4.1.45.1/1512).

35. "Robin Goodfellow, hobgoblins and pucks all belonged to the same group [genus?] of fairies. . . . Scot [*Discovery of Witchcraft*, 1584] lists all three as distinct and separate types of 'bug[bear]s'" (Holland 35).

36. Spellings vary: "Pu," "Puck," and "Pucke"; and "Ro," "Rob," "Robi," and "Robin." All could be Shakespearean. Some are instances of "decremental repetition," which occurs also in the Shakespearean pages of the MS of *Sir Thomas More* (see Clayton, "Today" 67, 73).

37. The word occurs with both '*d* and *ed* pronunciations in Shakespeare.

38. Cf. Brooks: at 5.1.371 "on his mission as Oberon's and the fairies' harbinger, he enters and speaks as 'Puck'; but he addresses the audience in the Epilogue in the folk-lore character familiar to them: the epilogue prefix is Robin, and the last line promises: 'Robin shall restore amends.' Yet in the course of his address he has called himself 'the Puck' and 'an honest Puck' (l. [431]). By this time, no doubt, both appellations, 'Robin' and 'Puck', were always present in Shakespeare's mind" (xxv).

39. No one seems to gloss "theme," but perhaps it is not superfluous to give *OED2* 1b: "A subject treated by action (instead of by discourse, etc.); hence, that which is the cause of or for specified action, circumstance, or feeling; matter, subject. Obs."—and note that the first examples are from Shakespeare: *Titus Andronicus* 5.2.80 ("See heere he comes, and I must play my theame"); and *Hamlet*. "*Hamlet*. Why I will fight with him vppon this Theme" (5.1.289) and "*Queen*. Oh my sonne, what Theame? *Hamlet*. I lou'd Ophelia [etc.]."

40. The other plurals of the kind are *Richard II* 3.3.202 and *The Taming of the Shrew* 2.1.318. Two misleading "concordance cousins" are *Henry VI, Part 3*, 4.6.38 and *The Two Noble Kinsmen* 5.3.109; in these the speaker asks for the hands of two in order to join them together (Henry VI to Warwick and Clarence, Theseus to Emily and Arcite).

Works Cited

Briggs, Katharine. *The Anatomy of Puck*. London: Routledge and Kegan Paul, 1959.

Bullough, Geoffrey. *Narrative and Dramatic Sources of Shakespeare*. Vol. 7 (Major Tragedies). New York: Columbia University Press, 1973.

Clayton, Thomas. "Today We Have Parting of Names: A Preliminary Inquiry into Some Editorial Speech-(Be)headings in *Coriolanus*." In *Shakespeare's Speech-Headings*. Edited by George Walton Williams. Newark: University of Delaware Press, 1997. 61–99.

Cressy, David. *Birth, Marriage, and Death: Ritual, Religion, and the Life-Cycle in Tudor and Stuart England*. New York: Oxford University Press, 1997.

Dawson, Anthony B. *Watching Shakespeare: A Playgoers' Guide*. London: Macmillan Press, 1988.

Dent, R. W. "Imagination in *A Midsummer Night's Dream*." *Shakespeare Quarterly* 15 (1964): 115–29.

———. *Shakespeare's Proverbial Language: An Index*. Berkeley: University of California Press, 1981.

Evans, Bertrand. *Shakespeare's Comedies*. Oxford: Clarendon Press, 1960.

Gurr, Andrew. *The Shakespearean Stage 1574–1642*. 3rd ed. Cambridge: Cambridge University Press, 1992.

Halio, Jay L. *Shakespeare in Performance: "A Midsummer Night's Dream."* Manchester and New York: Manchester University Press, 1994.

Hodgdon, Barbara. "Gaining a Father: The Role of Egeus in the Quarto and the Folio." *Review of English Studies* NS 37 (1986): 534–42.

Hunter, G. K. *English Drama 1586–1642: The Age of Shakespeare.* Oxford History of English Literature 6. Oxford: Clarendon Press, 1997.

Ioppolo, Grace. *Revising Shakespeare.* Cambridge, MA: Harvard University Press, 1991.

Kott, Jan. "Titania and the Ass's Head." Translated by Boleslaw Taborski. In *Shakespeare Our Contemporary.* Rev edn. 1965, 171–90. London: Methuen & Co Ltd., 1967.

Long, William B. *"John a Kent and John a Cumber:* An Elizabethan Playbook and Its Implications." *Shakespeare and Dramatic Tradition: Essays in Honor of S. F. Johnson.* Edited by W. R. Elton and William B. Long. Newark: University of Delaware Press, 1989, 125–43.

Maguire, Laurie E. *Shakepearean Suspect Texts: The "Bad" Quartos and their Contexts.* Cambridge: Cambridge University Press, 1996.

Selbourne, David. *The Making of* [Brook's] *"A Midsummer Night's Dream."* London: Methuen, 1982.

Shakespeare, William. *A Midsummer Night's Dream.* Edited by Harold F. Brooks. New Arden Shakespeare. London: Methuen & Co Ltd, 1979.

———. Edited by R. A. Foakes. New Cambridge Shakespeare. Cambridge: Cambridge University Press, 1984.

———. Edited by Horace Howard Furness. 1895. New Variorum Shakespeare. New York: Dover Publications, Inc., 1963.

———. Edited by Trevor R. Griffiths. Shakespeare in Production. Cambridge: Cambridge University Press, 1996.

———. Edited by Peter Holland. World's Classics. Oxford: Oxford University Press, 1994.

———. Edited by Gary Taylor (John Jowett, "Scrutinizer"). In *William Shakespeare: The Collected Works.* Oxford: Clarendon Press, 1986.

———. Edited by Stanley Wells. New Penguin Shakespeare. Harmondsworth: Penguin Books Ltd., 1967.

———. *A Midsummer Night's Dream 1600* [Q1]. Prepared by Thomas L. Berger. Malone Society Reprints. Oxford: Oxford University Press, 1995.

———. *The Norton Facsimile: The First Folio of Shakespeare.* Prepared by Charlton Hinman. New York: W. W. Norton & Company Inc., 1968.

———. *The Norton Shakespeare.* Edited by Stephen Greenblatt (general editor), Walter Cohen, Jean E. Howard, and Katharine Eisaman Maus. New York: W. W. Norton, 1997.

———. *The Riverside Shakespeare.* 2d ed. Edited by G. Blakemore Evans. Boston: Houghton Mifflin Company, 1997.

———. *William Shakespeare: The Complete Works.* Edited by Stanley Wells and Gary Taylor. Oxford: Clarendon Press, 1986.

Spevack, Marvin, comp. *A Complete and Systematic Concordance to the Works of [the Riverside, 1st ed.] Shakespeare.* Hildesheim: Georg Olms, 1968–80.

Taylor, Gary, and Michael Warren, eds. *The Division of the Kingdoms: Shakespeare's Two Versions of "King Lear."* Oxford Shakespeare Studies. Oxford: Clarendon Press, 1983.

Tilley, Morris Palmer. *A Dictionary of the Proverbs in England in the Sixteenth and Seventeenth Centuries.* Ann Arbor: University of Michigan Press, 1950.

Trewin, J. C. *Going to Shakespeare.* London: George Allen & Unwin, 1978.

Urkowitz, Steven. *Shakespeare's Revision of "King Lear."* Princeton: Princeton University Press, 1980.

Warren, Michael J. "Quarto and Folio *King Lear* and the Interpretation of Albany and Edgar." In *Shakespeare, Pattern of Excelling Nature.* Edited by David Bevington and Jay L. Halio. Newark: University of Delaware Press, 1978.

Wells, Stanley, and Gary Taylor. *William Shakespeare: A Textual Companion.* Oxford: Clarendon Press, 1987.

Wright, George T. *Shakespeare's Metrical Art.* Berkeley: University of California Press, 1988.

Young, David P. *Something of Great Constancy: The Art of "A Midsummer Night's Dream."* New Haven: Yale University Press, 1966.

"The gift is small, / The will is all": Musings for Jay Halio

Donald W. Foster

To outside observers of our academic enterprise, it may seem mysterious that some "Shakespeare" discoveries should register no impact on literary studies, even as a marginal consideration for editors, while a few others become hugely controversial, thereby supplying grist for the mill of academic discourse. In November 1985, Stanley Wells and Gary Taylor endorsed Shakespeare's authorship of a little-known jingle ascribed to Shakespeare in Bodleian MS Rawlinson poetry 160, a seventeenth-century manuscript miscellany. The announcement sparked a furor. Literary scholars, students, journalists, and stand-up comics made merry with the ping-pong prosody, the banal lyrics, while ridiculing the Oxford editors for having credited the manuscript attribution. Never has a poem been mocked in so many different languages, or denounced with such contempt, as "Shall I die, shall I fly."

In the spring of 1986, as the Oxford edition was going to press, Shakespearean authorship of "Shall I die" had already been shouted down. Those scholars having endorsed the Rawlinson attribution could be counted on one hand against loud, overwhelming, largely uninformed and sometimes mean-spirited opposition. In response to these developments, Wells and Taylor made a shrewd move. They credited Shakespeare with additional verses of seemingly undecidable authorship, citing the same kinds of evidence offered for "Shall I die" (manuscript attribution, biographical plausibilities, verbal parallels with canonical Shakespeare), and printed them all with Shakespeare's occasional verse in both the old- and modern-spelling versions of their *New Complete Oxford Shakespeare* (1986–88). The nondramatic canon stood thus to be enlarged, not only by "Shall I die," but by a whole collection of doubtfully attributed texts—this time, without involving the press. Amazingly, when these additional "Shakespeare" poems were gathered and published, they were met with virtual silence, even among the Oxford *Shakespeare*'s most vigorous critics. While the "Shall I die" debate raged on, a whole new parcel of poems was thus introduced to the Works without ensuing controversy, digested without scholarly dyspepsia, and reprinted, a decade later, in the *Norton Shakespeare*.[1]

Among the poems that Wells and Taylor advanced for inclusion in the canon is the shortest "Shakespeare" poem ever credited as authentic. The text is just twelve words long:

> The gift is small:
> The will is all:
> A shey ander [*sic*] Asbenall.
> > Shaxpaire vpon a peaire of gloues that maser
> > [*sic*] sent to his mistris

These lines upon a gift of gloves are a conventional posy or "presentative" epigraph, unremarkable except for the attribution to Shakespeare. The text and ascription are supplied by a seventeenth-century manuscript miscellany compiled by Sir Francis Fane of Bulbeck and dated 1629.[2] The caption is a scribal addition, possibly transmitted by a student or servant of Master Asbenall (but "master" and "mistress" are conventional in poem headings and need not signify here a literal relation to the scribe). The three-line posy cannot be Fane's own invention. Fane or an antecedent collector has recorded a local Stratford anecdote, perhaps after having seen an actual artifact preserved by the Asbenall family (i.e., the gloves or a subscribed parchment).

In *William Shakespeare: A Textual Companion,* Wells and Taylor defend the "Shaxpaire" attribution, observing that John Shakespeare (the poet's father) was a Stratford glover, and that the Asbenalls (hereafter, "Aspinall") were a local family whom the poet must certainly have known. (Alexander Aspinall, M.A., was master of the Stratford grammar school from 1582–1624.) Wells and Taylor remark further that "The pun on 'will' would be characteristic of Shakespeare," and that "previous commentators seem not to have noticed the striking parallel at *Pericles* Sc. 1.4.17/1373: 'Yet my good will is great, though the gift small.'" The last line is said to be obscure, "perhaps merely an error for 'Alisander,'" though "it may conceal some private joke."[3] Unpersuaded by Alisander but wishing to improve on a difficult line, Wells and Taylor emend the third line of their modern-spelling text to read, simply, "Alexander Aspinall," thus following Edgar Fripp.

If "A shey under" is to be read as a corruption of Aspinall's Christian name, the original must have been either "Alesaunder" or "Alisaunder"—medieval spellings for "Alexander" that are still found, rarely, in the Elizabethan period (most often as a comic archaism, as in Shakespeare's *Love's Labor's Lost* and Chapman's *Humorous Day's Mirth*). But even if "A shey under" were certainly a corruption of "Alisander," the editorial emendation is incompatible with the manuscript attribution. If the final line is indeed a signature ("My goodwill is greater than the gift—love, Alexander Aspinall"), then no one but Alexander Aspinall can be credited as the "author"; and if someone other than Aspinall wrote the posy, then the emendation must be wrong. But this brief text appears to have been misunderstood by the Oxford editors, as by Fripp. Archival evidence offers an economical solution to the puzzle: on 28 October 1594, Alexander Aspinall, a widower, married Anne Shaw (or "Shey"), the widow of Ralph Shaw, a Stratford wool-driver. In the parish register, the bride's name is spelled "Shaw"; but in other records of the period, the surname *Shaw* is frequently spelled *Shey* (also *Shaa, Shaye, Shea,* etc.), reflecting early modern pronunciation.[4] In short, apart from trivial slips ("under" for "ander," "maser" for "master"), the Fane text is substantively correct:

> The gift is small,
> The will is all:
> A Shey under Asbenall
>   (Shakespeare upon a pair of gloves that master sent to his mistress)

Fripp's "Alexander" may remain latent in the third line. Insofar as the assonance and rhythmic symmetry can drive a pun on *A Shey under* : *Alesaunder* (or even on *she* : *Shey*), the third line might even be viewed by some readers as a Shakespeare-like equivocation—but it requires no emendation.

The original text of this epigram appears to have accompanied a wedding present from Aspinall to his bride, or perhaps—if the scribal caption is partly mistaken—a gift to the Aspinalls from a third party (Shakespeare, or whomever). Though posies of this sort were a convention of gift-giving, few have survived. I have found only three presentative verses written expressly for a gift of gloves, the earliest of which is the Aspinall posy. A second, with border ornamentation as for a gift-card, appears in William Browne, *Britannia's Pastorals* (1613).[5] A third survives in a Bodleian manuscript, the original of which is said to have been placed inside one of a pair of gloves, a helpful report that indicates something of seventeenth-century convention.[6] The historical particulars of the Aspinall gift are unrecoverable. The gloves may have been embossed with the posy—but "upon" means only "written on the subject of." More likely, the gloves bore only the names, *Asbenall* over *Shey* (or *Asbenall* on one glove, *Shey* on the other), with the posy inscribed on a card. Either way, the epigram's wit is located in the final line: it was a ubiquitous jest of the Elizabethan period that the wife lies beneath the husband's authority, as beneath her husband.

When restored from modern editorial corruption, this "Shaxpaire" text is unambiguous and vaguely amusing, and yet less inventive than the Oxford editors have supposed. Fripp rightly describes "The gift is small, the will is all" as an Elizabethan "commonplace."[7] (Even today, one can purchase from some country-style giftshops a sampler pillow bearing the identical sentiment, or a book of folk art entitled *The Gift is Small, The Love is Great,* by Frederick Pastor.) The "verbal parallel" in *Pericles* is no more "striking" than, say, Richard Barnfield's version: "Small is the gift, but great is my good-will" (1595). A Harleian manuscript from the same historical moment (c. 1596) offers another variant: "Though a gift be small, yet goodwill is all."[8] Nor should the phrasing in *Pericles* carry much attributional weight for the Oxford editors: Wells and Taylor ascribe the first two acts of *Pericles* not to Shakespeare c. 1594 but to George Wilkins c. 1608. Nor can I hear a pun on the poet's name in "The will is all," which here would carry a bumptious connotation—"Not Alexander, not Anne, but the *Will* is all," as if to say, "I the poet am the one who matters on your wedding day."

Only when the text has been understood may the attributional problem be considered. Fane refers us to mistress "Shey" and master "Asbenall." Master "Shaxpaire" is referenced only as a writer of the epigram, or as a maker of the gloves, or both. Will Shakespeare as a young adult surely became acquainted with Mr. Aspinall, Stratford's new schoolmaster; and he may later have dashed off a rhyme for a gift given on the occasion of Aspinall's marriage—the Shaws were longtime friends of the Shakespeares, and neighbors in Henley Street. But if Fane's caption is entirely correct, then "Shaxpaire" merely served as Aspinall's amanuensis—and it is hard to imagine that one of Stratford's foremost scholars would deputize the son of John Shakespeare to compose a three-line posy for a wedding gift to his own bride.

If, however, Shakespeare (or any other third person) gave the gloves as a wedding gift in his own behalf to Anne or Alexander Aspinall, then Fane's caption is at least half-wrong. And if the caption lacks authority, the attribution may be wrong as well. The twelve-word epigram contains nothing that could not have come from Aspinall's own Muse or, for that matter, from a thousand other well-wishers. Shakespeare's name may have been linked to the posy decades later only because Shakespeare was Stratford's best-known poet, or even because the Aspinall wedding-gloves were identifiable as having been made in the Shakespeare glovery. Such hypotheses are no longer subject to empirical proof. Still, Fripp and the Oxford editors mistook when they discredited Fane's text, and it could be a mistake to discredit Fane's Shakespearean attribution. The Aspinall epigram, though conventional and brief, may be Shakespeare's. Or maybe not. What interests me is not the attribution, but our indifferent response to it within Shakespeare studies: in the seventy years since Fane's text was first brought to scholars' attention, no one has bothered to consider its probable mode of transmission, the convention that it represents, or even to read it very carefully.

In the *Workes* of James I (1616) is a frontispiece portrait of the King, with a four-line inscription in alliterative verse. The sentiment is unremarkable: James finds his true likeness to God not in the "earth" of his own flesh, nor in his crown and royal finery, but in that which cannot be adequately represented in his portrait—his divine knowledge:[9]

> *Crounes have their compasse, length of dayes their date,*
> *Triumphes their tombes, felicitie her fate*
> *Of more then earth, can earth make none partaker,*
> *But knowledge makes the KING most like his maker*

Simon Passæus sculp: Lond.   *Ioh: Bill excudit*

Whatever one makes of the "Shaxpaire" gloves and verses, here is one instance among many where it is the creator of the artifact, not the writer of an accompanying text, to whom the ascription refers. Simon Passe did the engraving of both the portrait and letter-plate, and John Bill, the copper-plate printing. The poet is unnamed unless Passe (*sculpsit*) or Bill (*excudit*) also wrote the verses.

Could William Shakespeare have written this four-line poem? Someone in the seventeenth century thought so. The meditation on James's royal image survives in multiple manuscript copies (sans portrait), most of which are unattributed. But in two manuscripts at the Folger—one compiled circa 1633–34, the other about 1650— "Crowns have their compass" is headed "Shakespeare on (upon) the King."[10] As with the Aspinall posy, this "Shakespeare discovery" is old news—or rather, no news at all. Since 1821, when James Boswell first drew attention to it, the attribution has engaged hardly anyone's interest.[11] Subsequent editors did not disprove the attribution—they simply ignored it.

"Crowns" has been nudged toward canonicity by its inclusion in the *Oxford Shakespeare*. Taking their text from the 1616 Passe engraving in James's *Workes,* and their attribution from two mid-seventeenth-century manuscripts, Wells and Taylor defend Shakespeare's authorship of "Crowns" with a noncommittal but one-sided argument. That Shakespeare would compose "such a poem in praise of the monarch" is plausible in that he "was the chief dramatist of the only theatrical company patronized by King James himself"; "in the absence of a poet laureate [Shakespeare] might have served such a function." His poem in praise of James "might have been written especially for the *Works,* or for some other occasion." For internal evidence, Wells and Taylor muster from canonical Shakespeare a dozen "verbal parallels, which seem not to have been recorded hitherto."[12]

A competing attribution is supplied by Bodleian MS Ashmole 38 (p. 39), where this same poem is subscribed "finis R. B." and headed "Certayne verses wrighten by mr Robert Barker / His ma^{tis} Printer vnder his ma^{tis} picture." Barker's authorship seems plausible—as the King's printer from 1603, and as co-publisher (with John Bill) of the King's *Workes,* Barker had found James to be a generous patron. The Oxford editors acknowledge the difficulty of the Ashmole ascription, but conclude that "'wrighten' is ambiguous: it may mean 'composed' or only 'engraved.'"[13] The Shakespeare attribution seems to have carried the day without a whisper of protest. In the new *Norton Shakespeare,* Walter Cohen quietly credits Shakespeare's authorship of "Crowns" without so much as noting the contrary attribution to Barker.

All informed readers—including Wells, Taylor, and Cohen—will agree that "Crowns" is a conventional exercise in eulogy. The four-line text will not pay dividends on close reading or formal exegesis. Indeed, had these verses ever been noted in the press as a "Shakespeare" discovery, the attribution might well have generated sufficient interest, or offense, to have prompted an immediate rebuttal. But Shakespeare is no longer idealized as a god too proud to flatter a king. His livelihood, after all, had depended on Elizabeth's and James's patronage. That the Bard would dash off a eulogistic epigram in praise of King James is a hypothesis easily reconciled with the William Shakespeare of poststructuralist and materialist criticism. "Crowns," though conventional, is the sort of poem that our Shakespeare might well have written. Perhaps that partly explains why the attribution has generated no ripple of controversy since being added to Shakespeare's complete works in 1986. But while scholars nod, Shakespeare himself provides a fatal objection: the first edition of

King James's *Workes* bears a 1616 publication date—yet the texts therein were collected, edited, illustrated, and decked out with prefatory material after Shakespeare was already dead. That chronological difficulty is manifest from the volume's title page to its *finis*.[14] Shakespeare can have played no part in its production.

Many of the commissioned verses that accompany Simon Passe's work elsewhere were written by John Davies of Hereford or George Wither.[15] None can be Shakespeare's. Still, authorial attributions do not ordinarily come out of the blue. Some seventeenth-century ascriptions to Shakespeare are mistaken but it is usually possible, by charting the lines of textual transmission, to construct an etiology for erroneous or fraudulent ascriptions, as is the case here. "Crowns" was printed in more than one venue.[16] The two Folger copies of "Crowns," with their attribution to Shakespeare, are not plausibly derived from King James's *Workes* but from a broadside engraving published by the English printseller, Compton Holland, in 1619 and still available for purchase in mid-century when the Folger manuscripts were compiled. By taking his text from James's 1616 *Workes,* and his "Shakespeare" attribution from the Folger manuscripts, Stanley Wells inadvertently short-circuited lines of transmission that would otherwise have directed him to John Davies.

Davies was a personal friend of Abraham, Compton, and Hugh Holland for many years, and a frequent contributor of verses for engraved prints, as for Compton Holland's 1613 portraits of the royal family. Sculpted by Cornelius Boel, the prints bear four-line verse inscriptions—for James ("Iacobus Magnus Brittains blessed Kinge . . .") and Queen Anne ("Great Empresse of the North . . .")—that were probably penned by Wither or Davies, both of whom later published independent and revised versions of "Great Empresse."[17] No companion print survives of Prince Charles. The corresponding print of Princess Elizabeth, last of the 1613 set, bears four Latin elegiac couplets, and eight lines of English verse signed "Io: Dauies."[18] Six years later, Holland reprinted the Boel engravings with new verses, "Great Empress" being replaced by the King's own funeral elegy on Queen Anne. "Iacobus Magnus" was replaced by "Crowns," which appears, even more strongly than "Great Empress," to belong to Davies.[19]

How, then, did "Crowns" come to be ascribed to Shakespeare a quarter-century later? The bibliographic history of the Holland prints may supply an answer.[20] King James was not for all markets. Overly optimistic about the sales potential of royal portraits in the year of Anne's death and of Elizabeth's coronation in Bohemia, Holland made far more prints of the royal family than he or anyone else could sell. By 1622, when he died or retired from business, there was unsold stock—quite a lot of it, in fact.[21] For the next fifty years, London printsellers tried one after another to unload Holland's 1619 overstock of that yellowing portrait of King James with the verse inscription, "Crowns have their compass." The most likely explanation for those mid-seventeenth-century "Shakespeare" attributions is that a London stationer, possibly Holland himself, traded on Shakespeare's growing reputation to help move the unsold copies: "Welcome, shoppers, such a deal—*Shakespeare upon the King!*" At least two seventeenth-century readers bought the attribution, if not the actual print.

It should not have taken long for scholars to investigate whether "Crowns" was indeed written by the same poet who wrote *Macbeth*. Nor is the question irrelevant to our larger critical enterprise—interpretive work is conditioned by one's understanding of Shakespeare's relations with his noble and royal patrons—yet in the two centuries since Boswell first alerted scholars to Shakespeare's supposed authorship of these lines on King James, the necessary research has been neglected, allowing "Crowns" to take a quiet place, since 1986, among the canonical poems. That this poem and others not by Shakespeare appear in the Oxford and Norton *Shakespeare*s is a matter of small consequence. For generations, editors have included in the Works un-Shakespearean poems from *The Passionate Pilgrim* and *Sonnets to Sundry Notes of Music*. The poet's reputation has survived. Nor will the reputation or relative weight of any future edition of the Works turn on the inclusion or omission of the Aspinall posy or "Crowns." These two poems—which I have selected from among dozens of texts doubtfully ascribed to Shakespeare from 1599 to 1997—raise a question that has scarcely anything to do with historical actuality or attributional methodology: Why have these texts and attributions proved so uninteresting to professional Shakespeareans, so manifestly uncontroversial—unlike, say, "Shall I die, shall I fly"? Almost everyone has thoughts about "Shall I die" (the same thoughts)—but are there five living Shakespeareans with any opinion about the Aspinall posy or "Crowns"? And would the quantity and thoughtfulness of scholarly commentary suddenly increase if these two poems had the ill fortune to be written up in *The Times?*

As stories go, the "Shakespeare discovery" is one with a familiar plot. A noncanonical text (play, poem, signature) seeks admission to the Shakespeare canon. The appellant text passes unnoticed in Shakespeare studies until the journalists are called in. The imposture is quickly smelled out. (Most new candidates for the Shakespeare canon are stinkers.) The journalists interview a few established scholars, who advise caution. Eventually, someone exposes the would-be "Shakespeare" with a systematic refutation—and there's an end. Some months or years later, another "Shakespeare" knocks on the door. It is the same story.

Nowhere was this narrative more succinctly played out than in 1988, when Peter Levi trumpeted to the press that he had found a lost Shakespeare poem beginning "As this is endless," appended to John Marston's Ashby entertainment of 1607.[22] In this instance, the initial headlines were followed in just two weeks by the rebuttal of James Knowles, showing that Levi was mistaken. The text was neither lost, nor Shakespeare's, but a poem by Sir William Skipwith. Nor was the manuscript attribution incorrect. As demonstrated by Knowles, Levi (following J. P. Collier) had misconstrued an italic "W. Sk." for "W. Sh."[23] Knowles's scholarship provided a satisfying finality: controversy was nipped in the bud, leaving no other business but a round of applause for Knowles and condolences to the attributor. "As this is endless" can have no bearing on our interpretation of canonical Shakespeare.

Scholars generally take interest in the Shakespeare apocrypha and dubia in brief flashes, on those rare occasions when a debatable attribution appears in the news. But there is a tendency to respond more directly to the publicity than to the evidentiary case, and to lose all interest as soon as the academic community has moved toward evident consensus, one way or the other. Most readers—when confronted with "Shall I die, shall I fly?" in the London, or New York, or India *Times*—had the same response to the poem's opening line: "Yes, *please!*" Everyone, it seemed, was eager for this bad "Shakespeare" poem to be buried its full 135 lamely anapestic feet deep—the sooner, the better, and by any means possible. Following articles I wrote on "Shall I die" in 1985 and 1987, my mailbox was crammed with congratulatory letters and thank-you notes, a majority of them from persons whose only evident interest in "Shall I die" was in seeing the attribution defeated.[24] Many came from persons outside the academy, addressing me as if I had saved the President. Several letters from Shakespeare scholars contained biting commentary or parody directed as much toward Gary Taylor as toward the poem, even after after the public controversy had subsided. I slowly grew uneasy with the cultural phenomenon to which I had lent myself.

I ought to have given my 1987 essay some other title than "'Shall I die' Post Mortem." The article seemed to indicate that the Shakespearean impostor was slain, the discussion officially over. But it was not my intention to squelch interest in the text. Contrary to the conventional wisdom, "Shall I die" is a valuable literary artifact, a poem of interest even if it is not a poem of quality. The Shakespeare attribution seems all wrong to most readers—but how many manuscript "Shakespeare" attributions have survived, even mistaken ones? Very few. Most of them reward thoughtful study, as I have tried to show with the Aspinall posy and "Crowns." Another such is the Elias James epitaph (1610), ascribed to "W. Shakespeare" in the same hand, and in the same manuscript, that assigns "Shall I die, shall I fly" to "William Shakespeare."[25] The James epitaph was similarly ignored for generations, until Leslie Hotson took interest in it. Subsequent research has turned up both internal and external evidence showing the attribution to be correct beyond reasonable doubt.[26]

In 1986 Peter Beal advised Gary Taylor's opponents against an old-fashioned contempt for manuscript attributions.[27] I was myself among those who pointed out errors in the Rawlinson, but my esteem for the Rawlinson manuscript has only increased since 1985. The Rawlinson supplies correct attributions for a number of poems wrongly ascribed in printed texts of the seventeenth century. One of its attributions thought even by Beal to be mistaken has turned out, on further study, to be correct.[28] The Rawlinson also contains good or excellent texts of poems by Jonson and other members of the Mermaid poets group, including Beaumont and Fletcher. A survey that collates the Rawlinson with other manuscript and printed texts reveals that several attributions and many texts in the anthology may derive from an authority no worse than Jonson himself, an inconvenient fact that invites new questions about the attribution of "Shall I die." For what reason and on whose authority did this densely rhymed anapestic lyric come to be associated with Shakespeare? If "Shall I die" is a song, could it be one that was performed during or after a Shakespeare play? Could "Shall I die" have anything in common with other anapestic dance-ditties in Shakespeare, such as "The Sailor" or "Thought is free" in *The Tempest* (2.2.42–54, 3.2.121–23)? Perhaps not. But why is it so easy to endure "Flout 'em and scout 'em," without caring who wrote it, while gagging on "Shall I die"? If a snatch of "Shall I die" had been quoted in a First Folio play, would that coincidence have conditioned the aesthetic judgments expressed by scholars in 1985, or have softened the attacks on Gary Taylor? A passing decade has allowed for cooler judgments to prevail. Stephen Greenblatt and Walter Cohen wisely resisted the advice of those who said that "Shall I die" must not be included in the *Norton Shakespeare* (1997). It was included—and without a fight, even in the absence of new evidence—as a text that invites further study.

As we move toward the 400th anniversary of *As You Like It*, the Shakespeare canon remains a coherent body of culturally significant and well-liked poems and plays. Any challenge to that entirely useful status quo—especially news of an unfamiliar "Shakespeare" text— must, and will, be met with scholarly resistance. Those "Shakespeare" attributions that make headlines (with or without the attributor's consent) will meet with resistance sooner rather than later— and they deserve to be resisted, even the "good" ones. Skepticism is a wonderful thing. The mere prospect of professional humiliation inoculates scholarship against frivolous and speculative attributions that might otherwise be advanced in journals or the popular press. But politic skepticism must be followed by sound scholarship of the sort administered by James Knowles to Peter Levi's "As this is endless," or by MacDonald Jackson in response to doubts about "A Lover's Complaint."

Our discipline's primary objective must be to study and to understand cultural production both in the early modern period and in our own not-quite post-modern moment. The important issues in literary studies rarely hinge on who wrote what. But if particular attributions are unimportant, attributional consensus, once established, serves as an organizing principle for our interpretive work, a fact not always acknowledged even by the most canny theorist. The meaning and value of a doubtfully attributed text can emerge only after the text ceases to be viewed solely as an attributional problem and comes to be viewed as an interpretive challenge (whether read as Shakespeare or pseudo-Shakespeare)—and that cannot happen until the attribution has been debated without passion, with a full and mutual consideration of the evidence, both pro and con. We're not quite there yet with most of the Shakespeare dubia, not even with "Shall I die."

I submitted my first book, *Elegy by W.S.: A Study in Attribution*, to the University of Delaware Press in February 1986, during the winter of our discontent with "Shall I die." Absolute indifference to "Shall I die" and its Shakespearean attribution—which were known to scholarship long before the poem ever became news—had turned to a frenzy, causing embarrassment for Oxford University Press. A text tainted by its brush with greatness, "Shall I die" was being described, far and wide, as the most ridiculous piece of rubbishy poetry produced in the seventeenth century. Stanley Wells and Samuel Schoenbaum had been drubbed for their endorsement of the attribution. Gary Taylor was being subjected to ad hominem broadsides assailing his English accent, his earring, his scholarly integrity.

In submitting *Elegy by W.S.* to the University of Delaware in 1986, I was not sanguine about the book's prospects. Coming on the heels of *The Birth of Merlin, Edmond Ironside,* and "Shall I die," any newcomer with another "Shakespeare discovery" was bound to look like the broom-and-wheelbarrow man at the tail end of a messy parade. No one had to instruct Jay Halio that "A Funeral Elegy" was a poem lacking Shakespeare's usual verve—a poem that other Shakespeareans were sure not to like. But whatever one thinks of "A Funeral Elegy," one must applaud the intellectual integrity and moral courage that it must have required for Jay to move forward with *Elegy by W.S.,* submitted by a new Ph.D. at a time when senior Shakespeareans around the world were still having a hoot over "Shall I die, shall I fly." Many editors would have dropped the typescript like a hot petardo, in mortal fear of being hoist with Wells and Taylor. But when properly considered, even bad "Shakespeare" and "bad" Shakespeare can be viewed as a small gift to literary studies. The most wise and cautious scholars are those who, like Jay Halio, labor quietly to facilitate free and open debate.

Notes

1. Stanley Wells, Gary Taylor, et. al., eds., "Various Poems," in *The New Complete Oxford Shakespeare,* Original–Spelling Edition (Oxford: Clarendon, 1986), 881–87; Compact [modern-spelling] Edition (Clarendon, 1988), 777–83; modern-spelling edition reprinted with intro. and notes, ed. Walter Cohen, "Various Poems," *The Norton Shakespeare,* ed. Stephen Greenblatt, et. al. (New York: Norton, 1997), 1991–2009.

2. Shakespeare Birthplace Trust Records Office, MS ER.93 (p. 177), compiled by Sir Francis Fane (1611–80). The MS subheading is to the side of the text. On the next page Fane records "Shaxpers Epitaft," given as "Blest be the man that shaides these Bones / And Curst be hee that moues these stones"; and the final couplet of the familiar epitaph on John a Combe, given as "Hay hay sayth Tom toule who is in this tome / ho ho quoth the deuill tis my John a Come" (p. 178). Wells and Taylor, eds., "Upon a Pair of Gloves" (1986), 885; (1988), 780; Cohen, ed., p. 1998.

3. Stanley Wells and Gary Taylor, eds., [Commentary on] "Various Poems," 449–60, in Wells and Taylor, *William Shakespeare: A Textual Companion* (Oxford: Clarendon, 1987), 455. In these observations Wells and Taylor are anticipated by Edgar I. Fripp, *Master Richard Quyny* (Oxford: Oxford University Press, 1924), 62–64. Fripp cites the analogue in *Pericles,* another in Harl. MS 6910; suggests the association between Alexander, Alisander, and "A shey ander"; and suggests the "Alexander Aspinall" emendation (Fripp, *Master Richard Quyny,* 62–64). Subsequent discussions of the epigram appear in Fripp's *Shakespeare: Man and Artist.* (Oxford: Oxford University Press, 1938), 401–2; E. M. Martin, "Shakespeare in a Seventeenth Century Manuscript," *The English Review* 51 (1930): 484–89; and Mark Eccles, *Shakespeare in Warwickshire* (Madison: University of Wisconsin Press, 1961): 57–58.

4. See, for example, Percy H. Reaney and R. M. Wilson, *A Dictionary of British Surnames,* 2nd ed. (London: Routledge, 1976), 316; "Shaw," "Shey" (alphabetical,

by county), *International Genealogical Index* (Salt Lake City: Church of Jesus Christ of Latter-Day Saints, 1988).

5. William Browne, *Britannia's Pastorals,* Book 1, Third Song, 471–74 (London, 1613), 58.

6. "Deliuered in a gloue," Bodleian MS Rawl. poet. 212, fol. 56: "Happy wert poor glove if thou didst know / . . . / That thou so sweet an hand, so oft dost kiss." Cf. "Verse made upon a pair of slippers sent for a New Years guifte 1631," Bod. MS Ashmole 781, p. 165.

7. Fripp, *Quyny,* 63.

8. Richard Barnfield, "To the Right Honorable . . . William Stanley, Earle of Derby," in *Cynthia* (London, 1595), ed. George Klawitter, *Richard Barnfield: The Complete Poems* (London and Toronto: Associated University Presses, 1990), 115. British Library MS Harl. 6910 (containing more than 400 such posies); reprinted in Edward Arber, *An Elizabethan Garner,* 7 vols. (London: Arber, 1977–83), 1: 611.

9. James I, *The Workes of Iames, King of Great Britaine, France, and Ireland, published by James [Montagu], bishop of Winton* (London: R. Barker and J. Bill, 1616 [i.e., 1617 n.s., *STC* 14344]); anr. issue, augmented, R. Barker and J. Bill, 1616–20 [*STC* 14345]); frontispiece is omitted in some copies. Reprinted in James I, *Serenissimi . . . Principis Jacobi, . . . opera, edita ab I. Montacuto, episcopo* [trans. and revised by T. Reid and P. Young,] (London: B. Norton and J. Bill [R. Barker and J. Bill], 1619–20 [*STC* 14346.3 only]). For additional details, see Arthur M. Hind, *Engraving in England in the Sixteenth and Seventeenth Centuries,* 3 vols. (Cambridge: Cambridge University Press, 1955), 2: 259–60, no. 31.

10. "Shakespeare on the King," Folger Library MS V.a.160, p. 2, 2nd series; and "Shakespeare Upon the King," V.a.262, p. 131.

11. James Boswell (the younger), ed., Plays and Poems, 21 vols. (London, 1821), 1: 481.

12. Wells and Taylor, *Textual Companion,* 459.

13. Ibid., 459. Neither the *OED,* nor other instances in the Ashmole manuscript, allow for "wrighten" to be taken as a substitute for *engraved* or *worked* or *wrought* (or, indeed, for anything but "written"); nor was Barker the engraver. The "Robert Barker" and "R.B." ascriptions are unambiguous but mistaken. No verse by Barker survives. His prose prefaces and dedications contain some alliteration but otherwise nothing to suggest his possible authorship of the Passe poem.

14. The volume was edited by "James [Montagu], Bishop of Winton" (but Montagu was not confirmed in the see of Winchester until 4 October 1616). The collection extends through the King's 1616 oration in the Star Chamber, delivered two months after Shakespeare's burial. Nor can any of Passe's English engravings from 1616 be dated earlier than Shakespeare's April 23 decease. The Passe portrait of Prince Charles (James I, *Workes,* sig. a3) was begun before but completed after 3 November 1616, the date on which Charles was created Prince of Wales. The accompanying portrait of James cannot be much earlier. In fact, the first printing of the English *Workes* was not until February 1617 (n.s.), with a second issue in 1619.

15. Abraham Holland, Nicholas Breton, and John Owen, friends of Davies and Wither, each served a turn as well. For a catalogue of engravings by the Passe family, see Hind, 2: 245–302.

16. "Crowns" appears with the Passe engraving in the English *Workes* (1616, 1620), and in the Latin edition of the Works (1619); the poem was later recycled (with minor revision of line 4) as the inscription for an engraving of King Charles made by Willem Passe, Simon's brother. The engraving of Charles by Willem Passe was sold by Thomas Jenner during Charles's reign (Hind, *Engraving,* 287, no. 2).

17. See "To the sacred Queene of Englands most excellent Maiestie," lines 5–8, *Microcosmos* (Oxford: J. Barnes, 1613 [*STC* 6333]), sig. A2v; and George Wither, "Certaine Epigrams (To the Queens Majestie, Epigram 3)," lines 1–4, *Iuvenilia* (London: J. Budge, 1622), sig. Y8v. Wither was an inveterate reviser of his work. Cf. earlier version in Wither's *Abuses Stript and Whipt* (London, 1613), with *your* for *thy* (2), *you do* for *thou dost* (3), *curt'sie* for *Bounty, true* for *thy*. Cf. Davies, "To the sacred Queene of England," lines 1–2, *The Muses-Teares* (London: J. Wright, 1613 [*STC* 6339]), sig. E1.

18. For the Boel prints of King James, Queen Anne, and Princess Elizabeth, see Hind, *Engraving*, vol. 2: James, 57–58 (no. 12 [London:] C. Holland, [1619], reprinted from "another version," Sutherland collection [London: 1613?]); Anne, Hind 59–60 (no. 13 [London: C. Holland, 1619]; reprinted from "a similar second version," Sutherland coll. [London: 1613?]); Elizabeth, 313 (no. 1 [London: [1613,] revised [London: C. Holland, 1619]).

19. Davies' verse supplies multiple instances of the *partaker / maker* rhyme, and of every word and several phrases, found in "Crowns"; *felicity* ("Crowns," line 2), is one of Davies' favorite "rare" words, appearing 17 times just in *Microcosmos*, 7 in *Summa Totalis*, 5 in *Wittes pilgrimage* (plus cognates). The orthography, use of capitals for emphasis, alliterative phrasing, and prosody, all point toward Davies. A "Robert Barker" attribution is explicable, "George Wither" defensible—but "Shakespeare," a virtual impossibility.

20. Boel, a recent immigrant, corrupted the English texts supplied by Holland in 1613. Holland in 1619 altered the portrait of Princess Elizabeth to show her wearing a crown, replacing the verses by Davies with a prose note about her recent coronation as Queen of Bohemia. For "Iacobus Magnus," Holland substituted "Crowns" (also, I believe, by Davies), taking his copy either from the *Workes* or from the poet himself (Davies is directly associated with the Holland brothers as early as 1613 and as late as 1625). For "Great Empresse" (by Davies or Wither), Holland substituted the King's own funeral elegy on Queen Anne ("Thee to invite, the great God sent a starre"), an authorized text printed without attribution (but Hind misreads the engraver's "Thee" for "Shee," p. 59; cf. plate 29).

21. The prints passed from Compton Holland to Hugh Holland about 1622. A decade later, the remaindered prints were acquired by Thomas Johnson, who erased Holland's imprint and sold them under his own name. After Johnson's death, copies were available from his widow, who kept the business running through 1654. From 1657 to 1663, Peter Stent sold the remaining prints, having replaced Johnson's name with his own. From Stent the remaindered copies passed on to John Overton, who added his imprint below Stent's and who continued to sell them until the Great Fire.

22. Peter Levi, *New Verses by Shakespeare* (London: Macmillan, 1988).

23. James Knowles, "WS MS," *TLS* (29 April–5 May 1988): 472+.

24. Donald W. Foster, "A New 'Shakespeare' Poem." *New York Times Book Review* (19 Jan. 1986): 4; "Shall I Die?" *Times Literary Supplement* (24 Jan. 1986): 87+; "Shall I Die?" *Times Literary Supplement* (7 March 1986): 247; "'Shall I Die' Post Mortem: Defining Shakespeare," *Shakespeare Quarterly* 38.1 (1987): 58–77.

25. Bodleian MS Rawl. poet. 160, "An Epitaph" ("When god was pleasd"), fol. 41 (Crum W-1110); "Shall I die,"108v (Crum S–333).

26. For a summary discussion of authorship and provenance, see Wells and Taylor, eds., *Textual Companion*, 458.

27. See Peter Beal, Letter, *TLS* (3 Jan. 1986): 13, responding to Robin Robbins, "And the Counter-Arguments" (20 Dec. 1985): 1449.

28. See "Disdain me still," Rawl. poet. 160, fol. 103v, ascribed to "J. D.," and John Dowland, "Disdain me still," *A Pilgrimes Solace,* no. 1 [Crum D–327] (London, 1612), no. 2. Published as John Donne's in *Poems* (London, 1633), and as William Herbert's in the *Poems of Pembroke and Ruddier* (London, 1660). Cf. Beal (1986): 1449. Dowland's claim to "Disdain me still" was overlooked even by the careful eyes of Margaret Crum.

Part Two
Performances

A Polish Gentleman's Visit to London Theaters in 1820–1821

JERZY LIMON

THE DIARY OF A POLISH GENTLEMAN AND MAN OF LETTERS, KAROL SIENKIEWICZ, in the manuscript collection of the National Library in Warsaw, is, to my knowledge, the earliest firsthand Polish account of Shakespearean productions in London. Acquired in 1948 from a private collector, this manuscript (MS 5680) is bound in dark-green leather and entitled *Charles's Diary in England 1820–21*.[1] It opens on 24 June 1820 and ends on 16 August 1821; along with Sienkiewicz's recollections of his stay in London, it includes an account of his travels to Scotland, Oxford, Cambridge, Stratford-upon-Avon and other places. At Stratford he visited what was thought to be Shakespeare's house, where he transcribed, among other things, some verses inscribed on the chimney by Lucien Bonaparte (1775–1840):

> The eye of Genius glistens to admire
> How memory hails the sound of Shakespeare's lyre.
> One tear I shed to form a crystal shrine
> Of all that's grand, immortal and divine.[2]

Karol Sienkiewicz (1793–1860) was born in the Ukraine to a Polish family of impoverished gentry. Having completed his formal education in 1812, he became a tutor of Prince Adam Czartoryski's nephew, with whom he travelled abroad. This journey provided Sienkiewicz with an opportunity to learn foreign languages and attend lectures at the University of Geneva, all of which naturally broadened his knowledge and stimulated his literary interests. After his return to Poland in 1818, the Prince appointed him deputy librarian in Czartoryski's famous library in Puławy (now in Cracow). Sienkiewicz's mission to England was connected with the Prince's intention of enlarging his collection with books and manuscripts connected with Poland and the Poles.

Sienkiewicz left Puławy on 13 October 1819, heading through Germany and Switzerland to Italy and France. Having arrived in Paris on

1 January 1820, he promptly showed himself to be a theater-lover, for one of the first things he did there was to see a play. He reached London towards the end of June 1820, and as will be clear from the evidence below, the London theater became an important focus of his interest. But his stay in Britain was fruitful in other ways as well. He had an opportunity to meet a number of interesting people: politicians, book collectors, librarians, scholars, journalists and writers. Among the names that recur throughout his *Diary* are those of Henry Brougham, Robert Owen, John Colin Dunlop, and Thomas Campbell. His search for rare books, prints, and manuscripts was fruitful too, for he brought several cases of these back to Poland, along with his completed translation of Walter Scott's *Lady of the Lake*, which was published in Warsaw in 1822. Throughout the remaining years of his life Sienkiewicz was active as a journalist, writer, and book collector. As a theater critic, and the founder of the influential literary and critical journal *Ćwiczenia Naukowe* (which in 1819 evolved into *Pamiętnik Naukowy*), he naturally had an impact on the growing popularity of Shakespeare in Poland, and created a favorable climate for productions and translations of his works.[3] After the failure of the November Uprising in Poland in 1830, he made his home in Paris, where he was one of the founders of the Polish Library.

Much of what Sienkiewicz experienced in the theater had to do with the timing of his visit to London, which coincided with the notorious trial of Queen Caroline. Married to George Prince of Wales in 1795, Caroline separated from him within a year, after giving birth to their only child. At his prompting, a Parliamentary committee in 1805–6 investigated her allegedly immoral conduct, but found no proof of guilt, even though rumors continued to be spread about her after she left the country and took up residence in Italy. Divorce proceedings started in 1819 but the situation changed drastically when George III died in January 1820. Hoping to prevent his wife's return to England for the coronation, George IV took quick action: he insisted that her name be omitted from the liturgy and had the ruling cabinet declare that, should she return, the government would begin divorce proceedings. Determined to insist on her rights, Caroline returned on 5 June and was rapturously received by crowds of thousands. As a result, the King ordered an investigation of her actions abroad, and a Bill of Pains and Penalties was brought in, intended to deprive her of all her titles and rights of rank and to dissolve her marriage on grounds of adultery. Its preamble included a direct accusation that the Queen had treated Bartolomeo Pergami as a favorite as long ago as 1814, that she had conducted herself toward him "with indecent and offensive familiarity and freedom, and carried on a licentious, disgraceful and adulterous intercourse with him."[4] These allegations had to be proved before the two Houses of Parliament; the debate on the second reading of this bill, which began on 17 August 1820, took a form similar to a trial, and was popularly known as "the Queen's trial."[5] The bill was finally thrown out on 10 November after failing to gain the necessary majority. Popular sympathy was overwhelmingly with the Queen, and the "trial" added fuel to an already tense political situation, bringing England, many believed, to the verge of revolution. However, the excitement was short-lived, and Caroline died soon after an unsuccessful attempt to attend George IV's coronation on 19 July 1821.

The excerpts which follow have been translated from the modern edition of Sienkiewicz's *Diary* by Bogdan Horodyński, with the omission of Sienkiewicz's own translations of English texts into Polish and his lengthy quotations both from Shakespeare and from Cibber's adaptation of *Richard III*, which he failed to distinguish from Shakespeare's. Words and phrases that Sienkiewicz quotes in English appear in italics below.[6]

8 July 1820, Saturday.
At dinner our landlady let her *misses* and Francis go to the theater.[7] They asked whether I would come along. I said no, but afterwards agreed to go. To Covent Garden Theatre. It is constructed of ashlar and is extremely grand in size and architecture. The front façade is in the Grecian style, but enclosed all around. After it burned down in 1808, this theater was rebuilt in ten months.[8] This speed of action and completion is characteristic of the English people. St. Paul's had only one architect and mason, whereas St. Peter's in Rome had so many of them. After the construction of the theater was completed, the prices [of tickets] went up, and the commoners were enraged, so they had to bring them down.[9]

The entrances to the theater are beautiful: separate ones to the boxes, to the pit, etc. Inside it is vast and ornate. I cannot tell which is the largest, Covent Garden,[10] or the Grand Opera House in Paris, or San Carlo in Naples.

The benches in the pit rise rapidly one behind another, so that even a person wearing a hat does not obstruct the view of those sitting behind. The fronts of the boxes are upholstered with costly crimson fabric. There are four rows there, and above them, slightly recessed, the galleries. But the most striking feature is the chandelier, giving beautiful and vivid light. Hydrogen gas is used there, which runs out in whole bouquets of light, densely clustered around the crystal chandelier. The latter is hung just below the vault and does not blind the eyes of any of the spectators. The stage is vast, suitable for productions on the Shakespearean scale.

We arrived at half past six, entering the pit. Women are also admitted there. The crowd was great, and one could not find a free place, so we had to go to the boxes. The pit costs 3 shillings and 6 pence, the boxes twice as much—that is, 14 *zloties* [Polish currency] per person. The boxes are separated from the pit and are let annually; the ones that are deeper inside are for people of distinction, with the exception of the first two benches in these boxes, which are for people going to the theater in a group and paying a little extra. These remain empty until the second act, awaiting the arrival of a group, and, if nobody comes by that time, they are occupied by the persons sitting on the back benches. And that was what happened in our case.

Mr Garrick's *Clandestine Marriage* was played.[11] I understood as much as I had managed to read in the book, and therefore I laughed little and cannot judge the actors.

After the first play I went out to cool off. The corridors surrounding the boxes are full of beautiful nymphs, who walk around in sundry directions. The buffet is very expensive: ices are twice, and oranges four times, as expensive as usual.

The second play was a farce, of which I understood nothing, because I had no book. Except that when an actor said: "The Queen commands you to throw down your arms", people began to clap their hands, because at present the word "Queen" excites everybody here.[12] This ended at eleven o'clock.

15 August 1820, Tuesday.
Kean, who is now the leading actor in England, is leaving for America, and, for two weeks before his departure, he is going to play leading roles in the best plays. Tonight, it is *Richard III* by Shakespeare, staged at Drury Lane Theatre. [The latter is] equal in size to Covent Garden, only less decorated. From the outside [it is] nothing beautiful.

I was seated in the pit and had my book with me—otherwise I would not understand. I have been anxiously waiting to see Shakespeare's tragedies in London. I remember last year, when I went to Puławy, the Prince,[13] when the subject of tragedy came up, said that he would like me to see some London productions.

At last, the curtain was raised. The stage represented the Tower prison and soon Henry VI of the House of Lancaster appeared, and he learned of the battle lost by his wife Margaret, the victory of Edward IV of York, and the assassination of his son by Gloucester, the future Richard III.[14]

Thus, the first mention of the hero of this tragedy shows him murdering the unarmed Prince. But soon he appears in person, lame and hunchbacked, with his face as ugly as his soul; Kean was Richard, and he was welcomed by prolonged applause. Now he is alone, and he utters his soliloquy.(. . .)

. . . *That dogs bark at me, as I halt by them* [1.1.23]—Kean utters these words in a low voice, rapidly, waving his hands and rushing to the side of the stage, as if these words were forced and involuntary. Hence the impression was moving.

In order to achieve his aim, he first kills Henry—the imprisoned king. This is shown on the stage. Henry, moved with grief and anger at the sight of his son's murderer, reproaches him, shouting. . . . During this speech Richard kills him, and when Henry fell and gave his last breath, he stabbed him several times more with a sword, saying: *Down, down to hell and say I sent thee thither.*[15]

Here the first act ended. In the second act Henry's funeral [was presented]. A procession appeared with banners and candles, then a coffin followed by the mourning Anne—the wife of the Prince murdered by Richard, and King Henry's daughter-in-law. . . . That murderer, Richard, is in love with her, and is confident of reciprocation. He stops the procession and threatens everybody with death if any of them takes a step forward. They set down the coffin.

With a polite and contrite face Richard greets Anne, and a scene follows in which Shakespeare, extravagantly bold and attempting to present in one scene the epitome of cunning, cruelty, and female frailty, goes a step too far, thus destroying the boundary between pathos and the ridiculous. And Richard, through the power of his oaths, his outpourings of love, kneeling in front of her, and handing over to her his sword so that she might kill him, contrives that Anne promises to return his love. . . .

I would have been convinced, had not Richard been so ugly. But after all, women are the ones to judge. I do not feel that Kean played well here. His tone, smacking of irony, was not proper here. Therefore, the pit often burst into laughter.

Scenes then follow, informing us of the death of King Edward IV. This strengthens Richard's hopes for the throne. There remain only Edward's two sons in the way, adolescent heirs. The third act shows the plots through which Richard wins the crown, having imprisoned the legal heirs in the Tower.

Act four begins with a sad scene in prison, showing the two Princes and their mother, who, on Richard's order, are to be separated. This is a very moving sight; the children ask their mother to take them with her when she leaves, because they are frightened to stay there alone. The mother kneels and prays for the children. Richard's dagger is hanging over them, and thus they part. Richard sends a murderer to kill the children, and he himself appears in the shadows, feeling uneasy, but calling this foolishness.

He is informed that the Earl of Richmond has hopes for the throne. Richard moves against him; he enters the stage accompanied by the sound of drums. His way is barred by his mother and the mother of the murdered children. He is enraged because they have stopped him. They ask him where are the innocent victims, where is Clarence? Where is Hastings? Where is Grey? Richard's only answer is: *A flourish, trumpets!*

strike, alarum, drums!, and then he cries at the top of his voice: *Strike, I say!* [4.4.149, 151] The drums rattle and the mothers exeunt.

Act V. Richard's camp is presented alternately with Richmond's camp. Richard's tent is located at the back of the stage. He is alone. He complains about the length of the night, he hears some groans; it must be the wind, he says, and then falls asleep. Above his bed the ghosts of King Henry, and of Anne, whom he had killed after their marriage, and of the young Princes, appear. These shades are shown by means of transparent canvases.[16] Richard awakes crying: *Give me another horse! Bind up my wounds!* [5.3.177], and then runs and falls on his knees, pale, staring, with trembling lips, reclines his weakened head on his hand. Then he speaks (. . .) The last words [*Zounds, who is there?*, line 207] Kean, or rather Richard, because at this moment there was no other actor there, utters screaming, having suddenly sprung to his feet trembling. He, the King who knows no fear, in the moment of affliction is frightened by the entrance of an officer [Ratcliff] who approaches him. The scene is played with true mastery.

The battle breaks out. Both armies alternately march over the stage. Richard, having lost his horse, comes running on to the stage, shouting in despair: *A horse! A horse! My kingdom for a horse!* [5.4.7] The impact was great, but Kean lost his voice. How this would have sounded if uttered by Talma![17] Then Richard meets with Richmond, and they fight excellently; Richard falls and here the tragedy ended, and, it should be added, so ended the war between the house of York and the House of Lancaster, because Richmond, the victor, who reigned under the name of Henry VII, united the rights of both houses in one.[18]

Then they presented a comedy, *The Liar*,[19] but it did not appeal to the spectators in the upper gallery, who began to whistle aloud, and an actor began to address the audience in a tone that I found irritating, but it pleased the pit. Pleased because people wanted to hear something funny, but pleased with nothing. What the actor said was: "You have already seen a tragedy, and if you do not like comedy—get lost!" This impudence in the mouth of a common comedian would have had consequences anywhere else. And although he was addressing those sitting in the upper gallery, the people sitting there had the same right to be here as those in the boxes. . . .

17 August 1820, Thursday.
I went to the theater, where Kean played Hamlet. I did not like him as much as in *Richard III.* However, I cannot understand the actors well without the book and therefore I do not consider my opinion authoritative, but the London theaters do not seem to me as wonderful as I had thought in Poland. Decorations and machinery are better in Paris.

The ghosts are very funny. The shade of Hamlet's father in pale armor wanders around the stage, and, because he says nothing, one has the impression that this is some theater attendant who has accidentally appeared on stage. A theater so crowded with apparitions should at least present them well. At least in Warsaw Hamlet [the ghost] appears in a net,[20] and here I had expected something extra. There is also a procession here, and a funeral, but very modest. After the funeral, when the scene had to be changed, the earth which was dug up during the gravedigging scene was quickly swept away by a caretaker. It was just what might have been done by our native Rosciuses who reign at country inns. The pit laughed at the wrong time, and yawned during the scenes of pathos. When Kean started the famous *To be or not to be* speech, the spectators began to eat pears and nuts. This is not to say that everything was bad. Some of the scenes were played by Kean with spectacular power.

After the tragedy and before the comedy began, there were shouts of "long live the Queen" and applause. And in *Hamlet*, when the King and Queen were seated on the throne, somebody shouted that this was Mr Brougham and the Queen.[21]

28 August 1820, Monday.
I went to the theater to see *Othello*. This is one of the best of Shakespeare's tragedies, and Kean was at his best here. Strangely enough, in moments of great passion, as in his speech to the Senate when he justifies the abduction of his wife and utters those famous lines:

> *She loved me for the dangers I had passed,*
> *And I loved her, that she did pity them.*
> [1.3.169–70]

I did not like him very much. But at the moment when the base Iago evokes his jealousy, the atrociousness is perfect.

Emilia, Iago's wife, not knowing about the crime of her husband, clears Desdemona [of his accusations] before [Othello] and speaks words which might have been deliberately written for today's circumstances. This raised a noise such as I have never heard in a theater. These are the words:

> *I will be hang'd, if some eternal villain,*
> *Some busy and insinuating rogue,*
> *Some cogging cozening slave, to get some office,*
> *Have not devis'd this slander; I'll be hang'd else*[22]
> [4.2.130–33]

and then:

> *Oh, heaven, that such companions thou'dst unfold;*
> *And put in every honest hand a whip,*
> *To lash the rascal [sic] naked through the world!*
> [4.2.141–44]

Othello enters with a lamp in his hand and puts it on the dressing table. Desdemona is sound asleep. Othello is also carrying a drawn sword. He has come to kill Desdemona, after having endured the cruel sufferings of jealousy. Kean made an impression on me in that beautiful monologue when he speaks to the light. However, there was so much light on the stage that the lamp flame was not visible. Othello speaks to the lamp. . . . He kisses Desdemona and she awakes. Othello asks whether she has prayed. Then a disjointed conversation follows, in which he accuses her of unfaithfulness and reveals his intention. She asks him to banish her, but to spare her, to wait till the following day, for half an hour, so that she can pray. All in vain. The stubborn Moor strangles her and then stabs her. Suddenly, Emilia knocks at the door. Othello speaks to himself for a long while before he lets her in: *My wife! my wife! What wife? I have no wife* [5.2.97]. The time and place and the sight make these words penetrating. Kean was excellent at that moment. At last, the others enter. Iago's treachery is revealed. Othello kills himself.

In the fourth act a funny thing happened. Desdemona's suitor, a stupid person [i.e. Roderigo], having attacked another, is killed himself and falls on the stage. When the scene was changing and the curtain was falling, something brushed against it and the curtain was stopped half-way. The dead man, thinking that it had fallen, jumped up and made us laugh at this resurrection.

25 May 1821, Friday.
I went to Covent Garden Theatre with Mr Blaman who is also staying here.[23] Shakespeare's tragedy [*sic!*], *The Tempest,* was shown and a new play, *Undine.*[24] I have never seen more beautiful decorations. The eruption of a volcano, playing fountains, the sea, the ship-wreck, the flood—everything was there.

To appreciate Sienkiewicz's comments on Shakespeare, it is important to be aware that the first Polish production of Shakespeare, a version of *Romeo and Juliet,* had taken place only in 1797; not until the 1830s would there be a translation based on the original texts rather than German or French renditions. It is not surprising, then, that his response to Shakespeare on stage is sometimes bemused, that he is apparently not aware of the heavily adapted nature of some of the plays he saw, and that he is primarily conscious of visual effects and audience reactions.

The most important aspect of the performances described by Sienkiewicz is their conspicuous, though unintentional, topicality. It gives rise to questions about the ways in which meaning is created during a spectacle and the importance of social context in any discussion of the contemporary meaning of a literary text. Sienkiewicz's accounts of audience behavior on 8 July and 17 August 1820 corroborate what other sources say about the public's response to plays through the prism of contemporary events.[25] In such cases, topicality does not have to be consistent with the remaining elements of the plot; it suffices to have one line or a brief scene "to sound to present occasions" for the performance to become allusive.[26] Audiences are apparently undisturbed by the contradiction, and treat the topical allusion as a meaningful aside made to them by the actors on stage. In other words, the fact that they may find one or more such allusions in the performance does not mean that the spectators necessarily treat the entire play as a comment on the politics of the day.

While Sienkiewicz's experience is nothing new in the history of Shakespearean (and other) productions, it may serve as yet further evidence that meaning is not an invariant element of a literary or theatrical text. Shakespeare will always be read from the perspective of the times when his plays are produced, and spectators and readers will always be amazed that Shakespeare is "so contemporary." Thus it should not surprise us that, say, *Coriolanus* will acquire a political function and local meaning in the Turkey of 2005, just as it seemed an ingenious commentary on local politics in the Poland of 1995, when it was successfully produced on national television. The *Richard III* Sienkiewicz saw in 1820 obviously evoked different political associations from those created in the 1997 production in Belarus (which naturally alluded to the dictatorship there). Thus, when we debate the "meaning" of a literary or theatrical text, we should bear in mind its mutability and the infinite number of possible contexts in which its meaning is created. We should also be more specific: instead of asking the meaning of, say, *Hamlet,* we should rather ask the meaning of the play in London in 1605, or in 1820, or in Germany anno 1933 or 1991, or in Bulgaria in 1996. And Sienkiewicz's account of the performances he saw in London in 1820, at the height of the legal and political controversy over "the queen's trial," shows us that topicality often results more from chance than from an artistic concept.

Notes

1. First edited by Bogdan Horodyński and published by the Ossoliński Publishing House in 1953.
2. Quoted in Horodyński's edition, 93.
3. The rise of interest in Shakespeare in Poland is detailed in Andrzej Żurowski, *Szekspiriady polskie,* Warsaw, 1976.
4. For a detailed account of the negotiations, see Flora Fraser's *The Unruly Queen: the Life of Queen Caroline* (Papermac, 1996), 322–41.
5. See E. A. Smith, *A Queen on Trial: the Affair of Queen Caroline* (Stroud, 1993).
6. The quotations are given as Sienkiewicz himself gives them; however, act, scene and line references in brackets are taken from the Riverside edition.

7. Sienkiewicz uses the English word "misses," but with the Polish declension ending (*missom*).

8. The new theater described by Sienkiewicz burned down in 1856. The present Opera House was opened two years later.

9. For the famous "Old Price Riots," see A. Nicoll, *A History of English Drama 1660–1900*, vol. IV (Cambridge, 1955), 224, and Mark Baer, *Theatre and Disorder in Late Georgian London* (Oxford: Clarendon Press, 1992).

10. The old Covent Garden (i.e., the one that burned down in 1808) held over 3,000 spectators, whereas the theater built on its site was a "trifle" smaller; see Nicoll, *History*, IV, 223–24.

11. The comedy is usually attributed to George Colman and David Garrick.

12. I have been unable to identify this piece. It may be noted that on this day it was announced that the King's coronation had been postponed indefinitely: it was clear to everyone that he wanted his wife out of the country before the ceremony took place. See Fraser, *The Unruly Queen*, 401.

13. Adam Czartoryski (1770–1861), one of the leading and most influential nobles of the period.

14. Sienkiewicz was seeing Colley Cibber's version (1700) of Shakespeare's play, which still held the stage in this period, although in 1821 Macready would make a brief, unsuccessful attempt to revive Shakespeare's original version at Covent Garden. Cibber's opening scene, described here, is in fact a conflation of two scenes from other Shakespeare plays, *3 Henry VI* 5.6, and *2 Henry IV* 1.1.

15. The line comes from *3 Henry VI* 5.6.67.

16. In the Polish original the word "transparent" is used, which in those times meant a drawing or an inscription on glass, paper, etc., sometimes illuminated from the back.

17. François Joseph Talma (1763–1826), the famous French actor.

18. According to Genest, the part of Richmond was played by the famous American actor, Junius Brutus Booth, who made a few appearances in London. John Genest, *An Account of the English Stage from the Restoration in 1660 to 1830*, 10 vols. (London, 1832; reprinted New York: Franklin, 1965), 9: 39.

19. I have been unable to identify this piece; it might have been the farce by Samuel Foote (1720–77).

20. This may refer to some kind of stage convention meant to indicate invisibility: in Thomas Kyd's *The Spanish Tragedy*, Hieronymo says that the villainous Lorenzo "marched in a net, and thought himself unseen" (4.4.117).

21. Henry Brougham (1778–1868), a lawyer, politician and writer. He was one of the Whig leaders in the House of Commons, and also the Queen's barrister at her "trial." Sienkiewicz saw Brougham in the House of Lords during the trial, on Monday, 21 August 1820, and later met him personally, as appears from a letter he sent to Prince Czartoryski on 21 June 1821.

22. Some weeks earlier exactly the same words had been used by Thomas Denman, the Queen's Solicitor-General, in an attack in Parliament on Sir John Leach, who represented the King's interests.

23. During his stay in London, Sienkiewicz stayed at 17 Bedford Place, Bloomsbury Square.

24. A play of unknown authorship, based on a fairy romance published in 1811 by Friedrich, Baron de la Motte Fouqué, a German poet, playwright and prose writer. Genest, who likewise fails to name the author, says that this afterpiece (which opened on 23 April) was acted 26 times: a high degree of success for this period. Genest, *Account*, 9: 109.

25. The fact that the prosecution's case included a number of Italian witnesses, and that the Queen's supposed lover was Italian, may have added to the effect of *Othello* at Drury Lane on 9 October 1820 (*The Times,* 10 October). It was certainly responsible for the frenzied reaction to Iachimo's slandering of a British Princess in *Cymbeline* at Covent Garden on 19 October 1820 (*The Times,* 20 October). See Smith, *A Queen on Trial,* 138–39.

26. Ben Jonson, *Hymenaei, or the Solemnities of Masque and Barriers at a Marriage, Ben Jonson: The Complete Masques,* ed. Stephen Orgel (New Haven and London: Yale University Press, 1969), 76.

How Revolutionary *Is* Cross-cast Shakespeare? A Look at Five Contemporary Productions

GRACE TIFFANY

BY "CROSS-CAST SHAKESPEARE" I MEAN PRODUCTIONS IN WHICH WOMEN PLAY male Shakespearean characters such as Hamlet or Richard II. This increasingly popular theatrical experiment is sometimes justified on the grounds that it repeats, in reverse, what Shakespeare did. Yet it would seem that today's cross-casting directors have something different at stake from what Shakespeare did when he coached (say) the boy playing Cleopatra. For Shakespeare, all-male casting was a social imperative[1] which he used to unparalleled artistic advantage, embodying androgyny and sex-confusion themes in the language and action of his plays. But Shakespeare cast boys, not men, as women, and when the boys' voices changed they no longer played women's parts. That is, despite Shakespeare's celebrations of the joys of drag in plays like *As You Like It, The Merchant of Venice,* and even *Antony and Cleopatra,* his productions—like virtually all Renaissance dramatic productions—were designed to sustain the audience's illusion that female characters *were* female. (*As You Like It*'s Rosalind, to be sure, performs an epilogue in which she reveals that "she" is really a boy actor, but this epilogue comes after the play proper.) In this the boys were helped by the absence from the stage of real women, with whom audiences might have unfavorably compared them. The modern employment of women in male roles is different, if not in intention, then certainly in effect. Shakespeare's audience would not have had a boy actor's sex at the forefront of their minds. But the sex of a woman playing Falstaff in *The Merry Wives of Windsor* next to *real* men playing Page and Ford demands audience attention, and conspicuously colors our response to her character. Nor does biology assist the actress in the illusion as it did the boy. A boy's voice can sound like a woman's—Shakespeare refers to "boys, with women's voices" in *Richard II* (3.2.113)[2]—but a woman's voice hardly ever sounds like a man's. Thus most modern cross-casting seems designed not to sustain, as did Shakespeare, the illusion of the character's sex, but to undermine that illusion.

For these reasons gender-blind casting, unlike colorblind casting, will remain an oxymoron. The best actor available to play King Lear could be black, but not female, because Lear's maleness is so deeply inscribed in his character that to cross-cast him would be to distort him. A *King Lear* with a woman as Lear would be signally *about* Lear's femininity, and this femininity would be a directorial rather than a Shakespearean invention. Whatever the director's intent, a woman playing a man among men playing men calls attention to the gap between actor and character. This gap is manifest not only because even women who are costumed as men tend to look like women, but because a woman playing a man has to mimic maleness in the midst of men playing men. Her maleness must be reached for; theirs is given. Thus her ability realistically to portray character is handicapped at the outset by the "co-ed" nature of the acting company.

Thus cross-cast plays which succeed theatrically exploit an "effeminacy" already scripted in a male character. In such productions, cross-casting opens a classic male Shakespearean role to a woman, seeming to challenge conventional gender definitions and constraints. But the woman impersonating the male character "plays into" traditional notions of femininity as lack of emotional control, fickleness, finely tuned sensitivity, and weakness, and these predominantly negative qualities, or their performance, become the basis of her success in the role.

To illustrate this point, I will discuss three contemporary cross-cast productions: Deborah Warner's 1996 *Richard II*, starring Fiona Shaw; Joseph Papp's 1982 *Hamlet,* starring Diane Venora; and Michael Kahn's 1990 *The Merry Wives of Windsor,* starring Pat Carroll.

Richard II and Femininity

Fiona Shaw's portrayal of Richard II in Deborah Warner's 1995–96 London production of *Richard II* was hailed as a feminist gesture, and one which marked Shaw as "the most challenging and controversial actress on the British stage."[3] Shaw herself spoke of having violated "an enormous taboo about women playing male roles" in assuming the part.[4] Yet as ground-breaking as the casting choice was in one way, in another it worked to reinscribe age-old stereotypes about "womanish" behavior or effeminacy.

Numerous lines in *Richard II* link Richard's weakness as king to his lack of masculine purposefulness, his changeableness, and his tendency to "sit and wail [his] woes" rather than "prevent the ways to wail" (3.2.178–79). York criticizes Richard for habits generally associated with women or effeminate men, stressing Richard's feminine openness to penetration by alien fashions and courtly flatteries: the king's ear is

> stopped with . . . flattering sounds
> As praises, of whose taste the wise are [fond],
> Lascivious metres, to whose venom sound
> The open ear of youth doth always listen;
> Report of fashions in proud Italy,
> Whose manners still our tardy, apish nation
> Limps after in base imitation.
> Where doth the world thrust forth a vanity—
> So be it new, there's no respect how vile—
> That is not quickly buzz'd into his ears?
>
> (2.1.17–26)

York presents Richard as feminized, "thrust" into by the world's vanities. In a similar vein, Bullingbrook describes Richard's lack of emotional (and financial) restraint as wantonness and effeminacy, both qualities that Bullingbrook fears infect his own son, whom he calls "young wanton and effeminate boy" (5.3.10). At Flint Castle, Richard himself bitterly wonders whether he and Aumerle should "play the wantons with [their] woes, / And make some pretty match with shedding tears" (3.3.164–65). Richard's language—playing "wantons" and making a "pretty match"—recalls to the audience Bullingbrook's suggestion of Richard's homosexuality, delivered two scenes earlier when Bullingbrook charged Lords Bushy and Green with having "with [their] sinful hours / Made a divorce between [Richard's] queen and him" and "Broke the possession of a royal bed" (3.1.11–12, 14). Thus, in ways both obvious and subtle, Richard plays the wanton female against the stern, masculine Henry Bullingbrook. These foils' characterization and their slow confrontation are realized according to conventional gender distinctions: the "womanly" king's position is invaded from without by the silent, emotionally restrained Bullingbrook, who, like Death, gradually "bores thorough his castle wall" (3.2.170).

Richard's "feminine" characteristics are not solely the negative qualities of vacillation, lack of restraint, and easy penetrableness. With the Bishop of Carlisle and (sometimes) with York, he also shows uncanny intuition, and an appreciation of beauty in language and music. To adapt Wordsworth's phrase, Richard "sees into the life of things," painfully aware even before Bullingbrook's demand for the crown that he is Bullingbrook's *de facto* subject (3.3.197), and that for Bullingbrook's usurping action "Ten thousand bloody crowns of mother's sons / Shall ill become the flower of England's face" (3.3.96–97). The poetic strain in Richard's language has long been acknowledged; apt metaphorical descriptions of his experience flow from him like water:

> Let's talk of graves, of worms, and epitaphs,
> Make dust our paper, and with rainy eyes
> Write sorrow on the bosom of the earth.
> (3.2.145–47)

> Down, down, I come like glist'ring Phaeton,
> Wanting the manage of unruly jades.
> (3.3.178–79)

And his last scene poignantly dramatizes his sensitive response to the "sweet music" he hears playing outside his prison cell (5.5.42). His intuitiveness and aesthetic and emotional sensitivity are attractive and even ennobling aspects of his character; they are also, however, qualities which enhance his stereotypical femininity.[5]

Given a king who is famously characterized by these conventionally feminine attitudes and behaviors, how revolutionary could his impersonation by a woman really be? Although Fiona Shaw's portrayal of Richard sets a precedent for women who want to play Shakespearean kings, it is significant, and unsurprising, that Shaw was not invited to play Bullingbrook, Claudius, or Richard III. Drama critic Jack Kroll refers to Shaw's "disregard of the precise gender of Shakespeare's 'Richard II',"[6] but it is more likely that Warner's casting resulted from a responsible scrutiny of Shakespeare's script. Richard *is* "feminine," according to the most traditional—if not the most accurate—understanding of the word, and Shaw's performance underscored that point. Tall and unusually deep-voiced though Shaw is, her obviously female sound and features confirmed the suggestions of Richard's delicacy in Shakespeare's lines, especially in contrast to the male actors playing Gaunt, Northumberland, York, and Bullingbrook. As theater critic John Lahr wrote, Shaw's "feminine qualities hint[ed] . . . at the coddled, pristine, almost mutant unreality of the boy king," who is "uneasy in his skin and in his ruling role. He lacks command. As Shaw plays him, Richard II doesn't quite know how to set his face or deploy his force when he is administering power."[7] Shaw's compelling performance was thus assisted by the audience's own powerful, if subconscious, habit of associating women with uncertainty, with hesitance and confusion, with uneasiness in a leadership or "ruling" role.

The tremendous affective power of the deposition scene also gained from archetypal feminine associations. Arraigned before Bullingbrook and the other powerful barons, Richard showed "unmanly" vanity when Shaw called for and then smashed a hand mirror. Gazing into it, she expressed with shock her dismay at the "deep wrinkles" which the glass revealed, emphasizing those words despite the fact that the lines literally suggest Richard's surprise that, given what he's been through, he isn't *more* visibly careworn. Shaw's ultimate shattering of the glass enacted the stereotype of the aging woman demoralized by her fading beauty. As Lahr noted, her line, "How soon my sorrow hath destroyed my face" "conflat[ed] a literal and metaphorical loss of face";[8] the line also aptly described the perceptible collapse of Shaw's face, since her makeup in this scene accentuated tiredness and pallor. Thus the audience's automatic tendency to find poignancy in the ravaging of a woman's youthful freshness merged into the political displacement Richard was shown to undergo, and enhanced the magnitude of his identity loss.

That Richard's femininity was not incidental to his portrayal in Warner's production but part and parcel of his appeal is evident from the fact that Shaw's femaleness (more than her reputation as a superb actor) was the attraction of this play. This was obvious from the reviews: both English and American critics focused on that femaleness and its bearing on her portrayal of Richard.[9] Being a woman, some implicitly suggested, strengthened her performance, allowing her to underscore and exploit the conventional femininity that informs Shakespeare's character. Clearly, director Warner knew her audience, and knew the play. Thus, despite its surface unorthodoxy, her production did not challenge but reinscribed stereotypical notions of femaleness.

Hamlet and Masculinity

If moral and aesthetic sensitivity and emotiveness are perceived as feminine qualities, then one would expect women's portrayals of Hamlet generally to succeed. In fact, such productions were well received in both England and America in the nineteenth century. Sarah Bernhardt, Millicent Bandmann-Palmer, Charlotte Cushman, Clara Fisher Maeder, Alice Marriott, Winetta Montague, Julia Seaman, Fanny Wallack, and Emma Waller were among the women who played Hamlet to large and enthusiastic audiences in the Victorian era.[10] In most of these performances, femaleness was not something for which the actresses had to compensate. On the contrary, their femaleness was perceived as integral to their interpretations of Hamlet's character, and, as a result, a selling point for the productions in which they appeared. The notion that Hamlet's emotional imbalance, sensitivity, and volatility were feminine qualities was widespread among nineteenth-century students of the play. For example, in his influential book, Edward Vining spoke of Hamlet's "daintiness and sensitiveness," and argued that Hamlet "lacks the . . . strength, the readiness for action that inhere in the perfect manly character."[11] While Vining's theory that Hamlet really *was* a woman was not widely accepted, his argument was taken seriously because of general Victorian agreement that relative weakness and indecision were indeed characteristic of women. Delicacy, sensitivity, and indecisiveness were "feminine" qualities even when seen in a man: by his own admission, Edwin Booth "endeavoured to make prominent the femininity of Hamlet's character," and doubted "if ever a robust masculine treatment of the character [would] be accepted so generally as the more womanly and refined interpretation."[12] When even male impersonations of Hamlet succeeded by their "femininity," it is no wonder that the role was highly accessible to the great actresses of the day.

Fiona Shaw's success as Richard II, however, suggests that the sensitive and indecisive Shakespearean male is *still* accessible to a woman actor: that, in fact, our conventional notions of intrinsic feminine qualities overlap considerably with those of a century ago. Why, then, did the New York critics unite, with rare camaraderie, to reject Joseph Papp's 1982 *Hamlet,* starring the award-winning actress Diane Venora in the title role?[13]

While much blame for Papp's production was directed at features unrelated to Venora's performance—the "inexplicable" split playing area,[14] the disjointed quality of Claudius's delivery, the "dreary and smarmy Ghost,"[15] and the "worst Polonius in living memory"[16]—it was the female Hamlet—more accurately, the femaleness of Hamlet—that bore the brunt of critics' scorn. To nineteenth-century critics, Cushman's and Bernhardt's literal womanhood strengthened their portrayals of the "sweet prince" (*Hamlet* 5.2.359). But to Venora's reviewers, her femaleness was a travesty. Reviews' titles signalled the nature of their attack: headings included "Female 'Hamlet' a nuisance, not a novelty,"[17] "Papp's pipsqueal 'Hamlet' is mostly pap,"[18] "Hamlette,"[19] and—a direct expression of shock— "A woman is Hamlet!"[20] Most fault was found with the stereotypically feminine behavior for which nineteenth-century actors—male as well as female—aimed in their portrayals of the prince: Venora's Hamlet was seen to express too much emotion, to cry too much,[21] to be "too girlish and tantrummy,"[22] or to behave, in Clive Barnes' harsh phrase, "like an effete homosexual."[23]

Edith Oliver suggested that "if a woman is pretending to be a man, it is probably a mistake for her to dissolve into sobs, as Miss Venora does in her 'too too solid flesh' soliloquy."[24] In other words, it is women who dissolve into sobs, but Hamlet *isn't* a woman. The critics' objections to Venora's conventionally feminine interpretation of Hamlet thus represented not a revolution in our concept of womanliness, but a radical increase in our appreciation of Hamlet's masculinity.

When did Hamlet become a real man? Certainly Laurence Olivier's 1948 film contributed crucially to this transformation of Hamlet's character. As Marvin Rosenberg writes, Olivier's Hamlet was

> no youth; he is a full-grown man, always in control of himself . . . . Of Olivier's foolish film epigraph, that Hamlet's is the story of a man who could not make up his mind: he explained apologetically that he needed a simple cue for the many film spectators who normally would not see *Hamlet*. . . . The phrase did certainly not apply to Olivier's powerful prince. He is a figure to be admired, for his mature, regal presence, for his gravity, and for his athleticism, as in his magnificent final plunge on Claudius.[25]

But perhaps most integral to Hamlet's "masculinizing" was Olivier's overt reliance on Freudian Oedipal theory in his enactment of the role, particularly in the erotic kiss which he and Gertrude shared in the closet scene. The Oedipal longing which, according to Rosenberg, has come to be associated with Hamlet's character "[s]ince Freud and Ernest Jones"[26] received special support from Olivier's celebrated film. Its long-lasting influence is evident from the fact that the next widely popular screen *Hamlet,* Franco Zeffirelli's 1990 version, virtually restaged the erotically charged closet scene of the Olivier film, including a long kiss between Mel Gibson's Hamlet and Glenn Close's Gertrude. Since Olivier's film, an Oedipal subtext to Hamlet's performance has become so expected that when Venora performed the role in 1982, critics found the erotic tension between Gertrude and Hamlet disturbingly absent, as though it had been Shakespeare and not Olivier who foregrounded it. Edith Oliver wrote, "Given the circumstances [i.e., a woman playing Hamlet], the strong Oedipal element is missing in the Queen's closet scene"; while Frank Rich thought Venora successful "[e]xcept in those scenes that contain sexual tension—those with Ophelia and Gertrude."[27]

The stage and film release—or invention—of Hamlet's Oedipal longing, seen by Freud as a basic mark of the male, has doubtless contributed to the modern masculinizing of Hamlet. The eroticism Freud made possible between Hamlet and his mother assisted in the development of the sexy, macho Dane. From the late 1940s to the 1980s, aggressive, energetic, assertive Hamlets dominated stage interpretations in both England and America, in productions starring actors renowned for their bluff attractiveness: Donald Wolfit, Richard Burton, Stacy Keach, and Nicol Williamson. Critics of these "power Hamlets"[28] stressed their conventionally masculine appeal. Of Wolfit, a British reviewer wrote, "His Hamlet knows no caressing, seductive trait. He gives it power."[29] Of Richard Burton's 1953 performance, one writer observed, "Gone is the introspective, melancholy young prince. . . . Instead we find an energetic young man who would serve well in his rugger fifteen." Of a later Burton performance, it was said, "his Hamlet is less a scholar-courtier than a virile peasant, poetic but slightly musclebound." Keach as Hamlet in 1972 was "so vigorous, so clearly in charge, that is hard to believe very strongly that he could ever be weak or scared."[30] Similarly, Nicol Williamson's 1969 performance was filled with "power and energy."[31] The "masculine" Hamlet of the '50s, '60s, and '70s gave Diana Venora tough acts to follow. Nor did her performance succeed in altering the trend. "Macho Hamlet" has continued to rule in '80s and '90s productions, in incarnations including Kevin Kline, Mel Gibson, Keanu Reeves, and Kenneth Branagh. As Douglas Watt somewhat brutally expressed in his review of Papp's cross-cast production: "whatever feminine . . . traits may, pointlessly, be ascribed to the prince's character, it must be remembered that Shakespeare's Hamlet is unequivocally a man."

Sexual Powerlessness in *The Merry Wives of Windsor*

Unlike Papp's *Hamlet* and like Warner's *Richard II*, Michael Kahn's 1990 *The Merry Wives of Windsor*, starring Pat Carroll as Falstaff, succeeded by exploiting weaknesses in the central male character which were especially expressible by a woman. In this play, however, it was the comic softening of Falstaff into a relatively harmless figure that provided this opportunity. In Carroll's own interpretation, the Falstaff of *Merry Wives* was older and less "frightening" than the Falstaff of the Henry plays, and hence more capable of impersonation by her. As for constituting any real sexual danger to his quarry, Mistresses Ford and Page, this Falstaff was, in Carroll's phrase, "past it."[32]

Carroll, like Warner, knew her play.[33] Shakespeare's characters indeed variously describe Falstaff as "well-nigh worn to pieces with age" (2.1.21–22), "old, cold," and "withered" (5.5.153).[34] And his sexual stalking of the merry wives proceeds not from virile rapacity but from a perceived economic necessity; he is "almost out at heels" (or, as his companion Pistol comically observes, "Young ravens must have food") (1.3.31, 35). Falstaff's primary desire is not to ravage the wives but to service them in exchange for money—to assume, that is, the conventionally feminine role of prostitute—since the women, he hopes, will give him access to their husbands' wealth. "I will use her as the key of the cuckoldy rogue's coffer," Falstaff boasts of Mistress Ford (2.2.237–74). Earlier, he has observed that "she has the rule of her husband's purse," and that Mistress Page "bears the purse too; she is a region in Guiana, all gold and bounty. I will be cheaters to them both, and they shall be exchequers to me" (1.3.52–53, 68–71). Thus the sexual danger which Falstaff's seduction scheme implies is mitigated at the outset by his libidinal dearth. Falstaff's easy duping at the hands of the wives, like his fourth-act humiliation as he escapes from Mistress Ford's house in drag, only reinforces the audience's sense of Falstaff's utter innocuousness.

Carroll's physical characteristics and her performance stressed Falstaff's comic powerlessness in the sexual arena. Her bulk was mostly composed of foam padding, which rendered her almost spherical, or (to quote drama critic Hap Erstein) "roly-poly,"[35] like a clown or child's toy. (She looked, by her own admission, "like Mickey Rooney."[36]) At five-foot-three, Carroll's Falstaff was significantly shorter than the other male characters (not to mention the women), which undermined any sense of "male" threat she might otherwise have embodied. Her Falstaff's utter ineptness at seduction and conquest was most comically evident in the scene when Mistress Page, warning Falstaff of her husband's approach. hides him in her buck (or laundry) basket. Carroll's twice-repeated failure to "mount" the sides of the basket (she had finally to be helped in) visually enacted her character's impotence.

Of course, just as Shaw's Richard worked because of Richard's scripted "effeminacy," Carroll's Falstaff worked because of her talent at exploiting a harmlessness that is written into Falstaff's character. "I wouldn't dare do Falstaff in 'Henry IV' or 'Henry V'," she told *New York Times* critic Mervyn Rothstein, "because that is totally male. You would have to believe that he womanized, that he was bedding every wench. But that was the younger man."[37] In contrast, the *Merry Wives* Falstaff's agedness (she played him "in his 70s")[38] suggested his waning sexual powers, an interpretation which made him accessible to an actress. The diminishment of the powers of sexual aggression, in other words, is comfortably linked with femininity. It was on this conventional understanding that Carroll's successful performance was built.

Carroll's later, more problematic performance in Kahn's 1996 production of Jonson's *Volpone* bore out her earlier suggestion that sexually aggressive male characters were unavailable to female actors. As Volpone, her attempted rape of Celia fell flat, in sharp contrast to her amusing foiled trysts with Mistress Ford in Shakespeare's play. In the harsher comedy of *Volpone,* hilarity is arrested and real fear generated when Volpone, a vigorous man pretending to be ill, rises from his bed to pursue Celia. But when Carroll played him, the androgyny that was appropriate to the "softer" Falstaff undermined the genuine virility and licentiousness Volpone was scripted to project, and rendered this scene not scary but silly (as opposed to funny). In casting Carroll as Volpone, Kahn hoped to accentuate the androgyny of Volpone's household (his servants include an hermaphrodite and a eunuch). Yet the cross-casting of Volpone attended insufficiently to the "masculine" violence intrinsic to Volpone's own character. The *Merry Wives* Falstaff, in contrast, profited from cross-casting, since impotence is Falstaff's paradoxical comic strength. The actor's femaleness, stereotypically associated with sexual lack, underscored rather than played against the script.

This is not to say that *Merry Wives* as a whole promotes—or, in Kahn's production, promoted—a regressive view of women as weak, passive creatures overall. There are, after all, the merry wives, strong figures who run rings around Falstaff and Master Ford, who is nearly emasculated by his fears of cuckoldry. My argument is simply that in making a cross-casting choice to accentuate Falstaff's lack of sexual potency, Kahn inadvertently promoted (and profited from) the stereotypical connection between women and *sexual* passivity: of female sexuality as a guarded, inert quantity rather than an active, aggressive force. The sexual danger represented by Mistress Ford is not the danger of incursion, but of overflow: if Falstaff breaches her fortress of chastity, her sexuality might spill forth. Thus to Ford, trusting his "wife with herself" is tantamount to trusting "an Irishman with [his] aqua-vitae bottle" (2.2.305, 303); he fears that Falstaff will "drive her ... from the ward of her purity, her reputation, her marriage vow, and a thousand other her defenses, which are now too strongly embattled" (2.2.248–51). The joke—on Falstaff as well as on Ford—is not just Mistress Ford's determination to repel the intruder, but the play's strong suggestion that Falstaff is not really equipped to (as it were) breach the fortress. His cross-casting in Kahn's production was regressive in feminist terms,[39] in that it was used to accentuate his non-threatening features: his powerlessness in all sexual arenas but the farcical.

And, again—as in Warner's *Richard II*—the cross-casting choice was so received. Critics gave their reviews of the production such titles as "Distaff Falstaff"[40] and "An Artful Falstaff Who Transcends Sex,"[41] and devoted most of their comments to the accommodation and appropriateness of Carroll's femaleness to the role, as though her femaleness *were* her performance. In a sense, they were right. Although Carroll herself "was concerned that the play would only work if she could convincingly be a man,"[42] she showed the paradoxical awareness that her femaleness helped convey something true about the character. With this Falstaff, she concluded, "[t]he possibility of anything but [sexual] bluster is remote.... I think the audience can feel safe."[43] The distaff—and retrograde—Falstaff helped communicate the comforting innocuousness that is part of his comic design.

In all three of the productions discussed above, actors and directors expressed the desire that their cross-cast characters be understood as characters first, with the sex of their performers in the background. "It's not a feminist or a feminine gesture," Fiona Shaw said of her performance as Richard. "I play Richard not from my gender center but from my imaginative center."[44] Of the Venora *Hamlet,* Joseph Papp claimed that "this casting is not a gender issue. If she had been male, I would still have wanted Diane's qualities in the character."[45] And Pat Carroll, as noted, wanted "convincingly to be a man." In light of the Shakespearean characters these artists chose—ones whose "feminine" qualities have long been critically acknowledged—these professions of gender-blind motivation are not entirely convincing. But whatever the directors' or actors' intents, the dominance of gender concerns in critical responses to their productions directly reflected the importance gender assumed *within* the productions, as women playing men contrasted sharply and inevitably with men playing the other male roles. These "co-ed" productions have strengthened and at times profited from conventional gender distinctions, allowing the "soft" qualities of the male characters—Richard, Falstaff—to appear in high relief, as women spoke "feminine" lines alongside men speaking "masculine" lines. When such a production fails, as did Papp's 1982 *Hamlet,* it fails because audiences are no longer receptive to a particular character's "feminine" side.

Two types of cross-casting are yet possible for directors who wish to avoid reinscribing conventional constructions of gender. In one, a Shakespeare play might be adapted so that male roles are made literally female, and female roles literally male. Such an experiment was made in Lee Breuer's and Ruth Maleczech's 1990 play *Lear,* which cast Maleczech as an aging matriarch who divides her property among three sons. Despite its radical changes in setting and situation—in Breuer's and Maleczech's version Lear was not a medieval monarch, but a twentieth-century American southerner—the production left Shakespeare's dialogue essentially unchanged, with the notable exception of the sex-related language. The result was a startling inversion of some deep-rooted themes. Lear's and Gloucester's misogynistic slurs became misanthropic expressions of revulsion from *male* sexuality, expressed in lines like "There is the sulphurous *rod* [not "pit"], burning and scalding" (my emphasis. See *King Lear* 4.6.128). Conversely, in the mouth of a female Tom O'Bedlam the joking reference to "Pillicock Hill" became "Pillicunt Hill" [see 3.4.76]). King Lear's daughters' reprehensible dominance of their husbands became, in *Lear,* men's invalid usurpation of their *wives'* natural headship. And finally, the good son "Cordelion" presented an unconventional image of proper "lion-hearted" masculinity as gentle obedience to his mother's will. The reversal of *King Lear's* husband-wife dynamic that *Lear* accomplished provided a genuine challenge to conventional understandings of appropriate masculine and feminine behavior, unlike the earlier and more famous re-gendered adaptation of *King Lear,* Kurosawa's film, *Ran.* In *Ran,* King Lear's daughters are reimagined as the sons of a medieval Japanese war lord who fight over their father's divided kingdom. But in focusing on the sons' conflict with each other rather than on their relationships with marital partners, Kurosawa colors his re-gendered characters with conventional masculine aggression, omitting gender concerns as a central theme. In contrast, through its preservation of all characters and its bilateral "gender swap," Breuer and Maleczech's *Lear* accorded traditionally masculine behaviors to women and feminine behaviors to men, allowing audiences the curious imaginative experience of a gender-reversed world. The play's most emphatic and memorable re-gendering was its transformation of Gloucester's sons Edmund and Edgar to daughters (named Edna and Envil); the final physical conflict between these leather-clad women, fought with huge wooden lances, was viscerally frightening. Its impact was the greater because the women—including the servant Kent—were the privileged physical aggressors in the play. Their physical altercations did not suffer by comparison with those of men, whose aggression was confined to the "feminine" Shakespearean activity of verbal combat.

Lear was, however, an adaptation, not an authentic Shakespearean performance. One option exists for the Shakespearean "purist" who, alternatively, wishes to challenge constructions of gender without rewriting Shakespeare's actual characters or plot. This option is unisex casting, or the female performance of all roles. In recent years *Henry V* has been attempted with all-female casts, usually in academic environments where female students numerically dominate programs. Such was the impetus for James Daniels' 1995 production of *Henry V* at Western Michigan University. Daniels' interest in gender issues, coupled with his need for a vehicle to employ his predominantly female student population, led him to experiment with this eminently "masculine" war play. Like Breuer and Maleczech's adaptation of *King Lear,* Daniels' production was successful not only because of his talented actors, but because the characters' stage conflicts could not suffer by comparison with men enacting conflicts with greater vocal and physical strength. In witnessing the all-female *Henry V,* I personally was reminded of my matriculation in an all-girls' school, where, in the absence of males, our qualities of character and personality were made visible and, for the first and last time, genderless. Not, of course, that we fought each other physically (much). But in this all-female environment, as the author Gail Griffin notes of her summer-camp days, "girls could be strong and weak, stupid and smart, silly and serious, plain and pretty, could learn and take chances and fail and triumph, all of it apart from . . . the sexual strait-jacketing of [the] Real World."[46] The Shakespearean play with an all-female cast creates this kind of "free zone," especially in works like the Henry or most of the Roman plays, wherein most characters are the same sex anyway. In such a free acting zone, strength, weakness, volubility, intuitiveness, sensitivity, purposelessness, and valor appear not as masculine or feminine traits, but as human ones.

Ironically, all-female Shakespeare, an expedient for woman-dominated theater programs, brings us close to the Shakespeare of the Elizabethans. In response to the demands of his theatrical environment, Shakespeare used one-sex casting to explore the limitless roles available to the capable actor. In his time, women watched from the stage's perimeter as the human parade passed before them. But in our time, with all-female casting, the parade (if we are women) is us. Unisex casting brings us full-circle to the unisex productions of Shakespeare's time. At the same time—paradoxically—it puts us on the other side of the Globe.

Notes

1. In *Erotic Beasts and Social Monsters: Shakespeare, Jonson, and Comic Androgny* (Newark: University of Delaware Press, 1995), I discuss Renaissance social

and stage cross-dressing conventions, a topic which has been exhaustively (and exhaustingly) debated by academics in recent years. See also Ann Jones and Peter Stallybrass, "Fetishizing Gender: Constructing the Hermaphrodite in Renaissance Europe," in *Body Guards,* ed. Julia Epstein and Kristina Straub (New York: Routledge, 1991), 80–111; Phyllis Rackin, "Androgyny, Mimesis, and the Marriage of the Boy Heroine on the Renaissance Stage," in *Speaking of Gender,* ed. Elaine Showalter (New York: Routledge, 1989), 113; Marjorie Garber, *Vested Interests: Cross-Dressing and Cultural Anxiety* (New York: Routledge, 1992); Kathleen McLuskie, "The Act, the Role, and the Actor: Boy Actresses on the Elizabethan Stage," *New Theatre Quarterly* 3 (1987): 120–130; Steve Brown, "The Boyhood of Shakespeare's Heroines: Notes on Gender Ambiguity in the Sixteenth Century," *SEL* 30 (1990) 243–63; Susan G. Shapiro, "Amazons, Hermaphrodites, and Plain Monsters: The 'Masculine' Woman in English Satire and Social Criticism from 1580–1640," *Atlantis* 13 (1987); Catherine Belsey, "Disrupting Sexual Difference: Meaning and Gender in the Comedies," in *Alternative Shakespeares,* ed. John Drakakis (London: Methuen, 1985), 167; Linda Woodbridge, *Women and the English Renaissance: Literature and the Nature of Womankind, 1540–1620* (Urbana: University of Illinois Press, 1984); and Stephen Orgel, *Impersonations: The Performance of Gender in Shakespeare's England* (New York: Cambridge University Press, 1996). Orgel argues that England was unique among European nations in its all-male acting convention, and even that the convention itself was a Renaissance innovation. But whatever the convention's origins, Shakespeare was constrained to observe it. If female actors had been socially acceptable, one assumes that he would have used them.

2. All Shakespeare quotations are from *The Riverside Shakespeare,* ed. G. Blakemore Evans (Boston: Houghton Mifflin, 1974).

3. Jack Kroll, "Her Majesty the King," *Newsweek* 127, no. 3 (15 January 1996): 67.

4. Ibid.

5. This "take" on what it is to be female is literally Victorian. For example, Edward Vining wrote in 1881 that "daintiness and sensitiveness to the weather and perfume" were feminine qualities in Hamlet (*The Mystery of Hamlet: An Attempt To Solve an Old Problem* [Philadelphia: Lippincott, 1881], 82–83), and Charlotte Cushman's 1846 performance as Ion was criticized because the character's masculine self-control prevented her indulging her emotions on stage (see *The English Gentleman,* 22 February 1846).

6. Kroll, "Her Majesty the King."

7. John Lahr, "Blues for His Majesty," *The New Yorker* 71, no. 19 (10 July 1995): 84.

8. Ibid., 85.

9. Not that all the comments were positive. Jack Kroll lists some of the responses, which included "gimmick casting," "not enough maleness to play Peter Pan," and "audacity." However, even when "panning" Shaw (pun intentional), reviewers drew primary attention to her sex.

10. For an extensive discussion of nineteenth-century female Hamlets as well as other Shakespearean "male impersonators" of this period, see Anne Russell's "Tragedy, Gender, Performance: Women as Tragic Heroes on the Nineteenth-Century Stage," *Comparative Drama* 30:2 (Summer, 1996): 135–57.

11. Vining, *The Mystery,* 46.

12. Quoted in Marvin Rosenberg, *The Masks of Hamlet* (Newark: University of Delaware Press, 1992), 109.

13. Similarly, the Cincinnati Shakespeare Festival's 1998 production of *Hamlet,* which starred Marni Penning as "the Princess of Denmark," bored and baffled the preponderance of its audience.

14. Douglas Watt, "Female 'Hamlet' a nuisance, not a novelty," *Daily News*, 3 December 1982.
15. John Simon, *"Hamlette," New York Magazine* (13 December 1982): 69–70.
16. Clive Barnes, "Papp's pipsqueal 'Hamlet' is mostly pap," *New York Post*, 6 December 1982.
17. Watt, "Female 'Hamlet.'"
18. Barnes, "Papp's pipsqueal 'Hamlet.'"
19. Michael Feingold, "Hamlette," *The Village Voice*, 14 December 1982; Simon, *"Hamlette."*
20. Linda Winer, "A woman is Hamlet!" *USA Today*, 2 December 1982.
21. Walter Kerr, "This Boyish Princeling Is an Unpersuasive Hamlet," *The New York Times*, 12 December 1982; Watt, "Female 'Hamlet'"; Frank Rich, "Theater: Diane Venora Stars in Papp's Hamlet'," *The New York Times*, 3 December 1982; Simon, *"Hamlette."*
22. Edith Oliver, "The Theatre: Off Broadway," *The New Yorker* (13 December 1982): 166.
23. Barnes, "Papp's pipsqueal 'Hamlet.'" cited above.
24. Oliver, "The Theatre."
25. Rosenberg, *The Masks of Hamlet*, 133.
26. Ibid., 73. Rosenberg's book exhaustively discusses the complicated stage history of Hamlet's character, in which the Oedipal association is one powerful strain.
27. Rich, "Theater: Diane Venora."
28. The phrase is Rosenberg's (*The Masks of Hamlet*, 132); see his essay in this volume, pp. 163, 167.
29. From the *Coventry Evening Telegraph*, 12 April 1945. Quoted in Rosenberg, *The Masks of Hamlet*, 132.
30. From *Plays and Players*, 1953; and Bernstein, *Season of Discontent*, 1965; and *Evening News*, 30 June 1972. Quoted in Rosenberg, *The Masks of Hamlet*, 135.
31. From *The New Yorker* (10 May 1969), quoted in Rosenberg, 148.
32. Pat Carroll, in a telephone interview, 1 November 1990.
33. Some paragraphs of this discussion overlap with my discussion of *The Merry Wives of Windsor* in "Falstaff's False Staff: 'Jonsonian' Asexuality in *The Merry Wives of Windsor*," *Comparative Drama* 26:3 (Fall, 1992): 254–70; reprinted in Tiffany, *Erotic Beasts*, chap. 4.
34. Scholars have also found the *Merry Wives* Falstaff relatively mild. Anne Barton sees the "Windsor version of Sir John" as "tame and unresourceful compared with his far greater self of Eastcheap, Shrewsbury, Gaultree, and even Gloucestershire" (see her introduction to the Riverside *Merry Wives*, 287). See also H. B. Charlton's *Shakespearian Comedy* (New York: Macmillan, 1938), which describes the *Merry Wives* Falstaff as a "cynical revenge which Shakespeare took on the hitherto unsuspecting gaiety of his own creative exuberance" (193).
35. Hap Erstein, "Distaff Falstaff," *The Washington Times*, 27 April 1990.
36. Quoted in Megan Rosenfeld, "Distaff Falstaff," *The Washington Post*, 29 April 1990.
37. Quoted in Mervyn Rothstein, "An Artful Falstaff Who Transcends Sex," *The New York Times*, 7 June 1990.
38. Quoted in Erstein, "Distaff."
39. But still hilarious.
40. Erstein, "Distaff," Rosenfeld,"Distaff Falstaff," and Bob Mondello, *City Paper*, 4–10 May 1990.

41. Rothstein, "An Artful Falstaff."
42. Quoted in Rothstein, "An Artful Falstaff."
43. Quoted in Erstein, "Distaff."
44. Quoted in Kroll, "Her Majesty the King."
45. Linda Winer, "A woman is Hamlet!"
46. Gail B. Griffin, *Season of the Witch: Border Lines, Marginal Notes* (Pasadena: Trilogy Books, 1995), 50.

Strands Too Far Remote: A Note on Translating the Political and the Politics of Translation

Avraham Oz

THE 1993 "OSLO AGREEMENTS" BETWEEN ISRAELI AND PALESTINIAN LEADERSHIP under Itzhak Rabin and Yasser Arafat, euphorically considered by many at the time as predicting a rapid resolution to the Middle East conflict, took a crucial turn on 25 February 1994. On the morning of that *Purim* festival (a traditional Jewish holiday, annually celebrating a Biblically alleged resolution of an attempted assault on the Jews in Persia achieved through "peaceful diplomacy"), a Jewish settler massacred over thirty Moslems kneeling in prayer in a Hebron mosque. Neither we, shocked and bewildered as we were, nor Jay Halio, who was staying with us on that fateful morning, could have taken in there and then to what extent the entire discourse of peace could be totally reversed by a single terrorist act. The Hebron massacre did bring to the surface, however, Hobbes' claim that peace was nothing but some restraining or mitigating measures designed to regulate the indispensable human drive toward aggression,[1] or Rousseau's wry notes on the Abbé de Saint-Pierre's utopian plan for "Eternal Peace," based on not incompatible sentiments.[2]

On the day of the massacre, I had taken Jay to a prearranged meeting with the director and actors of *The Merchant of Venice*, then at a preliminary stage of rehearsals at the Cameri Theatre of Tel Aviv. After a lively talk with the cast, the director, Omri Nitzan, confided in me (as his translator and dramaturg) that following that day's events he had decided to transform the vengeful Shylock of acts 3 and 4 (whom we already had conceived of as a kind of terrorist),[3] into the image of a Jewish settler in the West Bank. In the following notes, affectionately dedicated to Jay Halio, I propose to problematize the representation of the discourse of peace by relating the case of that particular moment in history to Jay's favorite area of study, Shakespearean theater in performance.

Like any other constituent in a theatrical revival, translation involves an emphatic act of interpretive regeneration. This paradoxical act of preserving the *stasis* of the original while exposing it to a dynamic process of *exertion* of meaning may perhaps be best understood in terms of what Andrew Benjamin would call "questioning of the origin," itself part of the process of *Nachträglichkeit*.[4] Whenever such a questioning of the origin transcends the inherent "interplay of *arché* and *telos*"[5] in involving a charged ideological bent, such a translating act will always have a marked teleological bias, whether self-conscious or not. What emerges is an interactive process of exchange and negotiation between at least two threads of meaning, evolving a number of open relationships with the never-ultimate origin, whose inevitable elusiveness is enhanced in the course of its dynamic linguistic enactment. Reworked verbal gestures, newly acquired connotations, repetitions simultaneously enunciating sameness and variety, even different articulations of the obvious, all take part in a dance of meanings which, breaking any sense of essential unity, may wind up not only eliciting inflected interpretive nuances, but giving rise as well to a totally renewed or modified sense of the original text. When, as often might happen as a result of premeditated choice, such a radical questioning of the origin finds its counterpart in a fertile ideological scene, Thurber's wry dictum, "it loses something in the original," may lose something of its oxymoronic ingenuity.

In the case of a theatrical performance, that dance of meanings is enhanced, and its translational complexity made acute, by its attachment to the immediacy of public ceremony, whereby a collective body of the audience simultaneously responds both to the text and to the grammar governing dramatic genres and conventions. In the case of keywords in which both ideological and performative meanings converge, such as the binary set of "action-passion" in *Hamlet*, translational policy must alert itself to the much-intensified nature of theatrical dialogism, involving directorial, no less than translational, strategy. What is at stake here is the balance between freedom of interpretation and demands of accuracy, the boundaries of which may be probed and stretched so long as the finished product is still accountable to the original text and context. I propose briefly to explore here, as a particular test case, the teleological features of one charged speech in Shakespeare's histories when it is transported to qualify an analogous, yet different moment in the canon, where the ideological premises of the new contextual pattern are inevitably bound to "question" the key concept of the origin. Here, that particular key-concept is "peace," variously read in the original and its charged translations; what seems to constitute an almost value-free act of semantic transformation is revealed to be ideologically charged.

A complex concept in its non-theatrical contexts, peace often pertains to the final concord sought by simple forms of theatrical plot. Like its trivial analogy with theatrical dénouement, it is easily claimed as the abstract desire of every nation, however aggressive or military-minded. Pacifist individuals such as the Abbé de Saint-Pierre, Tolstoy, Gandhi, Einstein, or Russell, among many others, have sought to phrase a code of ethics which might govern the dynamics of relations between nations. Whereas views of peace as total harmony (the Abbé de Saint-Pierre or Gandhi) seem somewhat naive with regard to historical reality, the discourse of peace as a pragmatic regulating strategy, far as it stands from pacifism, is a constantly viable option in the history of international relations as well as in its dramatic representation. Lord Burghley's strong anti-militaristic sentiments, expressed in his counsels to the Queen as well as in his precepts for his son,[6] can be aligned with Shakespeare's allocating the contempt for peace to the heroic villain of *Richard III:* Steven Marx reminds us that pacifist ideas "make their persistence known by the vituperation of attacks upon them in militaristic literature and religious propaganda."[7] Michael Butler, the producer who brought *Hair* to Broadway in 1968, remembers in his *Journal* how his conservative, military-industrial father intervened when he and his fellow revolutionary friends failed to find a common cause on which to focus their political energies: "'Wait a minute,'" said the father. "'You do have a common ground, peace. Without peace, all of your concerns are for naught. If you don't have peace, you cannot do anything about your concerns.' Peace won the night," Butler junior comments, "and because of a hawk who made me remember Eisenhower's last speech."[8] The discourse of peace is indeed a classic common ground, its blurred ambiguity enabling everyone to take part in a saintly doublespeak which is hardly committed to any definite political or moral parameters. Like "nation," it is a convenient banner, the very viability and effectiveness of which lies in its vagueness.

The ideological analogy of peace and concord is, of course, misleading. Peace is always negotiable, more often than not by hegemonic victor and marginalized victim.[9] As such, it is open to a charged prophetic immanence in which the discourse of peace is revealed in its full complexity and fragility. It is war which is unambiguously and inexorably finite ("war is the father of all things," says Heraclitus), whereas peace, though craving the absolute and eternal, remains a constant desire, compromising its alleged unity by lending itself to endless permutations and configurations. It is, for instance, gender-biased. Solid, essential peace, which is at best ironically represented as being made between Shakespearean men (Octavius and Antony, Coriolanus and Aufidius, Prospero and his former rivals), is demanded by male hegemonic reading as a postulate for the chastity and integrity of women (Desdemona, Lear's three daughters, Cymbeline's nameless queen). Essentializing peace means to empty it of its complex prophetic layers.

"Peace" ("*shalom*") is a complex word in Hebrew, where it serves both to denote the charged concept involving concord and reconciliation and to function as the most common greeting word in meeting or in parting—in which context, though drawing on an ancient Eastern greeting known since Hammurabi, it does not currently carry more ideological weight then "hi" or "'bye." In an area where the political climate of incessant wars had ruled out any possibility of imminent peace, there used to be too wide a gap between the two meanings for any close association to be possible. However, since some striking political moves in the early 1990s manifested a peace process as feasible, the semantic tension between the two uses of the word now looms more conspicuously. An Israeli satirical paper, *Davar Aher,* published a weird picture of the nearly dying Lubavicher rabbi, literally proclaimed Messiah by his disciples, sitting expressionless on his verandah, and faintly, almost mechanically, waving his hand toward his ecstatic Hassidim in Brooklyn; the accompanying headline read: "the Lubavicher makes peace" (a pun juxtaposing the gesture with the political act). In a recent, Stoppard-like Israeli fringe play, characters entering the stage, using the common greeting, "*Shalom,*" are repeatedly addressed by the surprising question: "In what sense?"[10] A new political reality has recently lent a growing number of contexts of signification, from political debates to commercial advertisements, to the multi-significant concept of "peace."

A production of *The Comedy of Errors* that opened in January 1996 at the Cameri Theatre in Tel Aviv, under the direction of Omri Nitzan, is a case in point. Except for the special case of *Troilus and Cressida,* where love and war are intertwined to form the main theme, *The Comedy of Errors* stands out among Shakespearean comedies in deploying the state of war as an active dramatic presence constraining the narrative throughout. "Enmity and discord" between Syracuse and Ephesus are enunciated by Duke Solinus at the very outset, with Egeon's open sentence hanging over the main action of the play when Antipholus of Syracuse is warned not to give out his true city of origin. From now on, his venture of finding "a mother and a brother" (1.1.5) is constantly marked by that danger.[11] The aggression of comedy is readily interchangeable with the aggression of war. The choice of a comic action exploring the interaction of marriage—rather than courtship, as is the usual case in Shakespearean comedy—may also have been influenced by the hanging tension. It exposes the ironic futility of the excessive desire of peaceful marriage as phrased in "if we two be one" (2.2.142).

The 1996 Tel Aviv production of *The Comedy of Errors* represented Shakespearean Ephesus in the shape of a Beirut-like eastern Mediterranean harbor city, thus turning the geographic location into an ideologically charged comment: in the political/ethnic/religious whirlpool which had long ago got out of hand, nobody figures any more who fights whom. Given the geo-political circumstances in the Middle East at that particular moment, with an officially proclaimed and partly signed peace process confusing the situation and creating new allies, the scene bore great affinity to the external political circumstances. Thus the focus on a charged location informing the consciousness of a specific target audience turns the conventional game of errors, however mildly, into a political statement. During the first run of this production, the inherent confusion of the Israeli-Palestinian negotiations underwent dramatic upheavals, from a wave of sympathy toward the breakthrough achieved by the assassinated Itzhak Rabin, through the crucial election defeat of his successor Shimon Peres (whose visit to the play was covered by the media, evidencing its topical significance), to the disillusionment spread by the new right-wing government of Benjamin Netanyahu.

In order to emphasize the fresh ideological reading of the original text, Egeon was accorded an additional speech. Addressing the Duke in the concluding scene immediately after Emilia, he relates human similarity (and hence, equality) to the need for lasting peace. This incorporated speech combined allusions to various Shakespearean contexts, such as the exchange between Arviragus and Imogen in *Cymbeline:*

> Are we not brothers? . . .
> [Though] clay and clay differs in dignity,
> Whose dust is both alike.
>
> (*Cymbeline*, 4.2.3–5)

to be completed by the Archbishop of York's sermon on peace:

> A peace is of the nature of a conquest,
> For then both parties nobly are subdu'd,
> And neither party loser.
>
> (*2 Henry IV*, 4.2.89–91)

To this contrived speech, which gained vast applause every night, the Duke was made to respond in the words of Shakespeare's King Henry IV, spoken at the outset of the first play bearing his name:

> So shaken as we are, so wan with care,
> Find we a time for frighted peace to pant
> And breathe short-winded accents of new broils
> To be commenc'd in stronds afar remote.
> No more the thirsty entrance of this soil
> Shall daub her lips with her own children's blood.
> No more shall trenching war channel her fields,
> Nor bruise her flow'rets with the armed hoofs
> Of hostile paces. Those opposed eyes,
> Which, like the meteors of a trouble heaven,
> All of one nature, of one substance bred,
> Did lately meet in the intestine shock
> And furious close of civil butchery,
> Shall now, in mutual well-beseeming ranks,
> March all one way and be no more oppos'd
> Against acquaintance, kindred, and allies.
> The edge of war, like an ill-sheathed knife,
> No more shall cut his master.
>
> (*1 Henry IV*, 1.1.1–18)

In Henry's speech, the meaning of "peace" is conditional: it is confined almost exclusively to the peace between brothers in flesh and blood. Thus when the pacified, newly established brotherhood turns to those imminent battles, "to be commenc'd in stronds afar remote," the shaken speaker, still "wan with care," may nevertheless go on undisturbed depicting the bliss and fruits of peace.

Shakespeare's *1 Henry IV* has only once been translated in full into the Hebrew—back in 1963, by Repha'el Eli'az,[12] as part of a project to issue a selection of Shakespeare translations. It was later produced in a cut version designed to condense the two parts of *Henry IV* into a rather sugared two-hour production, with which the translation, though not commissioned for that particular production, perfectly agreed. In the 1960s, when the translation was both published and produced, any imminent peaceful resolution of the Middle East conflict (like that of the Cold War) was so remote from probability that the only analogy that could be made between Henry's speech and the topical situation was in the same conditional terms as the original speech: peace is possible only between brothers in flesh and blood, allowing them "peacefully" to confront a common enemy. So much did this ideological position dominate the mainstream political consciousness of the play's given audience that, in the absence of any putative controversy, the alerted fragility of peace was conceived as inherent in the very ontology of the concept. It thus hardly evoked any sense of "questioning the origin" beyond the purely semantic and phonetic level. Eli'az's version of Henry's opening speech thus forms a part of the whole, and does not betray any token of intended topical meaning:[13]

Gam im Navokh halev hamesukhsakh,	Even if the heart is perplexed and embroiled,
Vahashashot Mekharsemim od Banu,	And fears are still gnawing at us,
Havu niten ketzat nofesh lashalom	Let us allow some repose to frighted
Hamevohal: yahalif onim uve'oz yari'a	Peace: let him[14] change powers, and bravely sound a call
Al hidushey keravot harhek mibayit.	Proclaiming renewed battles far away from home.
Veadmatenu bal tosif limshoah	And our soil no more will daub
Sefateyha hatsme'ot bedam baneyha,	Her thirsty lips in her children's blood,
Velo taharosh hamilhama sdoteyha	And will not war plough any more her fields,
Af lo yihyu od lemirmas praheyha	Nor will her flowers be trodden any more
Tahat parsot susey oiveyha.	Under the iron-hoofs of her enemies' horses.
Hayerivim, bney dam uvney basar ehad,	The rivals, of one blood and of one flesh,
She'eyneyhem kemo gitsey kokhav ba'arafel,	Whose eyes like flickering stars in the fog,
Ze lo mikvar pagshu ish be'ahiv	Did lately meet each his own brother
Betokh ritha shel krav vetevah am,	Within the rage of battle and civil butchery,
Od yitz'adu yakhdav komemiyut	Shall march, in mutual, well-beseeming ranks,
Baderekh ha'ahat mibli yarimu yad	All one way, without lifting their hand

Al re'a vekarov uva'al brit.	On acquaintance, kindred, and ally.
Hamilkhama, kemin sakin soreret,	War, like a rebellious sword,
Lo od tin'atz huda bive'aleyha.	No more shall cut her master.

Dan Almagor renewed and updated his 1964 version of *The Comedy of Errors*[15] for the 1996 Cameri production, while a tortuous yet hopeful peace process was developing between Israelis and Palestinians. Almagor freely exploited Shakespeare's licentious employment of topical allusions in the play to pun on the Hebrew sounds of PLO, Hammas, and similar terms, and finally translated anew, at the director Omri Nitzan's bidding, the inserted *1 Henry IV* speech. Thus in this version, Henry's opening speech is singled out to stand alone beyond its original context to form part of a didactic finale of the early comedy:

Belev Navokh, Hoshesh umehases	With perplexed heart, fearing and hesitating,
Niten lo, Lashalom hamefuhad	We will allow him, the frighted peace,
Linshom, lehithazek, lifros kenafayim.	To breath, to strengthen, to spread his wings.
Lo od Timshah ha'adama sefateyha Bedamam shel yeladeyha hee.	No more will the soil daub her lips In the blood of her own children.
Lo od yihyu peraheyha lemirmas	No more will her flowers be trodden
Lefarsotav shel gedud zore'a ketel.	By the hoofs of a death-spreading regiment.
Lo od tikhtosh hamilhama kol telem,	No more will war bruise any furrow,
Vehaeynayim, eyney hayerivim,	And the eyes, those eyes of rivals,
Shedam ehad zorem betokh besaram—	In whose flesh one blood flows—
Otan eynayim, she'ad ko ra'u Zo et zo mibe'ad laharakh,	Those eyes, that so far had seen Each other through the shooting hole,
Besa'arat hakrav, Betevah am—	In the rage of battle, in civil butchery,
Ata tir'ena eykh oivim mitmol Beyahad tso'adim, Berosh muram,	Now shall see how yesterday's foes Together march, with lifted heads,

Baderekh ha'ahat, mibli lishlo'ah	All one way, without stretching
Yadam bere'eyhem, bikroveyhem,	Their hands against acquaintance, kindred
Beva'aley britam.	and their allies.
Hamilhama, keherev mithapekhet,	War, like the turned sword,
Lo od tin'atz et lahava ba'adoneyha.	No more shall cut her master.

The first major change to strike the reader of Almagor's later version is the significant exclusion of the "new broils / to be commenc'd in stronds afar remote": what might serve as an overture to a patriotic enterprise would mar the didactic concord of a comic dénouement. Thus whereas Eli'az is following Shakespeare's Henry in allowing frighted peace to pant momentarily and then "breathe short-winded accents of new broils," Almagor's frighted peace is carefully fostered and caressed in order to enable it to "spread his wings." That is, it will spatially expand and reach "stronds afar remote," but never give way to new broils; rather, the only function of allowing peace to pant, or rather breathe delicately, is to enable it (him) to establish his constant reign, thus materialize its true ontology in concord.

Unlike Almagor's version of the speech, Eli'az's translation does not intentionally "question the origin" of the ideology of genuine or partial peace. However, the earlier version does betray some inherent ideological tokens. In Shakespeare, the fields of England's soil, which, it is hoped, will be channeled no longer by trenching war, are battlefields rather than agricultural; Eli'az (like Almagor after him) renders the act of channeling into ploughing, to match both the Biblical metaphor and the peasant ideal inherent in modern Zionist ideology. More telling, however, is Eli'az's rendering of Henry's image of the newly pacified brothers marching "in mutual well-beseeming ranks . . . all one way"; for "well-beseeming" Eli'az chooses the charged Hebrew term *"komemiyut,"* which draws simultaneously on two remotely related semantic fields: "upright" (with a connotation of pride as opposed to humility) and "revival" (raising of the fallen—Israel's 1948 war, usually referred to as "the War of Liberation" or "of Independence," was officially called "the War of *Komemiyut*"). In Almagor's dovish version no such heroic term will be used: his "lifted heads" positively restricts the image to the pride in the newly achieved peace, repressing the military connotations of the march and converting the whole image into a pageant of peaceful solidarity. Whereas Eli'az's version of "The edge of war, like an ill-sheathed knife, / No more shall cut his master" (lines 17–18) seems to follow the original text in stressing "master," Almagor's version seems to shift the emphasis to the very act of cutting. Questioning the origin aggressively, the questioning of Almagor's version must focus first on the directorial rather than the translational level. This may initiate an entirely different discourse, both enriching and transcending the field of theatrical translation.

Notes

1. Thomas Hobbes, *Leviathan, or the Matter, Forme & Power of a Common-Wealth Ecclesiasticall and Civill* (London: Andrew Crooke, 1651), 2:17–18, 85–94.
2. See, for example, Jean Jacques Rousseau, *The Political Writings*, ed. C. F. Vaughan (Oxford: Oxford University Press, 1962), 358–96.
3. See Avraham Oz, *The Yoke of Love: Prophetic Riddles in "The Merchant of Venice"* (Newark and London: University of Delaware Press, 1995), epilogue.
4. Andrew Benjamin, "Translating Origins: Psychoanalysis and Philosophy," in Lawrence Venuti, ed., *Rethinking Translation: Discourse, Subjectivity, Ideology* (London and New York: Routledge, 1992), 18.
5. Benjamin, "Translating Origins," 25.
6. See Ben Lowe, *Imagining Peace: A History of Early English Pacifist Ideas, 1340–1560* (University Park: Pennsylvania State University Press, 1997), 300–301.
7. See Steven Marx, "Shakespeare's Pacifism," *Renaissance Quarterly* 45 (1992): 56.
8. Taken from *Pages from Michael Butler's Journal: "Hair" & The State of the Nation,* http://www.michaelbutler.com/orlok/michael/nation.html. [cited 3 July 1996].
9. The term "negotiation" is put to telling use by Stuart Hall in his "Encoding/Decoding." See Barbara E. Bowen's lucid use of his sense of the term in her *Gender in the Theater of War: Shakespeare's "Troilus and Cressida"* (New York and London: Garland, 1993), xiv.
10. Yossef Al-Dror, *Self-Explained* (unpublished playtext, 1996).
11. Citations are from the Riverside Shakespeare.
12. See William Shakespeare, *Henry Ha'Re'vi'i, Helek Aleph [1 Henry IV]*, trans. Repha'el Eli'az (Tel Aviv: Sifriyat Po'alim & Hakibbutz Hame'uhad, 1963).
13. I have transliterated the Hebrew text (in the left column), and then retranslated it back into the English (in the right column), rendering literal meaning accurately, rather than trying to keep rhythm, alliteration and other phonetic devices, which may be appreciated from the sound of the Hebrew alone.
14. In the Hebrew all nouns are gendered: thus peace is masculine, while war and soil are feminine.
15. See William Shakespeare, *Commedia Shel Ta'uyot [The Comedy of Errors]*, trans. Dan Almagor (Tel Aviv: Dvir, 1996).

Beginning with Branagh: *Romeo and Juliet,* Hammersmith, 1986

RUSSELL JACKSON

WHAT FOLLOWS IS AN ACCOUNT OF WORK ON A PRODUCTION OF *Romeo and Juliet* staged in London at the Lyric Studio, Hammersmith, in August-September 1986. Kenneth Branagh, who also played Romeo, directed and co-produced. He had made his mark with roles in stage productions in the West End and with the Royal Shakespeare Company (including a remarkable Henry V in 1984–85), and already had some notable television performances to his credit. He decided, with fellow-actor David Parfitt, to put his energy and resources into an independent production company, with the aim of escaping the director-dominated culture of the "nationals"—actors would work under the direction of other actors, in this case Branagh himself. For this project, the production company was "Kenneth Branagh Limited," and the production budget was about £15,000. Branagh has described the results in chapter seven of *Beginning* (London: Chatto and Windus, 1989), the volume of autobiography he undertook (typically and frankly) to raise money toward establishing an office for the Renaissance Theatre Company.

Rather than being a comprehensive diary of the production, or an attempt at a critique of it (from which my involvement as "text adviser" disqualifies me), what follows is an account, written shortly after the event and now recollected (but not substantially altered) in tranquillity, of some of the rehearsal process, attempting to suggest the atmosphere in which our work took place and the kind of discussions we had. This was my first experience as a "text adviser," a role I have subsequently played in a series of productions with Kenneth Branagh, and it established the basic procedures. Most of my discussions with individuals hovered between "what does this mean?" and "how can I make it work?", with the corollary of "how does my character come to say it?"—which probably indicates the order of priorities of this group of British, classically trained actors. It soon became clear that some of the habits of academic criticism, relating the text to a perceived overall pattern of thoughts, images and situations (in the fashion of "new criticism"), were of limited relevance to the rehearsal room. Many of the points covered will seem relatively unimportant, but they are included to indicate the range of the work involved, and to suggest how seemingly trivial adjustments can have a bearing on larger issues of interpretation in performance. This is not by any stretch of the imagination a tribute to my sagacity, but rather an illustration of the actor's need to find the most effective way of using the text, given his or her own training and instincts and the circumstances of a particular production.

I

At the read-through on the first day of rehearsals, the dozen actors seated around the bar-tables and trestles in the middle of the studio were still sizing each other up; they began to accumulate the first of many collections of used plastic cups and ashtrays. Some actors gave what sounded like "finished" performances, completely convincing in every intonation but deceptively so because as yet they owed nothing to interaction with the others. Some held back, barely rising above a murmur. But when we read the first balcony scene, with cigarette smoke already thick in the air, the tables in the middle of the room seemed to be the barriers between the lovers, who instinctively strained to push them aside, to make some contact with each other across the ashtrays and cups and scripts and pencils. It was oddly moving, unsentimental, powerful: no prepared effects, beyond what they had done alone in private, but a charge that came from reading the lines at and with another person, and from the instinct to make them work *on* that person, giving the words a sense of performative action.

This first reading took one and three-quarter hours, and was preceded by a brief talk from the director and a viewing of the set model (as ever on such occasions, actors craned over to peer into its recesses, giving the designer a show of informed appreciation, but also anxious to see how they would be seen). After lunch on the first day came the first real rehearsal, setting the fight director loose on the first scene. We had three weeks of solid rehearsal: scene by scene through the play for one week; every scene over again and "solo calls" in the second; more solos and run-throughs in the third. In the final week we moved out of the theater while the set was built, and found ourselves in a church hall with the lines of the set marked out in tape, while ashtrays, coffee cups, copies of the script (now dog-eared) and the odd dagger and vial found a home among stacking chairs and hymnals. There were bright prints of bible scenes on the walls, and the inscription "Thy Word is Law" in gilded letters over the arch at the end of the room. Thus was established the habitual environment in which play rehearsals take place in London, and the schedule before us was packed but no less typical: in the production week Monday would be for the technical rehearsals (a slow drag from cue to cue, mainly for lighting adjustments), Tuesday for dress rehearsal, photo calls and a preview for an invited audience, Wednesday a "paying" preview and Thursday the press night.

What did we know so far? This would be a fast-moving production, and the script prepared by the director had lost about thirty percent of the play's lines (913 lines out of 2,974; see pp. 160–62). The major cuts included the opening forty-two lines (the servants' quarrel); a similar amount from the opening of the "feast" scene (1.5); the second act chorus; the whole domestic scene at 4.4; the first seven lines of the Nurse waking Juliet, with the musicians' lines at the end of that scene (4.5); fourteen lines of Romeo's speech about the apothecary; forty-nine from the opening of the final scene, as well as most of the watchmen's lines and a further sixty-nine lines from the same scene. There would be no elaborately contrived "period," either Renaissance or modern, and the precise nature of the "timeless" costumes wouldn't be settled until the designer, Kate Burnett, had seen the cast at work on the play. (This in itself was a direct challenge to the common situation in the "nationals," where sets and costumes are often being made before rehearsals have begun.) In an interview in *The Stage* (29 August 1986), Kate made it clear that "there had been a decision not to put [the play] in any period." This was a shirts-and-breeches rather than tights-and-codpieces Verona. Juliet's costumes were simple shifts, and apart from the hand-painted glove that emphasized Tybalt's left-handedness, most of the detail was restricted to simple color-coding to identify the rival houses. With eleven in the cast there would be some doubling and no crowds: consequently Verona would have short sharp fights and intimate parties. Tybalt and Paris would be doubled, as would the Friar and Mercutio, and Montague and Friar John. Prologue, Prince and Apothecary would be tripled. The first brawl, much abbreviated, would be between two servants, both played by women (as boys), one of whom then reappeared as Lady Capulet. Lines referring directly to them as men (including some bawdy) were cut, so as not to highlight what we hoped would be an acceptable sleight-of-hand. (In the event, we didn't really get away with it, and a few reviwers wondered about the somewhat *gamine* Peter.) Lady Montague was absent. We were not yet sure whether there would be an interval (in the event, there was). The set, scaffolding painted a dull red, had an upper level across the back wall of the studio's black box; there was a balcony on the audience's right, with a gate opening onto a flight of steps, and a similar structure on the left would serve for the Apothecary's shop and a few other locations. The gray-black floor was painted with lines in receding perspective and vivid red blotches, so that the overall coloring, echoed in most of the costumes, was dried blood-red and matte black. The audience (about 150) would sit along one wall, facing the acting area, which took up about two-thirds of the studio's floor space. In rehearsals the studio (during these hot weeks) seemed peculiarly claustrophobic, but we were able to colonize the bar and the upper staircases of the foyer during the day, so that solo calls might take place by an open window as planes roared upriver toward Heathrow at regular intervals. Out of a welter of minor problems, some mundane (do we have everyone's National Insurance number?), some more momentous (can we make something of the physical proximity of the households in our little space?), we moved into the real work of rehearsals. Already there was that all-important sense of a company coming together.

Day one, problem one. The brawl in the first scene was plotted as an encounter between two boyish servants, but as they were played by women, the references to their gender had to be omitted. However, "Do you bite your thumb at me" really benefits from the "sir" on the end: it gives the line a performative, aggressive, gestural value, and the point about class (using "sir" sarcastically) is useful. Still, the "sirs" had to go. Then a word was added to point up Tybalt's identity more crudely than is necessary when the part isn't doubled with another, and Benvolio named Tybalt when he asked him to put up his sword. Adjustments of this kind were made throughout; it is interesting to notice how they can affect the ways the words are *used*—rather than their strict lexical "meaning." A more interesting example is at the beginning of 1.2, where Capulet urges Paris to think seriously about wooing Juliet. We wanted to make the identification of Paris absolutely clear, by having Capulet name him earlier than the text indicates. The scene begins in the middle of a conversation, with Capulet (Andrew Jarvis) saying

> But Montague is bound as well as I,
> In penalty alike; and 'tis not hard, I think,
> For men so old as we to keep the peace.

To this Paris replies, with customary tact:

> Of honourable reckoning are you both,
> And pity 'tis you lived at odds so long.

Then he shifts to his own preoccupations—

> But now my lord, what say you to my suit?

and Capulet's reply begins

> But saying oe'er what I have said before
>
> (1–7)

If we wished to add some such phrase as "Sir Paris," it couldn't be inserted much later than this—the text has one at line sixteen, but we wanted it earlier. Our first attempt involved adding to the first line: "Good county Paris, 'tis not hard I think." This sounded about as authentically Elizabethan as a "themed" pub, and, even worse, was static. It didn't add to the movement of the line, and offered no "push"—a respect in which Shakespeare's opening was hard to better. Despite this discouragement we tried other ideas. "But saying o'er" became "Paris, I'll say," which is equally unforceful, and needs a clumsy, finger-jabbing pause after "Paris" as well as the hefty verbal alteration. In the end we settled for the addition of a half-line, which could at least be used to give Capulet a moment's breath, and additional beat to push along the next line:

> But saying o'er what I have said before:
> Sir Paris, [beat]
> My child is yet a stranger to the world.
>
> (7–8)

This seemed enough to fix the actor's new identity without bringing the scene prematurely to a grinding halt.

One other piece of minor surgery will stand for other similar cases. In the Mantua scene and the final scene of the play (5.1 and 5.3) the servant Balthasar was replaced by Romeo's friend Benvolio, who normally disappears from the play after giving his account of the deaths of Mercutio and Tybalt. This was done purely for reasons of economy, but it incidentally strengthened and altered the part of Benvolio. It also entailed the removal of the words in which Romeo addresses Balthasar as a servant, so "Take thou that" (5.3.41) went because the implied gift of money is inappropriate between friends, and the ever-useful "coz" replaced "sir" in Benvolio/Balthasar's lines.

Variant readings have an almost fatal attraction for some actors, who pounce on them as though Shakespeare is hiding in the footnotes like a living author lurking in the back stalls, available for rewrites. Some phrases not in the New Penguin text were seized on when I mentioned their existence. (I have since come to believe that they can often help to "take the curse" off a passage that is proving difficult.) In Q1 Benvolio cuts in on the beginning of the "Queen Mab" speech: "Queen Mab. What's she?" This is useful to give a "kick" to the speech that follows, and suggests a stronger sense of interplay between Mercutio and his listeners. The nurse had learned her part before rehearsals—as some actors prefer to—but from another edition, so she was saying "alone" in "For then she [Juliet] could stand high-lone" (1.3.37). The "new" reading, "high-lone" seemed useful to her, but the Elizabethan baby-talk usage of "it" as a possessive ("a bump upon it brow" 53) proved too fussy. A more radical decision was taken in "Gallop apace" (3.2), where Juliet preferred "he" to the Penguin "I" in "And when *he* shall die / Take him and cut him out in little stars" (21–22). We gave Mercutio's first "A plague of both your houses" the "your" that the New Penguin editor denies it (3.1.91), and in 3.3 the Nurse did not snatch away Romeo's dagger (the Q stage direction) because it seemed better for the Friar to disarm his erring pupil quietly. Andrew Jarvis as Capulet preferred the spitting, almost inarticulate effect of the broken rhythm preserved in the New Penguin to other editors' efforts to introduce regularity in a wrathful speech at 3.5.177–79:

> Day, night; hour, tide, time; work, play;
> Alone, in company; still my care hath been
> To have her matched

Another actor might of course prefer to let the tide of Capulet's anger flow more evenly—in such instances rehearsal makes one aware that different readings can suggest divergent acting choices rather than offering a simple "solution" to a crux.

Some of the lines cut by the director were restored as we worked, and my function here was that of resident pragmatist rather than defender of sacred writ. I accepted the broad principles on which the cuts had been made: many elaborate developments of imagery had been removed and the crowd scenes thinned out, but the original dramatic structure maintained. We cut within scenes and sequences, and were anxious not to favor Romeo and Juliet at the expense of the other characters. This was important to the self-respect of the company, and the director was insistent that the production would not be actor-managerial in the old sense of being a showcase for its "star" with "lesser" roles diminished. Some cuts resulted in the loss to a degree of the play's (and the characters') self-consciousness about poetic expression, but we had to believe that other aspects of the production would compensate. For example, Romeo's first conversation with Benvolio lost ten lines following 1.1.172:

> Alas, that love, whose view is muffled still
> Should without eyes see pathways to his will!
> [Where shall we dine? O me, what fray was here?
> Yet tell me not, for I have heard it all.
> Here's much to-do with hate, but more with love.
> Why then, O brawling love, O loving hate,
> O anything, of nothing first create!
> O heavy lightness, serious vanity,
> Misshapen chaos of well-seeming forms,
> Feather of lead, bright smoke, cold fire, sick health,
> Still-waking sleep, that is not what it is!
> This love I feel, that feel no love in this.]
> Dost thou not laugh?
>
> (171–83)

Omitting these lines weakened the play's overall sense of rhetorical patterns, with its repeated use of antithesis and, specifically, oxymoron ("feather of lead" etc.). Romeo's weary response to the evidence of a "fray" was taken out and Benvolio's cue for "weeping" (his joke in line 184) also went. All the reasons for keeping the lines in were considered, but among other arguments the one that prevailed was the director's anxiety not to retain lines for himself while asking others to give up theirs, and the need to keep the action moving.

The omission of thirty percent of the text meant that we inevitably lost some of the play's breadth and scale, along with its duration, but the circumstances of a studio production and a reduced cast made this more palatable. Often the physical limitations of the space and the lines of the text collided in such a way as to remind us how the playwright had responded to the conditions of his own theaters. When Juliet first visits the Friar, in 2.6, his line "Here comes the lady" (15) is followed by this:

> O, so light a foot
> Will ne'er wear out the everlasting flint.
> A lover may bestride the gossamers

> That idles in the wanton summer air;
> And yet not fall. So light is vanity.
>
> (2.6.16–20)

As so often at such moments, four or more lines cover the time it would take for the actor to arrive at the front after entering from the rear of the Elizabethan stage, but our set gave Juliet only a steep flight of a dozen steps to make the journey, and she might be expected to be in earshot immediately after "Here comes the lady." Without these lines, though, we would lose the "moment," with the Friar's recognition of Juliet and his sense of the impression she makes on Romeo: we reinstated the first two of the omitted lines, cutting only the moralizing development (17–20).

More difficult was the Nurse's line at 4.2.15, where she marks Juliet's return from the cell: "See where she comes from shrift with merry look." Juliet's appearance might be expected to correspond to the description, unless we wanted to indicate that the Nurse is speaking hopefully rather than truthfully, but what can "merry look" mean? Certainly Juliet cannot be smiling or laughing too openly, because she is about to show penitence to her father (in our production she prostrated herself before him). Her feelings can hardly warrant "merry" looks: how deceitful can Juliet seem? Is the Nurse's line one of those "markers" so useful on the large open stage of an Elizabethan public theater ("Look I so pale, Lord Rivers, as the rest?") but redundant in a small studio? After a lot of pondering, and with no real answer, we left the line in: the Nurse has to say something here.

These two examples illustrate the fine distinction between "functional" and (for want of a better word) "aesthetic" priorities in cutting the text. It is often easier to justify a hefty cut in a long speech (such as the first ten lines of the Friar's opening monologue at 2.3) than to lose a few words at such moments as the Nurse's response to Juliet's arrival. Moreover, the actor's instinct should be respected. Capulet found that he needed some lines back in 4.2 (31–32, on the city's indebtedness to the Friar) but felt no particular need for "My heart is wondrous light, / Since this same wayward girl is so reclaimed" (46–47: cut along with everything between 33 and the end of the scene). In the lamenting over Juliet's apparent death (4.5) we restored two cut lines that allow Paris and Capulet to participate more fully in the rhythms of the litany of grief: "Beguiled, divorcèd, wrongèd, spited, slain" and "Despised, distressèd, hated, martyred, killed" (55, 59). The stately *rallentando* was valuable for the scene's effect. One of the Nurse's lamentations, however (52), did not prove useful and we cut it. We ended up leaving in most of the passion (encouraging the actors to make it all as intense as possible) and cut some of the Friar's reasoning ("And all the better is it for the maid," 67–79).

II

It seems a good idea to give some account of the "finished product," by describing briefly the performance of two scenes: the "balcony scene" (2.2) and the lovers' parting at dawn (3.5).

Two major cuts were made in 2.2: Romeo's "two of the fairest stars . . ." (15–22) and Juliet's "Bondage is hoarse . . . " (160–63). Three lines were deleted from the final section of the scene (173, 175, 179) together with the final six lines ("The grey ey'd morn smiles on the frowning night") which New Penguin gives to Romeo but some editors attach to the Friar's speech at the opening of 2.3. Three other cuts, of six lines in all (58–59,76–78,186–87) were considered but not implemented.

The most striking features of the scene as performed were its variety of pace, notably the rapidity of some passages, and the emphasis on its wit and comedy. These lovers might have matured into a comic couple, delighting in each other's verbal dexterity. Romeo was at first apprehensive about the light breaking from the window: for all he knew it might be the murderous Tybalt or a watchman, and he'd never been in the orchard before and couldn't know the geography of the house. He positively glowed when he realized he had found Juliet. She knelt down to the edge of the balcony (as much for the sake of the audience's sight lines as for Romeo), resting her cheek upon her hand, but leapt up and darted back into the shadows when Romeo spoke:

> What man art thou that, thus bescreened in night,
> So stumblest on my counsel?
>
> (52–53)

This was rapid and nervous (an effect which requires precise enunciation from the actress!). Romeo, by contrast, leaned back happily, recklessly savoring the situation:

> With love's light wings did I o'erperch these walls,
> For stony limits cannot hold love out.
>
> (66–67)

Her questions were then fired urgently at him, and she did not begin to slow down—to enjoy the situation herself—until the longer speech beginning "Thou knowest the mask of night is on my face" (85). There were comic changes of direction on "Or if thou thinkest I am too quickly won" (95) and "I should have been more strange, I must confess" (102). The former was quickly cancelled by the slower, more earnest "But else, not for the world" (98), and the latter drew laughter because it was spoken thoughtfully, as though Juliet had just remembered the rules. ("I *should* have been"). Romeo was up beside Juliet on the balcony at "Lady! by yonder blessèd moon I vow" (107), and the wit of her interruptions of his attempt to swear was comic in effect. When she cut in with "Well, do not swear" there was a pause before her foreboding: "Although I joy in thee, / I have no joy of this contract tonight" (116–17). Then, in response to Romeo's "O, wilt thou leave me so unsatisfied?" the reply "What satisfaction canst thou have tonight?", was rapid and taken aback—another laugh (125–26). The quick exchange of lines was brought to a halt after "But to be frank and give it thee again" (131) by a longer pause before the greater intensity of "My bounty is as boundless as the sea" (33), followed by another beat of silence before the noise from within (136).

When Juliet returned—"Three words, dear Romeo" (142)—the particulars of her instructions were counted off on her fingers with comic urgency, as though she were simultaneously striving for self-possession:

> If that thy bent of love be honourable,
> Thy purpose marriage, send me word tomorrow.
> (143–44)

As she tried to combine answering the Nurse with seeing as much as possible of Romeo, hopes of a lingering goodnight faded, and she was gone before he could realize it. Romeo climbed down from the balcony and made for the far side of the stage, looking for a way out of the orchard. When Juliet called him back, he kept out of her sight, enjoying the sound of her voice, and then presented himself, grinning, at "My nyas?" (167). He was happy to stand in full view of the balcony—and of anyone who cared to look from the house—and the lovers' next exchange was timed for comic effect:

> *Juliet.* I have forgot why I did call thee back.
> *Romeo.* Let me stand here, till thou remember'st it.

> *Juliet.* I shall forget, to have thee stand there still.
> *Romeo.* And I'll still stay, to have thee still forget.
>
> (170–72, 174)

The humor of all this did not, we hoped, altogether outweigh the effect of the scene's lyricism, but rather allowed the actors to place it more precisely: "My bounty is as boundless as the sea" is a new note in the play, heard for the first time, and it seemed to surprise Juliet herself. At the same time, we wanted to preserve the wit of the lovers' first encounter, and the shared sonnet. The playing owed a lot to Branagh's capacity to endow Romeo with frank good humour and a corresponding quality, with a touch more sophistication, in Samantha Bond's Juliet. Neither was conventionally or naively "poetical": in Romeo's case that was something he had discarded along with his devotion to the unyielding Rosaline. In the first rehearsal of the scene, before we had the upper levels of the set to work on, the scene was played with Romeo standing at the side of the bank of auditorium seats and Juliet above him, leaning over the railing. There was a point where the lovers touched fingers, straining to reach one another, so that their hands were seen against a dark background. This was not played as a symbol of their separation, but simply as a moment of trying to get close, lingering in each other's company as much as possible. In fact the "moment"—a variation on which is not uncommon in performances of the play—disappeared in later rehearsals, and Romeo's climb to the balcony on our scaffolding set became less precarious, but the playfulness of the scene remained: in our version, Romeo climbed up to the balcony, rather than remain below; it seemed unavoidable. The *Stage* reviewer, Peter Hepple, commented that "seldom can the balcony scene have been played at such a clip" (21 August 1986), and this seemed of a piece with the two-and-a-half hours' traffic of the stage at Hammersmith. It is interesting that when Bond and Branagh played the same roles in a BBC radio production in 1993, the scene was taken at a less frenetic pace with no loss of the sense of urgency.

In the scene of their parting at dawn (3.5), Romeo and Juliet were in a more sombre mood. He came out onto the balcony, peering toward the rising sun, and she emerged from the darkness, a shawl across her shoulders, and embraced him from behind. She was now wearing the black dress adopted as mourning for the death of Tybalt. Moments of humor remained. He smiled at the conceit with which she desperately tried to explain away the dawn:

> Yond light is not daylight, I know it, I.
> It is some meteor that the sun exhales

> To be to thee this night a torchbearer
> To light thee on they way to Mantua.

Then after a pause, and deeply felt:

> Therefore stay yet. Thou needest not to be gone.
>
> (12–16)

The "meteor" idea was not a serious possibility, and they recognised the fact. Juliet's lines (31–34) about the lark and the "loathèd toad" were cut, along with the "pale reflex of Cynthia's brow" (20); this was done because we considered them potentially confusing. The pun on "division" (29), though, remained for the sake of its wit. Two adjustments stand out from rehearsals: Romeo's tone needed to be more reassuring to Juliet than it had been at first in "I doubt it not; and all these woes shall serve / For sweet discourses in our times to come" (52–53), and Juliet had to learn to avoid an instinctively colloquial (and modern) tone on the first two words of "Oh God, I have an ill-divining soul" (54). We cut the five lines in which she apostrophizes Fortune, so that the voice of Lady Capulet would cut in across the last moments of the parting. (Again this was partly because of the staging in a small space.) The scene precipitates the actress into events that call for all Juliet's ability to think on her feet, passing from equivocating with her mother to the urgent need to stop the plan for her marriage to Paris.

In ours as in many other stagings the second half of the performance had begun with "Gallop apace" (3.2), a formidable speech followed by yet another testing scene—news of Tybalt's death and Romeo's banishment. Romeo is offstage from the parting at dawn until his entrance in Mantua (5.1), and the play is powered by Juliet. After the parting Juliet has two scenes with her parents, one with the Friar (including some equivocating with Paris), and the "Potion" speech (4.3.20–59). Viewed in this perspective, the first 60 lines of 3.5 are both a calm before the storm, and the last real meeting of the pair.

III

As I remarked at the beginning of this essay, it is impossible for me to be objective about the production. It was an exciting few weeks, and had a good deal of the spirit (if none of the broad comedy) of the idealistic troupe of actors in Branagh's film *In the Bleak Midwinter* (*A*

Midwinter's Tale in the United States): there were not quite enough actors for the play, and the budget was tiny. On several occasions during the rehearsal period I slept on the sofa bed in the director's Camberwell flat, and my own most vivid memories of the time include an evening when I had gone home early and had fallen asleep in front of the television. I was awakened by an urgent knocking on the window: Romeo had climbed onto the balcony and was trying to wake his slumbering guest. *Romeo and Juliet* was my first exposure to Branagh's way of working with fellow actors, and in particular his talent for creating a productive atmosphere (never fraught, often jokey, but intense and supportive as necessary) and his habitual restraint in never visiting his own frustrations or anxieties on his colleagues. This is a faculty that every actor values, but which the public would not discern, except in so far as it contributes to a sense of ensemble in the finished product.

We could claim (and the more sympathetic reviewers agreed) that our production was swift, fresh, clearly articulated and—in its best scenes—moving and direct. In the spectrum of British theater in the 1980s it qualified as a "fringe" production only by virtue of its studio venue and low budget. Branagh strove to strike a balance between being unselfish in his treatment of his fellow actors and accepting that he needed to give a good performance because his name was the principal box-office draw. But the term "fringe," evoking a world of avant-garde experiment and the values of the counter culture, does not normally include actor-managers. Several reviewers took pains to remind their readers of this, sometimes to hostile effect, and it cannot be said that the production was overwhelmed with praise. It was roundly condemned in *Plays and Players* and *The Guardian,* praised kindly in *The Times* ("rewarding") and coolly in *The Financial Times* ("a must for Romeo-collectors, though not for Romeo-connoisseurs"), and recommended in *The Stage.* It attracted a good deal of press interest, though. The fact that it was made known that this would be Kenneth Branagh's only appearance in London that season may have helped the production to play to near capacity audiences. This *Romeo and Juliet,* like subsequent productions by Renaissance Theatre Company (of which it was the forerunner), made no effort to distance itself from commercial theater, and was not in any real sense avant-garde—although it was hoped that this did not preclude its being innovative in individual performances or achieving an ensemble. Nor was it driven by a sophisticated "concept," beyond a set design that was intended to suggest heat, passion and darkness (blood-red, black).

In the mid-1980s, there was a strong feeling among actors in the British "national" companies, fueled by Simon Callow's book *Being an Actor,* that directors and (worse) designers exercised too much power. Later productions by Renaissance included a season of three plays which were directed by well-known actors, but in which they did not appear. Throughout the company's lifetime, the basic principles of work on the text remained constant: plays were cut for time and clarity, and with the general intentions of keeping the architecture of the text intact, not favoring one actor at the expense of others, and removing some of the elaborations of figurative language. Similarly, there was the broad aim to set up good working relationships between actors and directors, based on the principle of having actors do the directing. In this *Romeo,* as subsequently, the main emphasis would be on actors working on text, and the involvement of Hugh Cruttwell (to advise on matters having to do with acting) and me (as text adviser) was as a resource for the actors. Readers of *Beginning* will realise the particular debt that Branagh acknowledges to Hugh as a judge of his acting. If I were to choose a single word to characterize our contribution, I would say that we were there in the rehearsal room to be "pragmatic"—and by way of amplification that we were an additional set of ears and eyes for the actor-directors, providing another two people who see the process through and to whom the actors can speak. In this respect, the *modus operandi* of the company remained the same throughout the subsequent work, including the films of *Henry V, Much Ado* and (after Branagh's departure from Renaissance Films plc) *Hamlet.* The *Romeo and Juliet* at Hammersmith was not a "major" production by any definition of the term, but for Kenneth Branagh's career as a Shakespearean actor and director, it was a significant beginning.

Appendix

Romeo and Juliet, Lyric Theatre Studio, London 13 August–6 September 1986
1. Cast and production credits.
   Prologue/Escalus/Apothecary: Leslie Southwick
   Mercutio/Friar Lawrence: Mark Hadfield
   Paris/Tybalt: Simon Shepherd
   Montague/Friar John: John Gray
   Romeo: Kenneth Branagh
   Benvolio: Ian Targett
   Capulet: Andrew Jarvis

Lady Capulet: Gay Hamilton
Juliet: Samantha Bond
Nurse: Anne Carroll
Peter: Nicola Wright

Directed by Kenneth Branagh
Assistant Director: David Parfitt
Lighting Design: Brian Harris
Music Composed and Directed by Jessica Higgs
Fight Director: Nick Hall
Text Adviser: Russell Jackson
Production Consultant: Hugh Cruttwell
Stage Manager: Graham Coffey

2. Summary of cuts, based on RJ's rehearsal copy, checked against the production prompt-copy (on deposit at the Shakespeare Institute Library). References are to the New Penguin edition (ed. T. J. B. Spencer, Harmondsworth: 1967) which was used for the production.

Act One, Scene One: 1–42; 46–48; 56–58; 61–62 ("Gregory . . . blow"); 64 ("put up your swords"); 73–75; 75–78 ("Give me . . . in spite of me"); 79–80 ("Hold me not . . . foe"); 83–86; 92–95; 102; 110–15; 122; 127–28; 144–53; 158–59; 173–82 (cut in promptbook); 190–94; 200–202; 209–11; 219–24; 230–36.

Act One, Scene Two: 38–41 ("It is written . . . his nets"); 46–48; 65–66 ("The lady widower . . . nieces"); 69 ("Lucio . . . Helena"); 87–90; 93–98.

Act One, Scene Three: 88–96.

Act One, Scene Four: 4–8; 19–21; 35–47; 100–103 ("who woos . . . South").

Act One, Scene Five: 1–41 (Except 26 "You are welcome . . . play"); 42–43 ("which doth . . . knight"); 48–51; 118, 122.

Act Two, Chorus: omitted.

Act Two, Scene One: 2; 8–14; 23–29 ("Twould anger him . . . to raise him up").

Act Two, Scene Two: 14–22; 160–63; 173; 175; 179; 188–93.

Act Two Scene Three: 1–10; 31–34; 46–50; 67–74.

Act Two, Scene Three: (lines 1–2 made into two speeches, one question each for Benvolio and Mercutio); 10–12; 38–43 ("now is he for ... purpose"); 43–44 ("There's ... slop"); 70–85; 92–96; 117–23 ("tell you ... wisely!"); 131 etc. (song); 141 ("Lady, lady, lady"); 154–57 ("if I had ... side"); 191–96 ("What sayest thou ... prating thing—O"); 199–207 ("anger her ... good to hear it").

Act Two, Scene Four: omitted.

Act Two, Scene Five: 22–24; 33–37; 39–44 ("Though his face ... as a lamb"); 46 ("But all this did I know before"); 59–61 ("How oddly ... mother?").

Act Two, Scene Six: 10–13; 15; 18–20.

Act Three, Scene One: 41–43 ("Thy head ... quarrelling"); 46–48 ("Didst thou not ... old riband?"—restored in promptbook); 36; 57–58; 89 ("Away, Tybalt!"); 115 (restored in promptbook); 117–18; 121; 137–40; 155–75 ("All this utterèd ... let Benvolio die."); 190–91; 196–97.

Act Three, Scene Two: 28–31 ("So tedious ... wears them"); 32–34 ("and every tongue ... what news?"); 36–37 ("Why dost thou ... he's dead."); 44–51; 58–60; 67–68; 73–74; 75–76; 80–84 ("O Nature ... So fairly bound?"); 93–95; 102–4; 114–21 ("Tybalt's death ... following Tybalt's death"); 130–31; 134–35; 142–43 ("Give this ring ... farewell").

Act Three, Scene Three: 1–7 ("Come forth ... company"); 20–23; ("Then 'banished' ... murders me"); 37–41; 48–52; 73–74 ("unless the breath ... eyes"); 75 ("Hark how they knock"); 77–78 ("By and by ... I come!"); 82 ("O holy friar"); 83 ("Where's ... lord?"); 110–13; 119–21; 122–34; 137–45; 156–57; 163; 165; 173–75.

Act Three, Scene Four: no cuts.

Act Three, Scene Five: 20; 31–34; 60–64; 68; 70–73; 75–77; 93; 103; 126–28; 130–37 ("In one little body ... tempest-tossèd body"); 183; 185; 206–11; 212 ("What sayest thou?"—cut in promptbook); 236–40 ("Ancient damnation! ... thousand times?").

Act Four, Scene One: 29–36; 44–45; 48–51; 58–64; 71–75; 79–86; 99–103; 118–21.

Act Four, Scene Two: 1–10; 30; 33–47.

Act Four, Scene Three: 1 ("Ay, those attires are best"); 6; 7–8 ("We have called . . . tomorrow"); 34; 39; 50.

Act Four, Scene Four: omitted.

Act Four, Scene Five: 1–7 ("Mistress . . . but little"); 10–11; 26–27; 31–32; 38–40; 44–45; 52; 61–62; 68–78; 79–80 ("Stick . . . corse, and"); 82–83; 96–144 (musicians' scene).

Act Five, Scene One: 3–5; 23; 42–56; 64–66; 84.

Act Five, Scene Two: no cuts.

Act Five, Scene Three: 13–15; 19–25 ("What cursèd foot . . . In faith, I will"); 28–39; 45–53; 72–74; 76–82; 87 (restored in promptbook); 97–101 ("Tybalt . . . cousin!"—restored in promptbook); 121–43; 156–57 ("Come . . . holy nuns"); 168 ("Lead, boy, which way?"); 172–77; 190–94; 198–201; 203–7; 219–21; 224–25; 229–30; 242; 249; 253; 255–62; 265–66 ("and to the marriage / Her nurse is privy"); 271; 279–90.

To Know a Shakespeare Character

MARVIN ROSENBERG

SCHOLARS HAVE STUDIED SHAKESPEARE'S WORDS AND ACTORS HAVE ACTED them—often without paying attention to each other. But when the two share insights, new depths have been plumbed.

An example: in the later seventeenth-century theater, when Shakespeare's tragic characters were all decomplicated, Hamlet, his inwardness minimized, was reduced to an extrovert hero who fiercely exacted his revenges. Then critics began to find in the play the man of sensibility; Goethe proposed the delicate metaphor of the vase too frail for its task; and many theaters and critics adopted this inward strain of characterization. Conversely, though it became popular in Russia, the actor Mochalov, while true to Hamlet's interior, rejected the then standard defeatist "Hamletism" interpretation. When he acted a Hamlet of power, as well as vulnerability, the critic Belinski, after attending the performance repeatedly, was won over, and espoused the more positive characterization.

Another example: in England in the nineteenth century, Helena Faucit as Lady Macbeth dared to deviate from the standard tyrannical Terrible Woman portrayed by Sarah Siddons and Hannah Pritchard. She insisted instead on the humanity in the role. She convinced the critic George Fletcher, and his stamp of approval converted, among other actresses, Ellen Terry.

My point: we do our part as scholar-critics—we continue to make available to actors our latest learning. We unlock as we can the secrets of Shakespeare's language; in his characterizations we examine the complex involvements with culture, authority, sexuality, gender, family, intimate relationships. We know a very great deal about Shakespeare's art, and we provide insights for actors to dramatize.

How can we as scholars learn from the actors? Many ways. We can see all the stagings available—in person, if possible, on videotapes if some luckily exist. (With *Hamlet* I was able to collect forty from around the world; for *Antony and Cleopatra* I have found only a half-dozen.) We can begin to learn something from the many records of performances—in reviews, interviews, memoirs. We can go hunting among old newspaper files; fortunately some national theater institutes, and some libraries, preserve clippings, and will make them available. Actors and directors often like to be interviewed.

But however much we learn about Shakespeare's characters from the experience of the staged plays, the characters remain at a distance from us: we know them only from the outside. Can we not learn also to share the actor's gift for entering the characters, as Mochalov and Faucit, for instance, did? Yes.

We all do this intuitively, in our armchairs; but a further important theatrical dimension is available to us, even if, as scholars, we are (usually) not practiced in acting and directing. Ideally we achieve this by forming a reading group, as many of us do, engaging in a series of rehearsals, where we get to play all the characters, as Bottom wished to. We live the lines with each other.

We in academe have a special resource: we can share the search for Shakespearean character with our students. They can discover with us the inner life of the characters, often the subtextual life.

I will use my classwork as an example, as in my senior seminar focusing on *Hamlet*. For a scholar's purposes, it could as well be one of our reading groups. The objective: to search for the essence of Shakespeare's art in the unforgettable verbal poetry, as it is mated with the incomparable poetry of the theater. Suit the word to the action, the action to the word: so we seek their fusion, their inseparable interplay in the characters, from the characters' own experience.

We read the play, as scholars and actors, looking for pregnant areas where new joinings of word and action could deliver illumination. So many mysteries yet to resolve, so many layers of meaning still to explore.

Inevitably we find that the plays' depths can best be plumbed by confronting the multiplicity in the language and action of the characterizations. So we begin with them. I will suggest here initial steps; your intuitions may already have lifted you higher.

From our first readings, we develop hypotheses. Then we test them, inside and out. What are the characters biologically, what do they wear, what do they hold in their hands?—for their physicality is often a first clue to identity. Are they tall, short, what of their habits? Then, most important, what do they hold in their minds, their emotions?

So to their language: any recurrent ideas or images? Do any key words or rhythms indicate tendencies, for instance, of approach or withdrawal, attack or retreat, synthesis or diffusion, confidence or fear, affection or hostility, retention or disposal? These from the spoken words; as important, sometimes more, the subtexts behind the spoken language: what thoughts, what feelings—hopeful, passionate, despairing, bruised, fierce, cruelly controlled—are simmering, repressed? What of the silences?

The subtexts can only be known in what the characters *do,* or feel, to sustain or mask their objectives. The actors' bodies and voices are Shakespeare's aural-visual instruments here. Verdi said of actors that gestures are their bodies' pronunciations. Shakespeare knew that; and often he provided objects to help make the pronouncing more eloquent.

Consider *Hamlet*'s "nunnery" scene as a laboratory. Ophelia sits while Hamlet says his soliloquy. When he considers suicide, he sometimes brings out his dagger. He is able to refuse death, appealing as the thought is to him—though one hand may stay restlessly near the hilt of that dagger.

What else may we find him characteristically carrying? Perhaps the script for the play-within-the-play, his immediate linear objective if he is to live? After his soliloquy, and his determination to go on living, he is on his way to produce his drama that will catch the conscience of the king. Until he is stopped by the sight of Ophelia.

Ophelia. What is—in Stanislavskian terms—her objective? What does she want, from scene to scene, and ultimately? Often no two of us can agree on every thrust—as indeed has been the case, as we learn, with critics and actresses.

She has been sitting with the book Polonius has given her to pretend at least to read. Her brain and emotions are alight with the coming confrontation with Hamlet. Has she been told by her father of his madness? Can we, as Ophelia, sit still, as she sees Hamlet wrestling with the urge to kill himself? Does she let us know she wants to intercede (as one stage Ophelia actually did)? Does she turn the book restlessly in her hand? What book is it? Does she read a word? Utter silent prayers?

Her gestures will pronounce her emotions about the other *things* she holds. Precious things: gifts Hamlet has given her, and almost certainly the love poems too ("with them words of so sweet breath compos'd"). How large a package? In the theater she often holds the *things* in one hand; when I entered the character, I found that my generous, loving Hamlet had given me *many* gifts and poems, and two hands could barely hold them. How about you? As Ophelia, what gifts do you hold?

How will Ophelia handle the treasured *things?* Hold them to her heart? She is about to offer them back. Was this all her father's idea? Does she chance a look toward the eavesdroppers? She had told

Polonius that Hamlet had spoken to her "almost all the holy vows of heaven." Does she hope for marriage? In the pursuit of her objective, what is her subtext, her hidden agenda, to use a current phrase, that colors everything she says and does?

At the Old Vic, Derek Jacobi spoke the *To be* . . . soliloquy directly to Ophelia; he told me she was the one person he could confide in then. But Shakespeare has Hamlet only at the end of the speech, when he finally puts away his dagger, turn and see Ophelia for the first time. What is Hamlet's objective now? Will he go to her? Wait until she gives a sign of recognition? Whisper his recognition of her, and try to slip away, so she must stop him? She hides her packed emotions, her stormy subtext, behind the most conventional of greetings.

Now two double agendas, surface and masked, clash. Ophelia had suddenly refused to see Hamlet, though they were sweethearts. She had turned back his letters; now she offers to return all he has given her. What bodily pronouncements convey her feeling and his at the simple, provocative offering? The superb critic Bradley, though not partial to the theater, insisted the only way we could really tell what was going on was to be present at the Globe when the scene was played.

We, more bravely, take on ourselves the imaginative task of realizing the scene. We seek Shakespeare's theater poetry. So we learn to advance to the confrontation charged with physical indications of the passions and purposes we find loaded into the characters by Shakespeare up to this moment.

To give a compressed example of this experience: I was invited to address the Duisburg Shakespeare Festival, in Germany. My subject was *Hamlet,* and I wanted to make the point that while we agree on the general outlines of his action, there is no single Hamlet: that so vast is what I call the polyphony of his character—the combination and interaction of the human tones invested in him—that we all endow him with the mix of special notes that we individually perceive. I demonstrated this with films of strikingly different Hamlets. But even more persuasive: I had asked my friend and host, Professor Wilhelm Hortmann, to see if he could find two students who would like to model the nunnery scene for me. When I arrived the morning of the lecture, two bright, intelligent young Germans from the University, a boy and a girl, were waiting. They had no acting experience, none at all; but they had conscientiously memorized the lines. When I asked them to do the scene, they stood at opposite ends of the room, and clearly, precisely, exchanged Shakespeare's words.

In the next few hours my wife Mary and I helped the students respond to the hot impulses with which Shakespeare had charged his words and actions. The students learned to mime the *things* as well as say the linked words with which Shakespeare compelled them to physical action, to bodily pronouncements. Thus:

> *Ophelia:* My lord, I have remembrances of yours
> That I have longed long to re-deliver.
> I pray you now receive them.
> *Hamlet:*   No, not I:
> I never gave you aught.
> *Ophelia:* My honored lord, you know right well you did,
> And with them words of so sweet breath composed
> As made these *things* more rich. Their perfume lost,
> Take these again . . .
> There, my lord . . .

Back and forth, word and action suffuse the scene: give, refuse; offer, reject; plead, deny; and underneath every speech a countering subtext.

In Duisburg, Shakespeare's language so energized the boy and the girl that they could no longer stand still. They learned who the characters were by *being* them. The girl, who had appeared in a stunning dress that she did not want to muss by moving around, was freed of that restraint by the commands of Shakespeare's language and action, that drove her to and away from Hamlet. The well-mannered boy was now jerked about by the passions of text and explosive subtext. He could not find peace.

In a kind of shorthand Mary and I gave these eager young people a glimpse of the flexibility, potentiality, and risks in their characters' polyphonies. So for the festival that evening they, who had never acted in their lives (and never again acted, Sandy Hortmann told me), truly lived the passions of the characters. Two versions: in one a sweet Hamlet appealed desperately to Ophelia to live an untainted life, and she grieved for his mental balance; in the other, a power Hamlet and Ophelia raged and pleaded across the stage, the minds of both tested to the limits of control. They awed the Festival audience. And me.

In this way, but in more leisurely detail, we can, in our groups or classes, follow the pattern that I myself experience when I study a play. As scholar-critics, we work to discover and absorb word and explicit or implicit action, text and subtext, for ourselves. Helpful, of course, is a critical reading list, and a library of reviews of the staged play, to assure familiarity with the best that has been thought and said and acted; and videotapes. We forage further for ourselves—most of all, we see if we can intuit individually new physical pronunciations of the text that actors and critics have not yet found.

Most important: we do not try to *act*—only to *be* the characters. *Acting* implies the noble purpose of communication with an audience; we are not concerned with conveying. I—and my students and associates—have been interested rather in *exploration:* what mixes of tones we can realize in us to flow in the characters as they interact. And besides the manifest tones of passion and thought in the characters' polyphonies, what subtle countering notes sound, what grace notes can be sensed?

Speak the lines in their interaction, and inevitably you voice their buried life. Following is a sample of what I've learned; you have perhaps already gone further. Are any or all of these tones sounded: Did Ophelia *want* to give back the gifts and the poems? In my experience with classes and groups, all agreed she did not. All Ophelias sensed complex tones, from past and present, conflicting inward: some measure of grief and guilt that she had broken with Hamlet; much wish to heal the breach; some hope that Hamlet in taking the gifts back would grasp the chance for a reconciliation. All felt that an undermining note in Ophelia's polyphony was her more or less constrained awareness of the lurking King and Polonius eavesdropping behind the arras. Ophelia would go mad—was any faint tone of instability sounding now? Signaled?

Being the character, we had to sense her subtext in her handling of the *things*—the gifts and poems. Some of my Ophelias held tight to them, even while offering them; some held them out and pulled them back; one or two tried to force them on Hamlet. One offered them with tears in her voice, one with pleading, one with command.

One, who as a strong Ophelia found she felt Hamlet should have dared Polonius and forced his way to her, threw them at him.

What do *you* find Ophelia will do, will feel? I believe you cannot fail to sense the central polyphonic torment in the troubled girl, if you say the lines as if you are Ophelia—and hold the *things* (real or imagined), and offer them.

May I ask you please, as you read, to test that now: please feel in your hands the (imagined) loving gifts and precious poems Hamlet gave you. Now offer them,

> My lord, I have remembrances of yours
> That I have longed long to redeliver.
> I pray you now receive them . . .
>
> . . . There, my lord.

Are you not there with her?

Hamlet's polyphony we recognize as most complex. Again, you individually will sense the tones that mix for you now. We wonder: does Hamlet still yearn for this woman to whom he had written love poetry, given rich gifts, almost asked to marry him? Is he at first ready to embrace her? Is his later scorn of her the reverse face of a wounded love? Caused by her apparent rejection of his letters, his visits? Her readiness now to return all his tokens of love? Has he little time for her, his mind recently on suicide, and on his father's ghost? Is he focused on the play he is going to put on to expose his father's murderer? On the horror of life? Does he sense, at some point in the dialogue (usually at "Where is your father?"), the presence of the eavesdroppers for whom Ophelia seems to be a decoy? Does he sense it in her behavior? Is he disgusted with all humanity?—"What should such fellows as I do crawling between earth and heaven?"— He will become so unbridled in his attacks on Ophelia that she will doubt his sanity; is he in fact overreacting to the point of instability? Performing?

We go on, asking, intuiting, being, becoming every character cast, in touch with their objectives, and their characterful *things*. Regardless of gender: men exploring both male and female roles, as they did in Shakespeare's time, women also doubling. So we get to share the gift actors have of knowing deeply Shakespeare's immortal characters.

The Readiness Was All: Ian Charleson and Richard Eyre's *Hamlet*

RICHARD ALLAN DAVISON

UNDER HIS INSPIRED DIRECTION, RICHARD EYRE'S PRODUCTION OF SHAKESPEARE'S *Hamlet* led to the truest Hamlet in my memory, in the short-lived performance by Ian Charleson. I remember more laughter than at many comedies, more tears than at most tragedies. We laughed with Hamlet and at the end even the men in three-piece suits wept openly for him. Here is the context and some key details for those who did not have the good fortune to attend that life-defining performance.

Richard Eyre's production of *Hamlet* opened on the Olivier Stage at the National Theatre on 16 March 1989 to mixed reviews. It was destined to have an unusual run involving three different Hamlets. Daniel Day-Lewis, who had come to rehearse the title roll straight from the rigors of filming *My Left Foot* (for which he was to win an Academy Award), was joined by Judi Dench (Gertrude), John Castle (Claudius) and Michael Bryant (Polonius),[1] along with other first-rate actors. Jeremy Northam understudied Hamlet and played Osric for sixty-five performances. When an emotionally stressed Day-Lewis left the stage about a half-hour into the sixty-sixth performance, Northam (at twenty-seven) immediately took his place and then played the last seven performances of the thirty-two-year-old Day-Lewis's contract. Meanwhile, Ian Charleson (at forty) was in rehearsal to take over the role on 9 October, intending to play it until the end of the National Theatre run. Charleson played Hamlet to great acclaim (with Northam as his Laertes) until he too was forced to leave the production permanently after his performance on 13 November. Northam then not only played Hamlet to the end of the National Theatre run but continued in the role for the Hong Kong tour.

When Charleson left the role he was called "the latest casualty of the jinxed National Theatre production," having "dropped out of the title role recently vacated by Daniel Day-Lewis because of a mystery illness. . . . Two months ago Day-Lewis walked off the stage. . . . Fellow actors said he refused to say why, but was suffering from exhaustion."[2] Another source reported that "behind the sudden exit . . . lies the uncanny story that the actor was seeing the ghost of his own father." He would "go white as the ghost itself. . . . The night he finally quit. . . . he was in tears saying not only was his father on stage with him but was telling him he had done well and not to fret."[3] Day-Lewis left his Hamlet in mid-performance and went back to film acting. Northam fulfilled his commitment to Hamlet and completed those of Day-Lewis and Charleson and is now in the midst of a film career. Charleson played his Hamlet as long as his deteriorating body allowed him and then left acting forever. Evidence suggests that while Day-Lewis's was uneven and Northam's was very good,[4] Ian Charleson's Hamlet was brilliant.

Daniel Day-Lewis's Sixty-five Performances

Daniel Day-Lewis began rehearsals hard upon finishing *My Left Foot*, still exhausted from the strain of playing a man who had to express powerful emotions and thoughts while almost wholly paralyzed and confined to a wheel chair.[5] Unlike either Northam or Charleson, who had been primarily stage actors, Day-Lewis, during the previous five years, had committed most of his energies to film acting. This stage Hamlet was trial by fire for the son of a celebrated poet and scholar of high artistic standards. It is no wonder that the specter of C. Day-Lewis would remind his son of the unreachable goal of the ideal Hamlet. The strain must have been harrowing. For whatever reasons, while his performance elicited positive responses from some audiences and from a few reviewers, most of the critics had serious reservations. I did not see this performance, but some of those who did said these things:

Kenneth Hurren thought that Day-Lewis "often failed to find either the rhythm or sense in the soliloquies," and gave a performance "to be seen and not heard."[6] Milton Shulman heard "a rather humorless Hamlet that gets marks for effort, sincerity and some promise" and complained that "the soliloquies were taken at a gallop with little evidence that Hamlet while making them was thinking reflectively and painfully."[7] Charles Osborne described Day-Lewis's voice as "rather unctuous . . . amateurish and unreal" and faulted his "tendency to pause in mid-sentence, like a BBC announcer."[8] Christopher Edwards acknowledged that Day-Lewis looked "the part to perfection: slim, romantic, saturnine, with hollow eyes and an air of brooding self-preoccupation," but faulted the delivery of the lines, his "blinking and twitching during Claudius's opening speech," the absence of "authority" in "a voice too light and monochromatic to control or shape the verse," "the soliloquies . . . taken at a headlong rush as if he wanted to get them out of the way . . . [the] spasms of antic madness . . . seem[ingly] merely tacked onto the performance for effect, rather than arising essentially from the character's internal disorder."[9] David Nowlan criticized Day-Lewis for "leaping like a frog when acting mad" and for, apart from the Oedipal moment [his kiss of his mother "full on the lips"] with Gertrude, establishing "contact with no one, not even his friend Horatio, so that his graveside protest that he had loved Ophelia was quite without credibility or purpose."[10] To Jim Hiley, Day-Lewis's invention was "uneven. But 'O, that this too solid flesh' is attacked with neurotic intensity, and subsequent agonies see Day-Lewis twirling about the stage—stomping, then crouching in an adolescent caper. . . . At one point, he tries (unsuccessfully) to tear out his hair."[11] David Nathan noted that, although he "moves a lot and after he kills Polonius he occasionally goes into a kind of spasm when he kicks and punches the air," that "inner tension that slowly builds until it is triggered into an irresistible surge of action is sadly lacking."[12] Jennifer Carrnoy called his performance, at best, "merely naturalistic[;] at worst the great speeches sound like after-dinner recitations. The resonance . . . is entirely missing, and the play becomes very two-dimensional in his hands."[13] *City Limits* pointed to his "Sheer sweetness" in "a performance lacking danger and a sense of expectancy, in need of the injection of energy. Day-Lewis's prince is neither a thinker nor a doer."[14] Jane Edwardes reserves her highest praise for the "brilliantly staged"[15] final duel with Laertes. The exceptions to the mostly negative notices of Day-Lewis's interpretation of Hamlet tend to praise Richard Eyre's direction rather than the actor's rendition. With Charleson in the role the acting and direction came close to perfection.

Ian Charleson in Rehearsal

When Richard Eyre asked Ian Charleson to take over for Daniel Day-Lewis, Charleson was in the glow of such recent stage triumphs as Brick in Tennessee Williams' *Cat on a Hot Tin Roof* and Eddie in Sam Shepard's *Fool For Love*. He was also dying of AIDS. Nevertheless, he threw himself into vigorous rehearsal and still managed to give witty and cheerful interviews. He talked of his as a modern Hamlet and of his plans to emphasize the character's modernity. Behind dark glasses covering the puffiness from a recent "sinus problem," Charleson said that Hamlet should be "cheeky, daring, fascinating."[16] This was the Hamlet that I saw with my wife Milena, my dear friend

Charles Bohner and my younger daughter Annie. But before I give my personal recollections, let me again record the responses of others.

During the rehearsals Charleson and those close to him lived through the physical disfigurements and psychic intensities that elevated Hamlet's torment. Here are the observations of some of those firsthand witnesses.

> When we embarked on rehearsals he was having regular, and immensely painful, acupuncture treatment and, later on, chemotherapy which exhausted and debilitated him. . . . [He] still had a chronic sinus complaint which gave him large swollen bags under his eyes. On bad days it was barely possible to glimpse the face beneath the swelling, a malicious parody of his beauty.[17] (Richard Eyre)

> [During rehearsal in September] his eyes and forehead were very swollen. [During a dinner with Ian after a rehearsal in September] his eyes were bad. They were slits in his head from which it was impossible to see either their color or even the direction of his gaze . . . he could not even see to eat without bending his head almost to his plate. . . . He still believed his facial disfigurement might improve, but even if it didn't, so what. It would do because the rest would be so compelling, so captivating, so energizing, so damn good, that he could walk on stage with bandages around his face for all the difference it would make. . . . He believed so much in what he was doing and why he was doing it.[18] (Kenneth Charleson)

> During rehearsals he was utterly without reserve. . . . There was a deep well of generosity of affection, a largeness of heart, and the only Scottish characteristics that he showed were his doggedness and his persistence.[19] (Richard Eyre)

> I remember him saying at his Dress-Rehearsal, "I bet this is the first time they'll have seen Hamlet played by the Elephant man. Maybe I should put a bag over my head."[20] (Judith Coke)

> "When I walk on stage," he told me before the first night, "all you'll hear is people turning the pages of their programs and saying, 'Who's that? Who's that?'"[21] (Hilton McRae)

> He was not an obvious Hamlet, and possibly too old, but looking back I realize he made a deliberate choice to play the part of a dying man—or, at least, a man in love with death, because he was in a unique position to do so. . . . As he said on another occasion, "I bet I'm the best qualified Hamlet they'll see—I'm not coming back from the bourn, either, and I want to see the truth of it."[22] (Judith Coke)

Ian Charleson in Performance

Finally then, a chronologue of responses to Charleson's Hamlet. Indeed, on the recollections of fellow actors and friends who were firsthand witnesses on his opening night, 9 October 1989, Charleson's sense that he was "the best qualified Hamlet" proved true.

> Walking on stage he would command the house in an effortless way, making the audience feel that everything was all right, that they were in safe hands.[23] (David Rintoul)

> With a tiny inflection, Ian could give a line a thousand innuendos.[24] (Ruby Wax)

> He seemed completely self-possessed. He brought his thoughts and his feelings together and offered them to the audience with clarity, intelligence and grace.[25] (Johanna Kirby)

> His voice had a new and vibrant depth, probably because he could no longer rely on his head voice and reached down for the breadth and resonance.[26] (Di Trevis)

> From the moment of his first entrance and his first line, said in that light but perfectly placed tenor, you knew you were in the presence of a great artist.... I have never felt the spiritual side of Hamlet so strongly.[27] (Peter Eyre)

> Nearly every time he was carrying a book—not in a studious way but in a rebellious way—as if saying "I know that the pen is mightier than the sword."[28] (Catriona Craig)

> With a noble heart and generous spirit he played the part, not with showy pyrotechnics, but with great clarity, simplicity and truth. I don't expect I'll ever see Hamlet so profoundly performed again.[29] (Suzanne Bertish)

> The revelation of the Charleson Hamlet was to show what he would have been like at university, bright and outrageously witty. It was obvious what a marvelously sympathetic friend he could have been and how easily Ophelia must have fallen for him.... It is not often, despite the plot, that Hamlet's intelligence is quite credible. Ian had a strong cast around him but he out thought them all.[30] (Richard Eyre)

Assessments from the professional critics and reviewers testify that the above observations from friends and fellow actors were grounded in solid truths beneath the deeply felt sentiments. For these observers were especially receptive to the transcendent integrity in the Charleson Hamlet.

> This is an audience-friendly Hamlet, a civilised, mature, witty and eminently decent prince with whom one would willingly discuss architecture. . . . Mr. Charleson gives us the reasonable man surrounded by unreasonableness, the civilised human plunged into barbaric nightmare.
> A buoyant "To be. . . . be" epitomizes his virtues. Every hypothesis, discussion and turn of the argument is clearly thought out and conveyed. . . . For humour, anger and intelligence, it is one of the best all-round Hamlets going.[31] (Martin Hoyle)

> Looking oddly like a young Claude Rains Charleson seizes on the wit of the character, developing the necessary gravitas almost by sleight of hand. He is a warm and generous prince who enters the play as if he really hasn't read the end of it. He suffers the slings and arrows of outrageous fortune with rare grace but the fury, when it comes—as with his grief over Ophelia—is strong and true.[32] (Paul Ryan)

> An experienced Shakespearean who is completely at home with iambic pentameter . . . Charleson sees the Prince as a man sunk in rampant melancholia, introspective, detached from Ophelia, his mother and Horatio, though lightened by flashes of sardonic humor. Inky black and hung-dog in the first scene his voice breaks on 'break my heart' and from then Charleson's Prince goes darkly, painfully through the attempts to revenge, always suggesting the struggle that drags him down. The "To be . . . be" becomes a speech which almost halts at the words "To sleep" and "to dream." This Hamlet promises great revengeful things but his voice and demeanour suggest he will never rise to them and his antic disposition is like a dry run for a nervous breakdown.[33] (Nicholas de Jongh)

> When you recast a production you conduct a brand new experiment. Actor and director are like chemical elements: change one of them and you change the reactions of both. . . . In the eight months since the production opened the actors have settled into their roles with increasing confidence. Michael Bryant's marvelous Polonius . . . has now grown into the most searching reading of this character I've ever seen. John Castle's Claudius has gained immensely in authority and stature; he has acquired a sullen, sinister gravity and a natural sense of command. Sylvia Sims replaces Judi Dench as Gertrude: a gentle, languorous woman, gracious but not very clever. . . .
> These shining performances revolve like planets around . . . Ian Charleson. . . . Technically he deploys clarity combined with a powerful dramatic drive. His delivery is steely but delicate; the words move with sinuous elegance and crackle with fire. This is a princely Hamlet, every inch the king he should have been. . . . Charleson makes no concessions

to dreamy, distraught romanticism.... He oozes intelligence from every pore: a restless inquisitive rationalist.... He has a natural alertness, which helps him to hear the silent sub-text of people's conversation: an essential intuition which cracks the coded language of the court....

The performance is laced and spiced by a dry, tough, often self-mocking wit. Charleson's Hamlet can afford to laugh grimly at himself because he has the natural, regal confidence of a man ... perfectly at home with himself; it is the world that is out of joint. ... Charleson's Hamlet ... is a brilliant exercise in mature judgment: his somber self-knowledge forms the true substance of his tragedy, and it enables us both to be moved by the experience and to judge it. ... The way ... Charleson can transform a production is a reminder that ... directors can only draw a performance from those who have one in them.[34] (John Peter)

Personal Memories from 3 November 1989[35]

I didn't recognize the name of Ian Charleson when the National Theatre announced that he was replacing Day-Lewis in the title role of *Hamlet*. I had taken my class to Richard Eyre's superb production with Day-Lewis's understudy Jeremy Northam performing Hamlet, as he did throughout the two-week interim while Charleson rehearsed with a new Gertrude (Judi Dench had left to do *The Cherry Orchard*) as well as a new Laertes and Osric.

I anticipated a repeat of one of the two or three best productions of *Hamlet* I had seen since my first by the Canadian Players in 1957. Everything from the staging to the set design and costumes had prompted a return visit. Even had I not desired to share the exhilaration with my family and friend, I still would have seen it again. Eyre's first two scenes had proved apt microcosms of the whole. The darkened, bare stage showcased the slowly revolving, armed and helmeted statue, looming over the shivering sentries whose defensive, hissed exchanges pierced the foggy night. The transition to a glowing courtroom showed off the colorfully costumed Claudius and Gertrude[36] who danced their entrance amid a shower of gold confetti coins into a room of wooden walls richly inlaid with scenes of ancient battles.

My return to *Hamlet* at the Olivier Theatre was only in part prompted by my thirteen-year-old daughter Annie who, having been delighted by both the National Theatre Student Day productions of Tom Stoppard's fifteen-minute and two-minute *Hamlet*, asked me to take her to the "fuller" version. In our fourth-row seats of a full house as the lights dimmed, we were enveloped by the nervous apprehension on the foggy battlements of Elsinore Castle, then caught by the gigantic statue of Hamlet's father who, in full armor, would quietly preside over so many scenes. We anticipated scene 2 and that spot of gloom carried over from scene 1 in the person of the mourning Prince in black set amid the brightly lighted and richly costumed courtiers, dominated by a loquaciously sinister Claudius. We waited for Hamlet, solitary in the crowd of sycophantic celebrants. Jeremy Northam's handsome face and athletic figure were foremost in my mind. What we saw was a slight, wraith-like figure with a distorted face, one eye half shut and the other reduced to a swollen blur.

Why cast such a physically disfigured actor? This was Annie's first full-length *Hamlet,* and he would be with us for almost four hours! But Charleson opened his mouth, and with his first words he was the real thing. He had us. Every body movement and every vocal nuance rang true, from his quiet "A little more than kin and less than kind" to his frantic jottings in a little notebook, his "one may smile, and smile, and be a villain," to "the rest is silence" and his collapse in Horatio's arms. When the soldiers laid his frail body gently at the feet of the statue of his father as a sacrifice to the gods of war and vengeance, the image was heartbreaking.

This was Friday 3 November 1989. Flu kept Charleson off the stage for a couple of performances, but he returned ten days later for what was to be his last performance of Hamlet or of any other role. Ian McKellen was in the audience. The next night, McKellen, while accepting the *Evening Standard* award for best actor for his outstanding portrayal of Iago in Trevor Nunn's RSC *Othello,* announced that he had seen "the perfect Hamlet" the night before—that not he but Ian Charleson was truly the best actor of 1989. Watching the awards on TV, I stood up in my living room and cheered, without realizing the tragic irony of McKellen's tribute.

Not until we had returned to the United States in early January, when a colleague reminded me of what I should have remembered, did I realize that Charleson was the courageous and quietly charismatic Scot in *Chariots of Fire.* Of course! But my memory of his ruggedly angelic film presence hadn't connected with the actor on the Olivier Theatre stage—unrecognizable even from row four.

I immediately rented the video of *Chariots of Fire,* to the delight of Annie. She had seen thirty plays in London with some of the best actors in the world, including Dustin Hoffman, Albert Finney, and Paul Scofield, but "Ian" was her hero. We were moved together at the film's end when the victorious Scot was carried off in triumph. Housman came to mind: "Man and boy stood cheering by, / And home we brought you shoulder-high. / To-day, the road all runners come / Shoulder-high we bring you home." That night we read Ian Charleson's obituary in the *New York Times,* and in a terrible shock of recognition it all made tragic sense: the dramatic weight loss, the infection-ravaged face—they were the devastating side effects of AIDS. But most of all, we recognized the beauty born of pain and adversity, the courage of a man who had taken on what may be the most mentally and physically demanding role in theater, a role Ian Charleson accepted when he knew he was dying! So many lines in the play about accommodation to death resonated with more relevance, perhaps, than ever before.

So I was left with indelible images from the performance. Charleson's slender, black-clad body was electric, a quivering island of protest in a courtly throng that had bowed en masse to the incest of monarchs; Charleson's first soliloquy spat fury and frustration. His deep affection for Horatio, shown in their first warm embrace (after a wonderful doubletake before "Horatio—or I do forget myself") reinforced his isolation. His reluctant dismissal of Ophelia showed a lover submerging his burning heart in a sea of duty and revenge. Hamlet's feigned madness was intensified by Charleson's drooping sock and dangling doublet. While Day-Lewis and Northam played the role clean shaven, Charleson's short beard, covering only part of his ravaged face, framed a swollen forehead and puffy eyes. The black volume Charleson carried with him and the commonplace book hung around his neck added weight to his "Words, words, words," in answer to Polonius' question about what he was reading, an answer that kept the wily politician off balance in his attempt to detect the cause of Hamlet's apparent madness. The mock alarm in his "Between who" response to Polonius' follow-up question "What's the matter?" brought outbursts of laughter from the audience. At the start of the play-within-the-play scene Charleson lounged comfortably on the King's throne until Claudius' and Gertrude's entrance, whereupon with a frisky jump he pulled Horatio down next to him on the stage to watch the King watch the play. Charleson's playful taunting of Rosencrantz and Guildenstern in the piping scene that followed the King's hasty exit rose to a crescendo of denunciation. He first signaled the lingering players to stop piping, took the recorder from one of them and gave it to Guildenstern. On "'Sblood" he snatched it back and directed the rest of the denunciation first at the tall Guildenstern, then at the short Rosencrantz. In the closet scene Charleson capped his anger toward Gertrude by tenderly kissing his mother's hand on "So again goodnight." Charleson's retreat to the pedestal of the statue of his father, when Rosencrantz and Guildenstern pursued him after he stabbed Polonius, was timed perfectly, as he then leaped down with startling alacrity and fled this uncertain sanctuary. During scenes of high tension Charleson repeatedly injected perfectly timed moments of comic relief. Threatened by the King in his demand to know the location of Polonius' body, on "Come, for England," he impulsively kissed Claudius on the lips—a kiss which proved to be a sentence of death. His spirited account of his adventure with the pirates in Act 5 was tempered by his concern over Horatio's troubled reaction to his deadly treatment of betrayal: "So Guildenstern and Rosencrantz go to't." In the graveyard scene on "Make her laugh at that," he threw the skull to Horatio who (on the night we were there) caught it handily. For the fencing match Charleson replaced his disheveled clothing with a strikingly different outfit appropriate to his new self-confidence. The melancholy and madness (feigned or otherwise) disappeared with his old apparel. The new well-fitting black leather vest over a white shirt, the smart black breeches neatly tucked into calf-high black boots and the black gauntlet on his fencing hand perfectly reflected the new man. His apology for the deaths of Polonius and Ophelia momentarily disarmed the volatile Laertes. After rosin was sprinkled on the floor, they fenced before the paneled doors against which sat (as they had during the play within the play) the royal thrones side by side. During pauses in the match, the seated King and Queen were framed by the profiled, dueling silhouettes of Hamlet and Laertes. They fought a thrilling fight with vigor and conviction in such an expert way that the frail Charleson's victory over the sturdy Northam was compelling. Wounded, he turned and out-muscled Laertes, seizing his poisoned sword and forcing him against a table before stabbing him. He rushed Claudius, cut his neck and pounced, forced the wine cup between his teeth and, despite Claudius' frantic struggles, poured the deadly potion down his throat. Drawing on his last reserve of strength as the poison flowed through his own body, in an adrenalin-charged movement Charleson knocked the deadly cup from the hand of Horatio (who had crossed the stage to join him in death) and slid slowly, feebly down the wall covered with the friezes of ancient battle scenes to a sitting position on the floor. He died cradled in Horatio's arms with the laughter of self-knowledge on his lips. Charleson's accommodation to death in Hamlet blended humor, pathos, and determination.

A year after his son's last performance (in response to my brief tribute kindly passed on to him by Ian McKellen) I received a letter from Ian Charleson's father. "By a coincidence my wife and I were at that performance too. . . . I remember thinking to myself when he came on the scene at first, 'Ian you're never going to get away with this,' and then gradually like the rest of the audience forgetting his face and becoming lost in the magic of his talent."[37]

We happy few who saw Ian Charleson and the company of Richard Eyre's *Hamlet* carry with us a standard of excellence for all the *Hamlets* to come.

Notes

My thanks to Jay Halio for urging me to write about the Eyre *Hamlet*. Parts of this article appeared in different forms in *Shakespeare Bulletin* and *Playbill*. See "A Tribute to Ian Charleson," *Shakespeare Bulletin* 8.2 (1990): 33; "Ian Charleson: The Perfect Hamlet," *Playbill* 91.2 (1991): 20.

1. I heartily agree with the critics who praised Michael Bryant's classic, perhaps definitive Polonius, having seen it twice with Northam's Hamlet and once with Charleson's. Bryant's Polonius deserves a full article in its own right. John Peter's view (see John Peter, "A Hamlet Who Would be King at Elsinore," *London Times*, 12 November 1989, sec. c, p. 9.) that Bryant's Polonius had "grown into the most searching reading of this character I've ever seen" supports other critics' earlier assessments:

> Instead of a boring old dodderer, Mr. Bryant gives us a self-important chamberlain with a habit of blurting out blunt truths "Your son is mad" which he then proceeds to qualify. . . . [T]he single most moving moment in the whole evening is also Mr. Bryant's touch of aphasia as he sets Reynoldo to spy on his son: instead of a cheap laugh, we get a sudden chilling glimpse of a public official facing the reality of old age. (Michael Billington, "Prince Charming," 1989. Unpaginated clipping in National Theatre Archives scrapbook. This and many of the following items are from a scrapbook of clippings about Richard Eyre's *Hamlet*. For some, the citations were incomplete).

> "Michael Bryant's superb performance: a worthy old man stricken with aphasia." (Gerard Van Werson, *The Stage*, 9 November, 1989. Unpaginated clipping in National Theatre Archives scrapbook).

> Michael Bryant's Polonius. . . . Inordinately fond of his son and coldly indifferent to his daughter, Polonius is a sharp witted authoritarian counsellor, tactless and brusque to his considerably less astute employer, who is having to come to terms with the fallibility of old age. (Christopher Edwards, *The Spectator*, 25 March 1989, 38).

> Michael Bryant's Polonius was valuable in the amount of texture and subtlety he was able to find between the lines. Pauses become meaningful, expertly drawn into stories of their own. His bitter aggressive closing down of possibilities enacted the brutality of the patriarchial order. (Dominic Gray, *What's On*, 29 March 1989. Unpaginated clipping in National Theatre Archives scrapbook).

Michael Bryant is one of those rare actors' actors. Every performance I have seen by him has been inventive, intelligent and unequivocally believable.

2. "Hamlet Jinx Hits Chariot's Ian Charleson," *Daily Express*, 8 December 1989. Unpaginated clipping in National Theatre Archives scrapbook.

3. *Today*, 23 October 1989. Untitled and unpaginated clipping in National Theatre Archives scrapbook.

4. An athletically trim but sturdy six-footer with superb control of his body, Jeremy Northam was certainly a better Hamlet physically than either Charleson or Day-Lewis. I have read no reviews of his Hamlet, as he had no opening night in the role. The two of his Hamlet performances I saw, one when he was filling in between Day-Lewis and Charleson, the other when he took over after Charleson's departure (with fourteen performances left), were both very convincing. Considering the pressures that were also on him, it is remarkable how good he was.

His fellow actors speak very highly of his courage and his talents. Judith Coke recalls that

> He never knew from day to day, whether it would be Laertes or Hamlet that night. It depended on Ian's strength and will power, but sometimes Jeremy didn't know if he was going to be Hamlet that night till he stepped through the door at the half. His temperament was wonderful, and his commitment and unselfishness, total. (Judith Coke, letter to author, December 1995).

Northam talked to my class (on 11 November 1989) very articulately about the play and production without saying a word about the unforeseen burdens that had been placed upon him. I would very much like to see his own Hamlet without the considerable restraints put on an understudy or a temporary replacement.

5. Day-Lewis's performance involved spasmatic movements of his character Christy Brown, who had suffered from cerebral palsy from birth. Appropriately, however coincidentally, Day Lewis's Christy Brown achieved his first big adult breakthrough as he painstakingly learned to communicate verbally by memorizing and reciting aloud Hamlet's "To be or not to be" soliloquy.

6. Kenneth Hurren. Undated clipping in National Theatre Archives scrapbook.
7. Milton Shulman. Undated clipping in National Theatre Archives scrapbook.
8. Charles Osborne. Undated clipping in National Theatre Archives scrapbook.
9. Christopher Edwards, *The Spectator*, 25 March 1989, 38.
10. David Nowlan, *The Irish Times*. Undated clipping in National Theatre Archives scrapbook.
11. Jim Hiley, *The Listener*, 30 March 1989, 32.
12. David Nathan, "Theatre." Undated clipping in National Theatre Archives scrapbook.
13. Jennifer Carrnoy, "Stage and Screen Review," *London Weekly Diary*, 10 April 1989. Unpaginated clipping in National Theatre Archives scrapbook.
14. *City Limits*. Unsigned and undated clipping in National Theatre Archives scrapbook.
15. Jane Edwardes, "Preview Theatre," *Time Out* (London). Undated clipping in National Theatre Archives scrapbook.
16. Dominic Gray, "Neither a Borrower Nor a Lender Be," *What's On* (London) 10 October 1989, 14.
17. Richard Eyre, "The Rest is Silence," *Manchester Guardian Weekly*, 21 January 1990.
18. Kenneth Charleson, *For Ian Charleson: A Tribute* (London: Constable, 1990), 112, 116–17.
19. Richard Eyre, "Silence."
20. Coke, letter.
21. Hilton McRae, *Ian Charleson*, 19.
22. Coke, letter.
23. David Rintoul, *Ian Charleson*, 50.
24. Ruby Wax, *Ian Charleson*, 58.

25. Johanna Kirby, *Ian Charleson*, 77.
26. Di Trevis, *Ian Charleson*, 31.
27. Peter Eyre, *Ian Charleson*, 83.
28. Catriona Craig, *Ian Charleson*, 101.
29. Suzanne Bertish, *Ian Charleson*, 105.
30. Richard Eyre, "Silence."
31. Martin Hoyle, *Financial Times*, 20 [October?] 1989. Unpaginated clipping in National Theatre Archives scrapbook.
32. Paul Ryan, *What's On* (London), 28 October 1989, 42.
33. Nicholas de Jongh, *The Guardian*, 20 October 1989. Unpaginated clipping in National Theatre Archives scrapbook.
34. John Peter, "Elsinore."
35. It is a truism that (unlike film performances) each stage performance is unique, never to be repeated, never to be recaptured wholly. Only 1000 or so people attended the 3 November 1989 *Hamlet*. For the details in this section I draw upon the memories of four of those audience members: my own, my wife's and daughter's, and that of Ian Charleson's father.
36. Michael Ratcliffe nicely captured the look of the costumes: "Liz da Costa dresses the king and queen in gorgeous abstract patterned velvets and the entire court in Renaissance clothes, varied along the way by leaps to the years on either side of 1800: jackets suggesting Sheridan, high waistlines from Austen and *Vanity Fair*. Poor Gertrude looks like Mrs. Bennett." See Michael Ratcliffe, 1989. Unpaginated clipping in National Theatre Archives scrapbook.
37. Jack Charleson, letter to author, 14 August 1990.

Stoppard's *Rosencrantz and Guildenstern Are Dead:* The Film

H. R. Coursen

Guildenstern: There's something they're not telling us.
Rosencrantz: What?

With all the new films appearing in 1995 and 1996, Stoppard's elegant production of 1991 is likely to be forgotten—assuming that it hasn't been already. It is an "offshoot," of course, as Ruby Cohn would call it,[1] but it interrogates an older play and, in fact, lives symbiotically within the world of the prior script. Films like this, as Douglas Lanier suggests, stage "contests . . . between historicity and contemporaneity, between theater and film [and thus] form a crucial and tacit context with which more conventional Shakespeare films are necessarily engaged."[2]

It may have been assumed that the film follows the stage play closely, but it does not. The film abandons the "waiting for Godot within the framework of another play" premises of the original and conducts instead a complicated analysis of the relationship between art and life. More than most plays that become films, this film establishes its independence of the stage, ironically by using film as a means of interrogating theater, showing how varied and ungraspable a medium theater is. The film demonstrates what the larger play, *Hamlet,* does—that live theater and "real life" interact with each other, that is, assuming that each is functioning within the dramatic continuum. It does so with highly sophisticated techniques that at once "frame" the action and erase the frames, forcing us to question what it is we thought we observed. The film is "free" of stage, free to do the things that film can do, yet it is always running into or becoming a stage or a theater. The film is a commentary on the differences between film and stage and a game played on the borders of the two media. Those "sidelined" characters, Rosencrantz and Guildenstern, find either that they are pulled into the game or that the game spills over and engulfs them.

Elizabeth Wheeler suggests that "the homage to Beckett did not survive the transition" from stage to screen play.[3] Indeed, the concepts of Herbert Marcuse seem to be the genesis of the film:

> Insomuch as man and nature are constituted by an unfree society, their repressed and distorted potentialities can be represented only in an *estranging* form. . . . Art breaks open a dimension inaccessible to other experience, a dimension in which human beings, nature and things no longer stand under the law of the established reality principle. . . . The encounter with the truth of art happens in the estranging languages and images which make perceptible, visible and audible that which is no longer, or not yet perceived, said and heard in everyday life.[4]

Rosencrantz, a great observer in the film, spots a gold coin as the two ride though a chalky mountain range—the "place without any visible character" for which the stage directions of the play call. The game of heads continues until probability is itself challenged. One of the options that Guildenstern offers for discussion is "probability is not operating as a factor." Having made camp in a stick-thin, late-autumn woods, they suddenly recall that they "were sent for" and ride off. They encounter the Players' wagon and are treated to a sampling of the Players' quality, including "rape and rapier," in which the transvestite boy, miming sexual activity, holds off a second attacker with a sword. They stand on the stage in front of the canvas backdrop, looking out at their horses, a bored audience that has been stopped "without a farmhouse near." They hear the cries of a woman. Through a curtain comes Ophelia, Hamlet pursuing. The curtain falls over two objects. They are Rosencrantz and Guildenstern, of course. They disentangle and walk into the great hall of Elsinore, trailing paper from the Players' chest—music and pages from old plays. Almost immediately they are greeted by Claudius and Gertrude.

They begin to move *toward* the estranging form on the way to Elsinore. The coin keeps coming up heads. As they leave the wagon, they collide with an estranging art form known as *Hamlet,* a form controlled by the Players. The Players, though, exist only in the eyes of people. Except for the Player and the tranvestite boy, we see them only as pushers of the wagon or as characters in play or mime. They cannot always control their audience, of course, or their own medium. After a portion of the Nunnery scene breaks literally through the Players' rehearsal of "Gonzago"—everyone pauses to bow to Claudius, who pays no attention as he says "He shall with speed to England"—the Player moves back to the stage to complain that "it doesn't seem to be coming. You're not getting it at all." Like

Claudius, the Players are at least trying to reassert control, a quality from which Rosencrantz and Guildenstern are estranged. Guildenstern keeps trying to regain the illusion of control. Rosencrantz is interested in what's going on in this zone of freedom from everyday life, this place dominated by the half-heard play that neither of them knows. It is Guildenstern, though, who wants to find out. His problem is that much of what he does hear is intended as nonsense, like Hamlet, in his antic disposition, talking to Polonius, or later insisting that Polonius agree about the shape of the cloud. Furthermore, as Sheidley says, "the assumptions about identity, causation, memory, and will underlying [some of the basic causative premises of the plot] have been called into question."[5] The only ghost here is the sheeted Halloween spook the Players conjure up as part of their initial sampling of possibilities. What happens to Rosencrantz and Guildernstern will occur within the continuum between art and life and not in any zone partaking of the supernatural.

Stoppard's play serves its ur-play by showing how Shakespeare develops an existential meaninglessness for two very minor characters. The film serves *Hamlet* in a very different way, by calling attention to the source play's analysis of art and life, of theater and the realities residing in an audience. In other words, the film moves back towards the source play and its archetypes instead of narrowing the meanings of *Hamlet* into the zone of "Shakespeare Our Contemporary." Perhaps the best illustration of the film's larger dimension is the actual "Gonzago" sequence. The murderer becomes "uncle to the prince," who is Lucianus. The film accepts the Hamlet-Lucianus conflation that Hamlet makes at "Gonzago." "Lucianus has a plan to catch the conscience of the king," the Player informs Rosencrantz and Guildenstern. "Gonzago" takes a step into the infinite regress of fictional formats. It is a puppet show, mimed for the masked player King and Queen. As the show imports its meaning to this fictional audience, the masks give way. An unmasked Claudius stands, Ophelia notices that "The King rises," Hamlet delights in this frighting "with false fire," Polonius commands unnecessarily that the play be given "o're," and Donald Sumpter's Claudius furiously demands light and stalks out, toppling the furniture as he goes. The camera catches the actors—not the puppet show—on stage, the murderer removing his mask. The audience explodes outward. Rosencrantz says, "It wasn't *that* bad." Levels of unreality move outward and wash backward to erase other levels of unreality, including that of *Hamlet,* until several inner plays—puppet show, mime, and *Hamlet*— deliver us to Stoppard's play and Rosencrantz missing the point of everything we have seen. He cannot get the point, of course, because he doesn't know the play in which he is a character. He inhabits another plane of unreality and can respond to what happens in *Hamlet* only by confusing a human reaction to a version of "this is your life, Claudius, King of Denmark" with an aesthetic response. As Sheidley says, the two seem to be implicated in "fragments of obscure texts from an ancient civilization, lacking a frame of reference to explain them."[6]

The film situates Rosencrantz and Guildenstern in a kind of limbo where neither can *use* his "head." They are impelled forward within a zone where no alternatives exist. The Player calls "heads" in his wager with them. They don't even bother to check the coin. It has come up tails, and "fictional time has started moving."[7] As of that moment, they have fallen into the Player's rules of probability and, specifically, into the baffling world of *Hamlet*. This is a scripted version of "unfree society," where probability is not suspended but reversed along the threshold beween what is "on stage" and what is "real." "We do onstage the things that are supposed to happen off," says the Player, "which is a kind of integrity if you look on every exit as an entrance somewhere else." The film studies exits and entrances, pulling us "backstage with the two minor characters," as Stoppard's play had done, even as *Hamlet* continues somewhere before an audience we imagine in an imaginary theater, *or* as *Hamlet* continues as a "reality" occurring within our suspension of disbelief. The two characters cannot control their entrance into the framing play or their exit from it. As Rosencrantz lets go of a rope holding a dumbwaiter, he and Guildenstern tumble down a story. Hamlet opens the door below and closes it as Rosencrantz says, "My lord!" After Rosencrantz has startled Polonius, getting the latter stabbed, the darkness behind the arras becomes the night of the voyage to England.

Time hurtles forward along the scheme of *Hamlet,* yet it has already happened. The deaths of the two characters have been mimed in a play that Guildenstern does not recognize. In the mime, Polonius is killed after the audience in a barn warns the Player that someone is behind him. Ophelia drowns, twisting away behind a blue scrim. A shipwreck rolls Hamlet back to a duel in Elsinore. The Player insists that eight people have died. Guildenstern insists that it has only been six. Two bewildered figures had wandered into the play after Rosencrantz and Guildernstern had inadvertently looked out from a backstage portal, to the audience's amusement. The Player points back to the stage where those figures mime being hanged. It has been eight. It is their "real" world—but the play, as Sheidley says, is already "*in* [the Player's] repertoire."[8] Hamlet himself, then, is also a character within a fiction that dictates every word he speaks, his life and his death. If Rosencrantz and Guildenstern are victims of the play in which they have their being, so is the character who gives his name to that fiction. That is their "justice," although they merely add to the body count at the end of the outer play.

"Audiences know what to expect and that is all they are prepared to believe in," says the Player. The film presses those limits, makes them elastic. Audiences do not create the fictions, but they accept the conventional fictions already created. Drama, then, is a recycling of stereotype and banality. The Players have just done *Hamlet* and made it a farce composed of totally expected actions in which spectators don't believe and with which they interfere. They are prepared to laugh at what they already know, so that there's a kind of epic degeneration at work. But neither of the minor characters wandering around within this knowing world can intervene on their own behalf. Both Guildenstern and Rosencrantz seek meaningful closure. The latter asks the Player, "Wasn't that the ending?" The Player chides him: "there's a design at work in all art. . . . It aims for a point when everyone who is marked for death, dies. . . . It is written." They view their mimed death, not recognizing that, as they participate in it, *Hamlet* is already written. They are actors trying to be real people, but as the Player says, "The simple assumption that makes our existence bearable [is] that somebody is watching. We are the opposite of people. We are actors." Actors know they are in a play and they know that "Blood is compulsory." Rosencrantz and Guildenstern attempt to escape their roles, of course, and so fulfill them. But the lines written for them come *to* them only in a sequence that denies them any control over what finally happens to them.

As Hamlet and Claudius vie to assert their contradictory interpretations on Elsinore, Rosencrantz experiences events that "disrupt authorised accounts of contemporary reality," a quality that Kiernan Ryan attributes to Shakespearean comedy.[9] The film addresses the question of art itself and its relationship to other modes of representation, even that of nature itself, as Rosencrantz brilliantly but fruitlessly experiments with it. His discoveries include gravity, a principle of harmonics, a principle of acceleration, hydraulics, the aerodynamic application of Bernoulli's Principle, steam power, the laws of equal and opposite reaction and of conservation of energy, and aspects of vector theory and convection. In addition, he sets a "new record," as he says of the coin, after seventy-eight tosses have come up heads ("seventy-eight"—a nice pun on "old records"), of forty-two seconds for keeping a paper plane in the air, shattering the old Guinness World Record of 18.80 held by Ken Blackburn.[10] He is finding meanings a century before Newton, but is a mute, inglorious

Newton, because as Wheeler says, "perception both on an individual and a societal level is necessary for awareness of significance."[11] Since no perception occurs, there is no "reality" either. It is not that perception *is* reality, but that reality, to be "real," must be perceived. Furthermore, as Bohr and Heisenberg have shown us, observation changes what is observed, physically and in translation into language and replicatable modes. Here what is observed drops into time to be reobserved into a new physics. In a sense nature is like the Shakespeare script—the "meanings" are there but the circumstances required for their formulation have not yet occurred. Rosencrantz, even as he demolishes Aristotelian physics in a way that would have pleased Thomas Kuhn, cannot bring his insights to completion. Rosencrantz' discoveries prove that probability *is* functioning within this world, but it emerges from a paradigm yet to be defined. Rosencrantz is *half*-fulfilling the prescription provided by Leo Braudy for the generic Shakespeare film: they "concentrate not on the reality of a society or the reality of the past, but on the individual's perception of those superhuman orders and what they mean."[12]

Ryan suggests that "One of the deepest pleasures of Shakespearean comedy comes from its disclosure of space and time we never knew we had."[13] Rosencrantz constantly explores that space but needs a confirmatory eye. He is potentially that person without an investment in the established system of belief who might engender a paradigm shift.[14] The academically "brighter" Guildenstern is trapped in his own paradigms, trying to move from "the known" to the unknown. He is a shadow of Claudius and Polonius in the outer—or inner—play. Guildenstern is a logical empiricist who erases all modes of learning anything in his rejection of what he considers irrelevant. He crushes Rosencrantz' biplane, like the infant in Hawthorne's "The Artist of the Beautiful," who destroys Warland's butterfly and leaves only "a small heap of glittering fragments, whence the beauty had fled forever."[15]

Finally, Rosencrantz attempts to retreat from all observation, that is, to estrange himself from his estrangement from any meaningful action. If he jumps overboard from the ship bound for England, he will "put a spoke in their wheel"—the unnamed "they" who control events. But what if his jumping overboard is in the plan? as Guildenstern asks. He will stay on the boat, Rosencrantz responds. He stoppers his eyes and ears and so sleeps through the pirate attack. He wakes up and takes off his eye-mask just as the figurehead of the pirate ship slides over him. It looks exactly like Kate Winslet, but as to embrace it he inclines, it slides away. He sees Hamlet for an instant above the figurehead before Hamlet is covered by a canvas sail, the same veil between fiction and reality the Players have on their wagon. At the end, as the wagon moves away, we see a ship's wheel tied to its back—a prop in an illusion created by the Players for Rosencrantz and Guildenstern.

The film emerges from questions about art, as opposed to existential considerations, and is *framed* to give closure, as opposed to leaving questions drifting over the theater at the end of a live performance. The film eliminates the Player's complaint about the man about to be executed, who kept crying and ruined the play of which he was a part, or Rosencrantz' about how dull the voyage is an instant before the pirates attack, or Guildenstern's about moving "idly toward eternity, without possibility of reprieve or hope of explanation." The film incorporates its Beckett and its Brecht, but it does much more. Discourse and disquisition become demonstration. The play becomes a film, visualizing what is discussed in the play. In the film, meanings hover around things—like the Players's manuscript chest, where Rosencrantz and Guildenstern wait to die again, perhaps only to be mimed before a jeering row of peasants.

Film is a more closed art form than theater. This one ends almost where it begins, circling back to beginnings to ask whether anything *did* begin. The wagon from which they stepped to the throne room of Elsinore rumbles off through the stick-thin woods in the same direction it had been going when they first encountered it. It is a moment after the initial encounter—but it never occurred. The wagon never stopped. It has all been an instant within the mind of someone—the Player? Some playwright we never see? It has been one of those ideas that flicker through a writer's mind and either go unrecognized or are dismissed like dreams at dawn, or are as irrelevant as the fingernails and hair that continue to grow after death, as Guildenstern points out. They retain that non-meaning. They require *Hamlet* to be perceived. *Hamlet* occurred only insofar as it included them. In important ways, however, in *explaining* the way in which they were included, for example, *Hamlet* did not include them.

Continuing to seek "rational" closure, Guildenstern complains on shipboard that they are "still finally to be denied an explanation." He rebels and plunges a knife into the Player's belly. *"That's* death!" he says. But it isn't. The knife is a prop. Or, if it is death, it is "the kind you *do* believe in," says the Player. "It is what is expected." They have become, one last time, an audience looking through a frame—this time the entrance to the hold of the ship into which the Player has fallen in a "merely competent" simulation of death, good enough to make Rosencrantz and Guildenstern believe in it, good enough to convince the latter that he has been an agent, not just a straight man in someone else's comedy.

Since the Player also plays the English King (who also, then, escapes Guildenstern's collapsing blade), he at once announces that politics is a kind of play-acting and that those who get on the wrong side of politics discover that even play-acting can deal out fatal consequences. The hanging of Rosencrantz and Guildenstern is to be "real" as compared to the death the Player has just feigned. But as the cart moves off we realize that Rosencrantz and Guildenstern have been executed for removing what keeps the Players alive—an audience. This is an extreme example of a fiction reaching out to touch its spectators, in this case with the scratch of a heavy rope around each neck, to be followed by the latent half-life, fictional fingernails growing, they have in the Players' manuscript chest. If the hangings *do* occur, they are summary executions for the desertion of which the Player accuses the two once they all meet again at Elsinore. That meeting does not occur, but is a function of the imaginations of Rosencrantz and Guildenstern during the time between the noose and the drop, as in "An Occurrence at Owl Creek Bridge."

Even the location of their execution shifts, although they do not notice it. The two are at first strung up on the yardarm of the ship sailing to England. The film does a montage summary of *Hamlet*—Ophelia drowning, the funeral and Hamlet looking at Yorick, the fatal duel, the poisoned wine and Hamlet's forcing it on Claudius—then returns to them in their nooses. The Player talks of "the deaths of kings and princes . . . and nobodies." The ropes are now back in the woods where Rosencrantz and Guildenstern had met the players. They never got out of the woods. The Ambassador arrives at Elsinore to pick up the empty chalice and tell a pile of bodies "that Rosencrantz and Guildenstern are dead." The event has already happened, of course. The Ambassador's is a line from an old play. But here, *after* the announcement, the nooses twang. The embedded execution awaits another performance of *Hamlet*. It doesn't matter whether that Ambassador's report comes before or after the event itself. It will occur. The timing of their execution—making them footnotes, as it were, to the ending—repeats that of the mime that they witnessed earlier, but in neither case do they recognize that it is *they* who make up eight. They never do understand that they are a fragment of the closure of *Hamlet*.

The wagon plies out of the woods and goes up the road along the chalky cliff-face of the "place without any visible character." Another level of the same road lies below. Its movement recreates a scene from Elsinore in which characters ran along an upper corridor above a lower one. "This place is a madhouse," Rosencrantz had remarked earlier, observing from the courtyard. Now the madness, momentarily released, has been put back in the wagon, back in the script chest. It is a magic wagon where *Hamlet* is locked up to reappear later at another place at another time, the same play with different meanings, different ways of being misunderstood—even if the end is always the same, that Rosencrantz and Guildenstern are dead. That is, unless they are lucky or unlucky enough to encounter a director, like Olivier, who erases them in advance.

It has all been a fiction, of course, whether madness or sanity. The film, like some types of madness and all versions of sanity, moves in and out of realities, none of which *is* reality. The question is not poised in the adolescent mode—What is reality?—but, How does art condition reality, transmit it, through various frames ranging from obvious artifice to imitation that comes close to showing whatever truth may be? Truth always involves blood, always death as closure, seldom an explanation. There never was a time when anyone could have said no. Death as *they* understand it, though, can only be fictional, since neither Rosencrantz nor Guildenstern exists.

Rosencrantz' disquisition on being alive or dead in a box comes half-true. Neither state is reached, since their existential bodies have been hanged, but their roles as characters remain inside the wagon on the stage that can be lowered at a moment's notice. They are alive *and* dead. They are inside the play, potentially inside another performance in which they will not recognize the play *this* time either. They are doomed to an endless repetition of the same questions without answers, to the same ending. "Blood," as the Player says, "is mandatory." They are in that script chest, their parts "written," as the Player says, as if the play were a book of fate. They are not dead exactly, but they can come alive only in the radically estranging world known as *Hamlet,* a play they do not know. Guildenstern recognizes "Gonzago," but not that "Gonzago" is a play within a play or that he is within a play, both Shakespeare's and Stoppard's. They can come out of the script box—"Hey you, what's your name, come out of there"—but it is a movement from stasis, suspended animation, into an unfree, scripted society that can only be experienced as estranging. When Hamlet escapes to the pirate ship, Guildenstern complains, "We need Hamlet for our release." What he means is that they "need *Hamlet* for their release." They will not get Hamlet to England, but *Hamlet* will get them to England and provide sudden closure. That closure, though, will occur in only one production. They are trapped in the repetition of the script. There never was a moment when they could have said "No," nor will there be. They will never understand the play in which they are involuntary participants. Nor will we, of course. The existential point rides out, making us much more like them than like Hamlet, who at least motivates much of what it turns out he does not understand either.

The *play,* as Maurice Charney says, shows "a distrust for naturalistic drama . . . constantly breaking the illusion and playing with the audience's expectations."[16] The film does the same thing, but with a camera that cuts quickly from shot to shot, sometimes changing what we expect to see, as in the "Gonzago" sequence. As Sheidley argues, the film is not "a cinematic version of that play, but a different meditation, this time on death and on a new medium, the cinema"; it contains the play, and, of course, much more.[17] The quick camera cuts do what montage *can* do—that is, make the whole much more than just the sum of its parts.

Wheeler claims that Stoppard's reputation will "continue to depend on his plays,"[18] and that may well be. But the splendid film version of *Rosencrantz and Guildenstern Are Dead,* which appeared some twenty-five years after the original stage version at the Edinburgh Festival in 1966, deserves to be a positive element in any assessment of Stoppard's achievement.

Rosencrantz and Guildenstern Are Dead. Brandenberg International Cinecom, 1991. Produced by Michael Brandman and Emanuel Azenberg. Directed by Tom Stoppard. Photography by Peter Biziou. Music by Stanley Myers. Costumes by Andreane Neofitou. Designed by Vaughan Edwards. Puppets by Zlatko Bourek. With Richard Dreyfuss (Player), Gary Oldman (Rosencrantz), Gary Roth (Guildenstern), Iain Glen (Hamlet), Joanna Miles (Gertrude), Donald Sumpter (Claudius). Running time: 118 minutes.

Notes

1. Ruby Cohn, *Modern Shakespearean Offshoots* (Princeton: Princeton University Press, 1976).
2. Douglas Lanier, "Shakespeare in the Age of Cinematic Reproduction: *In the Bleak Midwinter* and *Looking for Richard*" (Unpublished paper, Shakespeare Association of America, Washington, D. C., 1997.)
3. Elizabeth Wheeler, "Light It Up And Move It Around," *Shakespeare on Film Newsletter* 16/1 (December, 1991): 5.
4. Herbert Marcuse, *The Aesthetic Dimension* (London: Andre Deutsch, 1978), 9–10.
5. William E. Sheidley, "The Play(s) within the Film: Tom Stoppard's *Rosencrantz & Guildenstern Are Dead,*" in *Screen Shakespeare,* ed. Michael Skovmand (Aarhus, Denmark: Aarhus University Press, 1994), 102.

6. Ibid., 103.
7. Ibid., 103.
8. Ibid., 109; his emphasis.
9. Kiernan Ryan, "Playing for Time: Improvising and Anachronism in Shakespearean Comedy" (seminar paper, International Shakespeare Conference, Stratford-upon-Avon 1996), 1.
10. Kenneth Wheeler and Jeff Lammers, *Paper Air Plane Calendar* (New York: Workman, 1996).
11. Wheeler, "Light It Up", 5.
12. Leo Braudy, *The World in a Frame: What We See in Films* (Chicago: University of Chicago Press, 1976), 122.
13. Ryan, "Playing for Time," 5.
14. See Thomas Kuhn, *The Structure of Scientific Revolutions* (Chicago: University of Chicago Press, 1962).
15. Nathaniel Hawthorne, *Selected Tales and Sketches*, ed. Hyatt Howe Waggoner (New York: Rinehart & Co, 1950).
16. Maurice Charney, *Hamlet's Fictions* (New York: Routledge, 1988), 32–33.
17. Sheidley, "The Play(s) within the Film," 111.
18. Wheeler, "Light It Up", 5.

David Wright as Young Senator supporting the Coriolanus of Byron Jennings in *Coriolanus* directed by John Hirsch, July–September 1988, Old Globe Theatre, Balboa Park, San Diego. Photo credit: Will Gullette

Cori-Ollie-anus[1]: Shakespeare's Last Tragedy and American Politics in 1988

R. B. PARKER

I

ONE OF THE MOST EXTRAVAGANTLY PRAISED BUT LEAST KNOWN INTERPRETATIONS of *Coriolanus* in recent years was John Hirsch's production of the play for the Old Globe Theater of San Diego, which ran from 28 July to 4 September 1988. Although there was justifiable criticism of the liberties it took with Shakespeare's text (which will be discussed later), the critical consensus was overwhelmingly in the production's favor, with "awesome" as the most frequently recurring adjective. This was all the more gratifying because by 1988 the Old Globe had become known for rather stuffy "museum" productions of the classics, with its occasional updatings for contemporary relevance condemned as unsuccessful.

John Hirsch, however, who had not worked for the Globe before, was not only an exceptionally experienced Shakespearean director, having served as both Associate and Chief Artistic Director of the Canadian Shakespeare Festival in Ontario (and also head of C.B.C. drama), but was also someone with a fervent belief in the social importance of theater, which sprang directly from terrible experiences in World War II. A Hungarian Jew by birth, he lost both his parents, a brother, and a grandfather to the Nazi Holocaust, and of the 800 Jews who lived in the small town of Siofok, was one of only three to survive. Years as an orphan in the refugee camps of Germany and France followed before he was adopted, as a teenager speaking no English, by a family from Winnipeg.

Not surprisingly, such experiences impressed themselves indelibly, and throughout his thirty-five years' career as director, dramaturge, playwright, and designer, Hirsch showed an intense, though always extremely sophisticated, awareness of the effect of political decisions on the lives of ordinary people. His first great success was a production of Brecht's *Mother Courage* at the Manitoba Theatre Centre—the model for Canada's chain of regional theaters, of which he was co-founder—and it was for this sort of production that by 1988 he had become celebrated internationally.

His interpretations were invariably energetic, imaginative, and theatrically inventive, but always at their core were serious social and political concerns; he had no interest at all in art that was merely entertainment. "In this country," he complained to a California columnist, "there's a tremendous gap between what goes on in the streets—in life—and what goes on in art";[2] the theater, in his opinion, should be "a place where you ask questions, where you confront people with important issues—what kind of government ought we to have and how should we govern ourselves and choose our leaders, what we believe in and why."[3] So in directing *Coriolanus* during a crucial national election campaign, he aimed to close the gap between life and art by showing how this final tragedy—the play that T. S. Eliot described as "Shakespeare's most assured artistic success"[4]—raised surprisingly up-to-date questions about events in 1988.

II

Coriolanus is arguably the most brilliant political play ever written. In its subtle balancing of right- and left-wing points of view, its grasp of mutual influences between authority structures in the family and those in the state, and its awareness of the psychological distortions caused by concern for public "image" in politicians seeking to influence an electorate, there are insights which have led to its description as "perhaps the least dated of Shakespeare's plays."[5]

"When I was asked to do *Coriolanus*," Hirsch explained, "I realized it has to do with the issue of democracy, and America has been one of the most important democratic societies in the history of mankind. Its health and survival influence the whole world."[6] During the election year of 1988, however, this democratic ideal was gravely challenged by forces both within and without the United States. Not only were there sporadic but serious outbreaks of violence in the black and Hispanic ghettos of the inner cities, but also, more spectacularly, a key issue for the electorate had become the televised spectacle of a Congressional hearing about "Irangate"—the clandestine sale of arms by the U.S. army to Muslim extremists in Iran, technically

America's foes, in order to channel support to right-wing "Contras" aiming to overthrow the mildly socialist Sandinista government of Nicaragua, which was ostensibly one of America's allies. Hirsch began work on his production of *Coriolanus* during the televised testimony of Oliver North, a much-decorated Marine colonel responsible for the arms sale who was totally unrepentant about the illegality of what he insisted was a patriotic act.

Hirsch decided that here was a contemporary equivalent of Coriolanus, so the actor Byron Jennings, who resembled North physically, appeared in the play smartly dressed in a beribboned Marine dress uniform or contemporary camouflage fatigues, with a bristling military crew cut, ramrod bearing, and the curt, clipped, forceful speaking manner of an experienced field commander. In fact, with his greater blondness and icy blue intensity of gaze, Jennings was even more Aryan looking than North himself, and thus a striking contrast to the motley "Central American" casting and costuming that characterized the Volscians. In addition, clips of other deponents at the Congressional hearing—Bush, Meese, Fawn Hall—and such media opponents as Jane Fonda were shown on banks of television monitors at each side of the stage, so there could be no question of the parallel being drawn. Hirsch's intention was not to comment on the specific case, however, but to raise a wider, more recurrent problem. He explained that

> the ambiguity of America's attitude toward Oliver North is a testimony to the ongoing fascination with people who put themselves above the law. And this is a major vein in America's mythology and thinking: the outlaw, the person who goes against the law, and the country's more-than-sneaking admiration for people of that sort.[7]

In other words, the production was neither an attack on nor a defense of Oliver North *per se*, but a consideration of contrasting attitudes toward law within American democracy.

Such an approach agreed with Hirsch's perception that "the heart of [*Coriolanus*] . . . is profoundly ambiguous"[8]: "this is not a play that paints all these issues in black and white," he insisted, "it is also about how Coriolanus can be pushed into a job for which he is not really equipped and how power groups *of all kinds* can use him as a front."[9] Material that could be construed as critical of the Republican party, therefore, was balanced by details aimed at other targets. The sly, compromising, manipulative Menenius was played as a portly, white-suited Southern Democrat with a leisurely, anecdotal drawling style of speech that was admirably suited to Menenius's temporizing and his folksy parable of the belly and the members. But again, there was no one model: the figure, Hirsch said, was "a combination of Sam Rayburn, Sam Irvin, Tip O'Neill—all those great political walrusses."[10] And to convey the play's sense of dynastic control and the way that family hierarchy can influence politics at a national level, Hirsch went to the other extreme of the American political spectrum and borrowed from the Kennedys. The troubled Virgilia, struggling with contradictory emotions of love, sexual attraction, hurt, submissiveness, and anger, was given the looks and drinking problem of Joan Kennedy; while the relentlessly smiling, manipulative Volumnia was based on Rose, the matriarch of the Kennedy clan.[11] The latter's impact was made even more striking because Hirsch installed her in a Roosevelt-style wheelchair, which she used ruthlessly as a weapon, entering scenes "like a hand grenade" so that people scattered before her,[12] and adding the moral blackmail of a cripple to that of wronged mother. This was in line with the original text's protest that Coriolanus's rebellion is like treading on his mother's womb (5.3.124–26), and it was when she struggled painfully from her wheelchair to kneel at his feet in the pleading scene that Coriolanus's resistance crumbled. The Tribunes too were criticized by giving them sinister bodyguards in leather coats and dark glasses, like mobsters protecting shady union bosses.

Moreover, Hirsch was also interested more widely in "What happens to an empire that runs out of steam, out of energy."[13] As he prepared his interpretation, he explained, "I was reading Paul Kennedy's *Decline of Empire*, re-examining America's position in the world. And Gorbachev was becoming important as the Soviet empire began to change."[14] Accordingly, the Tribunes and plebeians wore badges identifying them with the "Solidarnocz" shipworkers of Gdańsk, whose strike was at that time returning democracy to Poland, while a hand note on the title page of the script instructs that "First Citizen" be moustached like the strikers' leader, Lech Walesa, who eventually became president of Poland (though photographs of the production suggest that this was ultimately not adopted).

Similarly, although the ragtag, paramilitary army of the Volscians, led by a charismatic, camouflage-clad Aufidius, was immediately associated by reviewers with North's target, the Cuban-influenced Sandinistas, Hirsch's original influence was actually more domestic. The Volscians were, in fact, a combination of American Hispanics and blacks, using the accents and street argot of both groups, and inspired less by Nicaragua than by Joan Didion's book on contemporary *Miami*. Imagining what it would be like if Didion's Florida seceded from the union, Hirsch said, "I began to think about all those minorities—the black and Hispanics—with a country of their own."[15]

It was this provocative range of reference that prevented Hirsch's production from being oversimplified by any single ideological position and allowed audiences of all political stripes to find the interpretation illuminating. "The approach I took can be called 'radical' Shakespeare," said Hirsch, "in that I unashamedly shaped the play in a certain way, but it was not a gimmicky production. All those [modern parallels] were not there because I wanted to show off or make it 'relevant' or 'contemporary' but to communicate the heart of the play which is profoundly ambiguous."[16] By this he meant *politically* ambiguous: "Everybody who sees the show," he claimed, "becomes focussed on its politics."[17] And he was quick to recognize and admit that this interpretation was not the whole of Shakespeare's play: "It is my adaptation," he insisted, "an essay by me *on* the play."[18] It oversimplified Coriolanus' relation to his mother, for example, and, particularly, his emotional bond to Aufidius;[19] but to compensate for this, it captured the original's political complexity and excitement so successfully that for one reviewer "suddenly [Shakespeare] seems to know our entire era to its inches,"[20] and for another the interpretation appeared "the definitive version of the play for this century."[21] Hirsch himself, however, considered that, for all its brilliant inventiveness and phenomenal success, the production would become quickly out of date precisely because of its immediacy.[22]

III

Besides the audacity of its modern parallels, the other main source of imaginative excitement in this Old Globe Theater production was Hirsch's *mise-en-scène*, which, combining his long experience in thrust staging with a dazzling use of electronic technology, overwhelmed the audience with rapidly changing, often overlapping scenes, headlong crowds of extras representing rioters or armies in mid-combat, and an unremitting barrage of multiple visuals and sound.

Uniquely, in my experience, the usual prompt book for the production was supplemented by a mammoth staging plan prepared separately from the script. This consisted of ten large ledger-size pages, each divided vertically into seven columns: "Scene and title" (sometimes with the exact timing of particularly brief scenes), "Location-general," "Scenic elements," "Props-Costumes," "Video," "Sound," and "Electrics-effects." These columns itemize in detail the many simultaneous effects that had to occur in every scene, and where script and staging plan diverge, as they do towards the end of the play, it is clearly the plan that is the later and more reliable guide to what eventually happened in production. Both agree, however, in replacing conventional act and scene divisions with forty-five short sequences in the manner of Brecht, each with its own title or *grundgestus* (e.g. "*SCENE THREE,* Home you fragments"), and in calling for only two intervals: the first after Coriolanus' triumphant entry into Rome (2.1 in the original), the second after his farewell scene as he leaves family and friends for exile (4.1 in the original).

With all his Stratford experience to draw on, Hirsch used the open stage like a master, with rapid, fluid changes of "location" and a constant flow of action. Scenes in the Forum or Capitol of Rome were identified by a large reversible archway of black marble surmounted with heroic gold statuary of rearing horse and rider, which was withdrawn upstage behind a curtain for scenes elsewhere. Halfway downstage, either war-scarred "concrete" walls or sections of high chainlink fence could be closed in from either side to reduce or divide the acting area, with sometimes only part of the upstage area blocked off to establish particular locales (e.g., "interior" scenes in Volumnia's or Aufidius' houses). Two retractable "bridges" were suspended across the acting area, one upstage, one down, which served effectively as locations for cheering crowds, hanging flags and huge portrait placards during Roman triumphs, and, more sinisterly, for vigilant armed guards in other scenes. And the latter's sense of oppressive, almost prison-camp surveillance was heightened by tall lighting towers on each side of the stage, from which roving spotlights could pick out particular areas or speakers. To move large groups quickly on and off stage, Hirsch relied particularly on the "vomitories"—entrances opening diagonally onto the forestage from two tunnels under the audience.[23] And most striking of all were sixteen television monitors in vertical banks to either side of the stage, whose non-stop video commentary provided a peculiarly modern "chorus."

These were used initially to establish the contemporary context. In a fifteen-minute "prologue" before the play itself began, the monitors interspersed clips of Oliver North, Fawn Hall, and Edwin Meese testifying before the Irangate Congressional committee with beer and car commercials identifying the "heartbeat of America" with Chevy trucks, while extracts from such extravagant television shows as "Wheel of Fortune" and "Lifestyles of the Rich and Famous" were juxtaposed with footage of inner-city riots, street people scavenging from garbage cans, and President Ronald Reagan signing an anti-poverty bill. Simultaneously an independent sound track broadcast big-band music of the 1950s mixed with 1960s protest songs and "contra dialogue," with the stage plan noting "SOUND AND VIDEO NOT NECESSARILY IN SYNC. WITH ONE ANOTHER."

Then, still in the "prologue," this mix of video and sound started to be matched by images and action on the stage. One side of the central arch had been converted to look like the window of a haute-couture boutique in which a mannequin displayed expensive furs, while armed guards protected the "plaza" where it stood against homeless street people trundling shopping carts filled with rags and bedding. There was then a sudden blackout ("less than 20 sec.") in which smoke was released, a "bomb" exploded, and shots were fired in a mounting bedlam of shattering glass, alarm bells, police sirens, and other sounds of riot. And when red "emergency lights" came on, with spotlights nervously raking the stage from the two side towers and the snarl of a receding motorcycle, the guards were dead, the mannequin was stripped and riddled with bullet holes, and a chain-link fence, reinforced by police with riot shields, had been drawn across the trouble spot; as jubilant looters hurried past with booty in palls of smoke upstage of the barrier, downstage, the citizens who begin Shakespeare's dialogue came on with homemade placards proclaiming "Down with the Rich," "Food not Talk," "Share the Power," "The Poor Are Romans Too." After Menenius's belly fable, this crowd was in turn dispersed by Coriolanus' shouting through a megaphone as he noisily arrived in a machine-gun-mounted jeep with its lights on full and siren blaring, accompanied by yet further riot police with shields.

Coriolanus' entrance was recorded live by a television "news" crew on stage, and appeared simultaneously in close-up on the banks of video screens; from this time on, these monitors began to mix on-stage visuals with clips from regular American programs. Thus, the speeches of Coriolanus and Cominius before the Senate with Menenius as chairman of the investigating committee appeared simultaneously on television; there were horrendous close-ups of battlefield carnage on stage intermingled with actual war footage; arguments during Coriolanus' later conflict with the Tribunes and plebeians were projected like newscast interviews; and the video presentation of events on stage was particularly and tellingly ironic in the political canvassing sequences, because, as Hirsch remarked, "Isn't it great in the middle of a national election, to hear what Coriolanus has to say about [political] campaigns!"[24]

Television was used especially ingeniously to provide a modern equivalent for the Roman "gown of humility" which Coriolanus has to wear when seeking plebeian votes. At the beginning of the canvassing scene (2.3), Coriolanus wore a bathrobe because he was being prepared for television by a makeup girl. It was in this robe (and makeup) that he had gingerly to shake hands with individual voters as, in hard hats and carrying lunch pails, they emerged at the sound of a factory whistle through a gate in the chainlink fence beneath a large sign reading "DYNATECH INDUSTRIES," as though knocking off from work in what the staging plan suggests should resemble "an industrial city like Pittsburgh."

Hirsch talked of such ironic media coverage as an aspect of his adaptation: "There are a lot of things in [the production] that are not in Shakespeare; the media plays quite a large role, because if you're talking about politics these days, then you have to consider the media."[25] But actually, of course, this media emphasis reflects a dimension already strong in the play: the sense that several characters have—particularly Coriolanus—of playing hypocritical roles in public life, which is extrapolated into a major motif of performance imagery in the language (for which *Coriolanus* is second only to *Hamlet* in the whole Shakespearean canon).[26] Moreover, the video monitors had a further effect that Hirsch may not have anticipated, but that one of the reviewers comments on.[27] The variety and pace of events on stage, the noise, flashing lights, and competing levels of live and video performance were as overwhelming for the audience as the overloaded impressions of real life, and this exposed the misleading simplifications of the media's sound bytes and selective imagery on the monitors: an effect totally appropriate for Shakespeare's theme.[28]

There were many startlingly effective examples of imaginative updating besides the big set pieces of battlefields, ticker-tape processions, urban unrest, and the Senate committee hearing. In the two Volumnia domestic scenes (1.3 and 3.2), for example, her house was characterized by black leather furniture with fittings of silver and glittering chrome—the staging plan notes that "John wants as much chrome and silver as possible"—and a statue of Coriolanus himself was wheeled into the living room upstage. This produced an impression of repellent chic which established the hard and coldly reifying context in which Coriolanus had been reared. In the first of these two scenes, the visitor, Valeria, was offered afternoon tea, served by a butler from a teacart with small cakes and cookies and a splendid silver tea service, while a pregnant Virgilia itemized receipts instead of sewing. In the second, it was the cocktail hour, with both General Cominius and Virgilia herself obviously a little the worse for drink.

An especially bold invention was to place the first "Who does the wolf love?" colloquy between Menenius and the Tribunes (at the beginning of 2.1, before Coriolanus's victorious return) among the benches, towels, steam jets, and Muzak—a nice touch—of the locker room in a Turkish bath, not only establishing the sybaritic nature of Menenius himself, but showing also how the Tribunes have already affected a luxurious mode of life far from that of the plebeians. Similarly, when Menenius was asked later to plead that Coriolanus spare Rome (5.1), the scene took place in a greenhouse on his estate where he was languidly tending orchids.

Particularly striking was Hirsch's use of technology in the scene in which Coriolanus makes it possible for Titus Lartius' reserves to storm Corioli (1.5), and the later scene of Coriolanus' departure into exile (4.1). The former always poses the problem of how Coriolanus, "bleeding" and alone (his companions in Plutarch having been eliminated by Shakespeare), can possibly open the heavy city gates while simultaneously being "assaulted by the enemy" (1.5.34).[29] At San Diego, this was solved by having Coriolanus swung up from behind Corioli's "cement" walls clinging to the enormous hook of a crane (which also featured as a factory prop in the canvassing scene discussed earlier). From this he fired an automatic rifle at enemies out of sight below, then lobbed down grenades to blow a gap in the defense wall. The smoke from the explosions masked the small set change required, which consisted merely of opening up the walls a bit and thrusting a pre-set trolley of "rubble" into the gap for the attacking force to storm over.

Coriolanus' departure from Rome, which provided a spectacular conclusion for the production's second act, took place at night on a helicopter pad, with his little group of mourning well-wishers clad in black mackintoshes and carrying umbrellas glistening with rain, surrounded by watchful guards. The chainfence was closed stage-right, and the presence of the helicopter offstage-left was suggested by a fuel line brought across from the right by an attendant clad in yellow coveralls with "Shell" on the back, by a flashing red light from the plane's presumed position, and the sound of its engine idling. This turned into a familiar beating roar as it "took off," and a wind-machine buffeted the watchers as they followed the diminishing sounds of its rise and departure into the distance. So persuasive was the effect that some spectators even claimed to have felt the plane's vibrations.[30] This airport location was then kept for the meeting of the two spies after the intermission (4.3), with Adrian, the Volscian agent, disguised as a baggage handler, and Nicanor as a confidential courier complete with handcuffed valise.

Finally, the *mise-en-scène* of the conclusion poses a problem of reconstruction because there were discrepancies between the production's script and its staging plan, and also between reviews. The script eliminated Volumnia's triumphant return to Rome (5.5) but kept the state funeral with which Aufidius finally honors his victim; and it is possible that such an arrangement was actually tried out (in late rehearsal, perhaps, or previews) because one—though only one—of the reviewers complains that Volumnia's triumph has been cut.[31] However, the staging plan included an elaborate set-up for "VOLUMNIA'S TRIUMPH" as *"Scene* 38," with instructions that her procession thread the central arch, a drop portraying Coriolanus be flown in, two flag poles be used, and there be "banners, big posters, streamers, ticker tape, trumpets, and a march" played over the speaker system, and also that "live cameras" focus on Volumnia so that her smiling face might appear in close-up on the video monitors. But after directions for Coriolanus's subsequent murder ("Enhance the Kill") by three masked gunmen in combat fatigues—two with "practical" M.16 semiautomatic rifles from the "bridge" and one with a "practical" revolver from the "deck"—there are no indications at all for a funeral cortege. Instead, there is a direction for the walls to open to reveal Coriolanus' son "in suit and tie," obviously tapping American memories of John Kennedy Jr. at his father's funeral.

That this was the ending eventually favored is proved by such reviewer's comments as:

> In the cannonade of scenes that follow [Coriolanus' submission to his mother], we have the chilling portrait of this iron maiden of patriotism parading through the streets of Rome—bands blaring—followed by a crescendo of rifle fire from the betrayed Volscians. The contrast between the image of the manic smile of the hero's mother basking in her moment of glory as if she were a Roman military hero and the image of her son riddled with bullets *lying unmourned* under a bloody sheet is a *coup de théâtre*.[32]

The staging plan marks the ending as "T. B. D." (to be decided), but a final focus on Young Coriolanus is confirmed by the fact that George Wernberg Harter concludes his review for *The Source* by remarking that the child actor, Kyle Wares, provided "a spooky homunculus of his father."[33] Like similar uses of the boy in more traditional productions,[34] the implication left by such an apparition is that nothing will be changed, that psychological warping of the ruling class will continue and will result in further violence. Or alternatively, of course, that a new generation of patriots will pick the torch up to continue the heroism of their fathers.

IV

Such staging was brilliantly inventive, but it was effected at considerable cost to Shakespeare's text, which Hirsch was willing to acknowledge as a trade-off but which most reviewers, to various degrees, regretted.[35] Textual alterations were made in two main stages. Functioning as his own dramaturge, Hirsch gave the text a thorough workover that is reflected in the production script. Then the actors playing minor roles, particularly the Volscians, were encouraged to increase authenticity by frequent ad libbing, which is not recorded in the script but is commented on by several of the reviewers.

Except for whichever section was ultimately dropped from the conclusion, the only other large units to be cut were the scene in which Volumnia and Virgilia harass the Tribunes after Coriolanus' banishment (4.2), and the ironic sequence in which the Tribunes complacently receive the plebeians' praise and tease Menenius before news arrives of the Volsces' renewed attack (4.6). Rather than cut whole scenes, Hirsch more typically pruned—often rather heavily—*within* scenes; and to focus sharply on the play's political issues he sacrificed memorable passages that are essential for a full poetic and psychological understanding of the play. For example, there was no horse-betting between Coriolanus and Titus Lartius, so no chivalric gift of a horse to set against Coriolanus' repudiation of other booty. Coriolanus was not raised aloft by Cominius' soldiers to give his psychologically revealing cry, "O me alone! Make you a sword of me?" Since medics cleaned him up immediately after the battle, the poetically important references to his bloody appearance were cut, as were Volumnia and Menenius' grotesque haggling over the number of his wounds and Virgilia's consequent distress. Volumnia no longer mimed how Coriolanus should woo voters (which gives a parodic dimension to his canvassing later); the Volscian servants who switch allegiance in 4.5 were transformed into three drunken soldiers (as in Brecht's adaptation), and their dialogue was curtailed to accommodate a war ditty that they left the platform singing—as dialogue elsewhere was often transformed to modernized "newscasts" on the video monitors. Aufidius, in particular, suffered from heavy cutting of his first two scenes (1.2 and 11)—the staging plan specifies that the former last no more than 30 seconds—so that the neurotic complexity of the relationship between him and Coriolanus was lost (particularly since his contradictory response to Coriolanus' death was also cut).

The list of such omissions could go on and on—in 5.3, for instance, Coriolanus' self-comparison to "a great sea mark" was cut entirely, and the marvellously subtle progress of Volumnia's persuasion speech was truncated—but there is no point in recording every item. And even when the substance of a speech was kept, it was often rewritten to reduce the thematic density of Shakespeare's imagery and bring the idiom closer to modern demotic. At their best, such changes produced an effect that one reviewer wittily called "a kind of Revised Standard version of much of Shakespeare's poetry";[36] at their worst, they translated the original to such quotidian banalities as "Meet us at our offices" or "He was a real fighting machine." When a disaffected soldier in Shakespeare snarls "To th' pot, I warrant him," for example, as his unpopular commander is trapped inside Corioli (which links with motifs of food and cannibalism throughout), this was reduced to the totally flat comment, "This is surely the end of him!" And, as was mentioned earlier, such banalities were compounded in performance by *ad libbing* from the plebeians, especially the Volsces, with added ethnic vocatives like "amigo" and "man" and frequent interpolations of the interjectory "shit!"

From a scholar's point of view the text was vandalized. Yet it was done intelligently, not carelessly, with a particular aim clearly in mind—to focus on the play's politics; and it worked well in production, as even reviewers who lamented the alterations admitted. A difference was created between the speech of Volscians and Romans, and among the latter between patricians and plebeians, that was certainly not Shakespeare's but was Shakespearean in effect. And this was ultimately the impression left by the production as a whole, despite its textual mayhem.

As Hirsch himself maintained, the San Diego production did not pretend to be Shakespeare's whole play, but was rather an "essay" on the original, sacrificing psychology and poetry for an insight into political complexity that was very close to Shakespeare's own—and which few modern productions have achieved to anything like the same extent. The remarkable result was that its pungent commentary on some of the most inflammatory issues of 1988—in a part of the United States not noted for political tolerance, moreover—was enthusiastically welcomed by *both* sides of the political spectrum, with the kind of leftwing response that is reflected impertinently in my borrowed title, shading through recognition of Coriolanus as in part a noble victim, all the way to rightwing responses that interpreted the production mainly as a warning about "how a country by maltreating North-like men puts itself in jeopardy."[37] And outweighing everything, whatever the political reaction, was exhilarated recognition of the brilliance of its staging: "an absolutely astonishing, preconception smashing, teeming, flashing, thundering, spectacular and glorious version of Shakespeare's seldom-produced historical tragedy," rhapsodized one reviewer, that was "intelligent, detailed, powerful, visionary, magnificent, and illuminating."[38]

Not an interpretation for all seasons, certainly; but one brilliantly calculated for the political climate of Southern California in the summer of 1988: a theatrical *tour de force* that, sadly, can never be repeated. John Hirsch admitted, "I think it's my best work so far,"[39] and welcomed an invitation to return and direct for the Old Globe Theatre again. But within a year he was dead, his immune system devastated by AIDS; records of this production must stand as his memorial.

Notes

N.B. (1) Line references are to my 1994 edition for the Clarendon Press, Oxford. (2) Reviews preserved in the theater's clippings collection generally lack page numbers and are hence recorded as "(n.p.)."

1. This rather cheeky title is borrowed from a review of the San Diego production by "C. M." in *Alarums and Excursions,* vol. 2 (Los Angeles Theatre Center, August, 1988): 30.
2. Hirsch in Arthur Salm, "Most theater bores Coriolanus' director," *The Tribune* (San Diego), 22 July 1988 (n.p.).
3. Hirsch in Nancy Churnin, "Historical Nightmare Evolved Into a Political Obsession for Playwright [sic] Hirsch," *Los Angeles Times,* 19 August 1988 (n.p.).
4. "Hamlet," *Selected Essays* (London: Faber, 1932), 124.
5. H. J. Oliver, "Coriolanus as Tragic Hero," *Shakespeare Quarterly* 10 (1959): 57.
6. Churnin, "Historical Nightmare."
7. Salm, "Most theater bores." For another reviewer, "One only has to visualize Jennings with a pipe and sunglasses to recognize a modern General MacArthur": Hal Braham, "Coriolanus'—modern, powerful, explosive," *Bernardo News,* 18 August 1988 (n.p.).
8. *The Free Press* (Toronto) 5:2 (Fall, 1988), 2.
9. Churnin, "Historical Nightmare"(emphasis added).
10. Hirsch in Welton Jones, "'Coriolanus': Mondo Shakespeare," *San Diego Union,* 14 August 1988 (n.p.).
11. Ibid.
12. Jeff Smith, "In Succession," *The Reader* (18 August, 1988), 24. Another critic extrapolates, "Although it is never stated, one gathers that [Volumnia's] injuries arise from an attack by bomb-throwing terrorists who detonate a device that rocks the theater at the top [i.e. beginning] of the play": Andrew Harris, *Stages Magazine* (August, 1988), 4–5.
13. Salm, "Most theater bores."
14. Jones, "'Coriolanus': Mondo."
15. Ibid. In a production of *Coriolanus* for the New York Shakespeare Festival in 1965, Hirsch's predecessor in Ontario, Michael Langham (then at the Julliard School), had mixed black and Hispanic actors for the Roman plebeians.
16. *The Free Press,* 2.
17. Jones, "'Coriolanus': Mondo."

18. Salm, "Most theater bores" (emphasis added).
19. Neglect of the play's homoerotic dimension was criticized by Chris Schneider, "Globe's *Coriolanus* By-passes Play's Gay Aspects," *Bravo*, 1 September 1988 (n.p.).
20. Smith, "In Succussion."
21. William E. Fark, "Modern Touch Gives Vivid Feel to 'Coriolanus'," *Escondido Times-Advocate*, 11 August 1988 (n.p.).
22. Churnin, "Historical Nightmare."
23. This crowd movement gave one reviewer the impression of "a cast of thousands": Beverly Ragsdale, "Shakespeare's Tragedy Set On Old Globe Stage," *Chula Vista Star News*, 14 August 1988 (n.p.).
24. Jones, "'Coriolanus': Mondo."
25. Salm, "Most theater bores."
26. Cf. my introduction in *Coriolanus* (Oxford: Clarendon Press, 1994), 84–85.
27. Smith, "In Succussion."
28. Another reviewer suggested that such video close-ups were helpful for California actors trained in film and television, not the stage: Christopher Schneider, "Globe Triumphs with 'Coriolanus'," *La Jolla Light*, 11 August 1988, C9.
29. Cf. William Empson, *Essays on Shakespeare*, ed. David B. Pirie (Cambridge: Cambridge University Press, 1986), 177–83; Parker, Introduction, 93.
30. Smith, "In Succussion."
31. Schneider, "Globe Triumphs" (emphasis added).
32. Harris, *Stages* (emphasis added). A similar shortening of the conclusion was used in Michael Bentham's traditionalist production at the *Old Vic Theatre* in 1954, with Richard Burton as Coriolanus.
33. George Weinberg-Harter, "On Stage: Rome with a View," *The Source* (San Diego), 4 August 1988 (n.p.).
34. In productions by the Old Vic in 1954 and the Royal Shakespeare Company in 1977 and again in 1989, Volumnia used Young Martius as the climax of her welcome back to Rome; see Parker, Introduction, 32.
35. The most savage attack was by the New York critic John Simon, as reported in Nancy Churnin's *Stage* column in the *Los Angeles Times*, 12 August 1988, Part 4, p. 2. He also took exception to ethnic mixing and to Volumnia's wheelchair.
36. Weinberg-Harter, "On Stage: Rome."
37. Schneider, "Globe Triumphs."
38. Weinberg-Harter, "On Stage: Rome."
39. Churnin, "Historical Nightmare."

Staging *The Tempest* as an Alchemical Experiment in the Theater

PEGGY MUÑOZ SIMONDS

KEITH STURGESS HAS ARGUED THAT "DESIGN, NOT NARRATIVE, IS *THE TEMPEST'S* major impulse and its structure is architectural, not dynamic."[1] Although I do agree that design, which will be the topic of this essay, is exceedingly important to any production of Shakespeare's magical play, I would also emphasize that the design chosen must agree with and help to explain to a modern audience the "strange" and politically significant *action* that we witness on the stage—that is, Prospero's successful completion of an alchemical "project" or projection to alter the moral nature of a king, his son, his courtiers, and three drunken servants, including one native wild man. An alchemical reading of *The Tempest* was casually suggested by William Rockett in 1973, but in quite another context, when he observed that "Prospero, after all, is a Christian magician and the success of his project, as with the projections of the spiritual alchemists of the Renaissance, rests upon his capacity through discipline for purging his soul and his motives of their impurities. Through labor one purges the spirit, mortifies the passions, and grows in understanding and grace."[2] For some reason, however, it did not occur to Rockett to notice that Prospero's labor in the play was precisely the *opus magnum* of alchemy. Not until 1985 did a doctoral candidate in Sweden notice clear textual references in Shakespeare's play to certain stages of the alchemical process, but his pioneer work has been essentially ignored by later critics and editors.[3]

Following in these exploratory footsteps, I have recently demonstrated elsewhere that *The Tempest* is not only bristling with alchemical terminology, as some editors had noticed previously, but also that the very structure of the tragicomedy is based on at least nine clearly indicated steps of the transmutational process.[4] Such a process is, of course, "dynamic" rather than "architectural," which would be an entirely non-dramatic structure inconsistent with Shakespeare's usual practice as a popular playwright. Instead Prospero, whose very name means "successful," manages through alchemy to return the lost Golden Age to his world. Since mystical alchemists were not interested in making literal gold, Patrick Scot defined the moral nature of the art in 1623 by arguing that alchemical Philosophy's

> refyning of us in *vertue*, is to a more pure *substance*, then of thrice purified *gold*: if wee would from *vice* extract *vertue, quintessence, content* and true *reputation* from *poverty* and *contempt*, Convert *exile* into our native *Country, bonds* into *liberty, want* into wealth, or would wee multiply some few short *earthly crosses* into *celestiall* permanent *ioyes*, all these can Philosophy doe.[5]

This, in a nutshell, is a fairly accurate description of Prospero's own alchemical "project" in *The Tempest*. For, unlike the Anabaptist in Ben Jonson's *The Alchemist*, Prospero knows that fallen human nature itself must be chemically perfected before the Golden Age can return, or any modern utopia succeed. His alchemical project is thus designed to perfect humanity itself before attempting to achieve a perfect society in Italy.

I have shown in my previously mentioned essay that Shakespeare actually dramatizes the following alchemical stages in *The Tempest*: (1) the separation or *divisio* of the elements during the storm, a process marked by the initial shipwreck and the cries "We split, we split" (1.1.61); (2) the marination of the King in salt water, resulting in a promised "sea change" from white bones to red coral (or the red Philosopher's Stone) and Ariel's offering of "golden sands" to the equally marinated King's son; (3) the *nigredo*, or putrefaction and *distractio*, which is literalized by the blackness of Alonso's grief for his apparently lost son as well as by Ferdinand's grief for his father, and by the psychological madness of the court party during Prospero's boiling of their brains; (4) *solve et coagula*, the repeated dissolutions and condensations into dew, or distillation, which is the result of such boilings and which removes all impurities; (5) calcination, often called "The Women Washing Sheets" or the cooking and drying, as well as re-dyeing, stage of the process, that is marked by Gonzalo's four observations on the miraculous renewal of their garments after a bath in the salt sea; (6) the *cauda pavonis* or peacock's tail, a marvelous display of colors in the alembic that indicates the empowerment of the alchemical opus and is dramatized in *The Tempest* by the wedding masque, including the descent of Juno with her peacocks to bless Ferdinand and Miranda with Golden Age perfection through a paradoxical wish that "Spring come to you at the farthest / In the very end of harvest" (4.1.114–15); (7)

the *conjunctio* or the chemical wedding between sulphur and mercury, which is symbolized by the Naiades and the Reapers in a dance that joins the opposites of moist and dry, cold and heat, female and male, moon and sun, body and soul, springtime and summer, Miranda and Ferdinand, and is followed by the sudden dissolving of the masque itself; (8) squaring the circle, which again symbolizes the chemical wedding and consists of the reincorporation of the divided elements and of the court party into the circle of perfection, as well as the adept's abjuration of magic or illusion;[6] and (9) the successful achievement of the *albedo* or the dawning after darkness through the appearance of the white stone, which is dramatically symbolized by the return of reason to the minds of the court party. The final achievement of the red Philosopher's Stone of perfection may not occur until the actual wedding ceremony in Naples, although Prospero's melancholy at the end of the play already indicates the reappearance on earth of Saturn, god of the Golden Age and of melancholy. In addition, a similar process of transmutation through fermentation or drunkenness, resulting in the symbolically "red-hot" faces of the clowns, has been simultaneously dramatized throughout *The Tempest* by the parodic subplot concerning Caliban, Stephano, and Trinculo. Caliban announces his own spiritual transmutation with a new and astounding determination at the end of the play to seek not for freedom but for grace as a good and willing servant, or as the ideal Christian man.

Nevertheless, we modern scholars have tended to miss this dynamic alchemical pattern of *The Tempest* because we have overlooked two essential factors: first, that famous Renaissance magicians such as Dr. John Dee, Cornelius Agrippa of Nettesheim, and Giambattista Della Porta of Naples were all practicing alchemists who were also skilled in the magical arts of illusion; secondly, that during the late Renaissance, alchemy was a popular artistic metonym for political, social, and spiritual change, which made it dear to Protestants in northern Europe and anathema to English conservatives like Ben Jonson up until the Restoration.[7] By boiling the brains of the King of Naples and his corrupt courtiers, and thus activating a conscience within them to guide their future behavior, Prospero succeeds in transforming the ruling hierarchy into ideal leaders who are quite unlike the real leaders, either of European kingdoms or of the actual seventeenth-century utopian experiments described by historians.[8] The servants of such reformed leaders must also undergo a similar alchemical process of reform through fermentation during the course of the tragicomedy. The possibility of such a transformation of the intellect through the operations of sack was suggested earlier by Falstaff in *2 Henry IV* (4.3.96–102).

It is, of course, impossible today for us to believe that the practice of alchemy (the art of achieving the material perfection of metals in glass or ceramic alembics heated on a primitive furnace) could possibly have any effect on the moral behavior of human beings, but then we no longer believe in a cosmos of correspondences or in the fundamental interconnectedness of the microcosm and the macrocosm, as illustrated in Isidore of Seville's *De natura rerum*. In contrast to our scientific skepticism, many members of Shakespeare's audience did believe that what happened in an alembic could indeed influence the human mind and heart, but only if the practitioner were a true alchemist and virtuous himself, rather than a mere faker or con-man, like Jonson's Subtle, in search of other people's gold. Since *The Alchemist*, a satire expressing our own modern biases, was produced by Shakespeare's company within the same year as *The Tempest*, the latter play might well have been written as an optimistic answer to the former's skeptical view of alchemy as a fraud.

In general, however, alchemy was highly regarded in Renaissance England.[9] As we know, Queen Elizabeth employed her own palace alchemist, and Jonson himself metaphorically bestowed the transforming powers of an alchemist on her successor, James I, in two court masques, *The Golden Age Restor'd* and *Mercury Vindicated From the Alchemists at Court*. Furthermore, since Martin Luther approved of alchemy's "secret signification"[10] as an allegory of Christian reform, regeneration, and transcendence, the Anglican Church offered no opposition to its practice by Paracelsian physicians and others. In fact, the English clergyman and Paracelsian apologist Thomas Tymme went so far as to compare the spiritual results of alchemy to Christ's Second Coming in his 1605 English translation of Joseph Duchesne's *The Practice of Chymicall, and Hermetical Physicke:*

> Moreover, as the omnipotent God, hath in the beginning, by his divine wisedom, created the things of the hevens & earth, in weight, number, & measure, depending upon most wonderfull proportions & harmony, to serve the time which he hath appointed: so in the fulnesse & last period of time (which approacheth fast on) the 4. Elements (whereof al creatures consist) having in every of them 2. other Elements, the one putrifying and combustible, the other eternal & incombustible, as the heaven, shall by Gods *Halchymie* be metamorphosed and *changed.* For the combustible having in them a corrupt stinking feces, or drossie matter, which maketh them subject to corruption, shall in that great & gen-

Tetragram from Isidore of Seville's *De natura rerum* (Augsburg, 1472). It illustrates the interrelation of the four elements with their two pairs of opposing qualities, hot and cold, moist and dry. Following an ancient doctrine from Hippocratic physiology, the diagram adds the four seasons of the year and the four humors of man to complete the image of cosmic harmony. Reproduced by permission of the Warburg Institute

erall refining day, be purged through fire: And then God will make new Heavens and a new Earth, and bring all things to a christalline cleernes, & wil also make the 4. Elements perfect, simple, & fixed in themselves, that al things may be reduced to a *Quintessence of Eternitie*.[11]

What God could do in the macrocosm, a virtuous man like Prospero could also accomplish in the microcosm of the human skull, which was sometimes called a limbeck (see, for example, *Macbeth* 1.7.61–67).

In *The Tempest,* the alchemist creates a "brave new world" not to enrich himself but in order to restore Golden Age purity to an old world corrupted through the fall of Adam. The only "vanity" (usually understood not as pride but as "emptiness" in the sense of Ecclesiastes) of this sacred art in *The Tempest* is the accompanying practice of magical illusions through spectacle, such as the vanishing banquet, the subsequent appearance of Ariel as a Harpy, and the colorful royal wedding masque, all of which must be abjured by the end of the action, as Agrippa and others had advised.[12] Although certain types of magic and the use of daemons like Ariel were admittedly dangerous occult activities, alchemy itself was believed to be an imitation of God's act of Creation that would be successful only when aided by the deity. Moreover, Prospero's echoing of Medea's famous invocation in Ovid's *Metamorphoses* is not an indication of evil, as is often claimed today.[13] Medea was not a witch for Renaissance adepts but rather one of the first great alchemists in human history, an example to be followed with reverence.[14] She produced the Golden Fleece for Jason, and she rejuvenated Jason's aged father Aeson by giving him the first blood transfusion that we know of, using for youthful healthy blood what seems to be the *aurum potabile* that she has alchemically achieved in her boiling cauldron. Medea was a respected adept in the "divine art" of sublimating matter into higher forms through the purgation of corruption and disease, especially because the final medicine of alchemy, the Philosopher's Stone or the Elixir, was believed to cure both mind and body. Even the play's title is an alchemical term for the "boiling process which removes impurities from base metal and facilitates its transmutation into gold," as John S. Mebane has correctly observed.[15]

The gold—or moral excellence—that Prospero seeks in the play is the return of the Golden Age of human innocence, but now tempered by wisdom through the purification and regeneration of human psychology, including his own. Indeed, the play's imagery constantly reminds us of an ideal state of human existence, of the Eden lost by Adam and Eve but now found again for the enjoyment of Ferdinand and Miranda. Prospero's success in his moral project is particularly noticeable in the behavior of the would-be rapist and murderer Caliban, a wild man called "Thou earth" (1.2.314) by the alchemist, who despairs of his transmutation until the very end of the play. In Hebrew, the name Adam means *clay, earth,* or that lowly stuff which must be transformed into gold by the alchemist. As Tymme explains in theological terms, the Philosopher's Stone begins as "Adam *mortall*," then passes through the four Elements to a Quintessence that is called "Adam *immortall,* because it will never decay, but purgeth & transformeth all imperfect bodies or Metalls."[16]

How can a director and a designer suggest all these complex and arcane matters to an audience in a modern production of *The Tempest?* As Sturgess reminds us,

> it is clear that in *The Tempest* Shakespeare was experimenting with graphic kinds of stage imagery. A special poetry is developed in place of the verbal richness of the earlier plays. The audience is given a series of stage pictures which, like the visions in a dream, have a sharp-edged clarity and a sense of careful composition. They seem, again as in a dream, to be both emblematic and not readily accessible to simple interpretation. For the play moves in a masque-like way, proceeding by way of a series of counterpointed events that act like revelations or epiphanies. Again, the relation to dream is insistent, and the characters themselves suspect they are inhabiting a dream. But the shows are not dreamwork but a species of art-work, created by artist Prospero. (136)

Now that we know what that "art-work" is, however, designers should be able to help it along with precise visual imagery. Since I do not believe that historically based literary scholars like me should tell creative theater people what to do in their area of expertise, I will offer only a few very general suggestions here, along with the reminder that alchemy was widely illustrated in published books of secrets during both the Middle Ages and the Renaissance.[17] Pictures, even emblems with texts as well as illustrations, are easy for a director or designer to come by, as Gareth Roberts has shown.[18] However, because the "divine art" is highly symbolic in all its aspects, I would have to advise against modern psychoanalytic interpretations by actors in a production following the alchemical reading suggested in this essay, nor should Prospero be confused with the malevolent "mad scientist" figure of nineteenth-century fiction. He is a stern but benevolent physician of the soul. Thus Prospero's sexuality is irrelevant to the Renaissance text, although his Christian virtue and his ability to "forgive" past injuries are essential to his eventual success, as Ariel gently reminds him (see 5.1.20). His constant attempts to "control" his daemon and all other aspects of his experiment are scientifically necessary, rather than a form of political tyranny or the result of a Freudian abnormality. He does suffer, on the other hand, from the Renaissance version of "melancholy," as did all true alchemists, and this should be taken into account. As for design, in the discussion that follows I shall concentrate on several staging problems that arise from the text, and on a few illustrative woodcuts that might help to solve them.

First, we might ask the question that almost everyone, except Srigley,[19] seems to avoid. Why does Prospero need all those logs that

Caliban, Ferdinand (under orders), and even Miranda (voluntarily) carry about with such effort? An alchemical reading of the text makes the answer to this problem very simple, since the *opus magnum* required an enormous quantity of wood with which to feed the adept's furnace or furnaces. Although some furnaces did take small sticks directly, the most efficient way to obtain the long, slow heating required by the divine art (often for forty days or more) was to burn charcoal. In his important manual for Paracelsian chemist-physicians called *The Jewell of Health: The Practise of the New and Old Physicke* (1599), Conrad Gesner provides detailed directions for the proper making of charcoal from logs.[20] This process is illustrated in a woodcut that seems very suggestive for what the actors might be doing on stage during the log-carrying scene, although an explanatory program note might also be helpful.

Gesner's symbolic woodcut of the alchemist in his laboratory, wielding the torches of enlightenment and of literal fire is equally suggestive—in this case, of how the original audience might have envisioned a true alchemist at work. The symbols of sun and moon (sulphur and mercury) that must be wedded in the heated alembic are ubiquitous in alchemical literature, as are the stars that determine the proper time for commencing the *opus magnum*. Such signs should appear somewhere in the scenic design, and/or possibly on Prospero's magic mantle. Because astrology was closely linked with alchemy, astrolabes were also associated with alchemists, and one should be visible on stage in at least one of Prospero's scenes. As Prospero himself points out: "I find my zenith doth depend upon / A most auspicious star, whose influence / If now I court not, but omit, my fortunes / Will ever after droop" (1.2.181–84). Furthermore, according to Caliban, Prospero has a number of such "brave utensils (for so he calls them) / Which when he has a house, he'll deck withal" (3.2.95–96). The term "utensils" probably refers here not only to an astrolabe but also to the usual contents of an alchemical laboratory. These would include crucibles, retorts, alembics, pelicans (or interconnected alembics for distillation), tongs, bellows, and furnaces of different sizes. Indeed, a bellows would be a useful property for Ariel at various moments in the play to indicate visually his association with the element of Air and his control of the winds. Gesner's woodcut of "Alchymia" includes images of most of what Prospero would need in order to complete his project. Another woodcut from the same manual indicates what an alchemical furnace might look like and how charcoal would have been fed into it. But, since *The Tempest* is hardly a realistic play, we need not ask how such "utensils" came to be on this mysterious Mediterranean island, which is

of Distillations. 10

the woode on the Hlles: and the woode in the balleys is the thynner, for which cause are the Coales the lyke, yet doth the fire lyghtly and soone waste all thynne matters. And in makyng the

best Coales, they ought not to be done vnder the Grounde (as the custome of many is) but made aboue the Earth, for that they burne better, and are more profitable. Also the Coales made of the Beeche, Birche, and Fyrre trée, are accounted best, for their sweeter and sooner burning, although Coles of the Iuniper trée, doe last farre longer, as of experience knowne: besides, the Coales made of the Oke and Ashe trée, are not in cases of necessitie to be refused, especially where the store of the Beeche, and other trées are not. Moreouer, it behoueth the Distillatour to haue a speciall regarde and care about the bestowing of fire vnder hys vessels, that the same be not made of cleft woode halfe rotten, or euill smelling (as we haue aboue declared) nor of Coales smoothered within a deepe pit or hole of the Earth, or euill burned, or of Coales gotten out of Caues, whether those be of Stone, or of Earth, for feare that the vessels of Distilling, and the lycours be not taynted and infected of their vapour, filthie and stynking. A lyke reason may be gathered, that if waters or Oyles be distilled with any of those, they after purchase a sauour and qualitie

C.ij. disagrée-

The art of making charcoal, a woodcut from Conrad Gesner, *The Jewell of Health: The Practice of the New and Old Physicke* (London: Henrie Denham, 1576), p. 10. Reproduced by permission of the Folger Shakespeare Library

¶ The seconde Booke of Dystillations, *conteyning sundry excellent secrete* Remedies of Dystilled waters.

The alchemist-magician in his laboratory manipulating the element of fire. A woodcut from Gesner, p. 39. Reproduced by permission of the Folger Shakespeare Library

¶ The newe Iewell of Health, wherein is contayned the most excellent Secretes of Phisicke and Philosophie, deuided into fower Bookes. In the which are the best approued remedies for the diseases as well inwarde as outwarde, of all the partes of mans bodie: treating very amplye of all Dystillations of Waters, of Oyles, Balmes, Quintessences, with the extraction of artificiall Saltes, the vse and preparation of Antimonie, and potable Gold, Gathered out of the best and most approued Authors, by that excellent Doctor *Gesnerus*. Also the Pictures, and maner to make the Vessels, Furnaces, and other Instrumentes thereunto belonging. Faithfully corrected and published in Englishe, by George Baker, Chirurgian.

Alchymia with her laboratory utensils on the title page to Gesner.
Reproduced by permission of the Folger Shakespeare Library

located somewhere between Tunis and Naples and is very reminiscent of Rabelais' Isle of the Quintessence (see *Gargantua and Pantagruel,* Bk. 5, xviii–xxv).[21] As David Kastan pointed out at the 1995 Shakespeare Association of America meeting in Chicago,[22] Prospero's island was certainly not in the West Indies, which the text tells us was visited by Ariel alone on one specific occasion to collect alchemical "dew" for Prospero (see 1.2.226–29), probably after one of the famous Bermuda tempests, or natural boilings of the salt sea water.

The greater problem for the designer to solve is the location of the laboratory itself. It could be within the cave and at least partially revealed to the audience, or it could be set up outdoors by the mouth of the cave, as many medieval alchemical furnaces were for obvious reasons of safety. Or, since the Folio gives a stage direction at one point for Prospero to be "on the top" while observing the banquet scene, the laboratory itself might likewise be located above the action. In modern theaters, the alchemical process as it occurs within an alembic could also be indicated by a slide image of an alembic projected on a backdrop, thus resulting in an insert effect much like the illustration of the *cauda pavonis* painted by an inventive artist for the 1582 edition of Salomon Trismosin's *Splendor Solis* (Harley MS 3469). This technique would allow the audience to see the fantastic color changes occurring within the alembic as the action progresses. Typical Golden Age scenery is depicted, along with music-making, dancing, and drinking, in this particular symbolic painting of the empowering alchemical moment, the sixth stage of the process or the *cauda pavonis,* that Prospero indicates by the colorful descent of the rainbow goddess Iris in his wedding masque for Miranda and Ferdinand. In any case, the succeeding descent of Juno (preferably in a chariot) must be marked for the audience by the appearance of recognizable peacocks in some form, since Iris clearly announces that "[Her] peacocks fly amain" (4.1.74), rather than by placing the goddess alone on a descending throne, as Sturgess suggests (93). He is surely correct, on the other hand, when he makes the following observation:

> Ariel, who probably owes his origins to Shakespeare's reading in Agrippa and other hermetic writings, is a type of Mercury, the winged god associated by Renaissance emblem writers with the notion, so germane to the play, that "Art is a help to nature". (In this role, Mercury is pictured mending a lute.) Ariel is the arch shape-changer in a play of metamorphosis. (85)

The first Booke

aforesayde. It shall be requisite and nædefull, to haue another great Glasse, able to receyue and holde eight or ten measures of lycour (to be as the receyuing vessell) which he shall verye well fasten with the necke of the Bodie hanging without, after such manner, that the necke of this be entred sufficient dæpe into the Receyuer : which twoo on such wyse ordered, lute diligentlye (rounde about) with the strongest lute, as the common manner is. But the figure following shall shewe to the eye all the sayde description of the Furnace, and the vesselles before mentioned. In which it behoueth to note, that the slowe Harrie ought not so exactly to extende vnto, and touche the Iron Grate: but sufficient it shall be, if the same caryeth the Coales thither, or to the Grate. A. representeth the doore, by which the Ayre entreth to nourishe and mayntayne the fire. B. the grate of Iron which sustayneth or beareth the Coales. C. the slowe Harrie, by which the Coales are poured in. D. the place where is layde the long Barre of Iron, which beareth the Bodie. E. the neck of the Bodie lying forth, whiche bendeth downewarde. F. representeth the great vessell receiuing. G. the bent or breathing holes, situated in the. iiij. angles or corners. H. the great hole, whiche is formed on the toppe of the Furnace. I. the couer seruinge for the greater hoale on the toppe.

After that the thinges shall be on such

Feeding charcoal into an alchemical furnace, Gesner, p. 18v. Reproduced by permission of the Folger Shakespeare Library

The *Cauda Pavonis* from Salomon Trismosin's *Splendor Solis* (Harley 3469, f28). By permission of the British Library

¶ The fourth Booke of Dyſtillations, *conteyning many ſingular ſecrete* Remedies.

An imaginative woodcut of an alchemical distillation vessel from Gesner, p. 211, illustrating the fruition of the alchemical Tree of Life from the body of the Green Dragon. Reproduced by permission of the Folger Shakespeare Library

As quicksilver, Ariel resists fixation with all his energies, which is why the island seems like a prison to him. On the other hand, Miranda must reflect the refined Mercury of the Philosophers, since she will participate in the chemical wedding, or the conjunction between purified Sulphur and Mercury that finally leads to the Philosopher's Stone. Some clear evocation of such alchemical symbolism is particularly important if the audience is to understand not only the alchemical nature of the play with its implications of social reformation, but also the political references to events in Shakespeare's time. In fact, Kastan has suggested recently that the exile of Prospero may be based on actual events in the life of the Holy Roman Emperor Rudolf II, who was deposed by the Hapsburg archdukes in favor of his brother Matthias. Rudolf was famous for his interest in magic and for maintaining alchemists at his palace in Prague, where he welcomed, among others, Gerard Dorn, Heinrich Khunrath, Martin Ruland, Oswald Croll, Michael Maier, and Dr. John Dee and Edward Kelly.[23] In 1606 the Archdukes jointly commented on Rudolf's "whole library of magic books," and justified the deposition as follows: "His majesty is interested only in wizards, alkymists, Kabbalists, and the like, sparing no expense to find all kinds of treasure, learn secrets, and use scandalous ways of harming his enemies" (quoted in Kastan, 98).

As Prospero's theatrical experiment in transmutation progresses on stage, even more fanciful alchemical imagery could be projected to the audience, as it was in actual alchemical texts. For example, a highly imaginative illustration of a distillation vessel as the tree of life appears in Gesner's manual. It depicts the purifying dew that is distilled from the mixture of Paracelsus' three principles—sulphur, mercury, and salt—as living blossoms, the flowers of the sacred art of alchemy.

In any case, the most important visual effect to be achieved in the last scene of *The Tempest* is that of gilding the costumes of all the actors. They should all literally glitter with gold during this scene, if the audience is to understand that Prospero has managed through his alchemical art to achieve the transmutation of both lead (King Alonso, who has compared himself to a leaden plummet) and earth (Caliban) and to re-create the Golden Age. Even if Prospero does not himself completely realize the fulfillment of his dream at this point, Miranda announces it quite clearly for everyone else in her famous exclamation, "O brave new world / That hath such people in't" (5.1.183–84). The modern audience should share as fully as possible in her wondrous vision of regeneration. Such a perfected world would be new to us all.

Notes

1. Keith Sturgess, "'A Quaint Device': *The Tempest* at the Blackfriars," *Jacobean Private Theatre* (London: Routledge and Kegan Paul, 1987), 73; hereafter cited parenthetically. This essay is reprinted in *Critical Essays on Shakespeare's "The Tempest,"* ed. Virginia Mason Vaughan and Alden T. Vaughan (New York: G. K. Hall, 1998), 107–29.

2. William Rockett, "Labor and Virtue in *The Tempest*," *Shakespeare Quarterly* 24 (1973): 83–84.

3. See Michael Srigley, *Images of Regeneration: A Study of Shakespeare's "The Tempest" and its Cultural Background* (Uppsala: University of Uppsala, 1985). In my own alchemical reading of the play, I have corrected some of Srigley's errors and have expanded on his insights with the help of emblem books and other visual materials of the Renaissance. Indebted as I am to his published dissertation, I disagree with his moralistic conclusion, which disapproves of Prospero's efforts to make a better world through his occult art.

4. See Peggy Muñoz Simonds, "'My charms crack not': The Alchemical Structure of *The Tempest*," *Comparative Drama* 31 (Winter 1997–98): 538–70. For a discussion of Prospero as Orpheus, who was also a magician and a renowned alchemist to the Renaissance, see my "'Sweet Power of Music': The Political Power of 'the Miraculous Harp' in Shakespeare's *The Tempest*," *Comparative Drama* 29 (1995): 61–90.

5. Patrick Scot, *The Tillage of Light: or, a True Discoverie of the Philosophicall Elixir, commonly called the Philosopher's Stone* (London: William Lee, 1623), sig. D1.

6. In the thirteenth century, Roger Bacon made a crucial distinction between experimental science like alchemy, and magic, which was clearly unlawful. William Eamon summarizes Bacon as follows:

> Magic, he argued is always illicit and sinful because it is either fraudulent as in the deceits perpetrated by jugglers and ventriloquists, or else it is accomplished with the aid of demons. Fraudulent magic is worthless and without power; it is simply sleight of hand. Demonic magic, while powerful, cannot be controlled by human agency; instead, through it demons exercise their power over human souls. Against magic Bacon upheld the power of nature and of "art using nature as an instrument."

See Eamon, *Science and the Secrets of Nature: Books of Secrets in Medieval and Early Modern Culture* (Princeton: Princeton University Press, 1994), 67.

7. At this time, royalty was the outsider, and Charles II returned to England with his personal alchemist. For a survey of the political uses of alchemy, see J. Andrew Mendelsohn, "Alchemy and Politics in England 1649–1665," *Past and Present* 135 (May 1992): 30–78.

8. Most of these are described by Charles Webster in *The Great Instauration: Science, Medicine, and Reform 1626–1660* (London: Duckworth, 1975).

9. For the widespread interest in the art and knowledge of alchemical language and practice during the Renaissance, see Lyndy Abraham, "The Alchemical Context," in *Marvell and Alchemy* (London: Scolar Press, 1990), 1–35; and Charles Nicholl, *The Chemical Theatre* (London: Routledge and Kegan Paul, 1980), 1–100.

10. Quoted in Stanton J. Linden, *Darke Hieroglyphicks: Alchemy in English Literature from Chaucer to the Restoration* (Lexington: University Press of Kentucky, 1996), 193.

11. Thomas Tymme, Dedicatory Epistle to Charles Blunt, Earl of Devonshire, *The Practise of Chymicall, and Hermeticall Physicke, for the Preservation of Health* (London: Thomas Creede, 1605), sig. A3.

12. See Cornelius Agrippa of Nettesheim, *Of the Vanitie and Uncertaintie of Artes and Sciences*, ed. Catherine M. Dunne (Northridge, Calif: California State University, 1974). Agrippa's ironic attack on alchemy indicates his own deep implication in the practice of this science. He was himself an adept.

13. Agrippa wrote an interesting paragraph on magicians (who were usually also alchemists) that is very similar to the speeches of both Medea and Prospero. Magicians, he said, who are

> inflamed by a religious love, adorned with hope, directed by faith—can see the whole truth of things: we though Natural, know those things which are above nature, and understand all things below ... Hence it comes to pass that though we are framed a natural body, yet we sometimes praedominate over nature, and cause such wonderfull, sodain and difficult operations, as that the evil spirits obey us, the stars are disordered, the heavenly powers compelled, the Elements made obedient; so devout men and those elevated by these Theological vertues, command the Elements, drive away Fogs, raise the winds, cause rain, cure diseases, raise the dead, all which things to have been done amongst diverse Nations, Poets and Historians do sing and relate.

See *Three Books of Occult Philosophy*, trans. J. F. (London: R. W. for Gregory Moule, 1651), sig. Aa3.

14. See Allison Coudert, *Alchemy: The Philosopher's Stone* (Boulder, Colo.: Shambhala Publications, Inc., 1980), 132. On the quest for the Golden Fleece as an archetypal myth of alchemy for the Renaissance, see "R. B." (R. Bostocke), *The Difference Betweene the Aunceint Phisicke ... and the latter Phisicke* (London: for Robert Walley, 1585), sig. Hii; and Antoine Faivre, "An Approach to the Theme of the Golden Fleece in Alchemy," *Alchemy Revisited*, ed. Z. R. M. von Martels (Leiden: E. J. Brill, 1990), 250–55.

15. John S. Mebane, *Renaissance Magic and the Return of the Golden Age: The Occult Tradition and Marlowe, Jonson, and Shakespeare* (Lincoln and London: University of Nebraska Press, 1989), 181.

16. Thomas Tymme, *A Light in Darkness which illumineth for all the **Monas Hieroglyphica** of the famous and profound Dr. John Dee, discovering Natures closet and revealing the true Christian secrets of Alchimy* (Oxford: Bodleian Library, 1963), 29.

17. For a survey of such publications, see Eamon, *Science and the Secrets of Nature*.

18. See Gareth Roberts, *The Mirror of Alchemy: Alchemical Ideas and Images in Manuscripts and Books from Antiquity to the Seventeenth Century* (Toronto and Buffalo: University of Toronto Press, 1994).

19. Srigley, 42–43.

20. Conrad Gesner, *The Jewell of Health: The Practise of the New and Old Physicke* (London: Peter Short, 1599), 10.

21. Srigley, 38–39.

22. David Kastan, "'The Duke of Milan / And his Brave Son': Dynastic Politics in *The Tempest*," in *Critical Essays*, ed. Virginia Mason Vaughan and Alden T. Vaughan, 93; hereafter cited parenthetically.

23. Srigley, 23.

Part Three
Text and Performance

Stage Directions as Evidence: The Question of Provenance

ALAN C. DESSEN

THE TERM *PROVENANCE* ("PLACE OF ORIGIN, DERIVATION") IS REGULARLY INVOKED by theater historians and editors in their treatments of Elizabethan, Jacobean, and Caroline plays. For scholars such as Andrew Gurr and Roslyn Knutson, to establish a play's provenance is to link it to a specific theater or dramatic company or both. Here is a straightforward and eminently clear use of the concept. For an editor or bibliographer, however, to establish the provenance of a printed play is to move onto slightly different terrain so as (ideally) to determine what kind of manuscript(s) or printed text(s) were used by the compositor(s) who actually set the type. Such analyses can be crucial for various projects, but the inferences can be tricky and the results murky.

A highly visible example of this second sense of *provenance* is found in the familiar division of Shakespeare's plays. The so-called "good" quartos (*Titus Andronicus, Love's Labor's Lost, A Midsummer Night's Dream,* Q2 *Romeo and Juliet, Much Ado About Nothing, Richard II,* 1 and 2 *Henry IV, The Merchant of Venice,* Q2 *Hamlet*) may stand at one remove from Shakespeare's initial script, the draft he delivered to his fellow players, the beginning of what I conceive of as his conversation with his colleagues that eventually resulted in a production. The short or so-called "bad" quartos (e.g., the first printed editions of 2 *Henry VI,* 3 *Henry VI, Romeo and Juliet, Merry Wives of Windsor, Henry V, Hamlet*) may reflect a performance of some version of the play as remembered by one or more actors and, if so, provide valuable evidence about the end of that conversation. Other printed texts (e.g., Folio *Hamlet,* Folio *King Lear*) may correspond to the performance text, an approximation of the words actually included in a performance. Other Folio texts (e.g., *The Tempest, Measure for Measure, Merry Wives of Windsor, The Winter's Tale, Two Gentlemen of Verona*) probably give us the play as transcribed (and perhaps edited or "improved") by scrivener Ralph Crane. Here are at least four different narratives about origins, any one of which may affect how a scholar reads or values a given stage direction. For example, a "good quarto" or "foul papers" play may include signals that demonstrate an author's conception but not what was actually staged; a Ralph Crane transcript may provide an elegant reshaping (for the benefit of a reader) and hence a possible distortion of an author's or book-keeper's stage direction.

Without doubt, then, provenance is a crucial, bedrock issue for 1) editors of English Renaissance printed plays and 2) those theater historians who seek to reconstruct specific buildings or stages. To see this provenance issue at work one need only look at editorial treatments of Juliet's "That which we call a rose / By any other **** would smell as sweet" (2.2.43–44)[1] or at such landmark works as G. F. Reynolds' book on the Red Bull and Bernard Beckerman's book on the Globe. When working with either texts or buildings, scholars must be as scrupulous as possible about "placing" the manuscript or printed play so as not to build edifices upon shifting sands.

This scholarly desire for precise distinctions then carries over to other related areas of investigation, for editors or theater historians readily transfer the same rigor and the same habits of thought to their consideration of the language used or assumed by whoever wrote the stage directions in a given text. Despite the efforts of scholars such as William Long, moreover, some canards persist that smooth over such a transfer—most notably a putatively clear and discernible distinction between the wording of a stage direction that might appear in authorial copy and the alternative wording that would be appropriate for a playhouse manuscript (the supposed "prompt-book") that would actually serve as the basis for a performance. That no such clear distinction can be sustained from the actual playhouse documents (including the recently rediscovered annotations by two different hands in *The Two Merry Milkmaids*) has apparently not made a significant dent in this formulation or set of expectations.

The varied editorial formulations linked to provenance are too complex to be summed up neatly here. A useful summary of a theatrical version, however, is provided by T. J. King. Given limited information from sources external to the playtexts themselves, theater historians who seek to reconstruct stages and staging attribute the greatest "authority" to those manuscripts or printed texts that demonstrate not the author's wishes but rather actual playhouse practice. For King, stage directions in printed texts derived from supposed "foul papers" may actually "represent the author's intentions not fully realized on stage." Therefore, the principal evidence for reconstructing Elizabethan stages and stage practice should come from "texts dependent on playhouse copy," while, conversely, "texts evidently not derived from the playhouse have no primary value as evidence for the study of staging" (8). Given the available evidence, King admits 276 plays from the period 1599–1642 into his charmed circle of "primary value" and excludes, as having no "primary value," such authorial texts as *All's Well That Ends Well, Coriolanus,* and *Antony and Cleopatra.*

As a particularly rigorous version of a widely held position, King's formulation warrants scrutiny. In his terms, a never-performed play, a play with no discernible connection to a theater, or a play written by an amateur would not seem solid evidence upon which to build inferences about theatrical practice. Similarly, a playtext known to be a scribal copy, or for some other reason at several removes from the playhouse, might also seem a chancy item to use as evidence. But can such a yardstick be rigorously applied to all situations? As Bernard Beckerman asks in his review of King's book: "Is the staging projected by an experienced dramatist less reliable a guide to playhouse practice than actual prompt copy?" King may assume "that demonstration of playhouse origin automatically endows a text with theatrical authority greater than that of all other texts," but Beckerman asks: "Is not the text of a mature Shakespearean play, whether or not of playhouse origin, likely to reflect staging practice more accurately than the prompt manuscript of a relatively inexperienced author such as Henry Glapthorne?" (243, 239–40).

Beckerman's questions become especially pertinent when the focus is upon recovering not the physical features of a given playhouse but rather the shared theatrical language used in stage directions. Scholars seeking to tease out the number of stage doors or the presence of flying machinery at the Rose cannot use as evidence scenes or stage directions from a playtext linked to the Red Bull. Should or should not the same stricture then pertain to the terms or signifiers (what I think of as the theatrical vocabulary) found in stage directions? When isolating and defining such terms, how much does it matter if the stage direction comes from: a play never acted? a play revised by its author(s) before publication? a Red Bull versus a Globe play? a play written for child actors? a masque? a play from 1588 versus one from 1635?

To pursue such questions that link the value or usability of the evidence found in stage directions to provenance, I will explore some case studies.[2]

Adrasta

Consider as an extreme case John Jones's *Adrasta,* a tragicomedy printed in 1635 and, according to its title page, "Never Acted." As G. E. Bentley notes (4: 603), the dedication provided by this otherwise unknown author conjures up the image of a university man who, *"encourag'd by the general good liking and content"* that his friends offered *"in the hearing of it,"* offered the play to the players who *"upon a slight and half view of it, refused to do it that right"* so that *"it hath again been under the file since they saw it."* Here then is a play by an amateur that not only was never acted but was in fact rejected by some theatrical company (*"The reason I well know not, unless perhaps it had not in it so much Witchcraft in Poetry, as, now 'tis known, the Stage will bear"*).[3]

Jones' dramaturgy is, to put it mildly, clumsy, most notably in two elaborate scenes. In the first, Lucilio helps his beloved Althea escape a death sentence by providing her with a disguise and then taking her place. The sequence of stage directions reads: *"Enter Lucilio with a bag, as if apparel were in it"*; *"He throws a stone up to the window; Althea looks out"*; *"she lets down a line, to which he fastens the disguise"*; *"She draws up the bag, and while she is clothing"* he speaks: "once more lend your line"; *"Having again let down the Line, she draws up a Ladder of Cords"* (he instructs: "Fasten those Hooks to your window, and come down"); *"She fastens the Hooks above, he below: And then coming down he receives her"*; finally *"He goes up into the window"* (19–22).

After all these maneuvers, Lucilio (somehow) disguises himself as Althea so as to be executed in her place. He therefore next appears with others *"as going to the Rock"* along with *"the executioner, Frailware and others with Halberds."* "The Executioner with one more leads him up to the Rock, where he begins to bind his hands," at which point Lady Julia (Althea's mother) enters *"running with her hair disheveled,"* *"sees them on the Rock,"* *"Runs up to them,"* tries to kiss what she thinks is her daughter, *"and putting by his Scarf he is known."* The mother *"throws off his Scarf,"* and Lucilio, who has kept up this disguise so as to facilitate Althea's escape, *"offers to throw himself off the Rock"* (29–31).

What, if anything, can be made of *Adrasta* as evidence? Even without the title page's "Never Acted" and the author's prefatory remarks, the level of ineptitude here is high, so that no responsible scholar is going to build a case for the staging of window-ascent-descent scenes or rock-execution scenes or disguise conventions solely upon this evidence. However, some of the terms used by Jones do correspond to the theatrical vocabulary found in playtexts linked to experienced professionals and performed by professional companies. For example, of the many execution scenes in this period, few if any call for a "rock" as the place of execution, especially one from which a figure can offer *"to throw himself,"* but many of these same scenes do call for distinctive figures, such as an executioner, and for figures bearing halberds (often presented elliptically as *"enter with halberds"*). Similarly, to bring on a female figure *"running with her hair disheveled"* is to invoke a stock stage effect (usually linked to madness, extreme grief, or recent violence such as rape); to use an *as [if]* construction (*"as going to the Rock"*; *"as if apparel were in it"*) is to invoke another widely used device that, as I have argued elsewhere (*Recovering*, chapter 7—though I do not invoke *Adrasta*), is an essential part of English Renaissance theatrical language. Whether from his reading of plays, his playgoing, or his native wit, even this amateurish author of the 1630s employs some signifiers in a theatrical vocabulary that stretches back to the late 1580s.[4]

The presence of such terms in playtexts not linked to professional companies and playhouses is a phenomenon that extends well beyond Jones and *Adrasta*. For example, the tragedies of Thomas Goffe have unquestioned academic auspices (according to the title pages of the 1631 Quarto of *The Raging Turk*, the 1632 Quarto of *The Courageous Turk*, and the 1633 Quarto of *Orestes*, all three were acted by the students of Christ Church Oxford), but their stage directions often are indistinguishable from those found in comparable professional plays. Similarly, the manuscript play *Tom à Lincoln* appears to be linked to Gray's Inn, not a playhouse, and may indeed be a spoof of the romance form, but the stage directions (in which Heywood may have had a hand or a main finger) are very much in tune with contemporary usage elsewhere. As examples from Goffe's *The Raging Turk* consider: *manet-manent* (205, 340, 870); *solus-alone* (367, 1182, 1732, 2268, 2522); *"at several doors"* (66, 1503); *"pass over the stage"* (536, 2777); *"drums and trumpets"* (563–64, 603); various forms of *"offers to"* (631, 1416); and *"Drum sounds. Enter soldiers severally, dropping in sweating, as from fight"* (2435–56).[5] From *Tom à Lincoln* consider: *"he offers to stab himself, and she holds his hands"* (38–41); two uses of *"a far off"* (167, 801–03); two uses of *"Exeunt at one door: Enter ... at another"* (386, 2031); three uses of *manet* (686, 1912, 2336); *"Enter ... with her hair about her ears"* (2252); two uses of *"as from"* (799, 2406); several uses of *within* (818–19, 829, 2171–72, 2459); and several distinctive *unready* signals, including *"enter ... in their night habiliments"* (2494–95) and "*Enter Rusticano with one hose off the other on, without any britches*" (2419).

The Devil's Charter

At an opposite extreme from the unacted *Adrasta*, the Oxford venue for Goffe's tragedies, and the likely Gray's Inn auspices for *Tom à Lincoln*, stands Barnabe Barnes's *The Devil's Charter* (published in 1606), which is clearly a Globe play and, as such, is regularly mined for useful nuggets by theater historians. Even though the provenance is clear, however, to trust in this printed text as firm evidence for playhouse practice requires a leap of faith. First, according to the title page the play has been "*reviewed, corrected, and augmented*" by the author since its performance by the King's Men "*for the more pleasure and profit of the Reader.*" Equally important, the play as printed contains many odd or special features: two or three times as many "study" scenes as any other play of the period; an unusually wide array of spectacular effects involving devils, battles (see I1v), papal pageantry, and violence (as with "*He draweth in Rotsi by the heels groaning*"—K4v); and a unique set of signals for a *vanish*. When looking at such scenes or stage directions, the theater historian cannot disentangle what was actually presented at the Globe from what has been "*augmented*" by Barnes for the published version.

Consider the *vanish* effect as set up by Barnes after Pope Alexander calls forth a devil to reveal how two figures had been murdered. For the first, the devil "*goeth to one door of the stage, from whence he bringeth the Ghost of Candie ghastly haunted by Caesar pursuing and stabbing it, these vanish in at another door*"; for the second, "*He bringeth from the same door Gismond Viselli, his wounds gaping and after him Lucrece undressed, holding a dagger fixed in his bleeding bosom: they vanish*" (G2). If only the second of these instant replays had survived, "*they vanish*" would be as unrevealing as most of many other comparable stage directions I have collected, but, unlike any other evidence I have found, the first set of figures "*vanish in at another door*" (i.e., at a door other than the "*one door of the stage*" from which the devil originally brought them). If one can trust Barnes, these two vanishings were therefore effected not by means of a verisimilar trick (e.g., a trap door, fireworks, or a mist) but by means of a movement across the stage and a "normal" *exeunt* through a stage door.

Some version of this play was performed at the Globe, so that, in at least one sense, provenance is clear. Moreover, Barnes (more often than Jones) invokes terms from a widespread theatrical vocabulary: "*in her night gown*" (C1); "*offereth to stab herself*" (C4); "*upon the walls*" (D2, D3v, H3). Unlike the many "study" scenes (and related discoveries) and special effects, Barnes's approach to a *vanish* situation requires no more than a stage door and, as such, would seem to be an elegant, efficient solution that would in turn shed considerable light upon stage practice in many comparable scenes (including eight in Shakespeare's plays). Despite such tempting evidence in a text with clear provenance, however, today's reader cannot be certain what in this printed text corresponds to the King's Men's staging practices and what has been "*augmented*" by Barnes "*for the more pleasure and profit of the Reader.*" To build a scholarly edifice primarily upon elements unique to this play therefore seems unwarranted, but to draw upon Barnes's terms to help to gloss other comparable terms elsewhere (as part of a shared vocabulary) would seem reasonable.

Ben Jonson

Barnes provides only one extant play, albeit, in theatrical terms, a highly provocative one. In contrast, Ben Jonson provides a large number of plays that span over thirty years and were performed by a variety of companies (including three by the child actors). Yet the staging signals in Jonson's printed plays are even less reliable as evidence about current playhouse practice than those of Barnes— not because of variations in provenance, but because of Jonson's own distinctive practice of augmenting his texts for a reader. Thus, the 1600 Quarto version of *Every Man Out of His Humour* (according to its title page "As it was first composed by the Author B. J. / Containing more than hath been Publicly spoken or Acted") may have little in common with the version staged by the Lord Chamberlain's Men in 1599. The first printed version of *Volpone* (the 1607 Quarto), in turn, contains no stage directions at all, not even an *enter;* the first printed version of *The Alchemist* (the 1612 Quarto) has only one ("*Dol is seen*" at 2.3.210). The various signals now familiar to readers (e.g., the entrance of Volpone to the trial in Act 4 "*as impotent*") were added in the 1616 Folio and arguably represent the author's gift to his reader.

Jonson, however, despite some well-known disparaging comments, was highly knowledgeable about his contemporary theater.

The stage directions he chose to insert in the 1616 Folio and in some of his Quartos can be bizarre at times (*"This Scene is acted at two windows, as out of two contiguous buildings"*; *"He grows more familiar in his Courtship, plays with her paps, kisseth her hands, etc."*—*The Devil is an Ass* 2.6.37.s.d., 71.s.d.) but nonetheless are regularly couched in a standard vocabulary to be found elsewhere. As with Barnes, to build edifices composed of elements found only in Jonson's signals would seem unwarranted, but to draw upon such materials when they do correspond to comparable terms used by other playwrights (as part of a shared vocabulary) would seem appropriate.

Ralph Crane and *The Tempest*

The stage directions in *The Tempest* have received considerable attention. Given their distinctive features (e.g., unusually elaborate details, terms not found in other Shakespeare plays), scholars have argued that they are a product not of Shakespeare but of scrivener Ralph Crane. John Jowett in particular has offered a closely reasoned analysis that, building upon both Shakespeare's and Crane's practice elsewhere, singles out fifteen specific phrases which for Jowett do not reflect Shakespeare's characteristic usages but rather seem "mostly effective literary embellishments" that "are inadequate for the theater" (114). Some of the assumptions here (e.g., about what is "literary" versus what is "theatrical," or about the specificity that the players expect from a playwright) strike me as suspect, but Jowett does single out a series of distinctive terms (e.g., "*A tempestuous noise,*" "*several strange shapes,*" "*with gentle actions of salutations,*" "*with mocks and mows*") in order to link them to Crane rather than to Shakespeare.

Let me concentrate upon one such phrase cited by Jowett (and earlier by W. W. Greg, 151–52)—the disappearance of the banquet in 3.3 by means of "*a quaint device*" as found in "*Enter Ariel (like a Harpy) claps his wings upon the Table, and with a quaint device the Banquet vanishes*" (TLN 1584, 3.3.52.s.d.). Greg states: "I cannot imagine an author writing notes for the producer, still less a bookkeeper, using the phrase 'with a quaint device': it is descriptive of the thing seen, a compliment to the machinist." Jowett adds (112): "'*Device*', like '*shapes*' and '*actions*', is of no practical value, and to someone involved in the theater nothing is gained by the phrase that is not implicit in '*vanishes.*'" Assumed here is that the details and phrasing in authorial signals are consistently directed at the players and are couched in practical terms, an assumption that belies the myriad "fictional" or descriptive signals from Munday, Heywood, and others that survive in playhouse documents.

Admittedly, the term "quaint device" *is* unusual and cannot be found in stage directions elsewhere—in part because such tricks themselves are not that common. The scene closest to the vanishing banquet in *The Tempest* is the denouement of *The Wasp*, a manuscript play from the 1630s, where a sumptuous banquet of "Viands" is suddenly transformed into something horrible to look at ("snakes toads and newts"—2220–21) and then, later in the scene, reverts to its original condition ("these comfortable viands"—2325). The stage direction for the first moment reads: "*the table turns and such things appear*" (2220–21); and for the second: "*Table turns*" (2324). In the induction to *Wily Beguiled* (printed 1606), a juggler, who specializes in "tricks of Legerdemain, sleight of hand, cleanly conveyance, or *deceptio visus*," provides "a trick of cleanly conveyance" for the Prologue by adroitly switching the title of the play to follow; the stage direction reads: "*'Spectrum' is conveyed away: and 'Wily Beguiled,' stands in the place of it*" (24–25, 41–42, 46–47). The closest to the "quaint device" wording I can offer is to be found in Lupton's *All for Money*, a moral play from the 1570s, where, in an allegorical "birth" scene: "*Here Money shall make as though he would vomit, and with some fine conveyance Pleasure shall appear from beneath and lie there apparelled*" (B1).

Of these four roughly comparable examples that range from the 1570s to the 1630s, the signals range from the practical and theatrical ("*Table turns*") to the very general or "permissive" ("*some fine conveyance,*" "*a quaint device*"). What is distinctive in *The Tempest* (here and in other comparable moments) is not the wording but the unusual stage effect. Although "fine conveyance" or "cleanly conveyance" would seem to be the terms of choice (though two references do not a pattern make), in such a context "quaint device" does not seem all that unusual. Regardless of who is actually responsible for the term (and, despite Jowett's closely reasoned formulation, I am not prepared to rule out Shakespeare), "quaint device" is not outlandish or even atypical as theatrical vocabulary.

The other terms singled out by Jowett as Crane's contribution also warrant investigation in terms of the larger context of comparable scenes. I can provide no exact equivalent to "*with mocks and mows*" (TLN 1617, 3.3.82.s.d.), but Fletcher's *Bonduca* has Junius sing a song with Petillius "*after him in mockage*" (6: 100) and two Caroline plays provide "*Dance an Antic in which they use action of Mockery and derision to the three Gentlemen*" (Brome, *The English Moor*: 2,

67) and *"tread a solemn measure with changes, the whilst Wittworth dances an antic mockway, then retires to his chair and sleeps"* (Clavell, *The Soddered Citizen*, 1916–18). For *The Tempest*'s "A tempestuous noise of thunder and lightning heard" (TLN 2, 1.1.0.s.d.), noises of all kinds are very common in stage directions (roughly 130 examples), and other storm scenes include *"Storm and Tempest"* (Folio *King Lear*, TLN 1584, 2.4.284.s.d.), *"Sound, thunder, and Tempest"* (Heywood, *The Golden Age*, 3: 78), and *"A Tempest, Thunder and Lightning"* (Fletcher and Massinger, *The Sea Voyage*, 9: 2). The manuscript of Heywood's *The Captives* provides *"Thunder"* in the left margin and then calls for figures to *"Enter after a great Tempestuous storm"* (456), with the first spoken line: "was ever known such a tempestuous night" (458). Similarly, *The Tempest*'s *"several strange shapes"* (TLN 1536, 3.3.19.s.d.) should be compared to entrances *"in a fantastical shape"* (Brome, *The Antipodes*, 3: 316), *"in the shape of a Dragon"* (Heywood, *The Brazen Age*, 3: 175), *"in odd shapes"* (Ford, *Love's Sacrifice*, 1847); *"four Boys shaped like Frogs"* (Fletcher, *The Fair Maid of the Inn*, 9: 201); and devils *"in a fearful shape"* (Dekker and Massinger, *The Virgin Martyr*, 5.1.122.s.d.), *"in a frightful shape"* (Dekker, *If This Be Not a Good Play*, 4.4.38.s.d.), *"in most ugly shape"* (Barnes, *The Devil's Charter*, A2v). *Shape* is also used regularly as an equivalent for *disguise*, as in Heywood's *The Silver Age*, which provides *"Ganymede shaped like Socia,"* *"Jupiter shaped like Amphitrio,"* and *"Juno in the shape of old Beroe"* (3: 98, 100, 148), or in Fletcher's *The Faithful Shepherdess*, where Amaryllis first appears *"in the shape of Amoret,"* then reappears *"in her own shape"* (2: 406, 408).

Such usages outside *The Tempest* raise several questions. First, are the terms attributed to Crane as unusual as claimed by Jowett? Are the situations or stage effects (involving supernatural figures and tempests) the distinctive feature rather than the theatrical vocabulary? If the supposedly eccentric terms and phrases linked to Crane can indeed be documented elsewhere, are quaint devices, tempestuous noises, and strange shapes potential signifiers in a shared theatrical vocabulary, rather than exotic products of the imagination of a professional scrivener?

The Masque

In contrast to the scattered and often frustratingly limited evidence about staging practices in the professional theaters, plentiful evidence does survive about the presentation of the Jacobean masques.

However, information about those no-expense-spared productions with their one-time-only effects tells us little about the exigencies of professional repertory theater in the same period, where any onstage devices or choices within the confines of the wooden O had to be practical and repeatable.

This distinction between repeatability and practicality in repertory theater and one-shot extravagant effects in the masque is no small matter. For example, in one of his masques, Campion calls for nine trees to be *"suddenly conveyed away,"* but a note in the printed text informs the reader, "Either by the simplicity, negligence, or conspiracy of the painter, the passing away of the trees was somewhat hazarded; the pattern of them the same day having been shown with much admiration, and the nine trees being left unset together even to the same night." As the editor notes: "Apparently a stagehand had forgotten to reattach the trees to the engine after displaying them to the nobility during the day" (222).

In contrast, masques designed to be included within plays that were to be performed as part of a professional repertory are particularly valuable evidence in suggesting how far the resources of a playhouse could be stretched for masque-like effects (as with *Tempest* 4.1, *The Maid's Tragedy* 1.2, *Women Beware Women* 5.2). In such instances, moreover, provenance could indeed be a significant issue (as with comparable special effects involving the supernatural or the spectacular), for some playhouses may have been better equipped than others. Nonetheless, the language used to signal such effects need not have varied significantly from one venue to another.

John Marston and the Child Actors

The provenance of stage directions can have demonstrable importance when the plays in question have been conceived with the child actors in mind. Since Lyly's plays provide very few theatrical signals, as a test case I have looked at the evidence furnished in eight plays linked to John Marston (*Jack Drum's Entertainment, What You Will, Antonio and Mellida, Antonio's Revenge, The Malcontent, The Dutch Courtesan, The Fawn, Sophonisba*). Clearly, a few of the terms invoked here *are* linked to distinctive physical features of Paul's or another private theater: *"Andrugio's ghost is placed betwixt the music-houses"* (*Antonio's Revenge* 5.3.49.s.d.); *"A treble viol and a bass lute play softly within the canopy"* and *"Syphax hasteneth within the canopy, as to Sophonisba's bed"* (*Sophonisba* 4.1.200.s.d., 218.s.d.). Similarly, given the limited number of boys available to an adult company, some of Marston's calls for personnel also point to a special venue: "*Company of Boys within*"; "*Enter as many Pages with Torches as you can*" (*What You Will* 2: 259, 290).

Other features of Marston's stage directions are also distinctive—especially when compared to those linked to the adult companies of the same decade. For example, among the stage directions in the Shakespeare canon can be found only one allusion to "the Act," the often cited signal in Folio *A Midsummer Night's Dream*, "*They sleep all the Act*" (TLN 1507, 3.2.463.s.d.), presumably because during the 1590s and early 1600s no such act breaks took place in the public theaters. In contrast, such references to "the Act," usually associated with music, are commonplace in Marston's plays. *Sophonisba* is especially rich in such signals (see 1.2.236.s.d., 2.1.0.s.d., 2.3.113.s.d., 3.2.84.s.d., 4.1.218.s.d.), but links between music and stage business are sprinkled throughout this canon, as in: "*While the act is a-playing, ... enter*" (*The Fawn* 5.0.s.d.); "*they clothe Francisco, whilst Bydet creeps in and observes them. Much of this is done whilst the Act is playing*" (*What You Will* 3.1.0.s.d.). Music cues without references to "the act" are also plentiful, even to the extent of "*Consort of music*" (*The Fawn* 1.2.102.s.d.).

Other distinctive terms found in these stage directions may be linked either to the child actors or, equally likely, to Marston's idiosyncrasies. For example, twice in *Antonio and Mellida* he uses *scene* in a fashion seldom found elsewhere: "*and so the scene begins*" (3.2.123.s.d.); "*They two stand, using seeming compliments, whilst the scene passeth above*" (1.1.115.s.d). Marston, moreover, like Field and Chapman (but not Middleton), regularly makes use of Latin words or phrases where many of his contemporaries would not: "*cantant*" (*Antonio and Mellida* 2.1.61.s.d., 3.1.108.s.d., 3.2.36.s.d., 4.1.149.s.d.; *Antonio's Revenge* 2.2.136.s.d., 3.2.52.s.d.; *Sophonisba* 4.1.212.s.d.); "*Cantat Gallice*" and "*Cantat saltatque cum cithera*" (*The Dutch Courtesan* 2.2.69.s.d., 5.1.20.s.d.); "*tacite*" (*Antonio and Mellida* 1.1.74.s.d.); "*tantum*" (*Antonio and Mellida* 1.1.98.s.d.).[6] Other bits of atypical stage business may be linked to the boy actors or merely to Marston's own special vocabulary. For example, in *Antonio's Revenge* the three revengers vow their revenge, "*wreathe their arms,*" "*Exeunt, their arms wreathed,*" and in a later scene "*Exeunt twined together*" (4.2.110.s.d., 118.s.d., 5.2.97.s.d.). A truly distinctive locution is provided twice in *The Fawn*: "*Enter Zuccone, pursued by Zoya on her knees*"; "*Enter Don Zuccone, following Donna Zoya on his knees*" (4.280.s.d., 5.89.s.d.).

The theater historian must tread carefully (or proceed "*on his knees*") when drawing upon such odd or even unique signals, for, especially with terms linked to specific playhouses or theater companies, provenance can be important. Overall, however, Marston's usages, although sometimes idiosyncratic, are nonetheless usually in the main stream (or at least close). As in *The Tempest,* some of the oddities can be linked to plot materials or distinctive personae. For example, given a large number of dumb shows (most notably in *Antonio's Revenge*), Marston makes unusually heavy use of *seems;* from one stage direction alone comes: *"seemeth to send out Strotzo; ... talks with her with seeming amorousness; she seemeth to reject his suit ... they go to her, seeming to solicit his suit"* (*Antonio's Revenge* 3.1.0.s.d.). In a few of the plays (especially the two Antonio plays) more details are spelled out than is the norm elsewhere in the period. Marston, moreover, will sometimes take a stock term and put his own twist on it. Thus, like his fellow dramatists he regularly uses *offers to:* "*offers to go out*" (*Antonio's Revenge* 3.1.0.s.d.); "*She offers to stab herself*" (*Jack Drum's Entertainment* F1); "*Antonio offers to come near and stab*" (*Antonio's Revenge* 3.1.139.s.d.); but less typically Marston often completes the action in the same signal: "*He draws his rapier, offers to run at Piero, but Maria holds his arm and stays him*" (*Antonio's Revenge* 1.2.217.s.d.); "*Offering to leap into bed, he discovers Vangue*" (*Sophonisba* 3.1.182.s.d.); "*Offers to go out, and suddenly draws back*" (*The Dutch Courtesan* 2.1.145.s.d.); "*They offer to run all at Piero, and on a sudden stop*" (*Antonio's Revenge* 5.3.105.s.d.).

In general, this learned dramatist who wrote exclusively for the child actors does share a common theatrical vocabulary with his contemporaries, to the extent that his usages often cannot be distinguished from those of Shakespeare, Dekker, Fletcher, Heywood, and Middleton. To cite a few examples, Marston's use of *far off* or *afar off* for offstage sounds is the same as Shakespeare's. Compare "*A march far off is heard*"; "*Cornets, a march far off*"; "*The cornets afar off sounding a charge*" (*Sophonisba* 5.1.71.s.d., 5.2.29.s.d., 5.3.0.s.d.) with "*March afar off, and shout within*" (Folio *Hamlet* TLN 3836, 5.2.349.s.d.) and "*A Tucket afar off*" (*All's Well* TLN 1602, 3.5.0.s.d.). Similarly, Marston's use of *at one door, at the other door,* and *at several doors* is typical of the period—although one use of "*at several doors opposite*" (*The Malcontent* 5.1.0.s.d.) is distinctive. Throughout the period dramatists call both for officers carrying halberds and the elliptical *halberds* where no officers are specified. Marston provides both usages but more commonly invokes the latter: "*Enter Aurelia, two Halberds before and two after*" (*The Malcontent* 4.5.0.s.d.); enter "*Malheureux pinioned, ... and halberds*" (*The Dutch Courtesan* 5.3.0.s.d.).

Other Marston terms also correspond to usages elsewhere. For example, he regularly signals for male figures to enter *unbraced* (i.e., with their clothes unfastened), with the term 1) sometimes standing alone (*Antonio and Mellida* 3.2.0.s.d.; *The Malcontent* 2.1.0.s.d.); 2) sometimes accompanied by further details: "*Enter Piero unbraced, his arms bare, smeared in blood*" (*Antonio's Revenge* 1.1.0.s.d.); "*in his night–gown and a nightcap, unbraced*" (*Antonio's Revenge* 3.1.0.s.d.); and 3) sometimes omitted in favor of alternative details: "*in his night–gown and nightcap*" (*Antonio's Revenge* 3.1.131.s.d.); "*in his shirt*" (*The Malcontent* 2.5.2.s.d.); "*half dressed, in his black doublet and round cap*" (*What You Will* 3.1.0.s.d.). All of these locutions are widely used by other dramatists regardless of venue. The same is true of the many permutations of *manet*. The term itself can be found twice in these eight plays (*Sophonisba* 5.4.59.s.d.; *Jack Drum's Entertainment* B2v) along with one use of *remanet* (*The Fawn* 1.2.317.s.d.), but also present are a range of comparable locutions: "*All go out but*" (*Antonio's Revenge* 2.1.0.s.d., 3.1.106.s.d.; *The Malcontent* 1.6.0.s.d.; *The Fawn* 4.423.s.d.; *Antonio and Mellida* 4.1.261.s.d.); "*Exeunt all saving*" (*The Malcontent* 3.3.71.s.d., 5.3.1.s.d., 5.4.14.s.d.; *Antonio's Revenge* 3.1.145.s.d., 4.1.67.s.d., 5.1.0.s.d.; *The Dutch Courtesan* 5.1.163.s.d.); "*Exit. Only ... stay*" (*The Dutch Courtesan* 4.1.22.s.d.; *Sophonisba* Prologue.29.s.d., 2.1.153.s.d.).

To sum up: a few of the terms invoked in the stage directions found in these eight Marston plays may indeed be linked to specific conditions limited to the child actors or their playhouses, but most of the locutions are either standard vocabulary or some variation that reflects not the provenance behind the plays but rather Marston's idiosyncrasies. Indeed, such authorial idiosyncrasy (rather than theatrical provenance or chronology) emerges as the major variable when confronting the thousands of stage directions available as evidence.

The Significance of Chronology

In building upon stage directions as evidence the historian cannot ignore chronology, for some locutions found in the 1580s and early 1590s are superseded or simplified in the playtexts that follow. Earlier signals are often longer, without the many ellipses or shorthand forms that later become commonplace. Representative of the earlier approach is *Locrine* (printed 1595 though probably to be dated earlier), which provides: "*Let him write a little and then read*" (341);

"*Let them fight*" (797, 832); "*let Strumbo fall down*" (833–34); "*Then let both of them fall into the water*" (963–64); "*Let him sit down and pull out his victuals*" (1629–30); "*Let him make as though he would give him some*" (1669–70); "*Then let Locrine and Estrild enter again in a maze*" (2064); "*Let her offer to kill herself*" (2153). Signals for fights, falls, and other actions are commonplace in subsequent plays, but this *let* construction is hard to find after the early 1590s.

To minimize the importance of chronology is not to argue that staging procedures and the terms used to signal those procedures stayed the same in all theaters between the 1580s and the early 1640s. Nonetheless, the fact that a host of playwrights (that includes such seasoned professionals as Shakespeare, Heywood, Dekker, Fletcher, Middleton, Massinger, Shirley, and Brome) in many theaters over many decades appear to be using the same shared language strikes me as significant and revealing. Some account of the changes over time (as with the *let* construction or with *proffer* as opposed to *offer*) can be useful and informative, as are any distinctive usages or procedures limited largely to Peele, Greene, and the 1580s, but if (as is often the case) Shakespeare-Heywood and Brome-Shirley are invoking the same theatrical vocabulary, the importance of chronological distinctions is greatly diminished. Rather, what is of greatest significance are those signifiers that remain useful and meaningful over the full stretch of Elizabethan-Jacobean-Caroline drama.

Conclusion

In assessing stage directions as evidence (or in building mosaics from snippets in italics), the provenance of individual plays cannot be completely dismissed (as shown in Marston's references to the music-house and the canopy), but in practice this yardstick is less of an issue than other variables. Indeed, after looking at thousands of such stage directions, I can discern no technical backstage vocabulary that is the exclusive property of theatrical professionals (as opposed to amateurs or academics) or is linked to specific venues, nor can I document telling changes in the terms used between the 1590s and the 1630s. Admittedly, some usages are more likely to turn up in texts annotated for performance (e.g., *ready, clear*), but examples of the former are sprinkled throughout printed texts of the period, and examples of the latter, although plentiful in the manuscript of Heywood's *The Captives*, are found in only two other texts.

What needs stressing is that 1) there is indeed a widely shared theatrical vocabulary, especially from the 1590s on, and 2) the major variations in that vocabulary seem to arise not from different venues or different decades but from authorial idiosyncrasy. For example, Chapman is more likely to use Latin terms than any other professional dramatist, but it is Massinger who is particularly fond of *exeunt praeter* (or *preter*), where another dramatist would use *manet* or *exeunt all saving*. Similarly, Massinger and others regularly use *aside* as we understand the term today, but Shakespeare, for one, prefers other locutions (e.g., "*to himself*"—Folio *Richard III*, TLN 792, 1.3.317.s.d.; *The Merchant of Venice*, E4, 3.2.62.s.d.) and uses *aside* primarily to denote onstage positioning (see Quarto *Love's Labor's Lost*, E2v, 4.3.20.s.d.; E3, 4.3.42.s.d.; *Coriolanus*, TLN 992, 2.1.96.s.d.).

The provenance of stage directions may therefore be of considerable importance for some scholarly endeavors, but this yardstick is less significant for an investigation of a shared language of the theater. The language used by a professional dramatist may not be exactly the same as that used by a scrivener, an amateur writer, an academic, or a professional refashioning his play for a reader, nor is there an exact correlation among varying venues or during disparate decades. Nonetheless, by proceeding carefully (and by not building edifices upon unique or highly idiosyncratic usages) the theater historian can recover a range of terms that would have made excellent sense to Marlowe, Shakespeare, Dekker, Heywood, Jonson, Marston, Chapman, Middleton, Massinger, Brome, Ford, and Shirley.

Notes

1. In singling out this particular passage I have in mind the strictures of Fredson Bowers who argues that "for some readings there is no excuse for the choice of the bad over the good text" and that for him the choice between *name* and *word* serves "as a touchstone to distinguish a textually untrained editor from a good one." See his *On Editing Shakespeare* (Charlottesville: University Press of Virginia, 1966), 120–22.

2. These questions about the links between provenance and theatrical vocabulary have been generated by work on *A Dictionary of Stage Directions in English Drama, 1580–1642* that I compiled with Leslie Thomson (forthcoming from Cambridge University Press). Our entries are constructed from evidence derived from roughly 22,000 stage directions in over 500 plays.

3. Here and in subsequent passages I have modernized the original spelling and regularized the use of italics (the procedure followed in our dictionary).

4. Also found in *Adrasta* and widely used elsewhere are a scarf for disguise (see also 124) and a bar for courtroom scenes (23, 124).

5. Academic plays are often neo-classical comedies, declamatory tragedies, or learned allegories that do not invoke the terms or staging of the professional theater, but Goffe's three plays (written and performed during the second decade of the seventeenth century) are the exceptions that test the rule. Indeed, the onstage effects

in Goffe's tragedies often match or top anything found in other Jacobean tragedies: for example, from *The Courageous Turk:* "*Here Amurath cuts off Eumorphe's head, shows it to the Nobles*"; "*Here Schabin calls in his soldiers, and each of them presents to Amurath, the head of a dead Christian*"; "*The Heavens seem on fire, Comets and blazing Stars appear*" (711–12, 779–81, 1603–04); from *Orestes:* "*Enter Pylades and Orestes with his arm full of a dead man's bones and a Skull . . . Stamps upon them*" (E1). Before actually killing Aegisthus and Clytemnestra, Orestes ties them to their chairs, stabs Clytemnestra's child, "*stabs it again, that the blood spurts in his face. Turns it to her . . . Pulls bones from his pocket . . . Fills two cups with the child's blood: gives it them*" (G4v). In short, here is one "academic" dramatist not wedded to neo–classical decorum.

6. The use in stage directions of Latin terms (other than such workhorses as *exit-exeunt, manet-manent, moritur, solus-sola*) is wildly inconsistent. Many usages occur only once: Field's *aspiciens* for "looking at" (*A Woman is a Weathercock* 1.2.271–72); Massinger's "*Exeunt Cario et Rustici*" (*The Guardian* 4.2.48.s.d.— though the scene had begun [0.s.d.] with "*Enter Cario and Country men*"). Among dramatists writing for professional companies, Chapman out-Latins the field, for his arsenal (mostly of one-time usages) includes: *abscondit se; amplectitur eum; ascendit* (although elsewhere he uses *ascends*); *aufigiunt; aversus* (as an equivalent to *aside*); *bibit Ancilla; Chorus Juvenum cantantes et saltantes; cum aliis* (although "*with others*" appears in the same scene); *cum Pedisequis; cum suis* (six times); *descendit; exiturus* (seven times); *osculatur; procumbit; prodit; redit* (three times in the same scene); *Retrahit se* (twice in the same scene); *surgit.*

Works Cited

Barnes, Barnabe. *The Devil's Charter.* Edited by John S. Farmer. Tudor Facsimile Texts. Amersham, 1913.

Beckerman, Bernard. Review of T. J. King, *Shakespearean Staging, 1599–1642.* In *Renaissance Drama,* n.s. 4 (1971): 239–43.

———*Shakespeare at the Globe 1599–1609.* New York: Macmillan, 1962.

Bentley, Gerald Eades. *The Jacobean and Caroline Stage.* 7 vols. Oxford: Clarendon Press, 1941–68.

Bowers, Fredson. *On Editing Shakespeare.* Charlottesville: University Press of Virginia, 1966.

Brome, Richard. *The Dramatic Works of Richard Brome.* 3 vols. London, 1873.

Campion, Thomas. *The Works.* Edited by Walter R. Davis. Garden City, N.Y.: Doubleday, 1967.

Chapman, George. *The Plays of George Chapman: The Comedies.* Edited by Allan Holaday. Urbana: University of Illinois Press, 1970.

———*The Plays of George Chapman: The Tragedies with "Sir Gyles Goosecappe,"* Edited by Allan Holaday. Cambridge: D. S. Brewer, 1987.

Clavell, John. *The Soddered Citizen.* Edited by John Henry Pyle Pafford. The Malone Society. London, 1936.

Dekker, Thomas. *The Dramatic Works of Thomas Dekker.* Edited by Fredson Bowers. 4 vols. Cambridge: Cambridge University Press, 1953–61.

Dessen, Alan C. *Recovering Shakespeare's Theatrical Vocabulary.* Cambridge and N. Y.: Cambridge University Press, 1995.

Field, Nathan. *The Plays.* Edited by William Peery. Austin: University of Texas Press, 1950.

Fletcher, John. *The Works of Francis Beaumont and John Fletcher.* Edited by Arnold Glover and A. R. Waller. 10 vols. Cambridge: Cambridge University Press, 1905–12.

Ford, John. *Love's Sacrifice.* In *John Fordes Dramatische Werke.* Edited by W. Bang. Materialien zur Kunde des älteren englischen Dramas. Louvain, 1908.

Goffe, Thomas. *The Raging Turk* and *The Courageous Turk.* Edited by David Carnegie. The Malone Society. London, 1974.

——— *The Tragedy of Orestes.* STC 11982. London, 1633.

Greg, W. W. *The Editorial Problem in Shakespeare.* Oxford: Clarendon Press, 1951.

Gurr, Andrew. *The Shakespearean Stage 1574–1642.* Third Edition. Cambridge and N. Y.: Cambridge University Press, 1991.

Heywood, Thomas. *The Captives.* Edited by Arthur Brown. The Malone Society. London, 1953.

——— *The Dramatic Works of Thomas Heywood.* Edited by R. H. Shepherd. 6 vols. London, 1874.

Jones, John. *Adrasta, or The Woman's Spleen and Love's Conquest.* STC 14721. London, 1635.

Jonson, Ben. *Ben Jonson.* Edited by C. H. Herford and Percy and Evelyn Simpson. 11 vols. Oxford: Clarendon Press, 1925–52.

Jowett, John. "New Created Creatures: Ralph Crane and the Stage Directions in *The Tempest.*" *Shakespeare Survey* 36 (1983): 107–20.

King, T. J. *Shakespearean Staging, 1599–1642.* Cambridge: Harvard University Press, 1971.

Knutson, Roslyn Lander. *The Repertory of Shakespeare's Company 1594–1613.* Fayetteville and London: University of Arkansas Press, 1991.

Locrine. Edited by Ronald B. McKerrow. The Malone Society. London, 1908.

Long, William B. "Stage Directions: A Misinterpreted Factor in Determining Textual Provenance." *Text* 2 (1985): 121–37.

Lupton, Thomas. *All for Money.* Edited by John S. Farmer. Tudor Facsimile Texts. Amersham, 1910.

Marston, John. *The Fawn.* Edited by David A. Blostein. Revels Plays. Manchester: Manchester University Press, 1978.

——— *Jack Drum's Entertainment.* Edited by John S. Farmer. Tudor Facsimile Texts. Amersham, 1912.

——— *The Selected Plays.* Edited by MacDonald P. Jackson and Michael Neill. Cambridge and N. Y.: Cambridge University Press, 1986. [*Antonio and Mellida, Antonio's Revenge, The Dutch Courtesan, The Malcontent, Sophonisba*]

——— *What You Will.* In *The Plays.* Edited by H. Harvey Wood. 3 vols. London: Oliver & Boyd, 1938.

Massinger, Philip. *The Plays and Poems.* Edited by Philip Edwards and Colin Gibson. 5 vols. Oxford: Clarendon Press, 1976.

Reynolds, G. F. *The Staging of Elizabethan Plays at the Red Bull Theater, 1605–25.* New York: Modern Language Association of America, 1940.

Shakespeare, William. *The Norton Facsimile: The First Folio of Shakespeare.* Edited by Charlton Hinman. New York and London: W. W. Norton, 1968.

———*The Riverside Shakespeare.* Edited by G. Blakemore Evans. Boston: Houghton Mifflin, 1974.

———*Shakespeare's Plays in Quarto.* Edited by Michael J. B. Allen and Kenneth Muir. Berkeley and Los Angeles: University of California Press, 1982.

Thomson, Leslie. "A Quarto 'Marked for Performance': Evidence of What?" *Medieval and Renaissance Drama in England* 8 (1996): 176–210.

Tom à Lincoln. Edited by G. R. Proudfoot. The Malone Society. London, 1992.

The Wasp. Edited by J. W. Lever. The Malone Society. London, 1976.

Wily Beguiled. Edited by W. W. Greg. The Malone Society. London, 1913.

Show Business: The Editor in the Theater

JILL L. LEVENSON

> It must be remember'd, a Play is to be seen, and is made to be Represented with the Advantage of Action, nor can appear but with half the Spirit, without it.
> —Richard Steele, Preface to *The Conscious Lovers* (1723)

ACADEMIC INTEREST IN SHAKESPEARE'S THEATRICAL CRAFT MUST HAVE REACHED some kind of watershed lately, because it has already begun to provoke revisionists.[1] Nevertheless, major editorial projects since the Oxford *Shakespeare* continue to advertise their theatrical "orientation," "understanding," or "perspective."[2] If the publicity is new, however, the editorial premise goes back to the eighteenth century. Even Alexander Pope used theater history to explain textual errors; he had no compunctions about making it up.[3] More objective, Samuel Johnson incorporated bits of theatrical data in some of his annotations. Of the editors who immediately followed Johnson, George Steevens and Edmond Malone offered the most extensive dramaturgical notes, much of their scholarship treating the Elizabethan theater and its conventions. In addition, Malone's commentary refers to his *Historical Account of the Rise and Progress of the English Stage,* the collection of theatrical evidence which accompanied his edition. By the late eighteenth century, editors as well as drama critics tried to re-create the physical conditions of early performances in order to interpret plays and resolve textual anomalies.[4]

Of course, modern editors also use information about theater as a means of access to Shakespeare's plays, but the angle of approach has shifted because of other change. In the late twentieth century, scholarship has advanced on early dramatic texts less to reveal their permanent literary values than to expose their indeterminacy. Postmodernism has encouraged the study of plays as collaborative processes subject to many contingencies. Every sign of instability—from textual variants to adaptations in performance—has become valuable evidence for defining and illustrating the genre. Collectively, such evidence helps to reduce the inconsistencies of the edition published as a book, the material object containing a volatile text. Organized for maximum effect, information about a play's life in the theater tells the reader that the printed script, familiar and authoritative, may not always resemble its staged performances.

Shakespeare's *Romeo and Juliet* provides an ideal test case for such editorial treatment. In the first place, the play originates in two substantive texts and has appeared in a variety of editions since the seventeenth century. In the second, it has had a remarkable career on the stage since its initial performances at the end of the sixteenth century. From the Restoration on, it has been in production—in one form or another—almost continuously. During certain periods, it has enjoyed enormous success. The second half of the eighteenth century was one of those times: its 399 performances in London between 1751 and 1800 eclipsed those of *Hamlet*. The second half of the twentieth century has been another: hundreds of performances, internationally, have been surpassed by *Hamlet* alone.[5] Between the texts and the stage history falls a striking contradiction. The stylization of *Romeo and Juliet*—its verse and symmetries—has never proven as inviting as its narrative of the doomed lovers. As a result, the success of this play in the theater has depended on adaptation, numerous adjustments to attract and entertain paying customers over more than three centuries.

The edition intended to exploit the whole theater history of *Romeo and Juliet*, like my own forthcoming from Oxford, proceeds through at least two phases. In one it probes the early quartos for staging clues; in the other it studies later theatrical texts and related materials for adjustments generated by performance. As it equips the dramatic text with this information, it looks both forward and backward, not only giving an impression of the play's indeterminacy, but also attempting to illuminate the text in the best eighteenth-century manner.

I

More than once, theater historians have described the printed texts of English Renaissance plays as vocal books whose language and inflection may baffle the modern auditor: "The original contemporary evidence is all that has real authority, and it often speaks with an uncertain voice."[6] Alan C. Dessen considers the extant texts conversations between a dramatist and his actor-colleagues exchanged in a vocabulary now difficult to understand.[7] Others agree that the playbooks may mislead readers because a key part of their theatrical background is missing: "what R. B. McKerrow called the text's 'accessories,' Fredson Bowers its 'paraphernalia,' and the editors of the new Oxford Shakespeare the 'para-text.'"[8] Together the playwright and the actors, his first readers, filled out the script:

> [Shakespeare] could . . . rely on those readers to bring to their reading much specialist knowledge about the conditions and working practices of the contemporary theatre. . . . The written text . . . thus depended upon an unwritten para-text which always accompanied it: an invisible life-support system of stage directions, which Shakespeare could either expect his first readers to supply, or which those first readers would expect Shakespeare himself to supply orally.[9]

Modern editors cannot fully recover what the actors did on stage beyond the dramatist's printed instructions.[10] Finally, there is an irretrievable dimension of performance connected with the actors, a larger vacancy than that of later theatrical texts.

Examining the early printed versions of *Romeo and Juliet,* an editor faces additional well-known limitations. The provenance and relationship of the first two quartos remain almost completely unknown, since bibliographers over the past two decades have posed serious questions about what had been the received narrative of the play's textual history. In the present context, only a few facts bear repeating. Both quartos were published at the end of the sixteenth century with variant title pages: "*AN* | EXCELLENT | conceited Tragedie | *OF* | Romeo and Iuliet." (1597), and "THE | MOST EX- | cellent and lamentable | Tragedie, of Romeo | and *Iuliet.*" (1599). They differ (famously) in length, the first (Q1) about one-fifth shorter than the second (Q2); and many details—linguistic and theatrical—vary between them. Effectively, there are two extant versions of *Romeo and Juliet* which represent the Elizabethan play, two witnesses to distinct aspects of its career in the sixteenth century.

Despite their vague history and strange idiom, the first two quartos of *Romeo and Juliet* reveal important facets of the play's original staging. As scripts, both have a flexibility characteristic of Shakespeare's practice: its "multiplicity which defies categorisation."[11] They seem typical Elizabethan playtexts, a reflection of the dynamic and versatile circumstances of production. On the one hand, they make demands which the theater had resources to fill; on the other, they themselves are tractable. In many ways, they allow for interpretation and variables, particularly in their directions to the actors. They have a wide range of requirements, some slightly more unusual than others, which would enrich the introduction and notes of any performance-oriented edition. Like the team who assembled the

Cambridge Webster, an editor can take advantage of the apparatus "to ventilate the various possibilities" for staging the play.[12] In this case, ventilation airs a large inventory of data from both texts in light of known theatrical conventions.

Because Elizabethan plays seldom used large movable properties, the appearance of at least one in *Romeo and Juliet* must have been striking: the bed central to the last scenes of the fourth act. In other ways as well, the tragedy took full advantage of late-sixteenth-century resources for staging. Andrew Gurr emphasizes the heavy demands that it made on contemporary theatrical venues, especially for its closing scene. Specifically, it required means to represent not only the bed but the balcony and tomb, all the symbolic enclosures which help to define the world and "architectonics" of the play.[13] Both quartos call for these features in the scenes where a lover is alone or the lovers are alone together, and scholarship has established that Elizabethan staging offered a number of solutions: a stage structure, a substantial property, or both. For example, the bed on which Juliet falls in 4.3 must have been some combination of bed, curtain, and space either on the main stage or in the discovery area; the tomb, if not evoked strictly by dialogue, could have materialized as a trapdoor, the rear stage, or a structure.[14] These resources would have permitted removal of the bodies at the end of 5.3, without a procession, by use of a trapdoor or curtain. Various arrangements could have disposed theatrical space metaphorically to mark the lovers' descent from balcony and nuptial bed to the tomb they occupy in the last scene.[15]

Typical of Shakespeare's printed texts, both quartos require a variety of modest but emblematic handheld properties. *Romeo and Juliet* calls for many such items and uses them in a particularly "controlled" way:[16] their symbolism not only deepens but often connects individual events, enhancing semiotic patterns in the narrative. Again and again the small properties signal violence. Most of them are weapons: swords and bucklers, rapiers, clubs, and partisans in 1.1 (only Q2 specifies the weapons in this scene); rapiers and apparently daggers in 3.1; Romeo's dagger in 3.3; Juliet's knife in 4.1 and 4.3; Peter's dagger in 4.4; rapiers and a dagger in 5.3.[17] At the end of the play, the Apothecary's vial of poison (5.1) and Romeo's container for it (5.3) effect violence of another kind; Romeo and Friar Laurence furnish themselves with crowbars, spade, and mattock to break into the Capulet tomb. In contrast, a number of other properties fill in the domestic tableau of Capulet's hospitality, from napkins, platters, trestle tables, and seats in 1.5 to spits, logs, baskets, and other kitchen supplies in 4.4 (variously specified by the two quartos).

Several items are stage images of verbal motifs central to the play: the torches appearing in 1.4, 1.5, and 5.3; the flowers and other plant life analyzed by Friar Laurence in 2.2 and strewn to memorialize Juliet in 4.4 and 5.3; the money exchanged by Romeo in 2.3 and 5.1; the rope ladder carried by the Nurse in 3.2 and used by Romeo in 3.5; the ring sent by Juliet in 3.2 and received by Romeo in 3.3. Finally, the early texts call for a few odds and ends: the invitation list in 1.2, a material sign of coincidence; whatever instruments the musicians need in 1.5 and 4.4; the Nurse's fan in 2.3, an item which allows for stage business; and Romeo's letter(s) in 5.3, a device to expedite closure of the narrative.

As J. L. Styan recognized several decades ago, "Shakespeare takes the conventional equipment of property and costume and uses them as a way of speaking to the audience." Another "dramatic opportunity," costumes indicated by the two early texts are also symbolic and not out of the ordinary; the degree of richness would have been determined by a character's social status.[18] On Shakespeare's stage, apparel always represented order and degree even as it identified a festive or liminal sphere which minimized such differences.[19] In *Romeo and Juliet* it creates ironies and fulfills both roles by the way it distinguishes the everyday world of Verona from the world of the lovers. The two quartos require distinctive but uncomplicated items among the stock of Elizabethan costumes: a black cloak for the Chorus; a dressing gown for Capulet in the first scene (Q2 only); appropriate garments for the masquers, including masks for Mercutio and Romeo, and (according to the dialogue in 2.3) baggy trousers and dancing shoes for Romeo; bridegroom's apparel for Paris in 4.4; rags for the Apothecary in 5.1; and "best array" for Juliet in 5.3, where she may appear for the last time in the same party dress she wore first in 1.5.

Instructions for the actors, like those for properties and costumes, allowed for changing circumstances of production. Comparable to many other playbooks, for instance, both quartos of *Romeo and Juliet* left the specifics of deploying supernumeraries and other minor parts to the company. Although Q1 may have fewer partygoers (1.4 and 1.5), servants (1.5, 4.2, 4.4), and watchmen (5.3) than Q2, it is equally permissive in the allocation of small roles. During the first scene Q1 calls for *"other Citizens"* (A4v) and Q2 for *"three or foure Citizens"* (A4); in 3.1 both have the stage direction *"Enter Citizens."* (F2, F4v). The two quartos can be similarly ambiguous: *"Enter watch."*, which occurs twice in the last scene of Q1 (K2v), corresponds with *"Enter Boy and Watch."* in Q2 (L4). Now and then Q1 reduces the minor roles to a single actor, avoiding the permissiveness of Q2: only one servant engages Capulet in 4.2 and 4.4 (H3v, I1), where Q2 brings *"two or three"* and *"three or foure"* on stage (I4, K1v); only *"one"* accompanies Balthasar in 5.3 (K3), where Q2 has no instructions about watchmen at all (L4). Yet once, Q1 is more permissive than Q2. In the later text the Prince enters 5.3 alone (L4v); in the earlier he arrives *"with others"* (K3).

The same adaptability is evident in the quartos' directions to performers. While each quarto has a distinct style of address, both permit the actors to exercise their skills in the representation of characters and events. They give directions unsystematically, leaving room for improvisation and presupposing actors who know what to do. A bit more assertive, Q1 is the more explicit text: it spells out cues in its own dialogue and that of Q2; it overadvises in the manner of an inexperienced playwright.[20] Despite its attention to these signals, however, Q1 only sketches the actors' stage business.

In both early quartos the dialogue contains many cues. During the first scene it marks the entrances of the Montague servants and Tybalt; at the end of the play it indicates Friar Laurence's arrival at the tomb, and it tells various watchmen when to enter and exit. More frequently it asks for particular motions or gestures: handling of properties like swords and torches, touching or kissing, kneeling and rising, stepping forward from a group. Its Shakespearean vocabulary has been itemized as "automatic demonstratives [as well as] every form of retrospective description, concurrent description, question, and command." As Ann Pasternak Slater concludes, "Actions vary with the character and the moment."[21] A Capulet servant bites his thumb in 1.1; Capulet's cousin sits in 1.5; Juliet leans her cheek on her hand in 2.1 and rubs the Nurse's back in 2.4; Romeo conveys Paris into the tomb in 5.3. Often the dialogue indicates how an actor might represent an emotional state. At the ball scene Capulet asks Tybalt "Wherefore storm you so?" and insists that he "put off these frowns" (1.5.59, 72). On news of his banishment in 3.3, the desperate Romeo directs himself to tear his hair and fall on the floor of Friar Laurence's cell. When Romeo prepares to return from Mantua to Verona in 5.1, Balthasar describes his appearance as "pale and wilde" (Q2, K4), "dangerous and full of feare" (Q1, I3v). The last speeches of Romeo and Juliet guide the performances of their suicides, the gestures leading to death and the posture of death itself.

Q1 adds stage directions to the dialogue at more than twenty points. A dozen times or so it supplements what the characters say and in the process makes timing more precise. At a climactic moment in 3.1 it describes Mercutio's deathblow several lines before he does: *"Tibalt under Romeos arme thrusts Mercutio, in and flyes."*

(F1v). Later it tells Romeo when to rise from the floor in 3.3 (G1), when to descend in 3.5 (G3v), when to open the tomb and fight with Paris in 5.3 (K1, K1v); it tells Juliet when to kneel in 3.5 (H1) and 4.2 (H4). Plainly it directs the Nurse to address Peter in 2.3 (E3) and to exit at the end of 3.5 (H2). As 5.3 begins, before Paris describes his act of remembrance, Q1 offers the stage direction *"Paris strewes the Tomb with flowers."* (I4v). Soon Friar Laurence *"stoops and lookes on the blood and weapons"* before he asks what blood stains the monument's entrance, and he will observe "The Lady sturres" immediately after the stage direction *"Iuliet rises."* (K2). In one notable instance, however, Q1 lacks dialogue to supplement: the passage in the first scene of Q2 between Benvolio's entrance and the Prince's. It has a stage direction instead:

> *They draw, to them enters* Tybalt, *they fight, to them the Prince, old* Mountague, *and his wife, old* Capulet *and his wife, and other Citizens and part them.*
>
> (A4v)

If the first quarto makes cues prominent, it still leaves a great deal to the actors' judgment. This openness distinguishes the stage directions which elaborate on the dialogue rather than repeating it. Often reprinted by editors, many of these stage directions have become familiar. They add detail to moments which are vaguer in Q2. In the Q1 version of 1.5, for example, Romeo's party make their farewells to Capulet with a particular signal: *"They whisper in his eare."* (C4). Mercutio adds a fillip of impudence to his exchange with the Nurse in 2.3: *"He walkes by them, and sings."* (E2v). When Romeo threatens suicide in 3.3, it is specifically the Nurse who intervenes: *"He offers to stab himselfe, and Nurse snatches the dagger away."* (G1v). Stage directions in 4.4 give a choric effect to the lamentations for Juliet and ritualize the mourners' exit: *"All at once cry out and wring their hands,"* *"They all but the Nurse goe foorth, casting Rosemary on her and shutting the Curtens."* (I2, I2v). Twice, characters hesitate before leaving the stage: the Nurse at the end of 3.3 (G2), Paris during 3.4 (G2v). At times they move *"somewhat fast"* (Juliet in 2.5, when she *"embraceth Romeo,"* E4) or *"hastely"* (the Nurse in 3.5, G3v).

As the illustrations show, stage directions in the first quarto are more descriptive than cues in the second, but they are hardly more prescriptive. In Styan's terms, the instructions are rich and precise in both texts but never indispensable, except for entrances and exits.[22] John Russell Brown is probably right to conclude that nothing subtle or elaborate in the actors' business, movement, gesture, pause, or inflection could have been fixed.[23] Moreover, it cannot be assumed that all printed stage directions were enacted or that all enacted stage directions were written down. When the two quartos are viewed in a contemporary frame of reference, it appears that *Romeo and Juliet* may have been staged and performed somewhat differently each time the Chamberlain's Men revived it. Obviously all plays change in the theater, influenced by the responses of actors and audiences to the text, but since the Restoration, staging has become more or less set for a series of performances. Like other dramatic works of its era, *Romeo and Juliet* may have changed more radically in its original productions than it would in later runs. It probably appeared in both long and short versions;[24] it certainly left performance decisions for each revival to the acting company. As G. K. Hunter writes,

> The actor reminds us that behind the clothes and the role there remains an unexhausted capacity for new inventions. Shakespearian parts encourage the actor to remain in touch with this ambiguity or "third dimension" and to continue to give us his sense of freedom, even though the inexorables are closing in around him.[25]

II

Since the Restoration, the theater history of *Romeo and Juliet* has assumed a pattern. Thomas Otway's *History and Fall of Caius Marius* (performed 1679, published 1680), the adaptation which combines 750 lines from Shakespeare's play with Plutarch's narrative about republican Rome, initiated the trend by displacing the Elizabethan format for more than sixty years; it inaugurated the long-run versions of *Romeo and Juliet* which have occupied English-speaking theaters through the late twentieth century. In the history of the play to date, five productions have held the stage or remained highly influential for at least a few decades: David Garrick's (1748), Charlotte Cushman's (1845/46), John Gielgud's (1935), Peter Brook's (1947), and Franco Zeffirelli's (1960 at the Old Vic, 1968 on film).[26] Assembling material on these key productions turns an editor into a theater historian, retrieving every scrap of relevant data. For three of the revivals there is a prompt-book or printed script, but Gielgud's pre-World War II production left few printed traces and Zeffirelli's Old Vic staging was improvised from a workbook with cuts only. Evidence to supplement the scripts is available from the usual sources: published reviews, criticism, interviews, and reminiscences; any visual records of stage design and costumes; information about music; and, for the later revivals, witnesses to the performance and members of the cast or production team willing to talk or correspond.

In this case, summaries of the key revivals add up to a survey of the play's life in the theater suitable for the introduction to an edition and adaptable for use in the commentary. But these revivals, in their pattern and number, fail to capture the play's vitality or continuing transformations on the stage. To give that impression, even faintly, an editor needs a larger sample of productions from the many hundreds recorded. Promptbooks help to fill in the gaps, although they have almost as many idiosyncrasies as the original texts of Shakespeare's plays. Charles H. Shattuck, who compiled the indispensable guide to Shakespeare promptbooks, describes these documents as another sort of vocal book with the potential to mislead auditors:

> Promptbooks are tricky, secretive, stubborn informants. They chatter and exclaim about what we hardly need to know: that certain characters are being readied by the callboy to make their entrances; that the scene is about to change or the curtain to drop; that the orchestra is about to play at the act-end. They fall blackly silent just when we hope to be told where the actor stood or how he looked or what he did.[27]

Working with promptbooks causes other difficulties. In the first place, Shattuck's catalogue is incomplete. Published in 1965, it has a terminal date of 1961. *Theatre Notebook* printed some additions within several years, but the descriptive list has not kept up with production.[28] Gary Taylor, singling out the year 1986 for Shakespeare reinventions, observes the quantity of stagings over recent decades in view of its effect: "Accelerated productivity and magnified exposure build instant obsolescence into every new production."[29] Shattuck had anticipated a swelling of the records, but not the outburst that has happened.[30] As a result, his guide is the starting point for any exploration of Shakespeare promptbooks, not a complete travelogue. Some of the collections he describes have increased their holdings, at times substantially, since the 1960s: they have acquired documents for new revivals or books formerly in private hands. At the same time, foreign-language productions have increased in number and significance beyond "[t]he very few foreign-language books" Shattuck relegated to the end of each section.[31]

In the second place, an editor who plans to rely on promptbooks must decide quickly what information to collect and how to apply it most effectively. Whether the promptbook can be viewed on site or on microfilm,[32] research usually costs money as well as time. When I began to study promptbooks of *Romeo and Juliet* in the mid-1980s, it seemed most sensible to make profiles of them: records of their cuts and staging notes. William P. Halstead had already compiled a collation of acting editions and promptbooks through 1975, but he was concerned more with the history of individual lines than with reconstructions of any play as a whole. Taking a different approach and following Shattuck from collection to collection, I accumulated profiles of 170 promptbooks, about five dozen more than the number he listed, although I did not see all of those he described.[33] These represent just a fraction of performances since the seventeenth century; they include only one (early) production both foreign and amateur.[34] Nevertheless, they provide a respectable sample from which to analyze revisions of *Romeo and Juliet* on the stage. The sample is large and detailed enough to need methodized access, a challenge met by technology. With the help of a colleague, graduate students, and a grant, it was entered on a data base later transferred to the World Wide Web.[35] Even on the database it proved very useful as I wrote commentary for the edition.

From the start I intended to use the information from the promptbooks in the notes. Shattuck and my own experience made it clear that recorded stage business (and therefore profiles) varied from era to era, ranging from exits and entrances in the earliest promptbooks, to detailed rationales for production in the late nineteenth century, to careful documentation of technical matters in the twentieth century.[36] With such variations in mind, I searched the data base to see what kinds of choices the theater had made when my control text, Q2, was less than specific about staging. Usually the choices were diverse but not surprising, and the evidence was circumstantial. If the original texts of *Romeo and Juliet* left most decisions to the actors, scripts since the Restoration seem to make up their own minds about large movable properties, stage structures, blocking, and gesture in particular.

For all productions, of course, staging has been affected by cuts and other changes to the lines. Differences between the quartos imply that such adjustments in any Elizabethan performance may have ranged over more than a fifth of the play. Later theatrical books often make at least as many adjustments, most of them staying in place during a run. At some performances Shakespeare's company may have emphasized a single dimension of *Romeo and Juliet,* yet the extant texts and early modern theater always permitted the actors to explore more than one. By contrast, productions since the Restoration have generally settled on a concept which isolates one component of the tragedy—the transcendental lovers, their rite of passage, sociopolitical tensions—and determines most aspects of staging. At some points an edition has influenced the process: for example, Garrick's version, which spans a century, owes much to Pope.[37] But the promptbooks do not engage with editors over textual cruxes. For the most part they adopt the readings of the editions which serve as their points of departure, and they collaborate with them in preparing the play for the stage.

Revivals since the seventeenth century have dealt with balcony, bed, and tomb in a number of ways, although each production has offered a specific and concrete arrangement of properties. In the second balcony scene, for instance, the original texts contain a well-known ambiguity which theater history eliminates: the management of action on two levels of the stage. According to Q2, Romeo and Juliet enter the scene "*aloft*" (H2v; Q1 has "*at the window*," G3), appearing together in the space which Juliet had occupied alone in 2.1. Changing standards of decorum and theatrical conventions have had an effect even on this clearly defined staging. In early productions the actors performed the opening of the scene in a garden; in most productions since the late eighteenth century they have been discovered on a balcony, in Juliet's chamber, on a couch, or (more recently) in a bed. Q2 staging becomes conjectural at line 64 and remains speculative for at least the next several verses, as Capulet's Wife enters. For this sequence the second quarto gives only one clue to staging, "*Enter Mother.*" at line 64 (H3v). The first quarto has "*She goeth downe from the window.*" immediately after the Nurse's warning (G3v), a direction for either the Nurse or Juliet and therefore uncertain. However vague the texts, the situation on stage seems to demand that the ensuing action, 175 lines of dialogue involving four characters, move to the lower platform. Elizabethan staging would have allowed Juliet to descend from upper to main level by an inner staircase, the audience imagining a change of scene from bedroom window to chamber itself. Later editions and performances have offered various alternatives, from setting the whole scene in either garden or chamber to dividing private from public dialogue between two acting spaces, sometimes in two scenes (set, for example, in garden and chamber). In a number of early productions, all of 3.5 takes place at stage level, with Romeo miming descent through a window or over a balustrade, or simply exiting the stage.

Q2 makes its demand for a bed in 4.3 and 4.4 quite casually: the property is not named until the Nurse mentions it in the latter scene when she tries to wake the drugged Juliet (K2). Although Q1 gives a stage direction after Juliet takes the potion in 4.3, "*She fals upon her bed within the Curtaines."* (I1), it does not reveal how or where the bed was situated on the Elizabethan stage. Neither early text indicates whether the bed visually foreshadowed the final scene, standing where the tomb would appear in 5.3.[38] By comparison, later scripts, which ignore the symbolism, show no commitment to the property. In revivals after the seventeenth century, Juliet has performed not only with a curtained bed but with a couch, an ottoman, or the sheets on a bed; she has fallen down steps or on the stage itself. Whereas the early scripts offer no sign when the bed is removed—it probably remains visible through 4.4—recorded productions give the end of 4.3 a sense of closure: usually the stage curtain falls or the actress pulls a drape around the bed; sometimes there is a blackout. When the episode of Juliet's apparent death opens, productions often discover Juliet on her bed or the Nurse in Juliet's chamber. For a period of fifty years from the end of the nineteenth century, some performances resolved the problem of continuity by completely omitting 4.4.

The original tomb in 5.3 remains a mystery: Q2 has no stage direction at all, and Q1 states only *"Romeo opens the tombe."* (K1). In the absence of facts at least two questions arise: when does Romeo open the tomb, and what does he open? Confronting the first question, editors offer a range of possible answers; they propose that Romeo opens or begins to open the tomb at several points between lines 44 and 83. Confronting the second, theater historians and other critics of early modern drama speculate that the tomb was represented by a stage structure or dialogue alone.[39] In promptbooks since the eighteenth century timing varies, as it has in the editions. Usually Romeo forces open a door or gate on the platform after striking at it several times with a crowbar. The monument has been complex to various degrees, occupying the entire stage at more than one level in some productions. Of these, the most well-known is probably Henry Irving's representation for his lavish revival at the Lyceum Theatre in 1882. Ellen Terry describes how Irving treated the tomb as a problem he felt compelled to solve:

> At rehearsals Henry Irving kept on saying: "I must go *down* to the vault." After a great deal of consideration he had an inspiration. He had the exterior of the vault in one scene, the entrance to it down a flight of steps. Then the scene changed to the interior of the vault, and the steps now led from a height above the stage. At the close of the scene, when the Friar and the crowd came rushing down into the tomb, these steps were thronged with people, each one holding a torch, and the effect was magnificent.[40]

Terry's description of the torches in 5.3 suggests how revivals have elaborated Shakespeare's simple and emblematic properties. In the mid-nineteenth century Adelaide Neilson dropped flowers to Romeo in the first balcony scene and set a trend;[41] from the late eighteenth century on, the Nurse's fan has prompted extended stage business at least once in 2.3; during the first half of the twentieth century Juliet handled a dagger at the end of 3.5 (taking it from a table, kissing it, placing it under a cloak), evidently in preparation for the next scene; in eighteenth-century performances Romeo threatened Paris with a crowbar before engaging him in a duel, an "attitude" which some observers considered inappropriate for a gentleman. With the advent of realism in the nineteenth century, as actor-managers from John Philip Kemble on attempted to stage Shakespeare's plays with some degree of historical accuracy, the theater also elaborated Shakespeare's costumes. Directors in the next century interpreted this component of production according to their tastes and conceptions of the text. For *Romeo and Juliet,* the interpretations have ranged from Gielgud's Italian Renaissance designs to Brook's emblematic images to Zeffirelli's ancient but familiar dress inspired by Veronese frescoes. Where the original quartos are specific, later scripts and other theatrical records are more specific.

Where the original quartos are permissive, later scripts tend to make decisions. If they do not entirely omit supernumeraries or minor parts (such as the servants at the beginning of 1.5), productions assign a number to them (for example, two servingmen at the beginning of 4.2, three musicians in 4.4). When timing or sequence is debatable, they fix it. In 2.2, for instance, they favor Romeo's appearance at the end of Friar Laurence's opening speech rather than two-thirds of the way through it. Like most editors, many productions adopt Q1 staging at the beginning of 3.3: first Friar Laurence enters alone, then Romeo appears after the third line. In the theater, Romeo has also been discovered (lying on a cot, sitting on a bench or behind a desk, set under stairs), or he and Friar Laurence have entered at the same time from different directions. Later in this scene most promptbooks observe the same timing as Q1 for the Nurse's entrance, making it clear that she speaks offstage before she appears at line 80. Two scenes afterward Q2 has no formal stage direction to indicate when Juliet kneels; Q1 has "*She kneeles downe.*" after her entreaty at lines 158–59 (H1). In most promptbooks Juliet sinks to her knees at line 158 and remains on the ground, like Romeo in 3.3, for much of the exchange which follows. Once the potion scheme has been devised, both quartos allow Juliet and Friar Laurence to exit separately or together from 4.1. Revivals, however, tend to choose among three options: Friar Laurence and Juliet go in different directions; Friar Laurence stays and Juliet leaves; or the scene ends in a blackout. During the discovery episode in 4.4, Q2 has no stage direction for the entrance of the musicians; Q4 and Q1 have different timing. In the theater, early productions often bring Friar Laurence and Paris on stage at line 59 without musicians; modern ones usually furnish them with music (two or three instrumentalists, an adult or children singing, even a live band). When Friar Laurence reappears in 5.2, the original directions for his entrance and Friar John's are ambiguous, but the theater has managed the opening of the scene efficiently in several ways: the actors enter "to" each other; one may be discovered before the other is heard or seen; they have also performed on different sides of a stage curtain, one in front and the other pushing his head through the middle.

Most promptbooks carefully orchestrate intricate passages, such as the entrances and exits during 1.5 and the fights in 3.1. At the transition from 1.4 to 1.5 (observed in most editions), a flexible Q2 stage direction indicates movement from outside to inside the Capulet house ("*They march about the Stage, and Servingmen come forth with Napkins.*", C2v), and performances have treated the shift in various ways. (Of course, promptbooks that reverse the order of 1.3 and 1.4 avoid this particular transition.) Many extant promptbooks omit the servants' dialogue (which does not appear in Q1); most have the masquers exit here. At this point Q2 suggests again that Romeo and his party have never left the stage, although theatrical tradition and some editors have them reappear for the dance. Q2's general stage direction ("*Enter all the guests and gentlewomen to the Maskers.*", C3), which does not specify Capulet's family and attendants, gives no indication of when or where the musicians take their places. In performance, however, the opening of the festivities is choreographed in some detail, whether the participants enter the stage, a curtain rises to discover them, or both. Certainly the promptbooks pay much attention to the fights themselves in 3.1, but they also notice key alternations of the actors on stage. At line 108, for example, the quartos do not specify how many actors leave with Benvolio and the wounded Mercutio. Some recent editors have assumed that all but Romeo exit; and a variety of productions since the eighteenth century have left Romeo alone. In a number of twentieth-century performances, this ambiguity disappears because Mercutio dies on stage.

The original texts of *Romeo and Juliet* leave blanks for staging or business which the promptbooks fill or otherwise eliminate. Perhaps the meeting of the lovers in 1.5 is the first striking illustration. At line

91, Q2 gives only the stage direction for Tybalt's exit, but promptbooks show that in production, business between Romeo and Juliet often occurs before Tybalt leaves. Usually Romeo takes the more active role, joining Juliet, leading her forward to the position where they will exchange their first words. Although Q2 makes no reference to Paris in this scene, quite a few productions since the early nineteenth century have introduced him as Juliet's partner in dance or conversation; and as the dance ends, Romeo takes Paris' place at Juliet's side. Another familiar instance of theatrical interpretation occurs at the beginning of the second act. With Benvolio's first words in 2.1 it becomes clear that Romeo has disappeared from the view of his friends, but the early texts fail to signal how or where. Edward Capell's direction, "*leaps the wall*" (in his 1768 edition), understands Benvolio literally in line 5; recent editors imagine the simplest and most fluid staging: Romeo conceals himself behind a stage post until his friends leave at line 42, when he reappears. In productions over the past two centuries, three solutions recur: some version of the uncluttered arrangement; the introduction of a wall; or omission of either Romeo's opening speech or the first forty-two lines. As a final example of action not mentioned in the quartos but specified in promptbooks, there are, in 5.3, three characters who "*retire*" (Capell's term, and Thomas Hanmer's in his 1743/44 edition) from the main action at various points. On the stage a character who does not exit from this scene finds a place to retreat on the set: behind a tree, at the gates of the tomb, on steps or a balcony, near a grille or wall.

At other points the theater specifies, extends, or omits stage business which the quartos imply or leave open to interpretation. For instance, when the masquers prepare to leave in 1.5, Capulet urges them to stay. Q2 does not indicate their reaction; Q1 prints "*They whisper in his eare.*" (C4). Extant promptbooks that annotate the polite rebuff stage it in a number of ways: Benvolio, Mercutio, or the group whispers to Capulet; Mercutio or Benvolio pantomimes that the gentlemen wish to be excused; the masquers bow a negative; the guests murmur; Capulet's lines are cut and the guests simply depart. In most productions, Peter spends his time between speeches during 2.3 dozing on a bench or step, against a wing or near a pillar. The Nurse wakes him for his dialogue by striking him with her hand, a cane, or the fan. Inevitably, productions add comic business to the exchange of money between Romeo and the Nurse at lines 172–74: the Nurse takes the coin or purse conspicuously as she says "not a penny," with her hand extended or behind her back and with accompanying gestures (for example, weighing the purse, putting the money in a pocket or satchel). On the stage, 2.4 is traditionally rather busy from the entrance of the Nurse. Usually she sits and rises more than once, and Juliet attempts to mollify her through physical contact: hugging, kneeling by her side, placing her head in the Nurse's lap, and rubbing the Nurse's aching head, ankles, knees, shoulders, and back. In 3.3, Q2 has no stage direction at line 107, allowing different kinds of business for Romeo's suicide attempt and disarming. In most modern productions, Friar Laurence removes the weapon. In many modern editions, however, the Q1 stage direction is reprinted (*"He offers to stab himselfe, and Nurse snatches the dagger away."*, G1v); some twentieth-century promptbooks follow such editions or direct the Nurse to snatch the dagger. Finally, gestures implied in the text are particularized in the theater. Paris' "holy kiss" at 4.1.43 is placed on the forehead, a hand, or (sometimes) the cheek. When Juliet calls for "this knife" at line 54 of the same scene, she draws it from various places on her person: a sheath, her cloak, around her neck.

Despite the elaboration of stage business, the promptbooks say little about the art of acting. Eighteenth- and nineteenth-century scripts give the actress playing Juliet detailed instructions for voice and gesture when she delivers the potion speech in 4.3, lines 14–57. Otherwise, the documents reveal nothing about voice and give only general directions about gesture. Worse, as Shattuck warns us, promptbooks "tell lies, as anybody knows who ever produced a play and failed to write into the book his own last-minute revisions or the happy inspirations that come to the actors midway in a run of performances."[42] Like the earliest scripts, that is, most promptbooks lack telling signs of a "para-text": certain crucial details always escape them. Together with the original texts, however, they help to define what we know and need to know about recorded productions since the late sixteenth century. For Shakespearean drama generally, such definition is the first step toward understanding how individual plays respond to the form and pressure of changing times.

Notes

1. For a summary of "performance" criticism and revisionist critiques, see Alan C. Dessen, *Recovering Shakespeare's Theatrical Vocabulary* (Cambridge: Cambridge University Press, 1995), 4, 225.

2. These illustrative phrases come from the advertisement for The New Cambridge Shakespeare in the *Times Literary Supplement*, 18 July 1997, 5.

3. Gerald Eades Bentley, Introduction to *The Seventeenth-Century Stage: A Collection of Critical Essays* (Toronto: University of Toronto Press, 1968), ix–x.

4. On the history of attempts to re-create Elizabethan conditions of performance, see my essay, "The Recovery of the Elizabethan Stage," in *The Elizabethan Theatre IX*, ed. G. R. Hibbard (Port Credit, Ontario: P. D. Meany Co., 1987), 205–29.

5. There are a number of guides to this series of revivals, among them three which offer theater history: Peter Holding, *"Romeo and Juliet": Text and Performance* (Houndmills and London: Macmillan Education Ltd., 1992); Katherine L. Wright, *Shakespeare's "Romeo and Juliet" in Performance: Traditions and Departures* (Lewiston, Queenston, and Lampeter: Mellen University Press, 1997); and my *Shakespeare in Performance: "Romeo and Juliet"* (Manchester: Manchester University Press, 1987). Two books give brief descriptive listings of twentieth-century productions: William Babula, *Shakespeare in Production, 1935–1978: A Selective Catalogue* (New York and London: Garland Publishing, Inc., 1981), 280–92; and Samuel L. Leiter, ed., *Shakespeare Around the Globe: A Guide to Notable Postwar Revivals* (New York, Westport, and London: Greenwood Press, 1986), 625–59. See also Charles H. Shattuck, *The Shakespeare Promptbooks: A Descriptive Catalogue* (Urbana and London: University of Illinois Press, 1965), 411–32; William P. Halstead, *Shakespeare as Spoken: A Collation of 5000 Acting Editions and Promptbooks of Shakespeare* (Ann Arbor: University Microfilms International, 1978), 9:711c–711nn; and Bryan N. S. Gooch and David Thatcher, eds., *A Shakespeare Music Catalogue* (Oxford: Clarendon Press, 1991), 2:1341–89.

6. George F. Reynolds, *On Shakespeare's Stage*, ed. Richard K. Knaub (Boulder: University of Colorado Press, 1967), 8.

7. Dessen, *Recovering Shakespeare*, 5–6.

8. Antony Hammond, "Encounters of the Third Kind in Stage-Directions in Elizabethan and Jacobean Drama," *Studies in Philology* 89 (1992): 71–99. See also Dessen, *Elizabethan Stage Conventions and Modern Interpreters* (Cambridge: Cambridge University Press, 1984), 29–30.

9. Gary Taylor, General Introduction to *William Shakespeare: A Textual Companion*, by Stanley Wells and Gary Taylor with John Jowett and William Montgomery (Oxford: Clarendon Press, 1987), 2.

10. On the difficulties of interpreting these instructions, see William B. Long, "Stage-Directions: A Misinterpreted Factor in Determining Textual Provenance," *TEXT* 2 (1985): 121–37.

11. Ann Pasternak Slater, *Shakespeare the Director* (Brighton and Totowa: The Harvester Press and Barnes & Noble Books, 1982), 49.

12. Hammond, "Encounters of the Third Kind," 91.

13. Andrew Gurr, "The Date and the Expected Venue of *Romeo and Juliet*," *Shakespeare Survey* 49 (1996): 15–25. The quoted term comes from Michael Mullin, "Motley and *Romeo*: The Designers and the Text," *Theatre Journal* 43 (1991): 469.

14. See Leslie Thomson, "'With patient ears attend': *Romeo and Juliet* on the Elizabethan Stage," *Studies in Philology* 92 (1995): 239–40 and 230–32, and Dessen, *Recovering Shakespeare*, 176–95.

15. On this symbolism see Thomson, "*Romeo and Juliet*," 234–37, and David Bevington, *Action Is Eloquence: Shakespeare's Language of Gesture* (Cambridge, Mass. and London: Harvard University Press, 1984), 111–13.

16. Slater, *Shakespeare the Director*, 182.

17. References are to John Jowett's edition in *William Shakespeare: The Complete Works*, gen. eds. Stanley Wells and Gary Taylor (Oxford: Clarendon Press, 1986). Jowett's scene divisions approximate those in my edition. Citations of the quartos come from *Shakespeare's Plays in Quarto*, ed. Michael J. B. Allen and Kenneth Muir (Berkeley and Los Angeles: University of California Press, 1981).

18. J. L. Styan, *Shakespeare's Stagecraft* (Cambridge: Cambridge University Press, 1967), 36, 32.

19. Bevington, *Action Is Eloquence*, 36–38.

20. On the correlation between experience and instruction in the preparing of early scripts, see Long, "Stage-Directions," 127.

21. Slater, *Shakespeare the Director*, 20.

22. Styan, *Shakespeare's Stagecraft*, 198, 53.

23. John Russell Brown, *Free Shakespeare* (London: Heinemann, 1974), 52.

24. Donald W. Foster draws this conclusion in his linguistic study "The Webbing of *Romeo and Juliet*," in Joseph A. Porter, ed., *Critical Essays on Shakespeare's "Romeo and Juliet"* (New York: G.K. Hall & Co., 1997), 131–49.

25. G. K. Hunter, "Flatcaps and Bluecoats: Visual Signals on the Elizabethan Stage," *Essays and Studies* 33 (1980): 47.

26. It remains to be seen whether Baz Luhrmann's film version (1996), which speaks so powerfully to adolescents in the late 1990s, will displace Zeffirelli's.

27. Shattuck, *Shakespeare Promptbooks*, 3.

28. See Charles H. Shattuck, *"The Shakespeare Promptbooks:* First Supplement," *Theatre Notebook* 24 (1969): 5–17.

29. Gary Taylor, *Reinventing Shakespeare: A Cultural History, from the Restoration to the Present* (New York: Weidenfeld & Nicolson, 1989), 306.

30. Shattuck, *Shakespeare Promptbooks*, v.

31. Ibid., 5.

32. Four major collections have been microfilmed by Research Publications: the Folger Shakespeare Library; the Harvard Theatre Collection; the Shakespeare Library, Birmingham Public Libraries; and the Shakespeare Centre Library, Stratford-upon-Avon. Some other collections will xerox or microfilm individual promptbooks.

33. As Halstead discovered when he tried to collect microfilms of all the promptbooks in Shattuck's catalogue for the University of Michigan Library, it can be difficult to gain access to some of these documents (see *Shakespeare as Spoken*, 1: xxxiii).

34. See G. Blakemore Evans, "The Douai Manuscript—Six Shakespearean Transcripts (1694–95)," *Philological Quarterly* 41 (1962): 170–71.

35. I want to record thanks in particular to Professor David Galbraith, Ms. Margaret McGeachy, and the Social Sciences and Humanities Research Council of Canada.

36. Shattuck, *Shakespeare Promptbooks*, 11–12.

37. See Nancy Copeland, "The Sources of Garrick's *Romeo and Juliet* Text," *English Language Notes* 24 (1987): 27–33.

38. On the staging of bed and tomb, see Brian Gibbons' edition for The Arden Shakespeare (London and New York: Methuen, 1980), 4.3.58s.d. note, and G. Blakemore Evans' edition for The New Cambridge Shakespeare (Cambridge: Cambridge University Press, 1984), 33.

39. See note 14.

40. Quoted in George C. D. Odell, *Shakespeare from Betterton to Irving* (1920; reprint, New York: Dover Publications, Inc., 1966), 2: 428.

41. Wright, *"Romeo and Juliet" in Performance*, 176.

42. Shattuck, *Shakespeare Promptbooks*, 3.

"Oh be some other name": Translating *Romeo and Juliet*

LAURIE E. MAGUIRE

Inside or between languages, human communication equals translation. A study of translation is a study of language.
—George Steiner

Language

*R*OMEO AND JULIET, AS HAS LONG BEEN REALIZED, IS A GENERIC PARADOX (A tragedy that begins as a comedy), a generic oxymoron (a city tragedy, a romantic tragedy). It is a play of contradiction, of contrast, of clashes: Petrarchan lyricism with a Roman comedic plot structure; artificial clichés of courtly love (Romeo on Rosaline) versus experimental metaphoric daring (Juliet on Romeo); brash commercialism versus spiritual outpouring; narrative choric ecphrasis in the unexpected form of a sonnet versus the witty conceits of the lovers in the same verse form;[1] images of books and reading versus empirical lived experience; a plot of aleatory chance within a pre-scripted narrative (arranged marriage, family feuds); a play where upstairs is juxtaposed with downstairs (in no other Shakespearean tragedy do the servants and their household duties receive so much stage time); a play where Juliet's domestic confinement (home, garden, family tomb) is contrasted with her unbounded imagination, which reaches to the solar system for images;[2] a play where the lovers declare their love in the very language they have just rejected as inadequate; a play where "womb" rhymes with its conceptual opposite, "tomb."[3]

These clashes and inversions find specific and localized representation in language: the play's dominant linguistic mode is oxymoron. "Parting is such sweet sorrow" (2.1.229); "The sweetest honey / Is loathsome in its own deliciousness" (2.5.11–12); "they are but beggars that can count their worth" (2.5.32); Romeo acknowledges that the street brawl has "much to do with hate but more with love"

(1.1.168); Juliet "speaks yet she says nothing" (2.1.54); Friar Lawrence's herbs are both poisonous and medicinal (2.1.23–24); Capulet jokes that "it is so very late that we / May call it early" (3.4.34–35); Escalus believes that "mercy but murders, pardoning those that kill" (3.1.191); when Romeo slays Tybalt, Juliet calls her husband a "beautiful tyrant, fiend angelical. . . . A damned saint, an honourable villain!" (3.2.76–79); to Romeo, merciful banishment is death; in Mantua he finds poison is cordial and gold is poison. Thus, the drama's extended paradoxes have local lexical equivalents. Language, it seems, can do what the plot cannot: reconcile opposites. This is true, however, only in a localized and fleeting way, for, as Friar Lawrence knows, fire and powder, as they kiss, consume.

Romeo and Juliet is, to a large extent, a tragedy of language,[4] alert to the aporetic ambiguities and material power of words. In the opening scene, Sampson and Gregory shelter beneath the legal protection of verbal ambiguity, the difference between biting one's thumb, and biting one's thumb "at us" (much virtue in a prepositional phrase). Romeo and Mercutio quibble over the interpretation of "burn daylight"; Friar Lawrence becomes impatient at Romeo's chiasmic persiflage ("One hath wounded me / That's by me wounded"), retorting "riddling confession finds but riddling shrift" (2.2.56); Mercutio is characterised as a quarreler, "as hot a Jack . . . as any in Italy" (3.1.11–12), whereas Tybalt is distinguished as a "duellist"; Mercutio loves to hear himself talk, but his words are meaningless (2.3.32); Paris prematurely calls Juliet wife ("That may be, sir, when I may be a wife," she corrects; 4.1.19). By the second half of the play, words have assumed the power of weapons. "Calling death 'banished' / Thou cutt'st my head off with a golden axe," weeps a desperate Romeo to the friar (3.3.22–23). Juliet falls down at the mention of Romeo "as if that name, / Shot from the deadly level of a gun, / Did murder her" (3.3.101–2).

But words, at least in their onomastic sense—Montague, Capulet— have had murderous power since 1.1 ("Draw thy tool. Here comes one of the house of Montagues"; 1.1.29), and, by implication, since before the beginning of the play. It is the lovers' attempt to negotiate an identity independent of family name which leads to Juliet's antinominalist soliloquy. However, the connection she debates between name and identity is but a subset of the larger (and equally problematic) relation between words and things, and the solution she proposes—anonymity—is no more practical than that offered by Swift's Laputans: "Since words are only Names for *Things,* it would be more convenient for all Men to carry about them, such *Things* as were necessary to express the particular Business they are to discourse on."⁵

Linguists have long recognized the paradoxes inherent in human speech.⁶ We speak to communicate, and to leave unspoken; thus, language reveals but it also conceals (it is, in fact, this capacity for mendacity that distinguishes us from beasts and, in part, ensures our survival). Language is power—both inter-lingually, where accents and pronunciation differentiate class, and intra-lingually, where conquerors impose their language on the conquered people— but so is its opposite, silence.⁷ Language is an issue of identity (in the case of conquest, national identity), but, although it represents selfhood, it also represents society. We create community and culture through language, yet language is reciprocally the creator of community and culture: in short, we act on language and it acts on us. Often, the more impoverished a culture, the richer its language.⁸ Language has the power to say and also to un-say, to name and un-name. To learn a language is to absorb it, but also to change it, to contribute to it. From contradictory statements we move to interrogative alternatives: is language the expression of thought, or is thought language internalized? Is language mimesis or "refusal of mimesis"?⁹ Does it create a reality or label a pre-existing entity? Indeed, are these binary questions alternatives or symbioses?

All civilizations have some version of the story of Babel, in which linguistic diversity, and concomitant failure to communicate conversationally, is inflicted on humankind as a punishment. Before this, linguistic homogeneity allegedly prevailed in an *Ursprache* which made discourse straightforward, not just because a single tongue was used and understood by all, but because it contained a perfect correlation between the word and the thing.¹⁰ This strikingly structuralist concept of the sign appears in Genesis (in the onomastic-ontological fit of Adam's naming of the animals), in the philosophers and dramatists of Athens in the fifth century BCE, and in the medieval scholasts.¹¹ Closer to home, Shakespeare too shows himself a Saussurian *avant la lettre* in plays such as *All's Well that Ends Well* where the abandoned, newlywed Helena finds herself "the name of wife and not the thing."

Language is a subset of communication, which relies additionally on gestures and silence; names are a subset of language. One of the first phrases we learn in a foreign language, as in our native tongue, is how to identify ourselves. Every culture has, as Michael Quigley points out, a ritual to name a new person, an occasion of celebration and optimism.¹² Writing, the reification of language, is a powerful act of naming, as Theseus acknowledges in *Midsummer Night's*

Dream: "The poet's pen . . . gives to airy nothing / A local habitation and a name." The metaphysical paradoxes of language are obviously equally true of naming, for, like words in general, a name confers identity, but it also labels a preexisting identity. It is thus impossible to talk of naming without invoking language, and vice versa; indeed, the two subjects are often treated metonymically or synecdochically (names as a paradigm of language).

In this essay I want to investigate the complexities of words and names in *Romeo and Juliet,* showing how the play embodies problems specific not to Verona or to sixteenth-century England, to young love or ancient grudge, but to language generally: the separation of signifier and signified, and the paradoxical co-dependence of onomastics and ontology. Thucydides states that in the Peloponnesian War words lost their meaning: recklessness became loyalty, prudence became cowardice, obstinacy became courage, an "irresponsible gamble" became "a brave and comradely venture." In justifying their actions, the leaders "reversed the customary descriptive meanings of words."[13] His description applies equally to the civil feud in Verona: no longer identifying patronymics (if ever they were, if ever surnames can be just labels), Montague and Capulet, fetishized into onomastic icons of enmity, have become rallying cries to battle.

Names

"What's in a name?" asks Juliet in the play's most famous soliloquy (2.1.85), contemplating the relation between onomastics and ontology, words and things, signifier and signified. "That which we call a rose / By any other word [Q2; name Q1] would smell as sweet," she responds to her own question, the textual variants ironically illustrating the very point she is making: that identity is independent of label.[14] But the language debate begins much earlier. The play opens with puns on collier/choler/collar, the pun being a rhetorical form based on the sounds of words divorced from meaning. In 1.2, Benvolio offers to rename a Rose (who, significantly, as James Calderwood points out, exists only as a name in the play[15]): he encourages Romeo to attend the Capulet feast to observe "admired beauties of Verona," an exercise in aesthetic collation that will translate Romeo's disdainful inamorata, Rosaline, from beautiful to ugly ("Compare her face with some that I shall show, / And I will make thee think thy swan a crow"; 1.2.86–87).

It is significant, as both Kiernan Ryan and Manfred Weidhorn have pointed out, that the protagonists are nameless when they meet and fall in love;[16] their subsequent identification by family labels brings with it emotional and cultural baggage. As if trying to recreate the liberating and unprejudiced anonymity of their first meeting, Juliet muses on a Romeo who is not a Montague. But her speech is fraught with difficulties, not just because of verbal and syntactical variants between Q1 and Q2, but because of the extreme nature of her vision, which posits a Romeo who is not simply not a Montague but also not a Romeo. Thus she moves from the prejudicial power of the patronymic to the limitations of the label, and rejects both.

The name of Montague is not problematic *per se;* it is so only because Juliet bears the name of Capulet. Therefore one of the two lovers must relinquish a surname if their love is to be feasible.[17] It is this choice which structures the first few lines of Juliet's soliloquy:

> Deny thy father and refuse thy name.
> Or if thou wilt not, be but sworn my love,
> And I'll no longer be a Capulet.
>
> (2.1.76–78)

However, Juliet's proposed alternative is not the namelessness implied by these lines, but another name. Even as Juliet is disassociating Romeo from Montague ("Thou art thyself, though not a Montague. / What's Montague? It is nor hand, nor foot / Nor arm nor face, nor any other part / Belonging to a man"; 2.1.81–4), even as she is avowing that names are irrelevant ("What's in a name?"), she is also paradoxically asserting their importance ("be some *other* name"; my emphasis), even as she did in her rhetorical question "wherefore art thou Romeo?" As Derrida points out, she does not say "Why are you called Romeo?"; she says "'why *are you* Romeo?' . . . his name is his essence."[18] Romeo's response—to tear the written word of Romeo—shows his awareness of this Platonic point: since he is his name, his offer is synonymous with suicide, as his frantic rephrasing of the offer in 3.3 acknowledges:

> In what vile part of this anatomy
> Doth my name lodge? Tell me that I may sack
> The hateful mansion.
> *Friar.* Hold thy desperate hand.
>
> (105–108)

Problem: to sack the hateful mansion is to kill the individual. The name is a physical self and, like the physical self, can give and receive wounds. Juliet's grief-stricken tirade against her husband is characterized as a physical act against his name: "what tongue shall *smooth* thy name / When I, thy three-hours wife, have *mangled* it" (3.2.98–99; my emphasis). It was the name of Rosaline that both attracted and wounded Romeo, as appears from his announcement to the Friar in 2.2.46: "I have forgot that name and that name's woe." Existence is predicated on a name, any name, as Romeo's statement in the orchard indicates. "Call me but love and I'll be new baptized," he says, offering to trade one offense-giving name for another. But when Juliet asks who is there, Romeo realizes his predicament: even if he does not call himself Romeo, he still has to find some identifying label to answer Juliet's question about who he is.[19] Derrida unpacks the paradox as follows: "Romeo is Romeo, and Romeo is not Romeo. He is himself only in abandoning his name, he is himself only in his name. . . . [H]e would not be what he is, a stranger to his name, without this name."[20]

As it continues, the orchard scene further demonstrates the simultaneous fissure between, and self-identification of, names and identity, words and things, language and communication. Juliet wishes to deny what she has spoken; by the rules of courtship and formal speech, such denial is not contradiction or mendacity but "compliment." In confessing that she would have spoken differently had she known she was overheard (2.1.144–46), she acknowledges the difference between public and private codes of speech. Her insistent factual questions and statements about Romeo's safety (e.g., "How cam'st thou hither tell me, and wherefore?"; 2.1.104) do not receive the satisfaction of a straight answer. Romeo's responses (e.g. "With love's light wings did I o'erperch these walls"; line 108) are intoxicatingly metaphoric; and metaphor, in this situation, serves only to evade and frustrate communication.

Jonson wrote that "*Language* most shewes a man: speake that I may see thee."[21] Mercutio anticipates this point less succinctly: as Romeo greets him with energetic wordplay in 2.3, Mercutio enthuses, "Why, is not this better now than groaning for love? Now art thou sociable, now art thou Romeo; now art thou what thou art by art as well as by nature" (76–78). Whereas Juliet felt Romeo had an identity independent of language and of name, here Mercutio recognizes the putative "true" Romeo through his speech. Although Mercutio's position seems incompatible with Juliet's, both, it seems, are correct: our identity is both separable and inseparable from language. And although the scene began with Juliet skeptically exploring the relation between words and meaning (in a soliloquy which of course, relies on words to express her skepticism), it ends with a trust in words and their meaning: "Dost thou love me? I know thou wilt say 'Ay,' / And I will take thy word" (2.1.132–34). Having asked Romeo not to swear his love because lovers' oaths are meaningless ("At lovers' perjuries, / They say, Jove laughs"), she immediately asks Romeo to take the one vow she will trust: the holy vow of marriage.

It is no accident of structure that the two scenes that frame the lovers' marriage, 2.1 and 3.5, ponder the question of language, the relationship between personal names and selfhood, nouns and quiddity. Marriage is, in Christian tradition, the gaining of an identity while losing an identity, the two-in-one of Ephesians. It is also, in traditional patriarchal societies, the moment when the woman abandons her family name to take that of her husband. In *Romeo and Juliet*, however, both Romeo and Juliet are viewed as capable of shedding their name in marriage ("refuse thy name, / Or if thou wilt not, . . . I'll no longer be a Capulet"; 2.1.76–78).

If in 2.1 Juliet experimentally muses on language, in 3.5 she confidently uses it, appearing as experienced an equivocator as any in Shakespeare:

> *Juliet.* Villain and he [Romeo] be many miles asunder.
> God pardon him—I do, with all my heart,
> And yet no man like he doth grieve my heart.
> *Lady Capulet.* That is because the traitor murderer lives.
> *Juliet.* Ay, madam, from the reach of these my hands . . .
> Indeed, I never shall be satisfied
> With Romeo, till I behold him, dead,
> Is my poor heart so for a kinsman vexed.
>
> (84–94)

In the orchard scene, Romeo's metaphorical equivocation playfully indicates his exhilaration; in 3.5, Juliet's equivocation is a survival strategy, concealing marital loyalty. Equivocation, like language in general, can be both poetic and duplicitous.

Translation

The slipperiness of language become even more pronounced when one enters the realm of translation. Translation is the turning of one language into another, but it is never a question of simple equivalence. Translation is interpretation and adaptation. The Elizabethans were unself-consciously aware of this. Thomas Drant prefaced his translation of Horace, *A Medicinable Moral, that is, the two bookes of Horace his Satyres* (1566), with the following explanation:

> I have interfarced (to remove his obscuritie, and sometymes to better his matter) much of myne owne devysinge. I have peeced his reason, eekede,

and mended his similitudes, mollyfied his hardnes, prolonged his cortall kynd of speches, changed, & much altered his wordes, but not his sentence: or at leaste (I dare say) not his purpose. (aiiir–v)

What the Restoration called "adaptation," and what we call "(re)appropriation," Drant called "translation." And for Drant, as for his age, translation was a creative act, a dialogue between the past and the present, a cultural linking, an intertextual moment.[22]

However, in the spirit of paradox which inheres in all levels of the language debate, translation was also perfidious, the "revealing of deep matters to others," and was associated etymologically with treason: *traduttore / traditore*.[23] In *2 Henry VI*, Jack Cade targets Lord Say as a traitor because he can speak French (4.2.150–51). Falstaff plots to "English" Mrs. Ford, to translate her from her husband's bed to his own, and Pistol comments that Falstaff has "studied her well (Q1; F: will), and translated her will, out of honesty into English."[24] Betrayal is how Brian Friel's *Translations* presents the central activity of its plot: the "standardisation" and Anglicization of Gaelic place-names in Ireland by the Ordnance Survey team in 1833. The play begins with Sarah (a woman with a "speech defect . . . so bad that all her life she has been considered locally to be dumb") struggling to articulate her name: "My . . . my . . . My name . . . My name is . . . My name is Sarah"; the offstage action concerns the baptism of Nellie Ruadh's baby. These two motifs punctuate the main action: "A hundred christenings! A thousand baptisms! Welcome to Eden . . . We name a thing and—bang!—it leaps into existence! Each name a perfect equation with its reality."[25] But "What's 'incorrect' about the place-names we have here?" says Manus to his brother Owen, who is now employed as the Gaelic-English translator to the English army. That translation represents a loss of culture, a severance from the past, a rewriting of identity, is made clear in the English army's onomastic error: they call Owen "Roland." Owen laughs it off: "Isn't it ridiculous? . . . Owen—Roland—what the hell. It's only a name. It's the same me, isn't it?" (32–33). As the play makes clear, it is not the same Owen at all; Owen the linguistic translator has inadvertently become Owen the cultural traitor. By act 2, Owen is defending the cartographic project to the English lieutenant, Yolland, who is having moral doubts: "Something is being eroded." Owen's response is a long speech explaining the confusing cultural history behind the name "Tobair Vhree"; since parish inhabitants no longer remember or understand its etymology, it is already "eroded" beyond recognition.

For the modern translator of Shakespeare, the linguistic contradictions in translation (fidelity to or betrayal/erosion of an original) coalesce in a position of theatrical rather than semantic logic. If a translation is not "conducive to performance, it remains essentially unfaithful to the original," writes Jean-Michel Déprats. Aligning himself with Drant and against Friel, he argues that "when translating into French, one should be trying less to manipulate the existing forms and usual turns of phrase than attempting to create new ones. And this to serve the demands of the original language rather than those of the language we are translating into." He concludes: "we are less concerned with translating *for* the theatre ... than with translating *theatre*."[26] Thus, by indirections the translator finds directions out. Not just a representation or a reproduction of meaning, translation is, as the Elizabethans well knew, a discovery.

Translation has cultural as well as semantic resonance; *trans-latio* is the carrying of material across cultures, and foreign directors often have remarkable success in discovering Shakespeare. One need think only of the original and imaginative Japanese productions of Ninagawa (*Macbeth* [1990], *The Tempest* [1991], and *A Midsummer Night's Dream* [1993]), of Seazer's *King Lear* by the Banyu Inryoko Company for the Tokyo Globe [1991], or of the Canadian Robert Lepage's controversial *Midsummer Night's Dream* at London's National Theatre (1992–93).[27] Lepage defended his approach:

> The British have always done Shakespeare but for them to restage Shakespeare is to set it in a different time. They will say, "I've set it in the twenties, just before the crash" ... It's like a recipe: you find a perfect time period and work within that. But that is not necessarily reappropriating Shakespeare.[28]

Lepage's "reappropriation" is Drant's "translation." And nowhere was the nexus between appropriation and translation more obvious than in the bilingual (French/English) *Romeo & Juliette*, codirected by Robert Lepage and Gordon McCall in Canada in 1989–90. To this production I now turn.

Romeo & Juliette

The Shakespeare-on-the-Saskatchewan festival, directed by Gordon McCall, was approaching its fifth birthday (1989), and McCall was looking for an anniversary production. Toying with the notion of a bilingual Shakespeare (McCall had already initiated four successful bilingual dramas between 1978 and 1984), McCall contacted Robert Lepage, the Francophone director in Québec, a founding member of Théatre Répère (1980), and the newly appointed head of French Theatre at the National Arts Centre in Ottawa. Peter Brook had influenced both men's directorial styles; thus, despite cultural and artistic differences, there was, as McCall explains, a "mutual fluency in the language of theatre."[29]

The directors assembled a cast of eighteen (twelve Anglophones and six Francophones) for *Romeo & Juliette*. The "ancient grudge" of the Capulets and Montagues was presented not as a specific feud or a linguistic confrontation (although it was certainly that), but more pervasively as a "clash between two cultures whose members have never really understood each other."[30] The set's long asphalt road, a ribbon of the trans-Canada Highway (the connection between eastern and western Canada), separated the estates of two prairie farmers: the Francophone Capulets and the Anglophone Montagues. The Capulet dialogue (about twenty percent of the play) had been translated into (non-modern) French by award winning Québec playwright Jean-Marc Dalpé. In a grim representation of what bilingualism means in Canada, the Capulets automatically spoke English to Anglophones; the Anglophones, by contrast, were consistently monolingual, apart from Mercutio, who offered Tybalt a few incendiary French taunts, and Romeo, who falteringly tried to communicate with Juliette, and, after his marriage, with his new kinsman Tybalt, in French.

Although the production was set in 1989–90 (the years in which it played), modernization was not the point. Lepage explains, "Directing is just finding where the winds are and then positioning yourself to say 'Well I think we should go there.' You don't decide where the wind blows."[31] As we have seen, the winds in *Romeo and Juliet* blow on the topic of language, communication, and translation. And in Canada, language, communication, and translation connote official bilingualism, and ongoing debates about the status of the province of Québec.

Canada has a four-hundred-year history of French-English disagreement. The first European to reach Canada and advertise his discovery in Europe was in the service of the British: John Cabot, in 1497. The Frenchman Jacques Cartier reached the Gaspé Peninsula in 1543, and planted a cross; in 1604 and 1608 the French founded settlements in what are now Nova Scotia and Québec. In the seventeenth century, the English made a claim on Canada through Cabot, and provoked a century of French-English hostility. The antagonism over land seemed decisively concluded by the fall of Québec to the

British in 1759; British rule was officially established in 1763. However, the French had inhabited the country for one and a half centuries, and the British were but newly arrived; the French were Francophone Roman Catholic and the British were Anglophone Protestant. Cultural hostility was inevitable. The British unknowingly created the milder Francophone-Anglophone unease of the present by ghettoizing the French in Québec. Thus Canada's constitution today, with its official policy of bilingualism designed to acknowledge the founding role of the French in the nation's white history, seems undemocratically to privilege a linguistic minority and a single province: Québec.

In 1987, the Canadian government put the province of Québec on the political agenda. The Meech Lake accord, a document on constitutional reform, dealt with eight principal matters, but the one that caused most controversy, received most media coverage, and eventually collapsed the accord in 1990, was the question of Québec as a "distinct society" whose government was committed to "preserv[ing] and promot[ing]" the province's Francophone identity.[32] *Romeo & Juliette* was thus conceived in an atmosphere of cultural tension, although the directors' aim was not to use the play for contemporary statement, but to allow it to speak "with its own political, social and cultural voice."[33] The production opened in Saskatchewan in 1989, and its success led to a tour of three Ontario cities the following summer. It opened in Ottawa, the nation's bilingual capital, in a venue pregnant with possibility or irony (depending on one's point of view): Victoria Island, a small island in the middle of the river that separates Ontario from Québec. Within twenty-four hours, the case was confirmed for irony: the Meech Lake accord officially collapsed. As English- and French-speaking Canada failed to reach constitutional agreement over cultural difference, the Capulet and Montague parents grieved for children who were sacrificed to an "ancient grudge."

The production's opening music—from the movie *Paris, Texas*—wittily established the cultural yoking of two contraries. Drifting over the set's empty road, it also evoked the film's opening shot and the parched conditions (Texan desert, Canadian prairie, Veronese square) blamed by Benvolio for the feuding families' public brawl in 3.1. As might be expected, some of the most resonant dramatic moments stemmed from characters switching languages within a single speech. Tybalt's challenge to Romeo in 3.1 initially read (in Dalpé's translation) "Romeo, tout l'amour que je porte pur vouse [sic] s'exprime le mieux ainsi: vous êtes une vilénie." Altered in the course of rehearsal, this last phrase became "thou art a villain": Tybalt's bilingualism painfully facilitated communication while severing social harmony. Romeo's conciliatory four-line response, in determined French, was rendered even more poignant by this context. The audience saw two characters adopting foreign languages for the contrasting purposes of inflaming and pacifying. This pattern characterized the ensuing exchange. Tybalt's French lines concluded in a command delivered in clear English, lest he be misunderstood—"therefore, turn and draw,"—and Romeo's five-line English response was punctuated with French phrases on "good Capulet—which name I tender / As dearly as mine own" (3.1.66–67).

Usually, however, speeches in two languages served to taunt, as in Sampson's lines in 1.1. To Grégoire's advice "Dis 'better,' v'là qui approche un parent de mon maître," Sampson responded "Oui, bien better, monsieur," the harsh unnaturalness of his bilingual collocation calling attention to itself and its incendiary purpose. Elsewhere, adoption of the French language expanded playful moments in Shakespeare's text, charging simple teasing with repressed malignancy. Mercutio used exaggerated French to curse "such *phantastims*, these new tuners of accent! . . . these strange flies, these fashionmongers, these '*pardon moi*' . . . O, their *bones*, their *bones!*"—amplifying the linguistic satire already implicit in Shakespeare's "pardon me" and bones ["bons"], and made more pointed in the continuation "Signor Romeo, *bonjour*. There's a French salutation to your French slop" (2.3. 25–40; my emphases). Elsewhere, the contiguity of French and English made one alert to the bilingual potential of Shakespeare's text as, for example, when Juliette's lament (in Dalpé's text) "Ah dieu" was followed by Romeo's farewell (in Shakespeare's text): "Adieu" (3.5.54–59). Such bilingual punning is rooted in the text. The lovesick Romeo is found under a sycamore (sick amour) tree, and Capulet acknowledges Juliet as the "Only lady of my earth" (1.2.15; "fille de terre" is, as Steevens first pointed out, the French term for heiress).[34] Pierre Iselin finds Latin-English puns on the Capulet name in phrases like "By my head—here comes the Capulets" (3.1.31; see also 4.2.16), and notes that such etymological paronomasia is characteristic of all the personal names in the play, which possess a quasi-Jonsonian legibility: Romeo (pilgrim [from French Roumieux]), Mont-ague (Mount high), Capulet (little head), Escalus (ladder and scales), Juliet (born in July), Paris (like his Trojan namesake, one of two suitors in a love saga which affects an entire city). Mercutio, Benvolio, Potpan, Susan Grindstone, Simon Catling, Hugh Rebeck and James Soundpost have yet more obvious legibility.[35] The Lepage/McCall production followed the dramatist's example in attaching resonance to names: Paris was able to speak fluent English but he was clearly a Francophone (as his name suggests).

The two languages on stage in *Romeo & Juliette,* and characters' use of one or the other or both, attuned the audience to linguistic change within a *single* language. Two characters in *Romeo and Juliet* experiment with different idioms and/or language: the satiric Mercutio and the romantic Romeo. Mercutio tries to appeal to Romeo in language that he will understand (and hence, to which he will respond):

> I conjure thee by Rosaline's bright eyes,
> By her high forehead and her scarlet lip,
> By her fine foot, straight leg, and quivering thigh,
> And the demesnes that there adjacent lie.
>
> (2.1.17–20)

Mercutio's parodic love-sick inventorying shows that he does not take this new language of Petrarchan idiom seriously; in fact, we know from preceding and succeeding scenes that it is not language with which he can identify (1.4; 2.3.34–38). More serious, although almost as brief, is the linguistic exchange in the debate between Romeo and Juliet the morning after the wedding night. Juliet identifies the birdsong as that of the nightingale, Romeo as "the lark, the herald of the morn," but, when she insists, her husband yields: "I am content, so thou wilt have it so" (3.5.18). He is not merely content to stay however, but to adopt Juliet's language:

> I'll say yon grey is not the morning's eye,
> 'Tis but the pale reflex of Cynthia's brow;
> Nor that is not the lark whose notes do beat
> The vaulty heaven so high above our heads . . .
> Juliet wills it so.
>
> (3.5.19–24)

In response to his *volte-face* Juliet now cedes:

> It is the lark that sings so out of tune,
> Straining harsh discords and unpleasing sharps.
>
> (3.5.27–28)

Marianne Novy comments that this scene uses "a verbal transformation of the world—a creation of a private world through words—as a metaphor for a relationship."[36] I agree that the scene is a positive metaphor for a relationship, but see the metaphor as bilingualism.

Romeo and Juliet agree to speak each other's language. Although Romeo knows it is the lark that sings, he is "content" to change languages, identifying the bird as the nightingale, whereupon Juliet reciprocally adopts her husband's language. They provide an example of linguistic reciprocity in love, making logical sense of Juliet's mixed metaphor in 3.2.26–28, where she is both subject and object, buyer and seller—and very different from the superficially similar scene of language exchange in *The Taming of the Shrew* (4.5), where Petruccio makes all the demands and Katherine all the concessions. Thus the motif that began as nominalism (or anti-nominalism) in the garden scene (2.1) of *Romeo and Juliet,* develops in 3.5 into something closer to foreign-language learning or translation.

That 3.5. is a scene of language exchange is made apparent by its source: John Eliot's *Ortho-Epia Gallica, or Eliot's Fruits for the French* (1593).[37] A series of dialogues (French on one page or column with an English translation facing), *Ortho-Epia* takes student-readers through daily situations—shopping, drinking, walking, thieving, book-buying, traveling, reading—introducing them, as language manuals still do, to basic functional vocabulary and dialogue, and to cultural aspects of the country whose language they are in the process of acquiring. The last chapter introduces the student to the poetry of Du Bartas, and provides a lyrical quatrain about the lark in the "vaulty heaven" (*R&J* 3.5.22; "la voute du Ciel," *Ortho-Epia,* *t*1v,p.146), followed by a change of ornithological subject:

> *Harke, harke, tis some other bird that sings now.*
> *'Tis a blacke-bird or a Nightingale.*
> *The Nightingale sings not but euening and morning*
> *Where is she I pray thee?*
> *Tis a Nightingale I heard her record.*
> *Seest thou not her sitting on a sprig?*
> *O how sweetly she sings without any stop,*
> *and ceaseth not!*[38]

Love means learning to speak the language of the beloved. This, at least, is the message from the *aubade* scene, and from *1 Henry IV* where the (politically and emotionally) captive Mortimer vows to learn the language of his (nameless) newlywed wife ("I will never be a truant, love, / Till I have learnt thy language"; 3.1.202–3).[39] *Romeo & Juliette* makes this point in the context of Canadian cultural history, and Brian Friel makes the same point in the different colonial history of *Translations.* The Irish Marie and the English Lieutenant Yolland fall in love. Although neither understands the other's language, they quickly find a way to communicate by reciting place-names. Yolland has learned the Irish names he was sent to standardise: "Carraig na Ri . . . Loch na nEan . . . Machaire Mor . . . Cnoc na Mona . . . Mullach. Tor" (51–2). Within a day, Marie has learned "Winfarthing—Barton Bendish—Saxingham Nethergate—Little Walsingham—Norwich—Norfolk. Strange sounds, aren't they? But nice sounds." (60) In fact, sounds (signs) have more meaning than do signifiers to the lovers:

> *Marie.* Say anything at all. I love the sound of your speech . . .
> *Yolland.* Say anything at all—I love the sound of your speech.
> (50)

To the audience this is a repetition. To the characters it is not, for they do not understand each other. Friel has brilliantly established a convention whereby the actors all speak English, although their characters speak Gaelic or English. The actors' monolingual representation of two languages deepens the play's resonance. Not just about a moment in Ireland's past when Gaelic speakers became English speakers, the play belongs also to the present, a period when two cultures who share a language—Northern Ireland and Britain, Northern Ireland and the Irish republic, Northern Ireland Catholic and Northern Ireland Protestant—fail to communicate.

As George Steiner observes in the epigraph to this essay, "Human communication equals translation."[40] In *Romeo & Juliette* the lovers' dialogue in the aubade scene took place in English; as the lovers exchanged language—lark, nightingale—the production showed that bilingualism is a motif for monolingual societies too. This was illustrated, sadly, in the McCall/Lepage collaboration in another way. McCall's confident memory of the directors' "mutual fluency in the language of theatre" compensating for cultural barriers was not shared by Lepage. Although McCall worked alone with the Francophone actors, he did not permit Lepage the reciprocal privilege of working alone with the Anglophone actors. Throughout, there were different ways of working "at every level, in every detail"; the actors even belonged to different unions. Consequently, Lepage felt that artistic/cross-cultural fertilization was frustrated. McCall's presence when Lepage worked with the English-speaking actors was, in Lepage's view, intended to prevent the possibility of contradiction. "But you have to allow people to contradict your work because that's when it thickens and becomes multilayered." Although Lepage anticipated that it would be "very exciting, the idea of working with both sides," in the end, he said, "I felt cheated."[41]

Conclusion

Using a sartorial metaphor, Juliet begs Romeo, "Doff thy name." But, as Mashay Bernstein points out, changing language or name is not "as benign as changing clothes."[42] It signals the relinquishing of cultural memory, identity, history, the past. Romeo and Juliet are prepared to give up such inherited identities in exogamous marriage, but their kinsmen are not. Arthur Brooke's (didactic) version of the tragedy (itself a translation of Bandello, but lacking Shakespeare's awareness of language and its problems) concludes by assigning punishments. Shakespeare's conclusion focuses on language:

> Go hence to have more *talk* of these sad things.
> Some shall be pardon'd, and some punished
> For never was a *story* of more woe
> Than this of Juliet and her Romeo.
>
> (5.3.396–99)

The couple's marriage and tragic deaths will be translated into narrative. The final paradox of language in *Romeo and Juliet* is that it can help assuage the sufferings it causes; a linguistic homeopathic remedy, it translates reality into art, senseless slaughter into tragedy.

Notes

1. See Gayle Whittier, "The Sonnet's Body and the Body Sonnetized in *Romeo and* Juliet," *Shakespeare Quarterly* 40 (1989): 27–41.
2. Ed Snow contrasts this with Romeo's kinetic energy and static images. See "Language and Sexual Difference in *Romeo and Juliet*," in *Shakespeare's Rough Magic* ed. Peter Erickson and Coppélia Kahn (Newark: University of Delaware Press, 1985), 170–75.
3. 2.2.9–10; Marjorie Garber, "*Romeo and Juliet:* Patterns and Paradigms," in *Romeo and Juliet: Critical Essays,* ed. John F. Andrews (New York and London: Garland, 1993): 126. All references to Shakespeare's plays come from the Norton Shakespeare (based on the Oxford edition), gen. ed. Stephen Greenblatt (New York: W. W. Norton, 1997), and are henceforth included parenthetically in my text. Note that the Norton-Oxford edition presents as one scene (2.1) what other editors usually (mistakenly) give as two scenes (2.1 and 2.2), and the rest of the Act is renumbered accordingly.
4. David Lucking narrows this to a tragedy of literacy. It is, as he points out, Romeo's ability to read that leads him to the Capulet feast. See Lucking, "The Balcony Scene in *Romeo and Juliet*," *English* 44 (1995): 1–16. However, failure to rely on the written word (the letter from Friar Lawrence) is also responsible for disaster: Romeo's trust in oral report brings him from Mantua to the Capulet vault in Verona (see Whittier, "The Sonnet's Body", 38). Pierre Iselin argues (in a position that, as will become apparent, I agree with entirely) that the play is a tragedy of

naming. See Iselin, "'What Shall I Swear By?': Rhetoric and Attitudes to Language in *Romeo and Juliet*," in *"Divers toyes mengled": Essays on Medieval and Renaissance Culture*, ed. Michel Bitot, with Roberta Mullini and Peter Happé (Tours: Université François Rabelais, 1996), 261–80.

5. Jonathan Swift, *Gulliver's Travels*, ed. Isaac Asimov (New York: Clarkson N. Potter, 1980), 175.

6. The paradoxes in this paragraph are indebted to Steiner, *After Babel: Aspects of Language and Translation* (Oxford and New York: Oxford University Press, 1975); James Boyd White, *When Words Lose their Meaning* (Chicago: University of Chicago Press, 1984); Ronald Wardhaugh, *Languages in Competition: Dominance, Diversity, and Decline* (Oxford: Basil Blackwell, 1987); John Edwards, *Multilingualism* (London and New York: Routledge, 1994); R. D. Grillo, *Dominant Languages: Language and Hierarchy in Britain and France* (Cambridge: Cambridge University Press, 1989); G. A. Wells, *What's in a Name? Reflections on Language, Magic, and Religion* (Chicago: Open Court, 1993); Richard W. Bailey, *Images of English* (Ann Arbor: University of Michigan Press, 1991); François Grosjean, *Life with Two Languages* (Cambridge: Harvard University Press, 1982); and Suzanne Romaine, *Bilingualism* (Oxford: Blackwell, 1989, 1995).

7. Literary examples of the power of silence include Chaucer's Griselda, where Griselda's uncomplaining acquiescence to Walter's repeated cruelty becomes increasingly subversive (see Elaine Tuttle Hansen, *Chaucer and the Fictions of Gender* [Berkeley: University of California Press, 1992], 188–207), and Shakespeare's French princess in *Henry V*, where Katherine's apparently benign incomprehension forces Henry into French.

8. It is no coincidence that the "savage" Caliban has one of the most poetic speeches in *The Tempest;* and, in a line richly aware of the Janus-like qualities of language, he declares "You taught me language, and my profit on't / Is I know how to curse" (1.2.366).

9. Seamus Deane, "Brian Friel: The Name of the Game" in *The Achievement of Brian Friel*, ed. Alan Peacock (Gerrards Cross, UK: Colin Smythe Ltd, 1993), 108.

10. Steiner, *After Babel*, and Einar Haugen, "The Curse of Babel," in Einar Haugen and Morton Bloomfield, *Language as a Human Problem* (New York: Norton, 1974), 33–35.

11. For ancient Greek contributions to the debate see Euripides' *Helen*, and Norman Austin, *Helen of Troy and her Shameless Phantom* (Ithaca, NY: Cornell University Press, 1994); for the medieval scholasts, see Mary Carruthers, *The Book of Memory* (Cambridge: Cambridge University Press, 1990).

12. Michael Quigley, "Language of Conquest, Language of Survival," *Canadian Forum* 42 (Nov 1982), 14.

13. White, *When Words Lose their Meaning*, 3.

14. Nonetheless, editorial preference for Q1's reading shows the difficulty of Juliet's position that ideas can be divorced from words. Earlier editors' promotion of the Q1 reading into their Q2 copy-text of *Romeo and Juliet* (see the editions of H. H. Furness [1899], Edward Dowden [1900], Peter Alexander [1951], John Dover Wilson [1955]) illustrates locally and textually the point the play makes largely and philosophically: names matter.

15. James Calderwood, *Shakespearean Metadrama* (Minneapolis: University of Minnesota Press, 1971), 88.

16. Kiernan Ryan, "*Romeo and Juliet* : The Language of Tragedy" in Willie van Peer, ed. *The Taming of the Text* (London: Routledge, 1988), 114, and Manfred

Weidhorn, "The Rose and its Name: On Denomination in *Othello, Romeo and Juliet, Julius Caesar,*" *Texas Studies in Literature and Language* 11 (1969), 671–86.

17. The Norton-Oxford edition emends from Q1 here. Q1 reads "Whats *Mountague?* It is nor hand nor foote, / Nor arme, nor face, nor any other part." Q2 reads "Whats *Mountague?* it is nor hand nor foote, / Nor arme nor face, o be some other name / Belonging to a man." See Stanley Wells and Gary Taylor et al, *William Shakespeare: A Textual Companion* (Oxford: Clarendon Press, 1987), 294 (2.1.83–4/ 814–5) for analysis of the alternatives.

18. Jacques Derrida, "L'aphorisme à contretemps," translated as "Aphorism Countertime," in *Acts of Literature*, ed. Derek Attridge (London: Routledge, 1992), 426. Cf. Catherine Belsey, "The Name of the Rose," *Yearbook of English Studies* 23 (1993): 126–42.

19. David Lucking, "The Balcony Scene in *Romeo and Juliet,*" *English* 44 (1995): 8.

20. Derrida, "Aphorism Countertime," 427.

21. Ben Jonson, *Timber: or, Discoveries,* in *Ben Jonson*, 11 vols., ed. C. H. Herford and Percy and Evelyn Simpson (Oxford: Clarendon Press, 1947), 7: 625.

22. See Jonathan Bate, *Shakespeare and Ovid* (Oxford: Clarendon Press, 1993), chapter 1.

23. See John Edwards, *Multilingualism* (London and New York: Routledge, 1994), 5.

24. See Patricia Parker, *Shakespeare from the Margins* (Chicago: University of Chicago Press, 1996), 116–22.

25. Brian Friel, *Translations* (London: Faber and Faber, 1982), 11, 45. As the British army and the Irish resistance resort to violent confrontation in the play's tragic ending, Sarah relapses into dumbness and Nellie Ruadh's baby is pronounced dead.

26. Jean-Michel Déprats, "Translating Shakespeare for the Theatre," in *Shakespeare and France*, ed. Holger Klein and Jean-Marie Maguin (Lewiston, NY: Edwin Mellen Press, 1995), 347, 353, 355.

27. For interesting discussions of this production see Barbara Hodgdon, "Looking for Mr. Shakespeare after 'The Revolution': Robert Lepage's Intercultural Dream Machine," and Denis Salter, "Acting Shakespeare in Postcolonial Space," both in *Shakespeare, Theory and Performance*, ed. James C. Bulman (London and NY: Routledge, 1996), 68–91 and 113–32.

28. Robert Lepage, interviewed by Christie Carson, "Collaboration, Translation, Interpretation," *New Theatre Quarterly* 9 (1993): 35.

29. Gordon McCall, "Two Solitudes: A Bilingual *Romeo & Juliette* in Saskatoon," *Canadian Theatre Review* 62 (1990): 40.

30. Barbara Crook, *Ottawa Citizen*, June 22 1990, C7.

31. Lepage, "Collaboration, Translation, Interpretation," 31–32.

32. James Robertson, "The Constitutional Accord of 1987: A Preliminary Analysis" (Ottawa: Library of Parliament, 1987); Mollie Dunsmuir, "The Meech Lake Accord Update" (Ottawa: Library of Parliament, 1989, revised 1990).

33. Denis St. Pierre, *"Romeo & Juliette* for 1990s," *Sudbury Star,* 14 July 1990, NN5.

34. *The Plays of William Shakespeare ... To which are added notes by Samuel Johnson and George Steevens* (London, 1773), 1.2.15n.

35. See Iselin, "'What shall I swear by?,'" 263, 272. As Iselin points out, bilingual punning has a long history. It appears in the New Testament in Christ's "You are Peter and on this rock I will build my church" (Matthew 16:18).

36. Marianne Novy, *Love's Argument: Relations in Shakespeare* (Chapel Hill: University of North Carolina Press, 1984), 108–9.

37. See J. W. Lever, "Shakespeare's French Fruits," *Shakespeare Survey* 6 (1953): 79–90.

38. *Ortho-Epia*, *t*3r, p.149; see Lever, "Shakespeare's French Fruits," 82–3. Eliot was a Warwickshire man, a near-contemporary of Shakespeare, and Lever speculates on the possibility that he and Shakespeare may have known each other. Whether the men were acquainted or not, it seems more than probable that Shakespeare was reading Eliot in 1593–4—for instance, towards its conclusion (*u*4r-*x*1r, 159–61), the dialogue offers a bathetic descent from poetic lyricism to a Mercutian-style "satire on the Petrarchan lover in which all the stock conceits of the contemporary sonnet craze are lumped together" (Lever, 83).

39. To late-twentieth-century readers, Romeo's and Mortimer's code-switching might seem an encouraging example of linguistic and sexual equality. But Romeo realizes that his love for Juliet has made him "effeminate": he turns the other cheek, prefers peace to fighting, love to hate, and consequently, though unintentionally, causes the death of his friend Mercutio. Mortimer is uninterested in politics, tardy in warfare, pacifist and passive rather than militarily aggressive.

40. In a recent *Globe and Mail* article on bilingualism, Victor Goldblum, Canada's Official Language Commsissioner, observed: "Québec's sense of collective destiny continues to clash with the rest of Canada's strong attachment to individual freedoms." Thus, *"even if we're bilingual and can communicate with one another we're ... not speaking the same language* when we talk about individual and collective interests" (my emphasis). See Murray Campbell, "Bilingualism: Canada Talks the Talk," *Globe and Mail*, 22 February 1997, D3.

41. Lepage, "Collaboration, Translation, Interpretation," 32.

42. Mashay Bernstein, "'What a Parrot Talks': The Janus Nature of Anglo-Irish Writing," in *The Text and Beyond: Essays in Literary Linguistics* ed. Cynthia Goldin Bernstein (Tuscaloosa: University of Alabama Press, 1994), 267.

Humor Out of Breath:
Francis Gentleman and the *Henry IV* Plays

LOIS POTTER

A CONTEMPORARY CALLED IT "THE WORST EDITION THAT EVER APPEARED OF ANY English author."[1] So perhaps it is fortunate that "Bell's Edition of Shakespeare" (1773–74) is known by the name of the publisher who commissioned it rather than by that of its editor, Francis Gentleman (1728–84).[2] The failure of Gentleman's brief editorial career was in keeping with the rest of his life. He was, among other things, an actor unsuited to major roles because of what he himself called his "inconsequential appearance,"[3] a playwright and adapter who had few real successes, and a critic whose habit of attacking almost anyone who happened to be in the limelight led David Garrick to write, though not to publish, verses referring to him as "only Gentleman by name."[4] What critics found particularly outrageous in *Bell's Shakespeare* was the extent of its cuts to the text of the plays and Gentleman's evident belief that these were a good thing. The contrast between his approach to Shakespeare and Garrick's stated determination "to lose no drop of that immortal man" made Gentleman an easy target for ridicule. Yet, as is well known, Garrick's enthusiasm for Shakespeare did not prevent him from cutting heavily; indeed, the line just quoted is the conclusion of the prologue to his adaptation of *The Winter's Tale*, which omits the first half of the play.[5] Gentleman's attitude, which corresponds with that of most film and video directors of Shakespeare, probably looks less shocking at present than it once did. But I am less concerned here with defending him than with examining the implications of his views on cutting, particularly with regard to the plays he considered most long-winded, the two parts of *Henry IV*.

It should be noted first that the cuts in Gentleman's edition were probably not his own. Based on acting texts supplied by the prompters of Drury Lane and Covent Garden theaters, *Bell's Shakespeare* claims to print what was spoken on the stage, at least in the case of plays in the current repertoire; one of its selling points was the ease with which it could be used at the theater by spectators who wanted to follow the performance in a book.[6] Gentleman made it clear that he considered most of the traditional cuts highly desirable, and he recommended shortening other plays which, because they had no acting editions, he had to print in full. But *Bell's Shakespeare* was not, as it has been called, "bowdlerized."[7] Since the theater's notion of propriety was not necessarily the same as Gentleman's, his edition often includes lines that he describes in his notes as "unpardonably gross."[8] In an essay of 1770 he had already protested against recent Shakespeare editions, with their increasingly heavy annotation; what was really needed, he suggested, was "a committee of able critics" (he proposed Garrick as its head) who would go through the plays and "strike out the insignificant and offensive passages which so often occur."[9] It was not, then, simply offensiveness that constituted the "gross." Wordiness might be just as bad. In the "Life of Shakespeare" which he wrote for the final volume of Bell's series (the *Poems*), he blames the dramatist for "indulging the redundancy of his own imagination" and directs those in search of examples to the "historical plays particularly."[10] His notes on these plays (especially the second tetralogy) are filled with complaints about the length of the speeches, culminating in the note—or exasperated sigh—on Burgundy's speech at the end of *Henry V:* "It is amazing *Shakespeare* should have run so much, and so often, into prolixity" (*Henry V,* 76).

Gentleman was thoroughly in agreement with the traditional cuts to the *Henry IV* plays, insisting that both of them were much better in the acting version than as originally written (*1 Henry IV,* 74; *2 Henry IV,* 78). Cuts in Part One were particularly noticeable in the speeches of Henry IV (the opening one, for instance, went from 33 lines to 10); performance texts omitted the play-acting in 2.4 and the whole of 3.1 involving Hotspur, Mortimer, and Glendower. Part Two, less frequently played, had been given its basic shape in the version attributed to Thomas Betterton, first published in 1720.[11] Because its opening scene had already been used by Colley Cibber for the opening of his immensely successful adaptation of *Richard III,* neither Rumour's speech nor the report of Hotspur's death to Northumberland linked Part Two with its predecessor; in fact, neither Northumberland nor Lady Percy reappeared at all, and the lines of the second set of conspirators were greatly reduced. The play now began with Falstaff's first entrance and was largely focused on him, although there were cuts and rearrangements in the scenes at Shallow's estate in Gloucestershire—scenes which Gentleman called "very insignificant" (*2 Henry IV,* 64). Although presumably unaware that 3.1 of Part Two may have been a later addition (it does not appear in the first issue of the 1600 quarto), the adapter deleted it.

The soliloquy on sleeplessness, one of the most admired passages in the play, was transferred to the opening of Henry IV's last scene.

What is interesting about Gentleman's comments on these scenes is the consistency of his language: he thinks that Part One's play-within-a-play scene "loaded the main business" (*1 Henry IV,* 33) and is glad to see the play "free of superfluities" (74); Part Two has been "considerably, and very well, purged" (Introduction, n.p.) but remains "laboured and heavy" (*2 Henry IV,* 78). He twice praises Falstaff's replies in Part One for being "pregnant" with humor (38, 57), although he finds one of his speeches in Part Two "unnecessarily fulsome" (10). Of Henry IV's long address to his son in 3.1 of Part One, he comments, "no actor could find breath to speak, nor any audience patience to hear his prolixity" (43). In short, without apparently seeing the implications of his own imagery, Gentleman is anticipating Patricia Parker's brilliant argument, in *Literary Fat Ladies,* about verbal and physical dilation—the entire play is a Falstaff: "a trunk of humours," fulsome, loaded, female in the sense of being overly talkative, pregnant, in need of purging—and, above all, out of breath.[12]

Gentleman's concern with breathing and breathlessness can be explained in part by the fact that, among his other careers, he had been a teacher of, and writer on, the art of speaking; he published an *Essay on Oratory* in 1771, and reprinted it in the first volume of *Bell's Shakespeare.* The contemporary craze for "Elocution" had already led to numerous essays and courses of lectures by actors and would-be actors, telling everyone else where to put the pauses and stresses in reading aloud.[13] Perhaps equally important, Gentleman, a man of almost skeletal thinness,[14] had played Sir Epicure Mammon in at least some performances of *The Tobacconist* (his own version of *The Alchemist*), and would thus have known at first hand the problems of playing an exhausting part while wearing heavy padding. Hence, his comment that most of the lines in the first scene between Hotspur and his wife could be cut, "Did not Sir John want some breathing time" (*1 Henry IV,* 27). The scene follows the one at Gadshill in which Falstaff frequently complains of shortness of breath, and finally runs away roaring, but Gentleman is clearly aware that he is talking about a problem for the actor himself.

The importance of breath control to acting must always have been obvious. Breathless entries were something of a convention: Alan Dessen's forthcoming dictionary of stage directions from English Renaissance plays includes directions for characters to "enter panting" (or sometimes "blowing"). The reason for this is usually character coding: a messenger who isn't out of breath cannot be a very good messenger. But a pause in a fight is a point at which not only the characters but the actors can "breathe."[15] Confusion between actor and character may even have been the object: drawing attention to breathlessness was a way of offering the audience one of those always popular glimpses (in reality highly edited) of the effort that lies behind a polished performance.

Gentleman's language draws attention to something which, I believe, has not previously been noticed: the relation of the longwindedness of the *Henry IV* plays to the constantly stated problem of breathlessness. The King's opening speech says that he wants to give "frighted Peace" time to "pant" while he himself will "breathe shortwinded accents" about the crusade he hopes to begin (1.1.2–3); in his final scene in Part Two, he refers to his lungs as "wasted" (4.5.216) and has too little breath to stir the feather on his pillow.

Gentleman's language also reminds us that, as Malcolm Parkes has most recently pointed out, punctuation began as a guide to breathing, with a "period" meaning a phrase that should be spoken without taking a breath until one came to a full stop, or "point."[16] The link between speech and punctuation was (in 1612) one of Thomas Heywood's justifications for the practice of acting plays in schools and colleges: public speaking would teach the scholar "to observe his commas, colons, and full poynts; his parentheses, his breathing spaces, and distinctions . . . ."[17] Not being able to see the point could be embarrassing, as in Peter Quince's prologue, or fatal, as in the letter of *Edward II* that has been "left unpointed for the nonce."[18] And if there was *no* point, as in the windy diatribes of which Puritans and bishops accused each other, the reader might be unable to breathe at all. Martin Marprelate told his episcopal antagonist that "a man might almost run himselfe out of breath before he could come to a full point in many places in your booke."[19] Breathlessness can thus be traced to several causes: not knowing when to stop (lack of intelligence), not being able to stop (lack of control), or not wanting to stop (egotism). The "longwinded" speaker is, paradoxically, the one most likely to become shortwinded.

It seems never to have struck Gentleman that the technical demands presented by the *Henry IV* plays might be evidence of the ability of the actors for whom they were written. Like his contemporaries, he took Shakespeare's "prolixity" to mean lack of control, an accusation which might seem to be supported by Jonson's famous comment in *Discoveries* ("He flowed with that facility that sometimes it was necessary that he should be stopped").[20] Though Gentleman knew more about comedy of humors than most of his contemporaries, his knowledge of the genre was confined to Jonson, from whom he had adapted several plays. Living as he did in a time when humors comedy had been banished from the mainpiece to afterpiece farces,[21] he was not aware of the Elizabethan taste for plays (like the anonymous *Look About You* of the late 1590s) which combined humor comedy with history. The *Henry IV* plays, like other humor plays of the 1590s, employ a dramaturgy of disguises, quick changes, and impersonation. They are very speech-conscious: characters frequently imitate one another's speech rhythms and Hal's tavern jokes exploit the predictability of human responses. Indeed, the trick Hal plays on Francis the drawer makes most sense in the context of a similar episode in Chapman's *An Humorous Day's Mirth* (1597), a play which is said to have inaugurated the fashion for humors comedy. Chapman's hero Lemot has a name which means "word," a fact that allows someone to point out that his name is "runne out of breath at euery word you speake."[22] In a later scene this becomes literally true: his rapid entrance is greeted with, "What, you are out of breath me thinks Monsieur Lemot?" (3.2.1) In a tavern not unlike the one in the *Henry IV* plays, he tells his friend that he will speak to each of five gallants separately, "and I will tell thee before[hand] what they shall answer me" (*An Humorous Day's Mirth* 3.1.182–85). He is right every time, to the admiration of his companion, because these gulls use clichés as a substitute for thought and their catchphrases and proverbs can be triggered by a suitably chosen keyword (*le mot juste?*).

Prince Hal's tavern joke is more obviously rigged than Chapman's. Francis replies, "Anon, anon, sir," to whatever Hal says to him, not really because—as Hal claims—he has "fewer words than a parrot" (*1 Henry IV* 2.4.96–97), but because Poins' offstage calling and Hal's frequent changes of subject destroy his train of thought and reduce him to an automatic catchphrase. In his subsequent conversation with Poins, who asks the point of this joke, Hal apparently changes the subject twice: first saying that he is now "of all humours that have shown themselves humours" and then caricaturing Hotspur's style of speech. Joseph A. Porter suggests that Hal's turning from Francis to Hotspur is a Shakespearean association of ideas: the word "parrot" recalls Hotspur's reference to the starling who is to drive Henry IV mad by being taught to say "nothing but 'Mortimer,'" and Lady Percy's comparison of Hotspur himself to a paraquito. Hal will compare Falstaff to a parrot in Part Two, where he and Poins again imitate the "anon, anon sir" joke.[23]

Predictability is one link between Falstaff and Hotspur; another is their breathless delivery, to which attention is constantly drawn. Falstaff's breathlessness is a standing—or running—joke. It results from his being full of words, which are made of air as he says (*1 Henry IV* 5.1.133–35), and hence also of wind, which he threatens to break. He visibly runs out of breath, or pretends to, as he exchanges insults with Hal: "O for breath to utter what is like thee!" (2.4.246), to which Hal replies, "Well, breathe awhile, and then to it again" (2.4.249).[24] Just as Falstaff is always thirsty and breathless, so the first thing Hotspur says about himself is that after the battle he was

> dry with rage and extreme toil,
> Breathless and faint . . . .
>
> (1.3.31–32)

In Part I his wife describes him as breathless even in his sleep:

> in thy face strange motions have appear'd,
> Such as we see when men restrain their breath
> On some great sudden hest.
>
> (2.3.61–63)

In Part Two she remembers him as "speaking thick, which nature made his blemish" (*2 Henry IV* 2.3.24). Although in this century there has been a theatrical tradition of interpreting this "blemish" as a stammer, the phrase actually seems to mean that the actor of Hotspur spoke unusually fast, even at a time when rapid speech was the norm on the stage. It seems odd, however, that Lady Percy should need to draw attention to it retrospectively. Was Hotspur so rapid as to be unintelligible to some auditors? One function of long speeches is that of showing off the actors' memories and lung power, qualities which tend to impress even the least sophisticated theatergoer.[25] As acting increasingly distinguished itself from oratory, in the 1590s, it may have become necessary to reassure the audience that deviant speech patterns were intentional, not an irritating "blemish." Part Two includes such a reassurance not only about Hotspur but also about Falstaff. When the Prince reads the beginning of Falstaff's letter—"I will imitate the honourable Romans in brevity"—Poins interjects, "He sure means brevity in breath, short-winded." (*2 Henry IV* 2.2.123–25). After this, we hear no more of Falstaff's shortwindedness, though presumably it remains part of the performance.

Why, then, all this stress on characters' difficulty in speaking? Gentleman himself had speculated, in a curious passage from his *Essay on Oratory,* that the difficulty of making oneself heard in a crowded room might result from "the conjunct respiration of so many people," producing "an essential density of air."[26] This sense of the competitive nature of speech is confirmed by a modern theorist. "Our participation in dialogue," writes Lev Yakubinsky, "is determined by our expectation of being interrupted, by our awareness that an interlocutor is preparing to respond, by our fear that we might not be able to say all that we want to say. Hence, ceteris paribus, the pace of dialogue is faster than the pace of monologue."[27] The ultra-competitive world of the histories is one in which failure to pause for breath reflects a fear of being interrupted and thus losing not only the floor but much more than that. The only one who can control his own air space is the king: able to silence interruptions, he can speak (as Gentleman noticed) at greater length than anyone else (in fact, many of his dialogues are really monologues); he can deny the right of reply to others. At the end of Part One Hal begins to take command, like his father, of the air space; having allowed both Hotspur and Falstaff to display themselves to their fullest extent, he then destroys them and their humor together. When he talks of his intention to let Percy "engross up glorious deeds on my behalf" (3.2.148), he is of course drawing on the language of finance, but "engross" also suggests a parallel with Falstaff's grossness and the lies Hal lets him tell—"like their father that begets them, gross as a mountain, open, palpable" (2.4.220-21)—until the time is ripe to put him down with a "plain tale" (251). The two characters are linked for the last time when Falstaff comments on their brief period of apparent death: "I grant you, I was down and out of breath, and so was he" (5.5.145-46). In Part Two, Northumberland is told that Hotspur had been "out-breath'd" (1.1.108) by Hal, as if the messenger knew that Hal had actually spoken his last word for him.

Medically speaking, the breathlessness of Falstaff and Hotspur could be explained by their being hot and dry, since Galenic medical theory held that the purpose of breathing was "the conservation of the innate heat" of the body, either by cooling the heart, or, in the case of someone naturally cold, by fanning its heat.[28] Characters who were unusually hot (choleric or sanguine) might be considered to need a greater supply of air than those who have the "cold blood" which Falstaff attributes to the Lancastrians (*2 Henry IV* 4.3.118). It is appropriate that Henry IV eventually dies of an apoplexy, since according to Galen this is a condition in which the "psychic pneuma" is "cooler than the norm."[29] Falstaff, who claims to have read about it in Galen, claims surprisingly that it is also "a kind of deafness" (*2 Henry IV* 1.2.117), perhaps alluding to the King's inability to listen to others, to take part in the circulation of air which Falstaff, characteristically, describes in terms of sack (*2 Henry IV* 4.3.94-115). Our sense of Falstaff as, despite his age, more *alive* than anyone else (Jay L. Halio calls him "the most youthful character in the play"),[30] comes from the sense that he is circulation personified, forever making us conscious of the process by which he takes in sack and air, transmuting it and expelling it at every orifice, whether as sweat, wind, or words. As Corbyn Morris put it in 1744, he is like perpetual motion: "continually detected and caught, and yet constantly extricating himself by his inimitable *wit* and *Invention*; thus yielding a perpetual *Round* of Sport and Diversion."[31] He is not put out of his humor, but his promises to amend in the future give the illusion of immortality. Although he has neither the authority nor the breath with which to silence others, the overcrowded air parts like the Red Sea for his famous speeches—until the end of Part Two, where the new King, following his father's example, forbids him to reply. His circulation cut off, deprived of the cooling function of breath, he later dies, and no wonder, of a "burning quotidian tertian" fever (*Henry V* 2.1.119).[32]

The fact that Francis Gentleman was both actor and editor gives his work a special relevance for a volume concerned with both text and performance. My argument has been that his obsession with breathing and his enthusiasm for cutting are related, and that, despite his objections to the "unnatural tragicomic mode of writing" in Part One (22) and to what he calls the "dramatic olio" of Part Two (78), these two concerns enabled him to intuit something like what would later be called the organic unity of the *Henry IV* plays. The question remains: why was he so enthusiastic about the "humour" of the plays but so negative about, and so eager to cut, their historical and political plot? The answer, I think, is not that he was not interested in their politics, but that he *was*.[33] His problem was that they were the wrong politics. Since 1688 it had become almost a cliché among British intellectuals to speak of their country's unique blend of liberty and humor. As Corbyn Morris wrote in 1744, the humorist "flourishes only in a Land of *Freedom,* and when *that* ceases he dies too, the last and noblest *Weed* of the Soil of *Liberty*."[34] In fact, the Renaissance concept of humor was much more imprisoning than empowering: to be predictable was to be manipulable. If Morris could turn Shakespeare into a Whig like himself,[35] Gentleman could not; in his "Life of Shakespeare", he reluctantly concluded that the playwright was a time-server.[36]

This political concern may explain his approval of two of the cuts which seem most surprising to a twentieth-century reader. One was the "Welsh scene" of Part One, which he describes as "strange, unmeaning, wild" and therefore—like Falstaff, one might say—"properly rejected" (*1 Henry IV,* 43). What he probably recognized (having played Hotspur for a brief period) was the way in which this scene reduces rebellion to humor, mostly expressed in such linguistic deviation as Hotspur's explosiveness or Glendower's exotic accent and the foreign language in which he speaks to his daughter. Phyllis Rackin has also pointed out that Mortimer, the key figure in the rebellion, is reduced to a different sort of humor: a lover "totally absorbed in his sensuality and his wife."[37] That Gentleman would have liked to cut the whole of the first scene between Hotspur and Kate in Part One is also not hard to explain. Both scenes showed the sillier side of Hotspur, and Gentleman did not want him to have a silly side. He did not mind that the plot required Hotspur to be defeated at last; indeed, although he sympathized with one who, "though a rebel, . . . seems to act upon just principles, and very aggravated provocation" (71), he admired the balance of sympathies in the final combat with Hal, where "we must rejoice at the success of one, and grieve for the fate of the other" (*1 Henry IV*, 71). His incidental comment that the recruiting scene in Part Two was "very applicable to the present time" (*2 Henry IV*, 38) reminds us that Gentleman was writing in 1774. What he wanted, in this pre-war era, was a noble if uncouth rebel, doomed, of course, to lose, but representing a cause for which many intellectuals of the late eighteenth century had a good deal of sympathy.

The other scene which Gentleman found "properly" omitted was 3.1 of Part Two, in which Henry IV and the Earl of Warwick consider the shape and meaning of recent history. Arguably, it is redundant, since it recapitulates events from earlier plays, and at a time when *Richard II* was no longer performed it may have been merely mystifying. Among other losses were the lines spoken by Warwick, often seen as a key to the English history plays:

> There is a history in all men's lives
> Figuring the nature of the times deceas'd;
> The which observ'd, a man may prophesy,
> With a near aim, of the main chance of things
> As yet not come to life, who in their seeds
> And weak beginnings lie intreasured.
> Such things become the hatch and brood of time;
> And by the necessary form of this
> King Richard might create a perfect guess
> That great Northumberland, then false to him,
> Would of that seed grow to a greater falseness,
> Which should not find a ground to root upon
> Unless on you.
> (*2 Henry IV* 3.1.80–92)

Warwick's account of the "history in all men's lives" is humor theory extended to politics, and made a key to all psychologies. It reduces the compulsively false Northumberland to the same level of predictability as his son, only slightly more dignified than Francis the drawer with his knee-jerk "Anon, anon sir." The speech would be still more ironic if Shakespeare thought (wrongly) that the speaker was the same "wind-changing Warwick" already portrayed in the *Henry VI* plays as guilty of the same kind of behavior which he now, without knowing it, predicts.[38] Gentleman, who objects that "predestination is . . . blameably inculcated" when the French King in *Henry V* refers to Henry's "fate" (*Henry V,* 30), may have been equally disapproving of Henry's response to Warwick's speech: "Are these things then necessities?" (93). The twentieth-century theater has found ways of playing the ideologically unacceptable—for instance, through "resistant readings," playing against the lines, and "alienation"—but the eighteenth and nineteenth centuries preferred simply to cut.

Richard Brinsley Sheridan had probably seen Gentleman's acting edition before he wrote *The Critic* (1789), which depicts an author, Mr Puff, watching the rehearsal of his tragedy. When the Under-Prompter tells Mr. Puff that the players have taken advantage of his permission to "omit whatever they found heavy or unnecessary to the plot," he is initially complacent: "Well, they are in general very good judges, and I know that I am luxuriant."[39] A few scenes later, of course, a reference to "the pruning knife" has him shrieking in anguish: "The pruning knife! Zounds, the axe! Why here has been such lopping and topping, I shan't have the bare trunk of my play left presently."[40] Puff (whose name occurs briefly in *2 Henry IV* as that of the only person fat enough to compare with Falstaff) visualizes his writing in terms of Edenic abundance; the players, like the skinny Gentleman, see it as overindulgence. Similarly, in the lean years of 1596–98, Falstaff's jokey argument—"If to be fat is to be hated, then Pharaoh's lean kine are to be loved" (2.4.472–74)—could have backfired on him.[41] If the eighteenth century preferred to see humor characters confined to the world of comedy, it was perhaps because the performance of humor could become a substitute for the stating of political grievances, both those within the play and those outside the play of which audiences might have been reminded.

Notes

Earlier versions of this paper have benefitted from comments by members of the Medieval and Renaissance Workshop at the University of Delaware and the

Shakespeare Association of America, Washington, D. C. (28 March 1997). Line references to Shakespeare's plays are to the Riverside Shakespeare.

1. David Erskine Baker, *Biographia dramatica, or, A companion to the playhouse.* 2nd ed., continued from 1764–1782 [by Isaac Reed]: London: Rivingtons, 1782, 1: 188. Cited in Colin Franklin, *Shakespeare Domesticated: the Eighteenth-Century Editions* (Aldershot, Hants.: Scholar Press, 1991), 137.

2. Gentleman, who wrote all the introductions and notes to the plays in this collection, receives credit on the title page only as one of "the Authors of the *Dramatic Censor*." The latter was a periodical published by Bell, first serially and then in a two-volume edition; Samuel Derrick had written one number of it in 1752 and Gentleman took it up again in 1770–71—hence, presumably, the odd use of the plural "Authors." F. N. Clary points out (privately) that the Dedication and Advertisement to Bell's edition are also signed "THE EDITORS."

3. Philip H. Highfill, Jr., "Francis Gentleman," in Highfill, Kalman A. Birnim, and Edward A. Langhams, *A Biographical Dictionary of Actors, Actresses, Musicians, Dancers, Managers, & Other Stage Personnel in London, 1660–1800* (Carbondale and Edwardsville: Southern Illinois University Press, 1978), 6: 138–53. For comments on his appearance, see 139, 142, 152. Highfill's excellent essay gives a very full account of Gentleman's career.

4. Ibid., 149. The poem can be found as Folger MS Y.d.120 (19). Gentleman's relation to Garrick was, however, complex. As F. N. Clary has pointed out in his "Garrick's 'Altered' *Hamlet* and the Editorial Rivalries of the 1770's" (seminar paper, Shakespeare Association of America, Cleveland, Ohio, March 1998), Garrick helped the struggling author financially and seems to have defended him, at least implicitly, when he was attacked by George Steevens. Indeed, Clary suggests (in a seminar paper given at the 1997 SAA meeting) that Steevens' attacks may have been an orchestrated campaign against what he perceived as a rival edition (the Johnson-Steevens edition was rushed through the press in 1773 in reaction to the appearance of Bell's).

5. "Prologue to *The Winter's Tale* and *Catherine and Petruchio*" (line 55), *The Plays of David Garrick*, vol. 3: *Garrick's Adaptations of Shakespeare, 1744–1756*, ed. Harry William Pedicord and Fredrick Louis Bergmann (Carbondale and Edwardsville: Southern Illinois University Press, 1981), 191.

6. Advertisement to vol. 1 of *Bell's Edition of Shakespeare's Plays, as they are performed at the Theatres Royal in London*, 9 vols. (London, 1774). Hereafter, *Bell's Shakespeare*.

7. Franklin, *Shakespeare Domesticated*, 137.

8. *Bell's Shakespeare*, vol. 4, *2 Henry IV*, p. 23. Volume 4 contains the two *Henry IV* plays and *Henry V*. Unless otherwise noted, all quotations from Gentleman's notes will be from this volume. As each play is separately paginated, I shall also give the name of the play and the page number of the note.

9. *The Dramatic Censor, or, Critical Companion* (London: J.Bell; York: C. Etherington, 1770), 1: 149–50. According to Janet E. Aikins, the suggestion that texts should be cut not only for performance but also in print derives ultimately from John Hill, *The Actor: a Treatise on the Art of Playing* (1750), 252–53 and 308. Pages 252–53 of Hill are reprinted in Brian Vickers, *Shakespeare, the Critical Heritage* (London and Boston: Routledge and Kegan Paul, 1975), 3: 373. A similar proposal was made by Samuel Derrick, Gentleman's predecessor on *The Dramatic Censor;* see Janet E. Aikins, Introduction to Samuel Derrick, *The Dramatic Censor: Remarks upon the Tragedy of Venice Preserved,* Augustan Reprint Society no. 233–34 (Los Angeles: Clark Library, 1985), viii.

10. *Poems Written by Shakespear* (London: J. Bell & C. Etherington, 1774), 14. This is vol. 9 of *Bell's Shakespeare*, but not described as such on the title page.

11. For a fuller account of the cuts, see Scott McMillin, *Shakespeare in Performance: Henry IV, Part One* (Manchester and New York: Manchester University Press, 1991), 6. As McMillin points out, these cuts, and the fact that the two plays seem never to have been performed in sequence, effectively prevented audiences from seeing them as a unified whole, with the complex ironic parallels that have been noted by twentieth-century critics.

12. Patricia Parker, *Literary Fat Ladies: Rhetoric, Gender, Property* (London and New York: Methuen, 1987), 43.

13. For the Elocutionists, see W. S. Howell, *Logic and Rhetoric in England, 1500–1700* (Princeton: Princeton University Press, 1956), chapter 4.

14. See the "Summary View of the Stage" prefixed to his *The Modish Wife* (London, 1774), 14.

15. I am grateful to Professor Dessen for showing me these entries from the *Dictionary of Stage Directions in English Drama, 1581–1642* (compiled by Alan Dessen and Leslie Thomson, forthcoming from Cambridge University Press).

16. Quintilian, quoted in M. B. Parkes, *Pause and Effect: An Introduction to the History of Punctuation in the West* (Berkeley: University of California Press, 1993), 65. I am very grateful to Professor Julian Yates for directing me to this book.

17. Thomas Heywood, *An Apology for Actors* (London: Shakespeare Society, 1841), 29.

18. *Edward II*, 5.5.16. Christopher Marlowe, *Complete Plays and Poems*, ed. E. D. Pendry and J. C. Maxwell (London: J. M. Dent & Sons, 1976).

19. *Oh read ouer D. Iohn Bridges (The Epistle)*, n.d. [Oct. 1588], in *The Marprelate Tracts*, Leeds: Scolar Press Reprint, 1967, 12. Cf. also "I was neuer so affraid in my life/ that I shoulde not come to an end/ till I had bene windlese." (*Oh Read ouer D. Iohn Bridges (The Epitome)* [Nov. 1588], C3v–C4). I owe these references to Professor Kristen Poole. For the idea of Falstaff as a "grotesque Puritan", see also her "Saints Alive! Falstaff, Martin Marprelate, and the Staging of Puritanism," *Shakespeare Quarterly* 46 (1995): 47–75.

20. As Ian Donaldson points out, Jonson is here imitating Seneca's characterization of another writer. *Ben Jonson*, ed. Ian Donaldson, Oxford Authors (Oxford University Press, 1985), lines 669–70 and 742n.

21. I should like to thank Professor Matthew Kinservik for pointing out this division, which was one effect of the Licensing Act of 1737.

22. George Chapman, *An Humorous Day's Mirth*, 1.5.61–62. Quotations from Chapman's plays are taken from *The Plays of George Chapman: the Comedies*, ed. Allan Holaday, assisted by Michael Kiernan (Urbana: University of Illinois Press, 1970). Subsequent references will be given by act, scene and line number.

23. Joseph A. Porter, *The Drama of Speech Acts: Shakespeare's Lancastrian Tetralogy* (Berkeley: University of California Press, 1979), 69–70.

24. The line was apparently a catch-phrase, since it also occurs in a marginal note at the point mentioned above in Marprelate's tract ("who who [whoa, whoa?]/ Dean take thy breath and then to it againe"). The emphasis on long-windedness may be yet another trace of Falstaff's origins as the Lollard Oldcastle.

25. Lois Potter, "Nobody's Perfect: Actors' Memories and Shakespeare's Plays of the 1590s," *Shakespeare Survey* 42 (1990): 85–97.

26. *Bell's Shakespeare*, 1: 51.

27. Lev Petrovich Yakubinsky, "On Dialogic Speech" (trans. and ed. Michael Eskin), *PMLA* 112 (1997): 250.

28. Galen, "On the Use of Breathing," in *On Respiration and the Arteries* (ed. and trans. David J. Furley and J.S. Wilkie, Princeton University Press, 1984), 131.
29. Ibid., 127.
30. Jay L. Halio, *Understanding Shakespeare's Plays in Performance* (Manchester: Manchester University Press; New York: St Martin's Press, 1988), 59.
31. Corbyn Morris, *An Essay towards Fixing the True Standards of Wit, Humour, Raillery, Satire, and Ridicule* (London, 1744; reprinted Garland Publishing, 1970), 27.
32. For a similar expression of the view of speech as part of the circulation of air, see Mowbray's impassioned reaction to his banishment, which, because he can speak no language but English, he sees as a way of stopping his breath: "What is thy sentence then but speechless death, / That robs my tongue from breathing native breath?" (*Richard II* 1.3.172–73).
33. This is clear from many of his notes; for instance, he comments on Worcester's speech (*Henry IV* 5.1.30–71): "There is a great share of good sense and pith of argument, in this justification of rebellion" (64).
34. Corbyn Morris, *Essay*, 20–21. Quoted in Stuart M. Tave, *The Amiable Humorist, a Study in the Comic Theory and Criticism of the Eighteenth and Early Nineteenth Centuries* (Chicago: University of Chicago Press, 1960), 118–19; see also Tave's discussion, 95. Curiously, Morris' image seems to derive from Henry IV's comment on Hal: "Most subject is the fattest soil to weeds" (*2 Henry IV* 4.4.54).
35. Morris' *Essay* is prefaced by a long and fulsome dedication to Sir Robert Walpole, the former Whig Prime Minister, whom he praises for having defended British liberty.
36. *Poems Written by Shakespear* (London: J. Bell & C. Etherington, 1774), 29. In an interesting footnote to his *History of England* (1754–62), David Hume put it somewhat more gracefully: although the Roman history plays expressed noble sentiments about freedom, "civil liberty" is never mentioned in Shakespeare's English histories, "an omission which cannot be supposed in any English author that wrote since the Restoration, at least since the Revolution." David Hume, *The History of England* (London, 1807), 5: 469n. I am grateful to Professor Burton A. Abrams for drawing my attention to this passage.
37. Phyllis Rackin, *Stages of History* (Ithaca, New York: Cornell University Press, 1990), 171. See Scott McMillin's comment on the unpolitical emphasis of the 1945 Old Vic *Henry IV* sequence, directed by John Burrell, in which Olivier played Hotspur: "If the King will not fuel a rebellion by behaving badly, one can always turn to that unfailing source of disorderly ambition according to some romantic temperaments, oneself. Hotspur is a role ripe for such inspiration" (19).
38. As J. Dover Wilson first pointed out in the New Cambridge Shakespeare edition of *2 Henry IV*, only one Neville was also an Earl of Warwick; see the note by A. R. Humphreys in his edition (London: Methuen, 1966), 3.1.66.
39. Richard Brinsley Sheridan, *The Critic*, in vol. 2 of *Dramatic Works of Richard Brinsley Sheridan*, ed. Cecil Price (Oxford: Oxford University Press, 1973), 2.1.23–27.
40. Ibid., 2.2.13–15.
41. A. F. Kinney suggests that Falstaff's fatness "is both a signifying cause and a haunting reminder of those that prey on others, and of those who feel it most when out at heels." See his "Textual Signs in *The Merry Wives of Windsor*," *Yearbook of English Studies* 23 (1993): 227. One might compare the exchange in *Nicholas Nickleby* about Wackford Squeers, the pampered son of a man who starves and exploits the children in his care. In response to the proud father's "Pretty well swelled out, an't he? . . . He has the fatness of twenty boys, he has,'" Newman Noggs replies, "he has—the fatness of twenty!—more! He's got it all. God help the others. Ha! Ha! O Lord!" (chapter 34).

Editing Informed by Performance History: The Double Ending of *Troilus and Cressida*

DAVID BEVINGTON

PERFORMANCE HISTORY IS INTEGRAL TO AN ATTEMPT TO UNDERSTAND THE TEXTS of *Troilus and Cressida* from the very start. The two states of the 1609 Quarto announce on their title pages not two different performances, but, it would seem, performance and non-performance. *The Historie of Troylus and Cresseida* (Qa) proclaims itself as having been "acted by the Kings Maiesties seruants at the Globe" and "Written by William Shakespeare." *The Famous Historie of Troylus and Cresseid* (Qb), issued apparently soon afterwards with a new title page and an advertisement from the publishers, drops all mention of the King's Majesty's Servants, describing the play instead as "Excellently expressing the beginning of their [Troilus' and Cressida's] loves, with the conceited wooing of Pandarus Prince of Licia." This decidedly literary characterization reads like an enticement to a reader, somewhat in the vein of the "sullen and assumed humor of Tom of Bedlam" trumpeted on the title page of the 1608 Pied Bull Quarto of *King Lear*.

The advertisement from "A never writer, to an ever reader. News" in this second state of the 1609 Quarto is even more blatant in its literary appeal. The "Eternal reader" is invited to acquire for his library, before the copies are "out of sale," "a new play, never staled with the stage, never clapper-clawed with the palms of the vulgar." Its author, the advertisement insists, is a writer of such "dexterity and power of wit" that even those who are "most displeased with plays" are sure to be "pleased with his comedies," since his works deserve to be ranked with "the best comedy in Terence or Plautus." The advertisement goes on to accuse "the grand possessors" of the play—presumably Shakespeare's acting company—of having attempted to withhold it from publication. This, evidently, is the version that the publishers intended to be read, since the changeover to the new title page and publishers' advertisement was apparently made before the text left George Eld's printing shop; only a few copies of the first state survive, having been sold along with the corrected copies because paper was expensive.[1]

Despite this insistently antitheatrical claim, we have little reason to doubt that the play was performed. The Stationers' Register entry of 7 February 1602/3 refers to "The booke of Troilus and Cresseda as yt is acted by my lo: Chamberlens Men," anticipating the claim of the Qa title page that the play was "acted by the Kings Maiesties seruants at the Globe." Heminges and Condell collected it into their Folio edition of 1623, albeit with apparent difficulties in obtaining the copyright that led to a hiatus in the printing of this play and finally an anomalous placement, unpaginated for the most part, between the histories and the tragedies. The Folio text substantially augments the stage directions of the Quarto, reflecting perhaps some attention in the theater to the demands of staging. Even the literary appeal on Qb's title page to "the conceited wooing of Pandarus Prince of Licia" may suggest that Pandarus had become something of a household name, like Falstaff. Pandarus' smarmy Epilogue, addressed to "Brethren and sisters of the hold-door trade," that is, to his fellow pimps and bawds, seemingly asks the audience to come back for more in a sequel: "Some two months hence my will shall here be made" (5.11.51–2).[2] No sequel exists, and most critics have concluded from this and from a lack of performance records that the play proved to be an experimental failure, but the Epilogue does suggest at least an initial production. The fact that a truncated version of Pandarus' last appearance on stage is to be found at the end of 5.3 in the Folio text may even suggest that the play was performed in different locales.

Perhaps the most challenging hypothesis of recent date about the two versions of the Quarto's front matter is Richard Dutton's contention that they reflect a divided sensibility in Shakespeare himself, or at least in his public reputation.[3] Was he simply, as a man of the theater, indifferent to seeing his play made available for readers, or was he conscious of their worth as deserving of literary fame? The early poems, *Venus and Adonis* and *The Rape of Lucrece*, show an avid interest in publishing his poetry, and the *Sonnets*, circulated "among his private friends,"[4] presumably in manuscript, thematize literary immortality. The conventional wisdom is to see Shakespeare as having drawn a sharp line of demarcation between these literary efforts and his plays written for the stage, which were (so the argument goes) scripts not unlike those for films today, whose authors we rarely can remember by name and whose scripts we almost never read.

Is the analogy a fair one, however? Plenty of play scripts were published in Renaissance London as texts to be read, including roughly half of Shakespeare's plays in quarto during his lifetime. Increasingly, they advertise his name, in ever-enlarged type, as an inducement to the buyer. His company (in which he was a business partner) undertook to bring out corrected versions of plays that had been printed without their authorization, and in what they evidently regarded as inferior versions. Shakespeare did not actually see his plays through the press, but he presumably was in agreement with his acting company's wish to publish corrected versions of them. Arguably, then, Shakespeare did care about some readership, perhaps a select one.

Troilus and Cressida seems to offer a unique instance of an attempt, by someone, to publish a play in 1609 that appealed first and foremost to sophisticated readers with no special love for the theater as such. If, as has been argued, the publisher's preface inserted in Qb was written by John Marston, a friend of the publisher Henry Walley,[5] then we may have a link to the Inns of Court and to that center of London intellectual life where literary reputations mattered. Even if Dutton pushes his evidence too hard at times, speculating that we have lost a number of manuscripts in which Shakespeare's plays were circulated among the cognoscenti, we do have the evidence of Qb in 1609 to suggest that Shakespeare did have a growing literary reputation among readers as a writer of plays in the highest cultural sense. Francis Meres' comparison of Shakespeare to Plautus and Terence lauds Shakespeare as a literary genius, not simply as one whose plays are to be seen. Gabriel Harvey speaks of *The Rape of Lucrece* and *Hamlet* as fare to please "the graver sort,"[6] making no distinction between poem and play in his praise of their literary qualities.

These considerations invite the question as to whether *Troilus and Cressida* was performed in a public theater "by the Kings Maiesties seruants at the Globe" (Qa title page) and also in a more select venue, such as the Inns of Court. Direct evidence is lacking, but the idea has its appeal. When Ulysses invokes the image of a "strutting player, whose conceit / Lies in his hamstring," in "to-be-pitied and o'erwrested seeming" and in hyperbolical rant "like a chime a-mending" (1.3.152–59), the diatribe is not unlike Hamlet's irritation at actors who saw the air with their hands and improvise lame jests not set down for them in their parts (*Hamlet*, 3.2.1–45). Speakers in both plays share a wariness of "groundlings" and the "unskillful" who seem "capable of nothing but inexplicable dumb shows and noise," thereby making the "judicious" grieve (*Hamlet*, 3.2.11–26).

Hamlet, to be sure, was publicly acted, but it was also reportedly a favorite at "the two universities" (title page of Q1). Might *Troilus and Cressida* also have been a darling of the smart set?

The two dismissals of Pandarus in the Folio text, one at the end of 5.3 and one at the conclusion of the play, do seem to suggest productions on separate occasions with textual alterations suited to match varying conditions of performance. The short three-line version at the end of 5.3—

> *Pand.* Why, but hear you?
> *Troy.* Hence brother lackie; ignomie and shame
> Pursue thy life, and liue aye with thy name.

—would appear to remove Pandarus from the play for good, thus obviating the necessity of his Epilogue at the end of 5.11. Lacking such an Epilogue (which is nevertheless printed in both Q and F at the end), the play would end on the bitterly tragic note of Troilus' lament for the death of Hector and his determination to fight on:

> Strike a free march to Troy! With comfort go.
> Hope of revenge shall hide our inward woe.
> (5.11.30–1)

To identify these moving lines as the conclusion of one acting version of *Troilus and Cressida* requires nothing more than the hypothesis that the three-line passage in 5.3 is intended to dismiss Pandarus from the play at that point, and that the Folio ending, with its nearly identical repetition of these three lines plus Pandarus' Epilogue, represents an alternative ending that should have been cancelled but was instead erroneously copied out when the printer failed to note the cancellation marks.[7] To be sure, one can regard the short passage in 5.3 as Shakespeare's first shot, which he then abandoned in favor of bringing on Pandarus at the end for an Epilogue,[8] but that hypothesis makes sense only if F as a whole represents an early version of the play and Q is some kind of revision. Other evidence renders this view (still maintained by some textual scholars)[9] uncertain, if not problematic and even improbable.

Perhaps then, the Quarto version of *Troilus and Cressida,* with its tawdry note of sexual disillusionment and hint of a sequel, was designed for an audience like that at the Inns of Court—an audience of spectators inclined to applaud the play's experimentalism and sexual daring, to share its aloofness toward public spectators, and to appreciate the play's literariness and classical sophistication. Even if we heed, as we must, the warnings of those who point out that Shakespeare cannot be proven ever to have written a play on commission for a private audience,[10] we can speculate that Shakespeare could have adapted a play written for his company in the first instance, but then selected for special performance at one of the Inns of Court, much as *The Comedy of Errors* seems to have been presented at Gray's Inn in 1594, not as a play written originally for those gentlemanly spectators, but as an entertainment chosen from the public repertory because it was well suited to their tastes in Saturnalia.

Troilus appears to require a larger than average number of actors (fourteen men and four boys, plus eight mute extras, by T. J. King's count),[11] although Quarto and Folio texts do not differ measurably in these requirements. Conceivably, Shakespeare added the Epilogue for a private occasion and then dispensed with it when the play returned to the Globe. (The argument, recently advanced,[12] that Pandarus' Epilogue might have been spoken at the end of 5.3 seems highly improbable; its jocose farewell to the audience and promise of a return engagement "Some two months hence" seem designed for a curtain call in the vein of other Shakespeare epilogues.)

What can twentieth-century performance history (there being none in the period from 1609 to about 1900 other than Dryden's extensive adaptation of 1679) add to our perspective on the early history of the play and its seeming bifurcation between a bitterly tragic *Troilus and Cressida* ending on a note of noble defiance, and a more satirical *Troilus and Cressida* ending with Pandarus as the final dispiriting spokesman? As Roger Apfelbaum ably demonstrates, performance history is not lacking in theatrical attempts to counter the disillusioning effects of Pandarus' Epilogue. Dryden transposed the material into an earlier scene, while at the same time expurgating Pandarus' bawdy song and syphilitic jesting. John Philip Kemble, in a promptbook designed for a performance that never took place, moved and cut the final soliloquy. Even William Poel, in 1912, for all his belief in restoration of Elizabethan texts and staging, preferred to locate the rejection of Pandarus in 5.3 and to end the play with Troilus' lament for the death of Hector. After all, Pandarus' smarminess had been one important factor in ruling the play off the stage for so long. At Stratford-upon-Avon, as the play began to gain acceptance, Ben Iden Payne in 1936, Anthony Quayle in 1948, and Glen Byam Shaw in 1954 all concurred in transposing to the end of 5.3 varyingly cut versions of the Epilogue—not without a rising tide of uneasiness from the critics as to the textual authority of such a move.[13]

Markedly to the contrary, directors and actors of the latter half of the twentieth century have found in Pandarus' sleazy farewell a key to the dispiriting play as a whole. The restoration of the Epilogue had been adventuresomely pioneered by Michael Macowan at London's Westminster Theatre in 1938. Tyrone Guthrie, at the Old Vic in 1956, also retained the Quarto arrangement of the rejection of Pandarus, followed by his Epilogue, at the end of the play rather than at the end of 5.3. Not coincidentally, as Apfelbaum points out, both Macowan and Guthrie set their productions in modern times.[14] Since then, Pandarus has sometimes been doubled with the Prologue as a kind of obscene chorus figure, introducing and then taking a final slick bow for the entire show. This kind of evidence does not amount to a conclusive proof as to how the play should end, but it certainly adds weight to those textual critics like Phebe Jensen who call attention to the inescapable fact that both Quarto and Folio versions end with Pandarus' soliloquy.[15]

In Howard Davies' production for the Royal Shakespeare Company at Stratford-upon-Avon in 1985, for example, Pandarus, played by Clive Merrison, was central to Davies' conception of the play as a monument to the collapse of civilization. Suavely hatted, Pandarus opened the play "by sitting at a table sipping wine and reading his paper"; by the end of it all, he was to be seen (as Michael Billington describes the moment) "picking out a wistful tune on the piano as the lights of battle blaze[d] and as structured society disintegrate[d]." He then rose from the piano, "pale, gaunt and half-blind," to discover that the piano was playing by itself. This "jaunty voyeur," and the play surrounding him, went out on a wry joke about self-annihilation.[16]

Norman Rodway doubled as Prologue and Pandarus in Sam Mendes' production of *Troilus and Cressida* at the RSC's Swan Theatre, Stratford-upon-Avon, in 1990. In both roles, Rodway was a natty chap in a blazer whose wheezing and giggling established the squalidness of the cause for which the Trojan War was fought. Pandarus was thus in effect Prologue and Epilogue; the play became his, and he saw to it that its potentially tragic story was cheapened from the start and then ushered sardonically to its demise in a mood of disillusionment and travesty.[17]

The RSC's most recent production, directed by Ian Judge at Stratford-upon-Avon in 1996, made a similar point through the framing of Prologue and Epilogue, this time involving Thersites. The Prologue, played by Richard McCabe and doubled with the role of Thersites, set about to debunk the whole business of war as if he were a "TV warm-up man," and the Epilogue picked up on this idea of disillusionment. The final battle scenes were staged under a blood-red sun. Pandarus (Clive Francis), mincing, queenly, wasted and diseased, spat out his final curses as a syphilitic voyeur; what had begun as a "jaunty comedy" ended, in Michael Billington's estimate, as "a soured, dispirited view of the devouring tyranny of time." The Epilogue, thus reinforcing the Prologue, showed how effectively the device of framing could speak for an interpretation of the play as a whole. The eloquent humanity shown in this production by Philip Voss's Ulysses appeared lost in a dreary world of cheap jokes and posturing.[18]

Another way to underscore the nihilism and tawdriness of Pandarus' Epilogue was developed by John Barton and Barry Kyle in their codirection for the RSC in 1976: that of melding the images of Pandarus and Thersites into a single garish and distorted amalgam. For his final appearance, Pandarus donned a death mask and "descended into a gravelike vault which revealed, when closed, Thersites clutching a life-sized female doll." The image seemed apt in a production that insistently portrayed the Trojan War as a pointless and bitter struggle between antipathetic enemies.[19] In still another production, that of Terry Hands for the RSC at the Aldwych in 1981, Pandarus (Tony Church) was seen at the end of the play draped across a barbed-wire fence, in vivid recollection of the killing fields of World War I.[20]

The Epilogue, in its final location as evidenced in both Q and F, is thus of vital importance for most late-twentieth-century directors, because it offers them a key to the play's distasteful view of war and sexuality. Even in earlier years, when directors were still reluctant to end the play with Pandarus' Epilogue, the impetus toward disillusionment was everywhere in evidence, as though laying the groundwork for the return of Pandarus to his position of dominance at the end of both the Quarto and Folio texts. William Poel, shortly before World War I (in 1912), used the play as a vehicle for his antiwar sentiments and dislike of military pomposity.[21] War-weariness and disenchantment were the hallmark of the Marlowe Society of Cambridge's postwar production by Frank Birch in 1922. In an early modern-dress version of the play in 1938, which, as we have seen, featured the reinstatement of the Epilogue, Michael Macowan directed Pandarus (Max Adrian) as a bon vivant of the languid 1920s clubbish set, accompanying himself on the piano in a Gershwin vein as he sang "Love, love, nothing but love" to Helen in a low-cut evening dress, while others, in formal attire, sat on stylish settees or stood at the bar sipping their aperitifs. Pandarus was, in the eyes of the reviewers, an "affected, elderly roué and society butterfly," a "chattering and repulsive fribble of the glassily squalid night-club type."[22]

In Robert Atkins' 1946 production at the Open Air Theatre in Regent's Park, similarly, Pandarus (Russell Thorndike) was a "perverted Punch."²³ Anthony Quayle, as Pandarus in Glen Byam Shaw's 1954 production at the Shakespeare Memorial Theatre, was not allowed his Epilogue, and yet was presented throughout as "a lisping, giggling, intriguing old fribble," a "very carefully managed study of senile blethering and fussing," and a "pathological nanny"; he unveiled Cressida for Troilus in 3.2 as though unwrapping a mannequin in a display window.²⁴ Paul Rogers wore a top hat and Ascot attire, complete with field glasses, for the part in Tyrone Guthrie's Edwardian production at the Old Vic in 1956 (which, as we have seen, did reinstate the Epilogue), and played Helen a love song on the piano as Max Adrian had done in 1938.²⁵ In Stratford, Connecticut, in a 1961 production commemorating the centenary of the American Civil War, Pandarus entertained the lovers on a mandolin as they met in the wisteria-draped garden of his home, visibly a mansion of the Old South.²⁶ Max Adrian returned to the part in John Barton and Peter Hall's 1960 production at Stratford-upon-Avon as a visibly older, diseased wretch urging on the coupling of Troilus and Cressida "with horrid zest that turns in the end to hollow disgust."²⁷

The image of disillusionment and waste thus embodied in Pandarus as pander and (increasingly in late-twentieth-century productions) as sardonic Epilogue, leagued in a number of productions with the Prologue and with Thersites as framing and choric figures for the play as a whole, has had important implications for the other characters as well. Cressida, in particular, has emerged as a victim of war and of male homosocial bonding under the specious guise of patriotic feeling and concern for personal honor. John Dryden, in 1679, portrayed her as not, in fact, guilty of the infidelity that Troilus is misled into believing. In 1912, William Poel saw Cressida (Edith Evans) as a matter-of-fact and resolute young woman determined to make the best of wartime's uncertainties and absurdities—a kind of Mother Courage. Ben Iden Payne was fascinated with Cressida as the object of a male gaze (1936); Robert Atkins' staging of Cressida's capitulation to Diomedes in 5.2 (1946) was voyeuristic, distancing, and disillusioning in its effect.²⁸ Anthony Quayle, in 1948, saw the young lovers as stripped of any illusions of poetic or romantic idealism.²⁹ In the American Civil War production of 1961 she was a flirtatious Southern Belle.³⁰ Helen Mirrin, in Barton's 1968 production at Stratford-upon-Avon, was a coarse tease surrounded by bare-torsoed warriors flaunting (in some cases) their homosexuality.³¹ In Barton's 1976 production, Cressida (Francesca Annis) was "symbolically disrobed" by Diomedes on her arrival in the Greek camp (4.5); as she left with Diomedes, a courtesan's mask worn at the back of her head was revealed to the audience for the first time.[32] Joseph Papp, in New York in 1965, saw Cressida as "a victim of men, their wars, their desires, their double standards."[33] Terry Hands' Cressida in 1981 (Carol Royle) was, more patronizingly, a "knowing and flirtatious virgin," but even here the emphasis was on the stereotypes of male attitudinizing that could be held accountable for the evils of war.[34] Suzanne Burden's Cressida, in Jonathan Miller's BBC Television production of 1981, brought her survival instincts into play: "There's got to be a way out of this and if I have to use my sex I will."[35] Juliet Stevenson's Cressida, in Howard Davies' 1985 production, quickly learned that her only choice of survival was to become a love-object like Helen after all.[36] For Amanda Root, in Sam Mendes' 1990 production, the question turned out to be not why Cressida betrayed Troilus "but why she ever entertained the possibility of faithfulness."[37] For both Helen and Cressida in Ian Judge's 1996 production, "sex is easy, but love and faith are out of the question."[38] The step from such a dispiriting view of women in time of war to Pandarus' Epilogue is an easy and inevitable one.

None of this performance history can definitively argue for the textual integrity of Pandarus' Epilogue as an integral part of the play. Textual evidence suggests in fact that *Troilus and Cressida* was performed on some occasions without it, especially in the early years of the twentieth century when directors seem to have been feeling their way toward what audiences would accept in the way of a dispiriting ending. Insofar as performance history does offer insight into directorial choices and a sense of what works in the theater, on the other hand, the vote is increasingly in favor of retaining the Epilogue in its assigned place in both Q and F at the end of the play. Its gloating and uncomfortably salacious mockery does not strike modern directors or actors as an anomaly devised for some special performance and thereafter abandoned. The Epilogue is by now an essential part of our vision of *Troilus and Cressida*.[39]

Notes

1. Philip Williams, Jr., "The 'Second Issue' of Shakespeare's *Troilus and Cressida*, 1609," *Studies in Bibliography*, 2 (1949–50): 25–33, and Fredson Bowers, "Running-Title Evidence for Determining Half-Sheet Imposition," *Papers of the Bibliographical Society*, University of Virginia, 1 (1948–49): 199–202. See also Peter W. M. Blayney, "The Publication of Playbooks," in *A New History of Early English Drama*, ed. John D. Cox and David Scott Kastan (New York: Columbia University Press, 1997), 383–422.

2. References are to *Troilus and Cressida*, ed. David Bevington, Arden 3 (Walton-on-Thames: Nelson, 1998).

3. Richard Dutton, "The Birth of the Author," in *Elizabethan Theater: Essays in Honor of S. Schoenbaum*, ed. R. B. Parker and S. P. Zitner (Newark: University of Delaware Press, London: Associated University Presses, 1996), 71–92.

4. Francis Meres, *Palladis Tamia* (London, 1598).

5. Philip Finkelpearl, "Henry Walley of the Stationers' Company and John Marston," *PBSA*, 56 (1962): 366–68, and William Elton, "Textual Transmission and Genre of *Shakespeare's Troilus,*" in *Literature als Kritik des Lebens*, ed. Rudolf Haas, Heinz-Zoachim Müllenbrock, and Claus Uhlig (Heidelberg: Quelle & Meyer, 1975): 63–82, esp. 65–69.

6. Gabriel Harvey, marginal notes written down some time between 1598 and 1601 in a copy of Thomas Speght's edition of Chaucer.

7. Gary Taylor, "*Troilus and Cressida*: Bibliography, Performance, and Interpretation," *Shakespeare Studies*, 15 (1982): 99–136, following a line pursued earlier by William Sydney Walker, *A Critical Examination of the Text of Shakespeare*, 3 vols. (London, 1860), 3: 203–4; Henry N. Hudson, ed., *The Complete Works of Shakespeare*, 2nd ed. 20 vols. (Boston: Ginn, 1880–86), 16: 358; and J. M. Nosworthy, *Shakespeare's Occasional Plays: Their Origin and Transmission* (London: E. Arnold, 1965), 81.

8. E. K. Chambers, *William Shakespeare: A Study of Facts and Problems*, 2 vols. (Oxford: Clarendon Press, 1930), 1: 438–49, seconded by, among others, Alice Walker, *Textual Problems of the First Folio: Richard III, King Lear, Troilus and Cressida, 2 Henry IV, Hamlet, Othello* (Cambridge: Cambridge University Press, 1953), and E. A. J. Honigmann, *The Stability of Shakespeare's Text* (London: E. Arnold, 1965), 78–99.

9. Notably E. A. J. Honigmann, "The Date and Revision of *Troilus and Cressida*," in *Textual Criticism and Literary Interpretation*, ed. Jerome J. McGann (Chicago: University of Chicago Press, 1985), 38–54. For fuller discussion on the difficulties of the Folio-first hypothesis, see the essay on "The Text of *Troilus and Cressida*" in Bevington, ed., *Troilus and Cressida*.

10. Among those who are skeptical of commissioning of the play for Inns of Court performance are Alfred Harbage, *Shakespeare and the Rival Traditions* (New York: Macmillan, 1952), 116; T. W. Baldwin, supplemental editor, *A New Variorum Edition of Shakespeare, "Troilus and Cressida,"* ed. Harold N. Hillebrand (Philadelphia: Lippincott, 1953), 356–57; Robert Kimbrough, *Shakespeare's "Troilus and Cressida" and Its Setting* (Cambridge, Mass.: Harvard University Press, 1964), 21–22; and Jarol W. Ramsey, "The Provenance of *Troilus and Cressida*," *Shakespeare Quarterly*, 21 (1970): 223–40. Various cases have been made for special commissioning of other plays, notably *A Midsummer Night's Dream;* see, for example, Paul A. Olson, "*A Midsummer Night's Dream* and the Meaning of Court Marriage," *ELH*, 24 (1957): 95–119. The argument essentially rests, however, on the appositeness of certain court marriages in the mid 1590s, rather than on any direct evidence of commissioning.

11. T. J. King, *Casting Shakespeare's Plays: London Actors and Their Roles, 1590–1642* (Cambridge: Cambridge University Press, 1992).

12. Stanley Wells and Gary Taylor, "The Oxford Shakespeare Re-viewed by the General Editors," *AEB: Analytical and Enumerative Bibliography*, n.s. 4 (1990): 6–20, especially 14–15, citing approvingly the idea as communicated to them by Wilbur Sanders. The idea was in fact proposed by Hudson in his 1880 edition; see n. 7 above, Hudson, 16: 358.

308 PART THREE: TEXT AND PERFORMANCE

13. Roger Apfelbaum, "'What verse for it? What instance for it?': Authority, Closure, and the Endings of *Troilus and Cressida* in Text and Performance," *Critical Survey*, 9.3 (1997). The author has graciously allowed me to consult a copy of his fine essay before publication. His work is prior to mine; I have belatedly taken advantage of his research, having written my essay originally without knowing of its existence. Our essays are, I hope, complementary to the significant extent that his production history focuses on the period up to the mid twentieth century, while mine focuses on the latter half of the century. Our arguments are not the same arguments. Nonetheless, he certainly deserves credit for being the first to bring together editorial questions and theatrical decisions in relation to the ending of *Troilus*, and I have learned much from his analysis of the ways in which directors and editors appear to have been involved in a continuous interchange of interpretive views. His essay makes instructive use of promptbooks by Payne, Quayle, and others.

14. *Ibid.*

15. Phebe Jensen, "The Textual Politics of *Troilus and Cressida*," *Shakespeare Quarterly*, 46 (1995): 414–23. On Quayle's 1948 production, see n. 27 below.

16. Michael Billington, *Guardian*, 27 June 1985. See also Vivian Thomas, *The Moral Universe of Shakespeare's Problem Plays* (Totowa, N.J.: Barnes & Noble, 1987), 135–36; Roger Warren, "Shakespeare in Britain, 1985," *Shakespeare Quarterly*, 37 (1986): 114–20; Nicholas Shrimpton, *Times Educational Supplement*, 5 July 1985; and Ros Asquith, *Observer*, 30 June 1985, 19.

17. Carol Rutter, "Shakespeare, His Designers, and the Politics of Costume: Handing Over Cressida's Glove," *Essays in Theatre / études théâtrales*, 12 (1994): 107–28, esp. 120–22; Martin Hoyle, *Financial Times*, 28 April 1990, Weekend FT XI; Nicholas de Jongh, *Guardian*, 28 April 1990, 21; Irving Wardle, *Independent*, 6 May 1990, 27; Peter J. Smith, *Cahiers Élisabéthains*, 38 (October 1990): 83–86; Elizabeth Beroud, *Cahiers Élisabéthains*, 39 (April 1991): 57–70; Iska Alter and William B. Long, *Shakespeare Bulletin*, 9.1 (1991): 18.

18. Michael Billington, *Guardian*, 25 July 1996; John Gross, *Sunday Telegraph*, 28 July 1996; Nicholas de Jongh, *Evening Standard*, 25 July 1996; Carole Woddis, *What's On*, 31 July 1996; Paul Taylor, *Independent*, 26 July 1996; Alastair Macaulay, *Financial Times*, 26 July 1996; Robert Hewison, *Sunday Times*, 28 July 1996; Jack Tinker, *Daily Mail*, 25 July 1996; Benedict Nightingale, *Times*, 26 July 1996; Robert Butler, *Independent on Sunday*, 28 July 1996; Robert Gore-Langton, *Daily Telegraph*, 26 July 1996; reprinted in *Theatre Record*, issue 15 (15–28 July 1996), 964–69. See also Dorothy and Wayne Cook, *Shakespeare Bulletin*, 15.1 (1997): 13–14.

19. Rutter, "Shakespeare, His Designers," esp. 116–17; Irving Wardle, *Times*, 19 August 1976, 5; Michael Billington, *Guardian*, 18 August 1976, 6; Robert Cushman, *Observer*, 22 August 1976, 20; Barbara E. Bowen, "*Troilus and Cressida* on the Stage," in *Troilus and Cressida*, ed. Daniel Seltzer, The Signet Classic Shakespeare (New York, 1963, rev. 1988), 265–87, esp. 283; and Ralph Berry, *Changing Styles in Shakespeare* (London: Geo. Allen & Unwin, 1981), 60–61.

20. Irving Wardle, *Times*, 8 July 1981, 11; Michael Billington, *Guardian*, 8 July 1981, 10; Robert Cushman, *Observer*, 12 July 1981, 33; G. M. Pearce, *Cahiers Élisabéthains*, 20 (1981): 114–15; and David Nokes, *TLS*, 17 July 1981, 810.

21. Jeanne T. Newlin, "The Modernity of *Troilus and Cressida:* The Case for Theatrical Criticism," *Harvard Library Bulletin*, 17 (1967): 353–73, esp. 359–62, quoting *The Daily Chronicle*, 11 December 1912, and Robert Speaight, *William Poel and the Elizabethan Revival* (London: Heinemann, 1954), 139. See also Edward Garnett,

Contemporary Review, 103 (1913): 184–90, and William Poel, *Shakespeare in the Theatre* (London: Sidgwick & Jackson, 1913), 98–116.

22. Newlin, 363–65. See also Desmond McCarthy, *New Statesman and Nation*, 16 (1938): 491; and Ivor Brown, *Observer,* 25 September 1938, 18.

23. *Times,* 29 June 1946.

24. Eric Keown, *Punch,* 21 July 1954, 130–31, cited in Newlin, 367–68.

25. W. A. Darlington, *Daily Telegraph and Morning Post,* 4 April 1956, 8; T. C. Worsley, *New Statesman and Nation,* 14 April 1956, 370; Brian Inglis, *Spectator,* 13 April 1956, 490; and Bowen, *Troilus and Cressida* on the Stage," 278–79.

26. Newlin, 369; Judith Crist, *New York Herald Tribune,* 25 July 1961; and Claire McGlinchee, "Stratford, Connecticut, Shakespeare Festival, 1961," *Shakespeare Quarterly,* 12 (1961): 419–23.

27. Eric Keown, *Punch,* 10 August 1960, 208; Bernard Levin, *Daily Express,* 27 July 1960, 4; Newlin, 368–69; and Robert Speaight, "The 1960 Season at Stratford-upon-Avon," *Shakespeare Quarterly,* 11 (1960): 451.

28. See notes 21–23 above.

29. Berry, *Changing Styles,* 52; *Times,* 5 July 1948; Ivor Brown and Anthony Quayle, *Shakespeare Memorial Theatre, 1948–1950: A Photographic Record* (New York: Theatre Arts Books, 1951).

30. See n. 26 above.

31. Rutter, "Shakespeare, His Designers," 115–16; Ronald Bryden, *Observer,* 11 August 1968, 21; Irving Wardle, *Times,* 9 August 1968, 10; Harold Hobson, *Sunday Times,* 11 August 1968, 41; Benedict Nightingale, *New Statesman and Nation,* 16 August 1968, 208.

32. Rutter, "Shakespeare, His Designers," 116–17; Irving Wardle, *Times,* 18 August 1976, 5; Michael Billington, *Guardian,* 18 August 1976, 6; Robert Cushman, *Observer,* 22 August 1976, 20.

33. Joseph Papp, "Directing Troilus and Cressida," in *The Festival Shakespeare "Troilus and Cressida"* (New York, 1967); and Bowen, *"Troilus and Cressida* on the Stage," 272.

34. Robert Cushman, "War Games," *Observer,* 12 July 1981, 33; Michael Billington, "Trojan workhorses," *Guardian,* 8 July 1981, 1; David Nokes, "In love and war," *TLS,* 17 July 1981, 810; G. M. Pearce, *Cahiers Élisabéthains,* 20 (October 1981): 114–15; Benedict Nightingale, *New Statesman and Nation,* 10 July 1981, 24–25; Mark Amory, *Spectator,* 18 July 1981, 26; and Sheridan Morley, *Punch,* 15 July 1981, 104.

35. Suzanne Burden in an interview with Henry Fenwick for BBC television, quoted in Claire M. Tylee, "The Text of Cressida and Every Ticklish Reader: *Troilus and Cressida,* The Greek Camp Scene," *Shakespeare Survey,* 41 (1989): 63–76, esp. 72–73.

36. Tylee, 68, citing Robert Wilcher, "Value and Opinion in *Troilus and Cressida,*" an unpublished lecture delivered at the Royal Shakespeare Summer School, Stratford-upon-Avon, 1985. See also note 14, and Rutter, "Shakespeare, His Designers," 118–20.

37. Irving Wardle, *Independent,* 6 May 1990, 27.

38. Steve Grant, *Time Out,* 31 July 1996.

39. For an alternate view, see Apfelbaum's interesting speculation as to whether, in years to come, directors may possibly take up the textual suggestion of Stanley Wells's and Gary Taylor's Oxford *Complete Works* (1986), and the more recent *Norton Shakespeare* with its alteration of the Oxford text by printing Oxford's "additional" passages in their QF position, but in italics. Will the pendulum swing back toward a more "tragic" *Troilus and Cressida?* Will we hear Pandarus' sleazy farewell at the end of 5.3, as Wilbur Sanders proposes (see n. 12 above)? Certainly the complex textual history of the play leaves open that choice.

Two Lears: Notes for an Actor

Alexander Leggatt

IN HIS AUTOBIOGRAPHY TYRONE GUTHRIE TELLS THE STORY OF A YOUNG ACTOR who had the opportunity to watch the legendary Max Reinhardt in rehearsal. As the actors ran through the scene, Reinhardt sat on a table, watching them, swinging his legs, and saying nothing. The young man waited eagerly for the great director to break his silence, to offer some brilliant insight or withering criticism. The scene was played to the end, and finally Reinhardt spoke: "*Quite* nice . . . . Go back to the maid's entrance; and you, dear, carry the tray in the *other* hand."[1]

Theater is detail. Although Guthrie tells the story to make the point that a great director works by evocation, not by talk or analysis, Reinhardt presumably had a reason for sensing the tray would be better in the other hand. From a Victorian actor making "points" to a modern director giving notes, theater practitioners build a performance detail by detail. Mother Courage counts out a few coins to pay for Kattrin's funeral, looks at them a moment, and puts one back in her purse. A new line is needed to get the timing of an exit right, and so Blanche duBois declares she has always been dependent on the kindness of strangers. Shakespeare's actors had nothing like the elaborate rehearsals of the modern theater, and their (to us) daunting repertory system must have meant that their performances were far less preset than ours, their delivery of the text less than word-perfect. But though their performances must have been more fluid and changeable, they too would have worked through detail, and their presentation of a play would have developed through, among other things, the cutting, adding and revision of lines and speeches.

We can glimpse this process at work when we have a play of the period in more than one version, although our speculations are of course complicated by the fact that changes would have taken place in the printing house as well as in the playhouse. *King Lear* has in recent years become a classic example of a play seen at two stages in a process of revision, as the old belief in the conflated text as our best approximation of a lost, perfect original has been replaced by the view that the Quarto and Folio versions need to be read as independent works, each with its own integrity. I want to explore, in detail, some of the implications of that belief for an actor playing Lear. My argument does not depend on any particular assumptions about the provenance of the two texts (foul papers, playhouse copy, authorial revision or revision by another hand), or try to say which text is "better."[2] Nor is it an attempt to reconstruct what happened in different performances at the Globe. I shall look instead at the guidance the two texts, however they came into being, now offer the actor, the different views of Lear they present, and the different manners of playing they encourage. My primary assumption is that what could happen in the theater now is as worthy of our attention as what could have happened in the theater, or the printing house, four hundred years ago.

When one looks at the overall movement of the play, the Folio, with its sometimes startling cuts—the mad trial, the servants comforting Gloucester, the whole of what is traditionally 4.3—seems a swifter text, more concerned to move the action along, less given to pause and reflection. But when we look at local details, particularly as they affect Lear, that impression, from the first scene onwards, is reversed. While the broad lines of the character are largely unaffected, the nuances change. The Lear of Q is more a creature of impulse, less reflective and less in control. The Lear of F is more inclined to stop, explain, listen and think, and more inclined to exert his will. Consider Lear's opening statement:

> 'tis our first intent
> To shake all cares and business of our state,
> Confirming them on younger years.
>
> (Q.1.1.37–39)

> 'tis our fast intent
> To shake all cares and business from our age,
> Conferring them on younger strengths, while we
> Unburdened crawl toward death.
>
> (F.1.1.37–40)[3]

In part, what he says is simply different. There is greater emphasis on his will in F: "first" becomes "fast."[4] In Q he measures himself against the youth of the young, in F against their strength. The most striking change, however, is Lear's reference to his own impending death, which brings a change not just in content but in rhythm. It adds a line, slows the moment down a little, and shows Lear thinking more sharply about his future. In this text (although not, as we shall see, in Q), this is also the last time Lear acknowledges his coming end. But it is enough to allow one to read the play as the experience of a man at the point of death. The play in either version is about dying, in that Lear struggles against the loss of power and the loss of identity.[5] At the beginning of the action the Lear of F has, if only for a moment, a glimpse of the last enemy, and to that extent he is both more reflective and more in control.

Another F addition that heightens his control is:

> our son of Cornwall,
> And you, our no less loving son of Albany,
> We have this hour a constant will to publish
> Our daughters' several dowers, that future strife
> May be prevented now.
>
> (1.1.40–44)

Far from leaving the future to the young (whom he seems not to trust), he wants to shape it himself. There is control of another kind in the sarcastic way "no less loving" plays off against "future strife." While he misreads the protestations of love from his daughters, Lear has no illusions about his sons-in-law, and for a moment he allows them to see this, using an irony that gives him an air of superiority.

The Lear of F is also more aware of what he has done in giving up his power. Q's "Tell me, my daughters, / Which of you shall we say doth love us most" (1.1.43–44) becomes in F:

> Tell me, my daughters,
> Since now we will divest us both of rule,
> Interest of territory, cares of state,
> Which of you shall we say doth love us most.
>
> (1.1.47–50)

He stresses the logic of what he is doing, getting control over his self-surrender by making it something he has thought about. The Lear of Q is at this point faster, more impulsive and arbitrary, less given to thinking about his actions. The additions in F make Lear slow down, reflect and explain.

This difference is particularly striking in the two versions of Lear's first confrontation with Cordelia:

> *Lear.* What can you say to win a third more opulent
> Than your sisters'?
> *Cordelia.* Nothing, my lord.
> *Lear.* How! Nothing can come of nothing; speak again.
>
> (Q.1.1.77–80)
>
> *Lear.* What can you say to draw
> A third more opulent than your sisters'? Speak.

> *Cordelia.* Nothing, my lord.
> *Lear.* Nothing?
> *Cordelia.* Nothing.
> *Lear.* Nothing will come of nothing; speak again.
>
> (F.1.1.84–89)

As the addition of "speak" slows the passage down (it could well be triggered by the first of Cordelia's silences) so the repetition of "nothing" freezes the moment, allowing Lear a pause of shock and incredulity before he issues his warning. The Lear of Q, faster and more impulsive, goes straight to the warning, with only the interjected "How!" to register the shock. In F the warning itself has more thought behind it, picking up and playing on the fatal word.

Small details in later scenes confirm the differing impressions made in the opening—particularly Lear's greater sense of control in F. Q's "O, my heart! my heart!" (2.4.96) becomes F's "O me, my heart, my rising heart! But down!" (2.4.110). Q offers an exclamation of helpless pain; in F, Lear conveys a more concrete awareness of what his heart is doing, and tries to control it, exerting his will over his own body. It is the same with his hand: Q's "Here, wipe it first; it smells of mortality" (4.6.128) becomes F's "Let me wipe it first; it smells of mortality" (4.5.128). In the Q-only mad trial, probably the most controversial of F's cuts,[6] Lear tries to get control over his daughters by arraigning them, only to watch helplessly as Regan escapes (3.6.49–52). In a passage peculiar to F Lear returns to the question of justice, and in a way gets firmer control over it:

> Plate sins with gold,
> And the strong lance of justice hurtless breaks;
> Arm it in rags, a pigmy's straw does pierce it.
> None does offend, none, I say none. I'll able 'em.
>
> (F.4.5.158–61)

In both texts Lear thinks critically about justice throughout this scene; but in F he comes to a firm and radical conclusion, with a characteristic repetition of "none" to hammer home the meaning. While in Q he thought of a trial as the answer, and watched helplessly as the prisoner escaped, in F he knows the system of justice is fundamentally corrupt and his conclusion, an assertion of his own will, is to pardon everyone and release all the prisoners himself.

Lear moves in and out of reality in both texts, but F gives him, on the whole, a little more contact with it. There are exceptions: Q reports, though it does not show, a few lucid intervals for Lear between his scene with Gloucester and his reunion with Cordelia at

4.3.38–47. This is cut in F. More characteristic of F is Lear's response to Regan's lecture about his relations with Goneril. Regan tells him, "You less know how to value her desert / Than she to slack her duty" (Q.2.4.114–15; F has "scant" for "slack"). In Q Lear replies "My curses on her" (115), a line he could have uttered without listening to a word Regan said. In F the curse comes five lines later; Lear's first response is "Say? How is that?" (2.4.129). He may be incredulous or uncomprehending, but at least he has noticed what Regan said. In act 4 of Q, when he sees Gloucester and Edgar, Lear mutters, "Ha, Goneril, ha, Regan" (4.6.95); he has seen two human figures, and he imposes his hallucination on them without noticing anything in their appearance that would contradict him; any two human figures will do (as in the Q-only mad trial, where he casts a joint-stool as Goneril). In F he is a little more alert: "Ha, Goneril with a white beard?" (4.5.95). The figure he sees is partly Goneril, partly Gloucester, and his linking of the adulterous Gloucester with his daughter may be a route into the searing disgust with female sexuality he shows a few moments later.

In F Lear's tendency to repeat words shows him more alert, more thinking. In a passage unique to F, Lear counters Gloucester's "Well, my good lord, I have informed them so" with "Informed them? Dost thou understand me, man?" F also adds, "Are they informed of this?" (2.4.87–88, 92). Like Coriolanus reacting to the tribune's "shall," Lear can scent political trouble in a single word (kings don't inform, they command) and he dwells on it. Q's "In such a night as this!" becomes in F:

> In such a night
> To shut me out? Pour on, I will endure.
> In such a night as this!
>
> (3.4.17–19)

Here the repetition allows Lear to dwell on the outrage, and forces the audience to dwell on it. Sometimes the repetition simply allows greater emphasis, as in the change from Q's "Hark, nature; hear, / Dear goddess" (1.4.261–62) to F's "Hear, nature, hear, dear goddess, hear" (1.4.245). Lear sounds more decisive in F; and in one case in which F reverses its usual practice and reduces Lear's repetitions the effect is, again, to make him more decisive. F's "So, so. We'll go to supper in the morning" (3.6.39–40) is much firmer than Q's rambling "So, so, so. We'll go to supper i'th'morning. So, so, so" (Q.3.6.77–78).

For the mad Lear, repetitions allow wordplay, letting words shift and expand their meanings. Q's "Peace, peace, this toasted cheese will do it" (4.6.88–89) becomes in F a word-association game: "Peace, peace, this piece of toasted cheese will do't" (4.5.88–89). The expansion of "Thou shalt not die for adultery" (Q.4.6.108) to "Thou shalt not die; die for adultery" (F.4.5.106) not only emphasizes the absurdity of the sentence, making the actor dwell on the key word, but allows a split second longer for the audience to catch the sexual pun. Interestingly, Edmund, whose energy drives the second scene of the play as Lear's energy drives the first, is, in his opening soliloquy, slightly more given to repetition in F than he is in Q; the words he dwells on are "base" and "legitimate."

The pattern I have been tracing is not absolutely consistent, and the reader would be properly suspicious if it were. At one point the F Lear seems more impulsive, less in control:

> *Lear.* Who is it that can tell me who I am?
> *Lear's* shadow? I would learn that, for by the marks
> Of sovereignty, knowledge, and reason
> I should be false persuaded I had daughters.
> *Fool.* Which they will make an obedient father.
> *Lear.* Your name, fair gentlewoman?
>
> (Q.1.4.218–23)
>
> *Lear.* Who is it that can tell me who I am?
> *Fool.* Lear's shadow.
> *Lear.* Your name, fair gentlewoman?
>
> (F.1.4.203–5)

As the F Lear wipes his own hand, the Q Lear at this point answers his own question; he also explains his own thinking more fully. F gives the Fool a much stronger role, and leaves some doubt as to whether Lear has really heard him.[7] It is a more cryptic moment, offering a choice for the actor. It breaks the pattern (relatively speaking, and remembering these are matters of nuance) of an impulsive, passionate, unthinking Lear in Q and a clearer, more self-aware Lear in F.

This prepares us for a more radical break in the final scene. In a play notorious for frustrating expectations, for building hope only to shatter it, the sharpest reversal comes toward the end. At this point the signals the text offers the actor are radically altered. We can see the change coming as Lear goes to prison with Cordelia, and word repetition begins to have a different effect from the one I have traced in earlier scenes. Q's "No, no. Come, let's away to prison" (5.3.8) is more firm and decisive than F's "No, no, no[,] no. Come, let's away to prison" (5.3.8), in which Lear's voice (as in the repeated "so" of Q.3.6) starts to acquire the wandering, dotty quality of Justice Shallow's.

It is in Lear's death that the divergence between the texts is sharpest and most significant, and the pattern of earlier scenes is decisively reversed:

> *Lear.* And my poor fool is hanged. No, no life.
> Why should a dog, a horse, a rat have life,
> And thou no breath at all? O, thou wilt come no more.
> Never, never, never. Pray you, undo
> This button. Thank you, sir. O, O, O, O!
> *Edgar.* He faints. My lord, my lord.
> *Lear.* Break, heart, I prithee break.   *Dies.*
>
> (Q.5.3.297–303)

> And my poor fool is hanged. No, no, no life.
> Why should a dog, a horse, a rat have life,
> And thou no breath at all? Thou'lt come no more.
> Never, never, never, never, never.
> Pray you, undo this button. Thank you, sir.
> Do you see this? Look on her, look, her lips,
> Look there, look there.   *He dies.*
>
> (F.5.3.279–85)

In F Lear's focus in his last moment is on Cordelia; he is unaware of his own impending death. He had that awareness, as we saw, in the very first scene; now, when death comes, he shows no knowledge of it.[8] In Q Lear's focus on Cordelia is less concentrated. He is more aware of himself, his own suffering; his last thought is fixed not on Cordelia's lips but on his own breaking heart. He wills it to break, not just aware of his impending death but doing what he can to bring it on. He is trying to exert that control over himself the Folio Lear attempted in commanding his heart down, and wiping his own hand.

It is here that "O, O, O, O!" is particularly important. As Maurice Charney has argued, Shakespeare seems to have thought of sighs and groans as shortening life.[9] The Folio Hamlet, having said "The rest is silence," dies with just such a groan, long suppressed even in conflated texts that purport to combine all the material. It is a fitting end to a role full of surprises and reversals that Hamlet, having declared a final silence, should break that silence himself.[10] He may also be, like Lear, willing his own death, doing literally what Ophelia earlier imagined him doing:

> He raised a sign so piteous and profound
> As it did seem to shatter all his bulk
> And end his being.
>
> (2.1.96–98)[11]

It is, perhaps, a form of self–slaughter that heaven will permit. Enobarbus' last words are "O Antony! O Antony!" (4.9.26). Moments later the watchmen find him dead. In Q (and only in Q) Edgar recounts that Kent, telling his story, seemed to be bringing on his own death in the same way: "He fastened on my neck and bellowed out / As he'd burst heaven. . . . His grief grew puissant and the strings of life / Began to crack" (5.3.206–11). Lear's groan has been seen as cryptic,[12] and as the expression of a final nihilism.[13] Arguably, it is quite clear and even functional. It is Lear's way of seeing that his own command, "Break, heart, I prithee break," is obeyed. This may guide the actor's reading of "Pray you, undo / This button," which could refer to Cordelia's button (undoing it will give her a chance to breathe, and counter the deadly constriction of the rope) or to Lear's button. Cryptic in F, it is pushed in one direction in Q. It is Lear's button; besides the echo of his attempt to strip in the storm, he is trying to release his spirit from his body, and even undoing a button will help let the final breath out. Like the crucified Christ, he does not just die; he gives up his spirit. His death is not something that happens to him, but something he does.[14]

When Lear enters with the dead Cordelia, Q has a fourfold "Howl," which F cuts to three. Q's version may anticipate the final, self-destructive sigh or groan: the sound is longer and takes more out of him. Q's "O, thou wilt come no more," as opposed to F's "Thou'lt come no more," similarly lengthens the sound and dwells on the pain. In the last scene, however, the Lear of F generally repeats his words more than does the Lear of Q; but now the effect is not to pause over the words and bring out their meanings, but to drain meaning away. (There is no need to repeat "Howl!" five times in order to do this; it is drained of meaning already; it matters more to do it with a word like "never.") In Q Albany says of Lear, "He knows not what he sees" (5.3.285); in F "He knows not what he says" (5.3.267). Q has "And my poor fool is hanged. No, no life." In the doubled "no" Lear could be answering a question he has silently asked in the depths of his mind. Is there life? No, there is no life. (Did the feather stir? No.) But the sense of answering a question is a little harder to see in F's "No, no, no life." The repeated "no" is less a part of a logical internal dialogue, closer to becoming a keen or a mantra, as articulate thought loosens into pure pain. Q's threefold "never" goes in the same direction; but not so far as F's fivefold "never." Q's three "never"s could still be a conscious, articulate Lear hammering the reality into his mind; but in F the word seems to lose its specific meaning and become pure hopelessness expressed in pure sound.[15]

What we have then, in the dying Lear of Q, is a will and a consciousness that are both operating powerfully. Lear is aware of his own suffering, and does what he can to make himself die. In F Lear's focus on Cordelia is much stronger, while his mind is less clear and his own will and self-consciousness are more suppressed. (This is in line with the fact that from his reunion with Cordelia onward Lear never speaks his own name.) He does not control his death, and does not even seem aware that it is coming, so little does he care about himself. In that way it is more truly a death than that of the Q Lear, who in making a stronger effort to die on *his* terms asserts his will and power to the end. In F meaning drains out of Lear's words, and accordingly his final "Look there, look there" is cryptic as the last words of the Q Lear are not. Since A. C. Bradley proposed that Lear sees returning life in Cordelia, and dies in "unbearable *joy*,"[16] readers and actors have made of this moment what they will: "an ecstatic vision that Cordelia is alive, that at last she speaks the words he wants so to hear; a vision of some supernatural aura about her, presumably beatific; even an apparent glimpse of her spirit, rising to heaven; or a horror of the ultimate silence that has stilled her."[17] Although it is less often debated, there is a further question: who is being told to "Look there?" The onstage spectators, the heavens, the audience?[18] In contrast to the decisive effect of Q, we are left with a mystery. Or so it is on the page; but can an actor play that mystery, or must he make a choice? One thing he *can* play, whatever emotion he finds in the line and however he directs it, is that Lear, who has been so fixed on himself, his pain, his injuries, is now totally fixed on Cordelia. For Jay L. Halio this new ability to direct his attention outward, away from himself, is one of those "redeeming elements that may rescue us from despair."[19] In Q the actor, having played a swifter, more impulsive Lear, is instructed to take hold in the final moments, to fix clearly on his own death and take control of it. In F, having played for control, the actor is given the harder and arguably more important task of letting go.

Notes

1. Tyrone Guthrie, *A Life in the Theatre* (New York, Toronto and London: McGraw-Hill, 1959), 154–55.

2. For a thorough overview of the textual questions, see the New Cambridge Shakespeare edition of *The Tragedy of King Lear*, ed. Jay L. Halio (Cambridge: Cambridge University Press, 1992), 58–89, 265–91. At the seminar on *King Lear* (chaired by R. A. Foakes and Dieter Mehl) at the 1996 World Shakespeare Congress in Los Angeles, a number of participants seemed to be converging on the view that the Quarto is based on the author's manuscript, while the Folio is a playhouse

revision which may be partly authorial but not exclusively so. A growing preference for the Quarto could be discerned. The present essay is a considerable (and purely authorial) revision of a paper presented at that seminar.

3. Because of its convenience for the present exercise, I have used *King Lear: A Parallel Text Edition,* ed. René Weis (New York and London: Longman, 1993); ordinarily I would have preferred the New Cambridge edition. It should be stressed that Weis offers an *edited* version of the two texts.

4. MacDonald P. Jackson notes a general tendency in F to emphasize Lear's firmness and resolve: see "Fluctuating Variation: Author, Annotator, or Actor?," *The Division of the Kingdoms: Shakespeare's Two Versions of "King Lear,"* ed. Gary Taylor and Michael Warren (Oxford: Clarendon Press, 1983; reprint 1986), 332–34.

5. Susan Snyder, "*King Lear* and the Psychology of Dying," *Shakespeare Quarterly* 33 (1982), 454–58, relates Lear's experience to the stages of dying as traced by Elizabeth Kübler-Ross: denial, anger, bargaining, depression, acceptance.

6. William C. Carroll's protest against the privileging of F, "New Plays vs. Old Readings: *The Division of the Kingdoms* and Folio Deletions in *King Lear,*" *Studies in Philology* 85 (1988): 225–44, bases its case largely on the mad trial and on changes in the part of Edgar.

7. John Kerrigan assumes he has, but needs to postulate a little extra work for the actor, a moment of silent self-discovery: see "Revision, Adaptation, and the Fool in *King Lear,*" (Taylor and Warren, eds., *Division,* 220).

8. Snyder, "Psychology," argues that Lear experiences his own death through Cordelia's (459). As she points out, this allows Lear to do the impossible, since strictly speaking one cannot experience death, which is the end of experience.

9. Maurice Charney, *Hamlet's Fictions* (London and New York: Routledge, 1988), 51–52. Charney gives a full discussion of what he calls "O-groans" in *Hamlet* and other plays of the period (48–58).

10. For a debate over Hamlet's last utterance, see *Connotations* 2 (1992): 28–29, 282–89, 278–85, and 3 (1993): 56–59. The participants are John Russell Brown, Dieter Mehl, Maurice Charney and Holger Klein.

11. References to Shakespeare's plays other than *King Lear* are to *The Complete Works of Shakespeare,* ed. David Bevington (New York: HarperCollins, 1992).

12. James P. Lusardi and June Schlueter, *Reading Shakespeare in Performance: "King Lear"* (Rutherford, Madison and Teaneck: Fairleigh Dickinson University Press, 1991), 143.

13. Thomas Clayton, "'Is this the promis'd end?' Revision in the Role of the King," Taylor and Warren, eds., *Division,* 133.

14. See John Marsh, *The Gospel of St John.* The Pelican New Testament Commentaries. (Harmondsworth: Penguin Books, 1968), 618–19.

15. Actors can make other choices than this: Laurence Olivier in his television performance breaks the line up; the word is meaningless at first; then the fourth "never" is a discovery and the last conveys resignation. But John Gielgud, having initially built the line to a climax, came to prefer a simpler reading: see Marvin Rosenberg, *The Masks of King Lear* (Berkeley, Los Angeles and London: University of California Press, 1972), 319.

16. *Shakespearean Tragedy* (1904; reprint London: Macmillan, 1957), 241. Bradley in effect conflates the texts, reading the repeated "O" as a cry of joy.

17. Rosenberg, *Masks,* 319. On the possibility that Lear sees Cordelia's escaping soul, see Ian J. Kirby, "The Passing of King Lear," *Shakespeare Survey* 41 (1989): 145–57. Kirby regards Q as too corrupt to base an argument on (154–55).

18. Lusardi and Schlueter, *Reading,* 145.

19. Halio, New Cambridge introduction, 28.

Staging *The Comedy of Errors*

ARTHUR F. KINNEY

OVER THE YEARS TWO COMMENTS CONCERNING SHAKESPEARE'S *COMEDY OF ER*rors have been for me unforgettable. One is by an experienced editor of the play who wrote in an introduction to it, "There is nothing new to be said about *The Comedy of Errors*." The other is by the singer and actor Roger Daltry of The Who whose first significant acting assignment was to play both the twin Dromios for the BBC production. When asked by the press what this opportunity had taught him, he replied, "I learned that Shakespeare was meant to be acted." The two remarks are actually two sides of the same coin, and together they embody the issue that is more or less explicit in all the essays collected in this volume. Does a playscript fix an overriding meaning or is it always susceptible to reinterpretation in performance? And where does meaning of a Shakespearean play finally lie: in the script carefully restored through editing and annotating, or in a given but fleeting, unrecorded performance? For a scholar like Jay Halio, himself one of the foremost editors of Shakespeare who nevertheless attended every production of a Shakespearean play he could, this must have been, and continues to be, a pressing question.

Perhaps the best answer to the question lies somewhere in the synergy of text and performance. In the case of *The Comedy of Errors*, we are lucky to have an account of an early—perhaps premiere—performance of the play at Gray's Inn on 28 December 1594. According to the *Gesta Grayorum or The History of the High and Mighty Prince Henry Prince of Purpoole,* Shakespeare's play was scheduled for the second "grand Night . . . intended to be upon *Innocents-Day* at Night; at which time there was a great Presence of Lords, Ladies, and worshipful Personages"[1] including one who played the ambassador from the Emperor Frederick Templarius (the neighboring Inner Temple).

> When the Ambassador was placed, as aforesaid, and that there was something to be performed for the Delight of the Beholders, there arose such a disordered Tumult and Crowd upon the Stage, that there was no Opportunity to effect that which was intended: There came so great a

number of worshipful Personages upon the Stage, that might not be displaced; and Gentlewomen, whose Sex did privilege them from Violence, that when the Prince and his Officers had in vain, a good while, expected and endeavoured a Reformation, at length there was no hope of Redress for that present. The Lord Ambassador and his Train thought that they were not so kindly entertained, as was before expected, and thereupon would not stay any longer at that time, but, in a sort, discontented and displeased. After their Departure the Throngs and Tumults did somewhat cease, although so much of them continued, as was able to disorder and confound any good Inventions whatsoever. In regard whereof, as also for that the Sports intended were especially for the gracing of the *Templarians*, it was thought good not to offer any thing of Account, saving Dancing and Revelling with Gentlewomen; and after such Sports, a Comedy of Errors (like *Plautus* his *Menechmus*) was played by the Players. So that Night was begun, and continued to the end, in nothing but Confusion and Errors; whereupon, it was ever afterwards called, *The Night of Errors*. (31–32)

This passage has long been interpreted as a factual account of a night of disruption; but there is at least another reading possible: that Confusion was the theme and the whole evening performed as planned. Certainly the confusion which mocks the student from another one of the Inns of Court, farcical in itself, leads nicely into the confusion of *The Comedy of Errors,* based on a farce of Plautus, and the exile of the ambassador of the Templarians is not unlike the arrest of Egeon of Syracuse for being in Ephesus. Indeed, the cozenage that Antipholus of Syracuse senses in Ephesus and the witchcraft that, following St. Paul's account of Ephesus, marks this city, look forward to the farcical exorcism of Dr. Pinch to rid the city of devilish witchcraft, anticipating in turn the following day's events at Gray's Inn when it is discovered that "some great Disorders and Abuses lately done and committed with High Highness's Dominions of *Purpoole* [a corruption of the manor of Portpool where Gray's Inn was located], especially by Sorceries and Inchantments; and namely, of a great Witchcraft used the Night before, whereby there were great Disorders and Misdemeanours, by Hurly-burlies, Crowds, Errors, Confusions, vain Representations and Shews, to the utter Discredit of our State and Policy" (32).

Such revelries of misrule were common features of the Christmas season, but Shakespeare may also have inside knowledge, since his patron, the Earl of Southampton, had been admitted to Gray's Inn with an M. A. from Cambridge in 1589.[2] In *The Comedy of Errors* the failure of Dr. Pinch leads to the success of the Abbess who sets wrongs to right again, but through reformation of the people involved. So too at Gray's Inn in the Christmas season of 1594: "When we were wearied with mocking thus at our own Follies, at length there was a great Consultation had for the Recovery of our lost Honour. It was then concluded, that first the Prince's Council should be reformed, and some graver Conceipts should have their places, to advise upon those things that were propounded to be done afterward" (34). What follows such reconciliation and reformation is harmony and brotherhood: "Then the Arch-Flamen did pronounce *Grayus* and *Templarius* to be as true and perfect Friends, and so familiarly united and linked with the Bond and League of sincere Friendship and Amity, as ever were *Theseus* and *Perithous, Achilles* and *Patroclus, Pilades* and *Orestes,* or *Scipio* and *Lelius*" (36)—or the twin Dromios, not one before the other, but hand-in-hand. The revels of 1594–95 continued, however, until Shrove Tuesday, ending in the pageant of Proteus and the theme of transformation in the performance before Queen Elizabeth herself, who like the Abbess, rules through love, fortune, and charity (83).

The protean ideas in Francis Davison's masque of Proteus are analogous to the transformative, even transcendent ideas in Shakespeare's early play, suggesting the complexity of the various revels, the play, and their relationship. The nonce princedom of Purpoole demands homage and tribute from all the localities surrounding it—Holborn, St. Giles's, Tottenham, Bloomsbury, Islington, Kentish Town, Paddington, and Knightsbridge (16–20)— and twice the revelers go in procession through the streets of London to secure their boundaries and reestablish order. Such perambulations, first established in 1559 by Archbishop Grindal to determine parish boundaries, go back to the rogation days of the medieval church, performed about three weeks before Corpus Christi in the liturgical calendar. But this apparently odd mixture of the farcical and serious—even of the secular and sacred—may also go back to the mix of traditions at the inns. In his *De Laudibus Legum Anglie* a century earlier, Chief Justice Fortescue writes that

> In these Inns there is, in addition to a school of law, a kind of academy of all the manners that are learned by the nobility. Here they learn to sing and to practice all kinds of harmonics. Here also they are taught to dance and to exercise themselves in all the games which are appropriate to those of noble birth . . . In the vacations most of them devote themselves to legal studies, and in holiday seasons to the reading of Holy Scripture and history. This is indeed an education in virtue and a banishment of all vice. And so knights, barons and other nobles and magnates of the realm send their sons to these Inns, not because they wish them

to be educated in the law, or to live by practising it, but for the sake of acquiring virtue and to discourage vice.[3]

The disruptions that characterize the annual Christmas revels at Gray's Inn, then, are grounded in the need for rational order just as the vice they display reaffirms the call to virtue. *The Comedy of Errors* shares this mixture in the practices of farce (the beatings of Dromio), the characters (the courtesan and the unfaithful husband; the upstart servant), and the ideas (the difficulty of marriage) with a narrative that suggests the mystery cycle, from the fall of Egeon to the reunion of the family before the Abbey. References to wizardry and farcical misidentifications align themselves alongside Antipholus of Syracuse's admission that he is a Christian (1.2.77), Dromio's plea to his rosary (2.2.188), Luciana's litany of God's creatures derived from the Established Church's Homily on Obedience (2.1.15–25) and the reference to Pentecost (4.1.1) as a means of charting time. Moreover, *The Comedy of Errors,* staged on 28 December, came at the calendrical moment that marked the change from classical to Christian, at the moment of the Nativity. "At Christs birth," Thomas Heywood writes, "all (pagan) Oracles were mute, / And put to lasting silence."[4] To begin to answer my initial question, then, *The Comedy of Errors* permits a range of performances because it is itself a mixture of the pagan and the Christian. And this is true, in turn, because it comes out of a profoundly unsettled cultural moment.

II

Like other schoolboys of his time, Shakespeare studied and perhaps acted Plautus at St. Edward's Grammar School on Chapel Street in Stratford at the same time he saw mystery plays, such as those at nearby Coventry as well as those on the Stratford village green. In 1576, James Burbage signed the lease for a plot of land in Shoreditch in the Liberty of Holywell just north of the city of London and began building the Theatre; in the very same year, in May, the Diocesan Court of High Commission in York sent a directive to the mayor and corporation of Wakefield effectively banning the Corpus Christi plays which had been planned for June.[5] "The Wakefield letter," according to Peter Womack, was

> part of the government offensive which brought the religious drama of the provincial towns to an end. The pageants were played for the last time at Norwich in 1564, at York in 1569, at Chester in 1575, and at

Coventry in 1579 [when Shakespeare, at 15, was preparing to set out on a career], and in most of these cases there was official pressure to close, whether from the ecclesiastical authorities, the Council of the North, or the Privy Council. All the major organs of state power were working against the plays, sometimes despite the apparent wishes of the urban authorities themselves. Burbage, on the other hand, seems to have made his risky investment *despite* the hostility of the City authorities [in London], and because he was reasonably confident that he had the support of the Privy Council. Government policy on theatre, then—whether or not there was anybody actually thinking it through in such terms—was to promote a particular kind of drama in the capital while suppressing another kind in the provinces. (96–97)

This is a fundamental change in English theater in Shakespeare's boyhood; and by the time the first Globe Theater was built for Shakespeare's company, the Lord Chamberlain's Men had completed the shift from sacred to secular entertainment, their tetralogy of chronicle history plays from the relatively recent reigns of Richard II to Henry V displacing the older sacred history of man staged in the Corpus Christi cycles.

This conceptual revolution in the understanding and presentation of human history had effects throughout the culture. On the political level, it can be seen in the imperialism of Henry VIII which stretched from London to Rome and which, in the newly-accentuated theory of the duplex royal body, merged the political with the metaphysical, as the mortal body of the king was merged with the immortal body of kingship. The sense of the human monarch as embodying the divine position of right rule, initially medieval in English origin, is another displacement—or perhaps invasion—of the sacred by the secular. Mervyn James puts it succinctly: "under Protestantism, the Corpus Christi becomes the Body of the Realm."[6] The Catholic calendar of saints' days gave way to an equally crowded calendar of profane national rituals and celebrations, while the newly rising theater was "seeking to draw its miscellaneous audience into a new kind of unity by rehearsing the fall and redemption of England."[7] The preacher John Stockwood must then have had much on his mind when he remarked, in 1578, that the Theatre was one of the "houses of purpose built . . . without the *Liberties,* as who woulde say 'There, let them saye what they will say, we wil play.'"[8]

This sweeping conquest of Corpus Christi by Corpus Regnum, which in retrospect characterizes English history from the advent of the Tudors to the Restoration of the Stuarts, did not come easily, did not proceed evenly across the island kingdom, and was forever being challenged, both by Puritans and by Catholics. Reflecting this transitional moment, *The Comedy of Errors* is staged both in the marketplace and before a priory; the platform on which the play is presented is both the customary Roman setting of farce and the kind of sacred setting which, in the Easter tropings, had been, in the churches, at the native birth of English drama. Just so: this long unsettled period of change belies Michel Foucault's understanding of history as neatly demarcated epistemes, for secular practices in performance began well before 1576, and sacred playing died out sometime later.

A number of contemporary records make this unsettled sense of priority and practice clear. John Aubrey writes in detail of Wiltshire revel feasts, as well as wassailings, midsummer bonfires, harvest homes, and sheep-shearings, all of them starting early in the Tudor years and stretching well into the Stuart ones. The antiquary Robert Plot describes the well-known Bromley hobby-horse dance which lasted into the Interregnum along with other Staffordshire festivals such as the "Court of Music" and bullrunning at Tutbury, church ales and perambulations. And David Underdown records that secular performances are popular "even in Puritan East Anglia: at Seething, Norfolk, for instance, there was a Christmas 'masque or mummery' in 1590" as well as harvest celebrations in Suffolk in 1603, Twelfth Night celebrations in Wiltshire in 1604, and dancing and sport to mark Whitsun itself in Maddington, Wiltshire, in 1608.[9] At the same time, the saints' days and Plough Monday celebrations were banned in the 1540s and an act of 1541 banned all sorts of public sports and spectacles. As the building of the Theatre suggests, the victory of secularism seemed destined.

Thus during the tense and uneasy years of the Reformation and just beyond, any visual church spectacle—the Rood cross, statuary, enacted mystery plays—could be seen as dangerously Jesuitical or papist. But that is not to say there was no opposition. When Archbishop Grindal wished to eradicate church drama by stopping the Corpus Christi plays at Chester in 1571, the mayor, John Hankey, allowed them to go forward claiming that the archbishop's inhibition had arrived too late to prevent the performances. Three years later, another Chester mayor, Sir John Savage, was doing the same, ignoring not only the archbishop but his secular counterpart, the Earl of Huntington, Lord President of the North. Indeed, during Shakespeare's boyhood the customary reredos of parish churches, as at Stratford, was displaced by large wall paintings of Doomsday, or the Last Judgment. This is the Judgment feared by Antipholus and Dromio of Syracuse, as well as Egeon, a Judgment which the whole of *The Comedy of Errors* transforms into salvation at the steps of the priory, moving from the thoughts of birth in act 1 to actual christenings just after the close of act 5. This should indicate that a cultural force such as the Corpus Christi plays was deeply foundational in Tudor culture and so pervasive to their sense of drama that no set of governmental acts could wipe out their meaning in personal and communal memory. We can measure such force. Alexandra Johnston has discovered, for instance, that the nearly fifty plays staged annually at York involved at least 300 local townspeople in their casts, not to mention the work of other gild members and their associates in preparing and costuming them, and at least twelve of those plays, performed simultaneously about the northern capital city, had Christ as a character; there were thus in a single year's presentation several hundred performances of his sacred role in a city of 8,000–11,000.[10] Womack comments on this evidence that

> something like one-tenth of the total male population must have been directly involved in the show, and even making generous allowance for visitors, an overwhelming majority of the rest of the people must have watched it, especially since it is hard to imagine much chance of doing anything else in the town while it was happening. It is thus not fanciful to suggest that this type of theatre involved the urban community *as a whole*. In that case, the spectacular proliferation of Christs, so far from being redundant, seems extraordinarily eloquent. The figure of the Redeemer permeates the town, endlessly subdivided, yet one and entire in each embodiment, just as, when the host is broken into pieces, the *verum corpus* is wholly present in each fragment. To perform that consecration of the ordinary environment is much more important than to achieve an economical rendering of the written text. The whole real town—its people, its material resources, its social structure and its topography—is organised into a single spectacle, in which it recognises itself as the mystical body of Christ. (99)

There is more than this for Womack: such plays are not only personal and communal but political, deliberately so.

> This can be seen in practice in the numerous points at which the show makes direct use of the presence of the crowd. In the York 'Entry into Jerusalem,' for example, it seems likely that Christ rides a real donkey in the street, and is formally welcomed by eight 'burgenses' positioned on the pageant-wagon. As recent editors have suggested, this arrangement makes the play resemble a ceremonial civic welcome in which the speakers *represent* the watching people: there is an accessible level at which Christ is riding into York. (99)

Similarly, the intercutting in the N-Town Passion Plays juxtaposing local council scenes with the betrayal of Christ makes another potential political statement about local rulers (100). Therefore when the Wakefield Letter of 1576 rules that

> no pageant be used or set furthe wherein the My^{t}ye of God the Father, God the Sonne, or God the Holie Ghoste or the administration of either the Sacramentes of Baptisme or of the Lordes Supper be counterfeyted or represented, or anything plaied which tende to the maintenance of superstition and idolatrie,[11]

the corporation of Chester could reply to such statements of the Privy Council that plays were staged

> according to an order concluded and agreed upon for dyvers good and great consideracons redoundinge to the comon wealthe, benefit and profitte of the saide citie in assemblie there holden, according to the auncyente and laudable usages and customes there hadde and used fur above remembraunce.[12]

We might, then, read *Comedy of Errors* as a reinstatement of the mystery cycle under Roman terms (for the most part), reversing the intentions of the Wakefield Letter and confirming the protests of the corporation of Chester.

The pagan and sacred also mingled in the dramatic performances in Coventry and Stratford. Extant records show visiting professional companies: Essex's Men and Worcester's Men in 1576;[13] Lord Delaware's Men, Lord Stafford's Men, and the Lord Chamberlain's Men in 1577 (281–82); Lord Derby's Men, Essex's Men again, and Worcester's Men in 1578 (286), and the Countess of Essex's Men, Lord Berkeley's Men, Lord Sheffield's Men, and Lord Strange's Men in 1579 (290). At the same time, chamberlains' and wardens' account book entries and gild records note the performance of mystery plays. In 1576 the cappers gild paid a total of 44s 10d to repair their pageant wagon and furnish it and they paid out 31s 5d to the players for wages and supper, including payments to "the prologe" (4d), "god and dede man" (20d), "ij bisshoppes'" (2s), "pylate" (4s 4d), iiij knyghtes" (6s 8d), "the spirite off god" (16d), "iij maries" a total of 2s, "ij angells" (8d), "the devell" (16d), and "the bisshoppes and knyghtes to drynck betwene the stagis" (9d) (277–78). In the same year under Account 100/17/1 the weavers gild records payments to Simeon, Joseph, Anne, Simeon's clerk, Mary and Jesus (each receiving 20d), 2 Angels (8d), a Child (4d) and for them gloves, bread and ale, butchery meat, 2 beards, and a cap (279). The ordinance book of the drapers' company describes their erecting "A Pagent House in the Same Street upon the South Side of the Same Street containing in breadth on the Street

Side six yard. & a half, Howsing 2 Bays with a Shoar & a Garden in breadth at the over End 6 yards & a half, and at the ne[ar] End 3 yards in breadth, in Leng[th] bounding East upon the M[. . .] upon Mr. Smallwood, butting South [. . .] Whitefriar Lane" (280–81). The cappers and weavers enter similar costs for 1577 when the smiths' account book also shows a new play for which they put out 3d "ffor a lase (noose) for Judas & a corde" (285), and the following years show similar entries. The peculiar mix of Roman farce that playing companies would perform professionally and sacred matters that townspeople would play as amateurs is thus embedded in *The Comedy of Errors,* as it is in the revels and the desire for reformation in the entertainments over Christmastide at Gray's Inn.

III

Perhaps to conceal, surely to complicate the Roman and Christian traditions in *The Comedy of Errors,* Shakespeare also keeps drawing attention towards the market and the marketplace. His play makes *possession* mean a necklace as much as the soul Dr. Pinch would try to liberate; the term *credit* is used to describe Antipholus of Ephesus whose "reverend reputation" is his "credit infinite"; just as the play enlarges through homonym or pun words like *travail,* so too with *deal* or *investment* which, in a play crowded with material goods, transforms such words from their older senses—*deal* as a "public, physical distribution of goods" and *investment* as a "garment, insignia, or office into which one was installed by ritual or communal fiat" to newer understandings in early modern England concerning negotiated transactions and commercial assets. The older, aristocratic, even feudal practice of owning slaves is re-addressed and interrogated by a newer lexicon of a bourgeois sense of property and exchange. The unsettling liquidity of money and of ownership makes the mercantile relations in *The Comedy of Errors,* involving most of the inhabitants of Ephesus we see, at odds with the familial and social concerns of the aliens from Syracuse. Although Egeon is arrested because as a merchant he has arrived at a port from which he and his trading are banned, he makes it clear that his arrival has nothing to do with trade or money; and, in turn, the Duke gives him time to exonerate himself, freed, however, by a ransom that is all too material. Both the medieval scholar V. A. Kolve and the early modern scholar Jean-Christopher Agnew remind us that theatrical ritual in Shakespeare's time was a dizzying shift of identities from Christian to commercial, social to personal, and imply that the drama alone, with its display of roles and transformations, could best accommodate and reenact such multiple matters.

That Shakespeare's *Comedy of Errors* makes itself current by stressing the Roman marketplace alongside Christian concerns arising from mystery plays is clear; but what of the play as a political statement? This too stems (for this play) from Acts—from Demetrius' confrontation with the temple of Diana in Ephesus in Acts 19:24–38. To understand the force of this in the early modern productions of *The Comedy of Errors*, we need to recall that Diana was predominantly a figure for Queen Elizabeth, the allusion in Shakespeare bringing her into his play much as Davison's allusion to Elizabeth brings her into his masque at Gray's Inn. Sir Walter Ralegh, for instance, wrote casually to Sir Robert Cecil in July 1592 that he saw Elizabeth I "riding like Alexander, hunting like Diana, walking like Venus"; in 1603 Ben Jonson caroled to the new Queen Anne, "Long live ORIANA / To exceed (whom she succeeds) our late DIANA." One of Nicholas Hilliard's miniatures, according to Sir Roy Strong, repeats the comparison in a jeweled locket of 1586–87 presented to Elizabeth by Sir Francis Drake, showing the Queen with a crescent moon and arrows of the huntress goddess nestled in her hair.[14] Various portraits and various virginals extended the comparison indefinitely; Spenser too seems to make the connection through Britomart. But as Margaret Aston has recently pointed out, "To a good many of Queen Elizabeth's subjects—those well-versed in scriptural priorities—Diana was [also] *the* idol of the New Testament, whose ill-fame radiated from Acts 19" (205). She comments further that

> This chapter describes the uproar caused by the craftsmen of Ephesus who feared for the loss of their trade, making silver shrines for Diana, as the result of St. Paul's preaching that the great goddess was a mere man-made idol whose magnificent worship ought to be destroyed. Doubtless it was this passage that was in the minds of the ministers of Kent who about 1584 objected that the painted and gilded seven-sacrament font at Ashford, a superstitious monument which they found most objectionable, had been quite ineffectually defaced, "being slubbered over with a white wash that in an houre may be undone, standing like a Dianaes shrine for a future hope and daily comforte of old popish beldames and yong perking papists, and a great offence to all that are Christianly minded." (205)

Diana also showed up in a fountain at the foot of Cheapside Cross, inspiring Ben Jonson to comment in *Cynthia's Revels* (1.4.94–95) that one might question London's magistrates "in pulling downe a superstitious crosse, and advancing a VENUS, or PRIAPUS, in place of it." "If you wanted to give anything a dreadful idolatrous name," Aston concludes, "nothing was worse than Diana. In the 1640s the Prayer Book was said to have become 'the most abominable Idoll in the land,' doted on 'as much as the Ephesians upon Diana.'" The Temple of Diana in Shakespeare's Ephesus before which all the characters congregate in the closing scene of *The Comedy of Errors* is the play's last transformation: this temple, presumably erected to a goddess figuring Elizabeth I, is turned into a Catholic priory whose Abbess alone can mend the play's confusions, save Egeon's life, release Antipholus of Ephesus from arrest, and redeem and restore her own family. Here, then, in the last great scene, both a political and a religious comment fuse visually, through spectacle. And how would this have been understood? Is Shakespeare harboring a support of Catholicism at the end of his play by suggesting that only an abbess can transform the Roman temple and set things right by Pauline charity? Or is he, more likely, passing from Roman beliefs through Catholic ones to those of the Established Church when Emilia steps down from the abbey and disrobes herself to become a more secular mother about to celebrate the christening of her secular sons? Either way, it surely paves the way for the appearance of Elizabeth herself at the final set of transformations, the masque of Proteus that will conclude the 1594 revels of Gray's Inn at Shrovetide.

In light of our original question, it would be difficult to stage *The Comedy of Errors* in a way that would make all of these meanings—classical, religious, political, commercial—equally forceful. The playscript here, then, suggests many possibilities for many different kinds of performances of the play, from roustabout farce to serious romance, one that looks forward to the statue of Diana and the Ephesus of *Pericles,* or a statue coming to life in *The Winter's Tale,* or a salvage thing of darkness who finally chooses to seek for grace. But at the same time that the script loosens itself to such a variety, it keeps a firm direction of narrative and, to a large degree, of character. Shakespeare was indeed meant to be acted and, to that extent, there is always something fresh and new to see in each performance of *The Comedy of Errors,* but all of it, finally, will derive from the script Shakespeare has left us. To that extent, there is nothing new to be said about the play because what we discover even now was always already there.

Notes

1. *Gesta Grayorum or The History of the High and Mighty Prince Henry Prince of Purpoole,* ed. Desmond Bland (Liverpool: Liverpool University Press, 1968), 29. The account was first published by William Canning in 1668.

2. I am grateful to Roger Strittmatter for supplying this fact.
3. Quoted by Bland, xviii. Fortescue's treatise was written in 1470.
4. Thomas Heywood, *The Hierarchie of the Blessed Angells* (1635), 24; quoted in C. S. Patrides, *Premises and Motifs in Renaissance Thought and Literature* (Princeton: Princeton University Press, 1982), 116.
5. Peter Womack, "Imaginging Communities: Theatres and the English Nation in the Sixteenth Century" in *Culture and History: 1350–1600: Essays on English Communities, Identities and Writing*, ed. David Aers (Detroit: Wayne State University Press, 1992), 96.
6. Mervyn James, "Ritual, Drama and Social Body in the Late Medieval English Town" in *Society, Politics and Culture: Studies in Early Modern England* (Cambridge: Cambridge University Press, 1986), 41.
7. Womack, 137.
8. Quoted by Steven Mullaney, "Civic Rites, City Sites: The Place of the Stage," in *Staging the Renaissance: Reinterpretations of Elizabethan and Jacobean Drama*, ed. David Scott Kastan and Peter Stallybrass (London and New York: Routledge, 1991), 21.
9. David Underdown, *Revel, Riot, and Rebellion* (Oxford: Clarendon Press, 1985), 47. My examples here are all from Underdown, 46–47.
10. Alexandra F. Johnson, "The York Corpus Christi Play: A Dramatic Structure Based on Performance Practice" in *The Theatre in the Middle Ages*, ed. H. Braet, J. Nowé and G. Tournoy (Leuven: Leuven University Press, 1985), 362–73.
11. Quoted by Womack, 98.
12. Ibid.
13. R. W. Ingram, ed., *Records of Early English Drama: Coventry* (Toronto and Buffalo: University of Toronto Press, 1981), 276. All page references in this paragraph are to this volume.
14. These references are from Margaret Aston, "Gods, Saints, and Reformers: Portraiture and Protestant England" in *Albion's Classicism: The Visual Arts in Britain, 1550–1660*, ed. Lucy Gent (New Haven and London: Yale University Press, 1995), 205–6.

A Checklist
Jay L. Halio

Professor of English, University of Delaware

Compiled by **BARBARA SILVERSTEIN**

Principal Books on Shakespeare and Elizabethan and Jacobean Drama

Approaches to Macbeth. Belmont, California: Wadsworth Publishing Company, 1966.

Twentieth Century Interpretations: As You Like It. Englewood Cliffs, NJ: Prentice-Hall, Inc., 1968.

Jonson's *Volpone;* Shakespeare's *Macbeth, King Lear* (critical old-spelling editions). Fountainwell Drama Texts. Edinburgh: Oliver & Boyd, 1968, 1972, 1973.

As You Like It: An Annotated Bibliography, 1940–1980. New York: Garland Publishing Company, 1984. (With Barbara C. Millard)

Understanding Shakespeare in Performance. Manchester: Manchester University Press; New York: St. Martin's Press, 1988.

King Lear. New Cambridge Shakespeare (Folio-based edition). Cambridge: Cambridge University Press, 1992.

Eastern and Central European Studies in Shakespeare and His Contemporaries. Newark: University of Delaware Press, 1993. (With Jerzy Limon)

The Merchant of Venice. New Oxford Shakespeare. Oxford: Oxford University Press, 1993; World's Classics edition, 1994.

The First Quarto of King Lear. New Cambridge Shakespeare, Supplementary Series. Cambridge: Cambridge University Press, 1994.

Shakespeare in Performance: A Midsummer Night's Dream. Manchester: Manchester University Press, 1994.

Shakespeare's Romeo and Juliet: Texts, Contexts, and Interpretations. Newark: University of Delaware Press, 1995.

Critical Essays on King Lear. New York: G. K. Hall, 1996.

All's Well That Ends Well. New Variorum Shakespeare. (With Joseph Price; in preparation)

Henry VIII. Oxford Shakespeare (in preparation).

Honors

Phi Beta Kappa, 1949

Fulbright-Hays Senior Lecturer in American and British Literature, University of Malaya, 1966–67; Buenos Aires, Argentina, 1974

Central Executive Committee, Folger Institute of Renaissance and Eighteenth Century Studies, 1975–

NEH Fellow, Symposium on "Shakespeare in Performance," University of Illinois, November 1977

Project Director, "The Humanities Semester at the University of Delaware" (funded by NEH), 1978–81

Danforth Associate in Teaching, 1981–1986

Academic Council, Globe Theatre Centre, 1982–

Advisory Committee, Center for Renaissance and Baroque Studies, University of Maryland, 1989–

Advisory Committee, *College Literature,* 1989–

Folger Fellowship, Spring 1994

NEH Research Grant, New Shakespeare Variorum *All's Well That Ends Well,* 1996–98

Numerous articles and chapters in books; biographical articles in *The Dictionary of Literary Biography;* book reviews in such journals as *Shakespeare Quarterly, Shakespeare Studies, Modern Language Review, JEGP,* and *Renaissance Quarterly.*

Contributors

DAVID BEVINGTON's books include *From "Mankind" to Marlowe* (1962), *Tudor Drama and Politics* (1968), and *Action is Eloquence* (1984). He has done editions of the complete works of Shakespeare for Bantam in individual paperbacks (1992) and for HarperCollins (now Longman, 4th edition, updated, 1997). He has edited *Medieval Drama* (1975), *The Macro Plays* (1972), *1 Henry IV* for Oxford, *Antony and Cleopatra* for Cambridge, and *Troilus and Cressida* for Arden 3.

TOM CLAYTON, Professor of English at the University of Minnesota, has edited Suckling's non-dramatic works (Oxford University Press, 1971) and *The Cavalier Poets* (Oxford, 1978). His more recent work has been on the Shakespearean text. It includes *The Hamlet First Published*, a collection of essays on the first Quarto (University of Delaware Press, 1992).

H. R. COURSEN attended Amherst College, Wesleyan University, and the University of Connecticut. A fighter pilot in the USAF, he was an early opponent of America's policy in Vietnam and an original member of Veterans for Peace. His recent publications include *Shakespeare: The Two Traditions*, from Fairleigh Dickinson, and his twentieth book of poetry, *The Green of Spring*, from Mad River.

RICHARD ALLAN DAVISON is Professor of English at the University of Delaware, specializing in American literature. He has published a book on Charles G. Norris (Twayne U.S. Authors series, 1986), edited the correspondance of Charles and Kathleen Norris (1993), and published essays on, among others, Hawthorne, Hemingway and Edward Albee. He is currently working on a book about the New York theater in the 1950s.

ALAN C. DESSEN, Peter G. Phialas Professor of English at the University of North Carolina-Chapel Hill, is the director of ACTER and the author of six books on English Renaissance drama, most recently *Recovering Shakespeare's Theatrical Vocabulary*. His current project (with Leslie Thomson) is *A Dictionary of Stage Directions in English Renaissance Drama, 1581–1642*, forthcoming.

DONALD W. FOSTER, Associate Professor of English at Vassar College, published *Elegy by W. S., a Study in Attribution* with the University of Delaware Press in 1989. He is also compiling a database (SHAXICON) intended to facilitate the study of Shakespearean attribution. As a result, he has frequently been called upon either to debate the authorship of the *Funeral Elegy* or to help in the attribution of other anonymous or pseudonymous works.

RUSSELL JACKSON is Deputy Director of the Shakespeare Institute of the University of Birmingham in Stratford-upon-Avon. His publications include *Victorian Theatre: a New Mermaid Sourcebook*. He also edited (with Jonathan Bate) *Shakespeare, an Illustrated Stage History*, and (with Robert Smallwood) two volumes in the series *Players of Shakespeare*. He has worked with Kenneth Branagh on a number of Shakespearean projects, including the films of *Henry V, Much Ado About Nothing* and *Hamlet*.

ARTHUR F. KINNEY is Thomas W. Copeland Professor of Literary History at the University of Massachusetts at Amherst, Director of the Massachusetts Center for Renaissance Studies, and Adjunct Professor of English at New York University. He is the founding editor of *English Literary Renaissance* and Massachusetts Studies in Early Modern Literature; his books include *Humanist Poetics, John Skelton: Priest as Poet*, and *Renaissance Historicism*.

ALEXANDER LEGGATT is Professor of English at University College, University of Toronto. His publications include *Shakespeare's Comedy of Love* (1974), *Shakespeare's Political Drama* (1988), *Harvester/Twayne New Critical Introductions to Shakespeare: King Lear* (1988), *Shakespeare in Performance: King Lear* (1991) and *Jacobean Public Theatre* (1992).

JILL L. LEVENSON, Professor of English at Trinity College, University of Toronto, edited the anonymous play *The Weakest Goeth to the Wall* in 1980 and is the author of the volume on *Romeo and Juliet* in the Shakespeare in Performance series for the University of Manchester (1987). She has also published on Shakespearean performance, on Marlowe, and on Stoppard.

CONTRIBUTORS

JERZY LIMON, a well-known Polish scholar and novelist who teaches at the University of Gdańsk, is the author of several books, most recently *The Masque of Stuart Culture,* published by the University of Delaware Press. In 1993 he co-edited *Shakespeare and His Contemporaries: Eastern and Central European Studies* with Jay L. Halio.

LAURIE E. MAGUIRE, Associate Professor of English at the University of Ottawa, has written essays on Renaissance, textual, and feminist subjects. Her book, *Shakespearean Suspect Texts: the "Bad" Quartos and their Contexts,* was published in 1996. She is currently working on a book on onomastics in Shakespeare.

AVRAHAM OZ heads the Department of Theater at the University of Haifa. He has also served as an Associate Artistic Director at Israel's Cameri Theatre and dramaturg for the Haifa Municipal Theatre. Among his publications are *The Yoke of Love: Prophetic Riddles in "The Merchant of Venice,"* and two forthcoming collections of essays on Shakespeare. He is the general editor of the Hebrew edition of the works of Shakespeare.

R. B. PARKER is an Emeritus Professor of English at Trinity College, University of Toronto, where he served as Director of the Graduate Centre and Director of Graduate English Studies for the University, and Dean of Arts and Vice Provost of Trinity College. His most recent books are the Oxford edition of *Coriolanus* (1994), and a festschrift for Sam Schoenbaum (1996) co-edited with Sheldon Zitner.

LOIS POTTER is Ned B. Allen Professor of English at the University of Delaware. Her publications include the Arden 3 edition of *The Two Noble Kinsmen* (1997); she recently edited *Playing Robin Hood: the Legend as Performance in Five Centuries* (1998). An experienced theater reviewer, she is currently writing the volume on *Othello* for the Shakespeare in Performance series.

MARVIN ROSENBERG has been publishing on Shakespearean performance for over forty years and is best known for his four books, *The Masks of Othello* (1961), *The Masks of King Lear* (1972), *The Masks of Macbeth* (1978), and *The Masks of Hamlet* (1991). A collection of his essays (*The Adventures of a Shakespeare Scholar,* 1997) and a festschrift in his honor, *Shakespearean Illuminations,* edited by Jay L. Halio (1998), were published by the University of Delaware Press.

Contributors

BARBARA SILVERSTEIN, a graduate of the Philadelphia Musical Academy, Philadelphia, is an opera conductor and the founder-director of The Pennsylvania Opera Theater, for which she translated a number of opera libretti. She is now a Ph.D. student in English at the University of Delaware, specializing in Renaissance literature.

PEGGY MUÑOZ SIMONDS is Professor Emerita of English, Montgomery College, Maryland. Her book *Myth, Emblem, and Music in Shakespeare's "Cymbeline": An Iconographic Reconstruction* (University of Delaware Press, 1992) won the Press's 1990 award for the best manuscript in Shakespeare studies. She has also published *Iconographic Research in English Renaissance Literature: A Critical Guide* (Garland, 1995).

SUSAN SNYDER is Gil and Frank Mustin Professor Emerita of English at Swarthmore College and Scholar in Residence at the Folger Shakespeare Library. Her books include *The Comic Matrix of Shakespeare's Tragedies* and, more recently, *Pastoral Process: Spenser, Marvell, Milton*, as well as editions of Sylvester's *Du Bartas* and Shakespeare's *All's Well that Ends Well*. She is currently preparing an edition of *The Winter's Tale*.

GRACE TIFFANY has taught Shakespeare and Renaissance drama at Notre Dame, Fordham, the University of New Orleans, and currently Western Michigan University. Her book, *Erotic Beasts and Social Monsters: Shakespeare, Jonson, and Comic Androgyny*, was published by the University of Delaware Press in 1995. Her work has appeared in such journals as *Shakespeare Studies, The Huntington Library Quarterly*, and *Comparative Drama*.

STANLEY WELLS is General Editor of the Oxford Shakespeare, editor of *Shakespeare Survey*, chairman of The Shakespeare Birthplace Trust, and Vice-chairman of the Governors of the Royal Shakespeare Theatre. From 1988 to 1997 he was Professor of Shakespeare Studies and Director of the Shakespeare Institute of the University of Birmingham.

GEORGE WALTON WILLIAMS (B.A., Yale; PhD., Virginia) is now retired from Duke University where he has been teaching since 1957. With T. L. Berger he is preparing the MLA Variorum edition of *Henry V*. He served two terms as the reviewer of textual studies for *Shakespeare Survey* and is now Associate General Editor (for the history plays) of the Arden Shakespeare. He serves also on the Advisory Committee of International Studies in Shakespeare and his Contemporaries.

Index to Works by, or Attributed to, William Shakespeare

All is True, 24–25, 30
All's Well that Ends Well, 10, 33, 36, 231, 241, 268
Antony and Cleopatra, 24–25, 28, 35, 120, 163, 231
As You Like It, 24, 35, 102, 120

Comedy of Errors, The, 24–25, 302, 320–30; Dir. Omri Nitzan, 139–40, 143
Contention betwixt the two Famous Houses of York and Lancaster, The, part 1 and 2, 30; See also *2 and 3 Henry VI*
Coriolanus, 24–25, 31, 117, 231, 314; Dir. John Hirsch, 194–207
Cymbeline, 140

First Part of the Contention, The, 25. See also *2 Henry VI*
Funeral Elegy, A, 103

Hamlet, 20, 26, 27–29, 35, 50, 63, 82, 115, 117, 120, 137, 159, 163–66, 183–92, 202, 229, 241, 249, 300–301, 316; Dir. Richard Eyre, 170–80; Dir. Joseph Papp, 121, 124–27, 130; Dir. Franco Zeffirelli, 126
Henry IV, part 1, 20, 51, 57, 141, 143, 229, 279, 285–93
Henry IV, part 2, 20, 29, 39, 40, 57–58, 140–41, 212, 229, 285–94
Henry V, 20, 25–26, 29, 31, 45, 132, 159, 229, 286, 292, 294, 324; Dir. James Daniels, 132
Henry VI, part 1, 25, 29, 294
Henry VI, part 2, 20, 25, 29, 39, 132, 229, 273, 294
Henry VI, part 3, 20, 25, 29, 229, 294
Henry VIII. See also *All is True*

Julius Caesar, 24–25, 84

King John, 20, 25
King Lear, 10–11, 20, 25–27, 29, 38, 53, 121, 131, 229, 238, 310–18; *Ran* (Kurosawa), 131; Dir. Ruth Malaczech, *Lear*, 131–32; Dir. Seazer, 274

Love's Labor's Lost, 93, 229, 244
Lover's Complaint, A, 102

Macbeth, 38, 74, 82, 99, 213; Dir. Yukio Ninagawa, 274
Measure for Measure, 24, 35, 39, 40, 229
Merchant of Venice, The, 10, 20, 29, 80, 83, 120, 136, 229, 244
Merry Wives of Windsor, The, 20, 24, 29, 39, 120, 229; Dir. Michael Kahn, 121, 127–30
Midsummer Night's Dream, A, 10, 20, 27, 29, 33, 35, 62–85, 229, 240, 266–67; Dir. Chris Bond, *Dream*, 72; Dir. Peter Brook, 75; Dir. Robert Lepage, 274; Dir. Yukio Ninagawa, 274; *The Dream* (rock-musical), 72
Much Ado About Nothing, 20, 26, 29, 33, 159, 229

Othello, 20, 24–25, 29, 35, 37, 39, 40, 83, 115; Dir. Trevor Nunn, 177

Passionate Pilgrim, The, 99
Pericles, 20, 23–24, 29, 93, 95, 330
Phoenix and Turtle, The, 19

Rape of Lucrece, The, 23, 299–300
Richard II, 20, 29, 120–25, 127, 293, 324; Dir. Deborah Warner, 121, 129
Richard III, 20, 27, 29, 55, 111, 114, 117, 138, 244, 286

Romeo and Juliet, 11, 20, 28–29, 55, 115, 249–63, 266–81
Romeo & Juliette, 274–81

"Shakespeare upon the King" ("*Crowns have their compass*"), 98–99, 101
Shall I Die, 92, 99–103
Sonnets, 19, 23, 299
Sonnets to Sundry Notes of Music, 99

Taming of the Shrew, The, 20, 24, 279
Tempest, The, 25, 27, 31, 39, 40, 84, 101, 116, 209–26, 229, 236–39; Dir. Yukio Ninagawa, 274
Timon of Athens, 25, 39, 40
Titus Andronicus, 20, 25–26, 29, 229

Troilus and Cressida, 20, 26–27, 29, 62, 139, 298–306
Troublesome Reign of King John, The, 20, 24
Twelfth Night, 24, 36, 56
Two Gentleman of Verona, 24, 39–40, 229
Two Noble Kinsmen, The (With John Fletcher), 23–24, 29
True Tragedy of Richard, Duke of York, The. See *Henry VI, part 3*

Venus and Adonis, 23, 299

Winter's Tale, The, 25, 31, 39, 40, 229, 285, 330

General Index

Adams, Davenport, 51
Adrian, Max, 304–5
Agnew, Jean-Christopher, 328
Agrippa, Cornelius, 211
Alchemist, The, 287
Alexander, Bill, 80
Almagor, Dan, 143–45
Andrews, John F., 48
Anne, queen to James I, 98, 329
Annis, Francesca, 305
Apfelbaum, Roger, 302–3
Arafat, Yasser, 136
Arcimboldo, Giuseppe, 50
Asbenall/Aspinall, Alexander, 93–96, 99
Atkins, Robert, 305
Aubrey, John, 325
Auden, W. H.: *The Sea and the Mirror*, 30

B., R.: *Greene's Funeral*, 17
Bailey, Samuel, 52
Bandello, Matteo, 281
Bandmann-Palmer, Millicent, 124
Barber, C. L., 11
Barker, Ernest, 51
Barker, Robert, 97
Barnes, Barnabe: *The Devil's Character*, 234–36, 238
Barnes, Clive, 126
Barnfield, Richard, 95
Barton, John, 304, 305
Basse, William, 19
Bateson, F. W., 50–51, 54, 56, 58
Beaumont, Francis, 19, 101, 238; *The Maid's Tragedy*, 239
Beckerman, Bernard, 230–31
Beckett, Samuel, 184, 189
Belinski, Vissarion, 163
Benjamin, Andrew, 137
Bentley, G. E., 232
Bernhardt, Sarah, 124–25
Bernstein, Mashay, 281
Bertish, Suzanne, 174

Betterton, Thomas, 286
Bevington, David, 57
Bill, John, 96
Billington, Michael, 303–4
Birch, Frank, 304
Birth of Merlin, The, 103
Blackburn, Ken, 187
Blayney, Peter, 25
Boel, Cornelius, 98
Bohner, Charles, 173
Bohr, Niels, 188
Bonaparte, Lucien, 109
Bond, Chris, 72
Bond, Samantha, 156
Booth, Edwin, 125
Boswell, James, the younger, 99
Bowers, Fredson, 250
Bradley, A. C., 318
Bradley, Herbert, 52
Branagh, Kenneth, 31, 127, 146, 156–59; *Beginning*, 146, 159; *In the Bleak Midwinter (A Midwinter's Tale)*, 157–58
Braudy, Leo, 188
Brecht, Bertolt, 189; *Mother Courage*, 196
Breuer, Lee, 131–32
Briggs, Katharine; *Anatomy of Puck*, 82
Brome, Richard, 243–44; *The Antipodes*, 238; *The English Moor*, 237
Brook, Peter, 62, 75, 255, 260, 274
Brooke, Arthur, 281
Brooke, Nicholas, 38
Brooks, Harold, 81, 83
Brougham, Henry, 110
Brown, John Russell, 254
Browne, William; *Britannia's Pastorals*, 94
Bryant, Michael, 170, 175
Burbage, James, 323–24
Burbage, Richard, 18
Bulloch, John, 52
Bullough, Geoffrey, 64

Burden, Suzanne, 306
Burnett, Kate, 148
Burton, Richard, 127
Bush, George, 197
Butler, Michael, *Journal* (online), 138

Cabot, John, 275
Caldecott, Thomas, 54
Camden, William, 17
Campbell, Thomas, 110
Campion, Thomas, 239
Capell, Edward, 34, 54, 262
Caroline, queen to George IV, 110–11, 115
Carrnoy, Jennifer, 172
Carroll, Pat, 121, 127–30
Cartier, Jacques, 275
Castle, John, 170, 175
Cecil, Robert, 329
Cecil, William, Lord Burghley, 138
Chapman, George, 240, 244; *A Humorous Day's Mirth*, 94–95, 289
Chariots of Fire, 177
Charles I, 98
Charleson, Ian, 170–80
Charleson, Kenneth, 173
Charney, Maurice, 192, 316
Chaucer, Geoffrey, 19
Chekhov, Anton; *The Cherry Orchard*, 176
Church, Tony, 304
Cibber, Colley, 111, 286
Clarke, Helen, 48, 54
Clavell, John; *The Soddered Citizen*, 238
Close, Glenn, 126
Cohn, Ruby, 183
Coke, Judith, 173
Coleridge, Samuel Taylor, *Biographia Literaria*, 23
Collier, J. P., 48, 51
Condell, Henry, 18, 21–24, 26–27, 30, 299
Coulson, E. G., 51
Coward, Noël; *Present Laughter*, 30
Craig, Catriona, 174
Craik, T. W., 54, 57
Crane, Ralph, 21, 25, 30, 35, 39–40, 63, 229–30, 236, 238, 244
Creighton, C., 50–51
Croll, Oswald, 224
Cruttwell, Hugh, 159

Cushman, Charlotte, 124–25, 255
Cutts, John P., 56
Czartoryski, Prince Adam, 109

Dalpé, Jean-Marc, 275–76
Davies, Howard, 303
Davies, John; *Orchestra*, 73
Davison, Francis; *Masque of Proteus*, 322, 329
Dawson, Giles E., 55–56, 85
Day-Lewis, Cecil, 171
Day-Lewis, Daniel, 170–72, 176, 178
Dee, John, 211, 224
Dekker, Thomas, 17, 241, 243–44; *If This Be Not a Good Play. . .* , 238; *The Virgin Martyr*, 238
Delius, Nikolaus, 51–52
Della Porta, Giambattista, 211
Dench, Judi, 170, 175–76
Dent, R. W., 62
Déprats, Jean-Michel, 274
Dessen, Alan C., 249, 287
Devereux, Robert, Earl of Essex, 17
Didion, Joan; *Miami*, 198
Digges, Leonard, 23
Donne, John; *Poems*, 19
Dorn, Gerard, 224
Drake, Francis, 329
Drant, Thomas, 274–75; Translation of Horace's satires, 272–73
Droeshout, Martin, 22
Dryden, John, 302, 305
Du Bartas, Guillaume, 279
Duchesne, Joseph; *The Practice of Chymicall, and Hermetical Physicke*, 212
Dunlop, John Colin, 110
Dutton, Richard, 27, 299
Dyce, Alexander, 35

Eagle, Roderick, 50
Edmund Ironside, 103
Edwardes, Jane, 172
Edwards, Christopher, 171
Einstein, Albert, 138
Eisenhower, Dwight, 138
Eld, George, 298
Eli'az, Repha'el, 141, 144
Eliot, John; *Eliot's Fruits for the French*, 279; *Ortho-epia Gallica*, 56, 279
Eliot, T. S., 196

Elizabeth I, 20, 97–98, 138, 212, 322, 329–30
Erstein, Hap, 128
Evans, Edith, 305
Eyre, Peter, 174
Eyre, Richard, 170, 172–74, 176

Fane, Francis, 93, 95–96
Faucit, Helena, 31, 163–64
Finney, Albert, 177
Fitzgerald, Percy, 47
Fleissner, R. F., 50–54, 57
Fletcher, George, 163
Fletcher, John, 101, 238, 241, 243; *Bonduca*, 237; *Cardenio*, 24; *The Fair Maid of the Inn*, 238; *The Faithful Shepherdess*, 238; *The Sea Voyage*, 238
Foakes, R. A., 69
Fogel, Ephim C., 50
Fonda, Jane, 197
Forbidden Planet, The, 30
Ford, John, 17, 244; *Love's Sacrifice*, 53, 238
Fortescue, John, 322
Foucault, Michel, 325
Francis, Clive, 304
French, G. R., 38
Freud, Sigmund, 126–27, 215
Friel, Brian, *Translations*, 273–74, 279–80
Fripp, Edgar, 93
Funeral Elegy, A, 103

Gandhi, Mahatma, 138
Garrick, David, 31, 255, 258, 285–86; *The Clandestine Marriage*, 112
Genesis, 268
Gentleman, Francis, 285–94; "*Bell's Shakespeare*," 285–87; *Essay on Oratory*, 287, 290; *The Tobacconist*, 287
George III, 110
George IV, 110–11
Gesner, Conrad; *The Jewell of Health*, 216–19, 221, 223–24
Gesta Grayorum, 320–21
Gibson, Mel, 126–27
Gielgud, John, 31, 255, 260
Glapthorne, Henry, 231
Goethe, Johann Wolfgang Von, 163

Goffe, Thomas, 233–34; *Courageous Turk*, 233; *Orestes*, 233; *The Raging Turk*, 233
Gollancz, Israel, 54
Gorbachev, Mikhail, 198
Greene, Robert, 17, 243
Greg, W. W., 39, 52, 55, 78, 236
Grenville, Richard, 50–51
Griffin, Gail, 132
Grindal, Edmund, 322, 325
Gurr, Andrew, 54, 56, 85, 229, 251
Guthrie, Tyrone, 303, 305, 310

Hair (Gerome Ragni and James Rado), 75, 138
Halio, Jay L, 9–12, 31, 62–63, 92, 103, 136, 292, 318, 320
Hall, A., 49
Hall, Fawn, 197, 200
Hall, Peter, 305
Halliwell, J. O., 51
Halstead, William P., 257
Handel, Georg Friedrich; *Messiah*, 38
Hands, Terry, 304, 306
Hankey, John, 325
Hanmer, Thomas, 262
Hardison, O. B., 11
Hardy, Thomas; *Under the Greenwood Tree*, 30
Harrison, G. B., 51
Harter, George Wernberg, 204
Harvey, Gabriel, 300
Hawthorne, Nathaniel; *The Artist of the Beautiful*, 188
Heisenberg, Werner, 188
Heminges, John, 18, 21–24, 26–27, 30, 299
Henry VIII, 324
Hepple, Peter, 156
Heraclitus, 138
Herbert, Philip, Earl of Montgomery, 22
Herbert, William, Earl of Pembroke, 22
Herford, C. H., 54
Heywood, Thomas, 233, 237, 241, 243–44, 288; *The Captives*, 238, 243; *The Golden Age*, 238; *The Silver Age*, 238; *The Heirarche of the Blessed Angells*, 323
Heyworth, P. L., 52, 55
Hiley, Jim, 172
Hilliard, Nicholas, 329

Hobbes, Thomas, 136
Hoffman, Dustin, 177
Holland, Abraham, 98
Holland, Compton, 98
Holland, F., 81
Holland, Hugh, 23, 98
Holland, Peter, 64
Honigmann, E. A. J., 37, 40
Horodyński, Bogdan, 111
Hortmann, Wilhelm, 166–67
Hotson, Leslie, 50
Housman, A. E., 177
Howard-Hill, T. H., 39
Hoyle, Martin, 175
Hulme, Hilda M., 49, 52, 57
Hunter, G. K., 38, 255
Hurren, Kenneth, 171
Huxley, Aldous; *Brave New World*, 31

Irvin, Sam, 198
Irving, Henry, 259
Isaiah, 38
Isidore of Seville; *De natura rerum*, 212–13

Jackson, MacDonald P., 53–54
Jacobi, Derek, 166
Jaggard, Isaac, 39
Jaggard, William, 19–20; *The Passionate Pilgrim*, 19
James I, 97, 99; *Workes*, 96, 98
James, Elias, 101
James, Mervyn, 324
Jarvis, Andrew, 149, 151
Jenkins, Harold, 48, 51, 54, 56
Jennings, Byron, 194, 197
Jensen, Phebe, 303
John a Kent and John a Cumber, 78–79
Johnson, Richard; *Tom B Lincoln*, 233–34
Johnson, S. F., 47–48, 53
Johnson, Samuel, 248
Johnston, Alexandra, 326
Jones, Ernest, 126
Jones, John; *Adrasta*, 232–35
Jongh, Nicholas de, 175
Jonson, Ben, 17, 19, 39, 101, 211, 235–36, 244, 271, 288, 329; *The Alchemist*, 210, 212, 235; *Cynthia's Revels*, 329; *The Devil is an Ass*, 236; *Discoveries*, 288; *Every Man Out of His Humour*, 235; Folio of 1616, 21–22, 39, 236; *The Golden Age Restor'd*, 212; *Mercury Vindicated From the Alchemists at Court*, 212; *Volpone*, 129, 235
Jonsonus Virbius, 17
Jowett, John, 236–37
Judge, Ian, 306

Kahn, Michael, 121, 127–30
Kane, John, 85
Kastan, David, 220, 224
Keach, Stacy, 127
Kean, Edmund, 112–16
Keightley, Thomas, 51, 53
Kellner, Leon, 53, 55
Kelly, Edward, 224
Kemble, John Philip, 31, 260, 302
Kennedy, Joan, 198
Kennedy, John Jr., 204
Kennedy, Paul, 198
Kennedy, Richard, 33–34
Kennedy, Rose, 198
Khunrath, Heinrich, 224
King, T. J., 230–31, 302
Kirby, Johanna, 174
Knight, Charles, 54
Knutson, Roslyn, 229
Kolve, V. A., 328
Kott, Jan, 62, 75
Kroll, Jack, 123
Kuhn, Thomas, 188
Kyle, Barry, 304

Lahr, John, 123–24
Lanier, Douglas, 183
Lepage, Robert, 274–75, 277, 280
Liar, The, 114
Locrine, 242
London Prodigal, The, 20, 23
Long, William B., 230
Look About You, 289
Lupton, Thomas; *All for Money*, 237
Luther, Martin, 212
Lyly, John, 17, 239

Macowan, Michael, 303–4
Macready, W. C., 31
Maeder, Clara Fisher, 124
Maguire, Laurie, 78
Maier, Michael, 224
Maleczech, Ruth, 131–32

Malone, Edmond, 23, 49, 52, 54, 248; *Historical Account of the Rise and Progress of the English Stage*, 248
Marcuse, Herbert, 184
Marmion, Shackerley, 31
Marriott, Alice, 124
Marx, Steven, 138
Marlowe, Christopher, 244, 304; *Edward II*, 288
Marprelate, Martin, 288
Marston, John, 100, 239–44, 300; *Antonio and Mellida*, 239–42; *Antonio's Revenge*, 239–42; *The Dutch Courtesan*, 239–42; *The Fawn*, 239–40, 242; *Jack Drum's Entertainment*, 239, 241–42; *The Malcontent*, 239, 241–42; *Sophonisba*, 239–42; *What You Will*, 239–40, 242
Massinger, Philip, 243–44; *The Sea Voyage*, 238; *The Virgin Martyr*, 238
Matthias (brother to Rudolph II), 224
McCabe, Richard, 303
McCall, Gordon, 274, 277, 280
McFarland, Thomas, 52
McKellen, Ian, 177, 179
McKerrow, R. B., 250
McLeod, Randall, 78
McRae, Hilton, 173
Mebane, John S., 214
Meese, Edwin, 197, 200
Mendes, Sam, 303, 306
Meres, Francis, 300
Merrison, Clive, 303
Middleton, Thomas, 17, 20, 240–41, 243–44; *The Witch*, 39; *Women Beware Women*, 239
Miller, Jonathan, 306
Mirrin, Helen, 305
Moberly, Charles, 51
Mochalov, Pavel, 163–64
Montague, Winetta, 124
Morris, Corbyn, 292
Mowat, Barbara, 33, 51, 53
Munday, Anthony, 237; *Sir Thomas More*, 55
My Left Foot, 170–71

Naso, Publius Ovidius; *Metamorphoses*, 214
Nathan, Norman, 49
Neilson, Adelaide, 260

Neilson, William Alan, 34
Netanyahu, Benjamin, 140
Newton, Isaac, 187–88
Ninagawa, Yukio, 274
Nicholson, Brantley, 52–53
Nitzan, Omri, 136, 139, 143
North, Oliver, 197, 200
Northam, Jeremy, 170–71, 176–78
Novy, Marianne, 278
Nowlan, David, 172

Oh, Calcutta, 75
Oliver, Edith, 126
Olivier, Laurence, 31, 126, 191
O'Neill, Tip, 198
Osborne, Charles, 171
Otway, Thomas; *History and Fall of Caius Marius*, 255

Pafford, J. H. P., 39
Papp, Joseph, 130, 306
Parfitt, David, 146
Paris, Texas, 276
Parker, Patricia, 287
Parkes, Malcolm, 288
Passe, Simon, 96, 98
Passionate Pilgrim, The, 99
Pastor, Frederick; *The Gift is Small, The Love is Great*, 95
Pavier, Thomas, 20–21
Payne, Ben Idan, 302, 305
Peele, George L, 243
Peres, Shimon, 140
Pergami, Bartolomeo, 110
Peter, John, 176
Plautus, Titus Maccius; *Manaechmi*, 321
Plot, Robert, 325
Plutarch, 64, 255
Poel, William, 302, 304–5
Poole, Kristen, 57
Pope, Alexander, 47, 52, 248, 255; *The Dunciad*, 48
Porter, Charlotte, 48
Porter, Joseph A., 56, 289
Pritchard, Hannah, 163

Quayle, Anthony, 302, 305
Quigley, Michael, 258

Rabelais, François; *Gargantua and Pantagruel*, 220

GENERAL INDEX

Rabin, Itzhak, 136, 140
Rains, Claude, 175
Ralegh, Walter, 329
Ran, 131
Rann, Joseph, 49
Rayburn, Sam, 198
Reagan, Ronald, 200
Reeves, Keanu, 127
Reinhardt, Max, 310
Return to the Forbidden Planet, 20
Reynolds, G. F., 230
Rich, Frank, 126
Richmond, Oliffe, 57
Rintoul, David, 174
Ritson, Joseph; *Cursory Criticisms*, 49
Roberts, Gareth, 215
Roberts, John, 47, 54
Rocket, William, 209
Rodway, Norman, 303
Rogers, Paul, 305
Rooney, Mickey, 128
Root, Amanda, 306
Rosenberg, Marvin, 126
Rothstein, Mervyn, 128
Rousseau, Jean Jacques, 136
Rowe, Nicholas, 33–34, 47–48, 52
Rowley, William; *The Birth of Merlin*, 103
Rudolph II, 224
Ruland, Martin, 224
Russell, Bertrand, 138
Russell, Thomas, 23
Ryan, Kiernan, 187–88, 269
Ryan, Paul, 175

Saint-Pierre, Charles Castel, Abbé de, 136, 138
Savage, John, 325
Sayers, Dorothy; *Gaudy Night*, 30–31
Schanzer, Ernest, 54
Schoenbaum, Samuel, 11
Schubert, Franz; *Who is Sylvia?*, 30
Scofield, Paul, 177
Scot, Patrick, 210
Scott, Walter; *Lady of the Lake*, 110
Seaman, Julia, 124
Seazer, J. A., 274
Selbourne, David, 75
Shakespeare, John, 95
Shattuck, Charles H., 256–57, 263
Shaw/Shey, Anne, 93–95
Shaw, Fiona, 121, 123–24, 128, 130

Shaw, Glen Byam, 302, 305
Shaw, Ralph, 94
Sheidley, William E., 185–86, 192
Shepard, Sam; *Fool For Love*, 172
Sheridan, Richard Brinsley; *The Critic*, 294
Sheriff, R. C.; *Journey's End*
Shirley, James, 243–44
Shulman, Milton, 171
Siddons, Sarah, 31
Sidney, Philip, 17
Sienkiewicz, Karol, 109–17; *Diary 1820–21*, 109
Singer, S. W., 54
Sir Thomas More, 55
Skipwith, William, 100
Slade, Julian; *Salad Days*, 30
Slater, Ann Pasternak, 253
Soane, George; *Undine*, 116
Sonnets to Sundry Notes of Music, 99
Spedding, James, 52
Spence, R. M., 52
Spenser, Edmund, 17, 19, 329
Steele, Richard; *The Conscious Lovers*, 248
Steevens, George, 248
Steiner, George, 266, 280
Sternhold, Thomas, 57
Stevenson, Juliet, 306
Stewart, G. R., 51
Stockwood, John, 324
Stone, P. W. K., 53
Stoppard, Tom, 139, 176; *Rosencrantz and Guildenstern Are Dead*, 183
Strong, Roy, 329
Sturgess, Keith, 209, 215
Styan, J. L., 252
Sumpter, Donald, 185
Swift, Jonathan, 267

Talma, François Joseph, 114
Tawyer, William, 79
Taylor, Gary, 19, 21, 53–56, 79, 92–93, 256
Terry, Ellen, 163, 259
Theobald, Lewis, 38, 47, 49, 52, 54–56; *Shakespeare Restored*, 47, 53
Thirlby, Styan, 52
Thorndike, Russell, 305
Thorpe, Thomas, 23
Thurber, James, 137

Tolstoy, Leo, 138
Trevis, Di, 174
Trismosin, Salomon; *Splendor Solis*, 220, 222
Troublesome Reign of King John, The, 20, 24
Tuckey, John S., 60
Two Merry Milkmaids, The, 230
Tymme, Thomas, 212, 214

Underdown, David, 325
Ure, Peter, 57

Venora, Diane, 121, 125–27
Verdi, Giuseppe, 30
Vining, Edward, 125
Voss, Philip, 304

Walesa, Lech, 198
Walker, Alice, 37
Walker, Roy, 51
Wallack, Fanny, 124
Waller, Emma, 124
Walley, Henry, 300
Walter, J. H., 57
Wanamaker, Sam, 31
Warburton, William, 47, 52, 56
Wares, Kyle, 204
Warner, Deborah, 121, 123–24, 127

Warner, Marina, 30
Wasp, The, 237
Waterhouse, Ellis, 49
Watt, Douglas, 127
Wax, Ruby, 174
Webster, John, 17; *The Duchess of Malfi*, 39
Weidhorn, Manfred, 269
Wells, Stanley, 19, 92–93
Werstine, Paul, 51, 53
Wheeler, Elizabeth, 184, 188, 192
White, R. G., 54, 56
Williams, Tennessee; *Cat on a Hot Tin Roof*, 172
Williamson, Hugh Ross, 51
Williamson, Nicol, 127
Wilson, J. Dover, 37, 57, 66
Wily Beguiled, 237
Winslet, Kate, 188
Wither, George, 98
Wolfit, Donald, 127
Womack, Peter, 323, 326
Wordsworth, William, 122
Wright, David, 194

Yakubinsky, Lev, 291
Yorkshire Tragedy, A, 20–21, 23
Young, N., 51

Zeffirelli, Franco, 126, 255, 260